Globus® Toolkit 4
Programming Java Services

The Elsevier Series in Grid Computing

Series Editors: Ian Foster, Argonne National Laboratory & University of Chicago, and Carl Kesselman, Information Sciences Institute, University of Southern California

The Grid is a rapidly developing computing structure that allows components of our information technology infrastructure—computational capabilities, databases, sensors, and people—to be shared flexibly as true collaborative tools.

The Elsevier Series in Grid Computing examines how the Grid Computing vision is being made a reality and the implications of Grid technologies for computing, industry, science, and society. Titles in the series are authored by leading experts and make the necessary connections between Grid Computing and Networking; Information Technology; Database Management; Programming Languages, Tools and Compilers; Security; Artificial Intelligence, Computer Architecture and Design and other computing disciplines.

The Grid: Blueprint for a New Computing Infrastructure
Edited by Ian Foster and Carl Kesselman

The Grid 2: Blueprint for a New Computing Infrastructure
Edited by Ian Foster and Carl Kesselman

Globus® Toolkit 4: Programming Java Services
Borja Sotomayor and Lisa Childers

Forthcoming Titles

Grid Portals: Enabling Collaborative Problem Solving
Dennis Gannon and Marlon Pierce

Related Titles

Grid Computing: The Savvy Manager's Guide
Pawel Plaszczak and Richard Wellner, Jr.

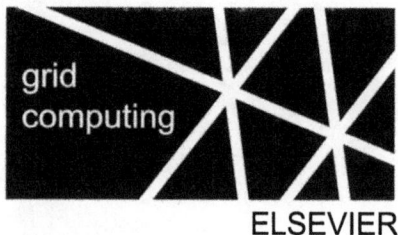

grid
computing

ELSEVIER

Globus® Toolkit 4
Programming Java Services

Borja Sotomayor

University of Chicago
Department of Computer Science

Lisa Childers

Argonne National Laboratory
Mathematics and Computer Science Division

AMSTERDAM • BOSTON • HEIDELBERG • LONDON
NEW YORK • OXFORD • PARIS • SAN DIEGO
SAN FRANCISCO • SINGAPORE • SYDNEY • TOKYO

ELSEVIER   Morgan Kaufmann Publishers is an imprint of Elsevier

MORGAN KAUFMANN PUBLISHERS

Senior Editor	Rick Adams
Publishing Services Manager	Simon Crump
Assistant Editor	Rachel Roumeliotis
Project Manager	Brandy Lilly
Cover Design	Eric DeCicco
Composition	Cepha Imaging Pvt. Ltd.
Interior printer	Phoenix Color
Cover printer	Maple Vail Book Manufacturing Group

Morgan Kaufmann Publishers is an imprint of Elsevier.
500 Sansome Street, Suite 400, San Francisco, CA 94111

Library of Congress Cataloging-in-Publication Data
Application submitted

ISBN 13: 978-0-12-369404-1
ISBN 10: 0-12-369404-3

For information on all Morgan Kaufmann publications,
visit our Web site at www.mkp.com or www.books.elsevier.com

Transferred to Digital Printing 2010

To Leon Kuntz
In memoriam

Contents

Foreword   xiii

Preface   xv

Part I   Key Concepts   1

   1   Grid Computing   3

   2   OGSA, WSRF, and GT4   13

   3   Web Services   19

   4   WSRF   29

   5   The Globus Toolkit 4   39

Part II   GT4 Java WS Core   45

   6   Writing Your First Stateful Web Service in 5 Simple Steps   47

   7   Singleton Resources   81

   8   Multiple Resources   95

   9   Logging   129

   10   Resource Properties   137

11 **Lifecycle Management** 177

12 **Persistent Resources** 193

13 **Notifications** 211

14 **Implementing Your Own Operation Providers** 241

Part III GT4 Security   255

15 **Fundamental Security Concepts** 257

16 **GSI: Grid Security Infrastructure** 271

17 **Writing a Secure MathService** 283

18 **The Security Descriptor** 297

19 **Authentication** 305

20 **Authorization** 325

21 **Resource-Level Security** 337

22 **Run-as Modes and Delegation** 347

Part IV The FileBuy Application   381

23 **Design** 383

24 **Implementation** 401

Conclusion 427

Part V Appendices   429

A **Installing the Globus Toolkit 4** 431

B **A WSDL Primer** 449

C **Command-Line Clients** 461

D **Examples** 475

E **globus-build-service Script Reference** 491

List of Figures

1	Chapter precedence diagram	xvii
1.1	The Large Hadron Collider, at CERN, is the largest machine ever built	4
1.2	An organization and its resources	5
1.3	Virtual organizations	5
1.4	Grid architecture	8
2.1	Relationship between OGSA, WSRF, and Web Services	14
2.2	Relationship between OGSA, GT4, WSRF, and Web Services	16
2.3	Layered diagram of OGSA, GT4, WSRF, and Web Services	17
3.1	Web Services	20
3.2	A typical Web Service invocation	21
3.3	The Web Services architecture	22
3.4	Client and server stubs are generated from the WSDL file	25
3.5	A typical Web Service invocation (more detailed)	25
3.6	The server side in a Web Services application	26
4.1	A stateless Web Service invocation	30
4.2	A stateful Web Service invocation	31
4.3	The resource approach to statefulness	32
4.4	A Web Service with several resources. Each resource represents a file	32
4.5	WS-Resource	33
4.6	Endpoint reference	33
4.7	WS-Resource-qualified endpoint reference	34
5.1	GT4 components	40
5.2	The Java GT4 container. Based on Figure 5 in Ian Foster's "GT4 Primer"	42
5.3	GT4 service overview	43

6.1	Generating a GAR file with Ant	72
7.1	Relationships between the Service, the Resource Home, and the Resource	82
8.1	The WS-Resource factory pattern	96
8.2	Relationships between the Factory Service, the Instance Service, the Resource Home, and the Resource	97
8.3	Sequence diagram for resource creation	99
8.4	Sequence diagram for WS-Resource invocation	101
13.1	Keeping track of changes using polling	212
13.2	Keeping track of changes using notifications	213
13.3	A typical WS-Notification interaction	214
13.4	A WS-Notification interaction where subscriber and the consumer are different entities	215
13.5	A typical brokered WS-Notification interaction	216
15.1	Key-based encryption	260
15.2	Key-based decryption	261
15.3	Key-based symmetric algorithm	262
15.4	Key-based asymmetric algorithm	263
15.5	Public key generation	264
15.6	Digital signatures	265
15.7	A digital certificate	266
15.8	Digital certificate chain of verification	269
16.1	Transport-level security	272
16.2	Message-level security	272
16.3	Alice, Bob, and Charlie	276
16.4	Alice, Bob, and Charlie (2)	277
16.5	A proxy certificate	277
16.6	A proxy certificate with a limited lifetime	278
16.7	Validation of a proxy certificate	281
17.1	TCPMonitor interface (1)	292
17.2	TCPMonitor interface (2)	293
22.1	The PhysicsService example	358
23.1	Three organizations with resources	384
23.2	A virtual organization based on our three organizations	385
23.3	Index service	386
23.4	Resource brokering	387
23.5	Example FileBuy VO	388
23.6	FileBuy use cases	389
23.7	Sequence diagram for advertising a file	390
23.8	Sequence diagram for finding a file	392
23.9	Sequence diagram for purchasing a file	394
23.10	FileBuy deployment diagram, with communication dependencies	396

List of Tables

13.1	Parameters specific to **wsn-subscribe**	238
16.1	Comparison of transport-level and message-level security	273
C.1	Common command-line parameters	461
C.2	Security parameters	463
C.3	Parameters specific to **wsn-subscribe**	468
C.4	Parameters specific to **globus-start-container**	470
D.1	Services	488
E.1	globus-service-build parameters	492

Foreword

Grid computing is an increasingly popular topic, and numerous books have appeared that describe grid applications and technologies. Indeed, we have contributed to this number, via the two editions of "The Grid: Blueprint for a New Computing Infrastructure," published in 1999 and 2004, respectively, and via the establishment of the Morgan Kaufman Series on Grid Computing, which has already released a guide to Grid computing for the "Savvy Manager."

However, what has been desperately lacking (until now) is a book that addresses the needs of the *programmer*. For the programmer, all previous books are just plain frustrating—they describe beautiful concepts and powerful applications, but say nothing about the nuts and bolts of how to write real programs that solve real problems.

The aspiring Grid programmer need be frustrated no longer. Borja Sotomayor and Lisa Childers have produced, in *Glolbus Toolkit 4: Programming Java Services*, a masterly tutorial text that is surely destined to find a place beside every Grid programmer's keyboard. Combining readable step-by-step tutorial text with bullet-proof code examples, Borja and Lisa introduce, one by one, the key programming concepts, technique, and tools needed to build "Grid services"—Web services that implement Grid patterns—in Java. The mysteries of both Web Services specifications and security are all explained in a precise but engaging exposition. It seems inevitable that Borja and Lisa will find themselves mobbed by autograph-seeking fans at future Grid events—and also within many companies and universities, as the book is adopted by both professional software developers and within university courses.

What makes us confident that this book will be well received is the extensive testing that the material has received over the past two years. The first version, released online as the "GT3 Programmer's Tutorial" in May 2003, became the primary point of entry for many new Grid programmers. The material has subsequently been field tested in numerous tutorials that Borja and Lisa have taught to hundreds of students around the world. The resulting extensive feedback has guided the evolution of the tutorial through many intermediate versions, ultimately producing the polished product that you see here.

We'd also like to point out that the book's publication now, at the end of 2005, is remarkably timely. The year 2005 saw both the finalization of key Web services specifications relating to Grid and the release of the open source Globus Toolkit implementation of those specifications, GT4. If the book had appeared earlier, it would have soon been out of date. As it is, it appears just when needed for the many programmers starting to develop applications based on Web services and GT4. While both specifications and Globus will surely continue to evolve, we expect the concepts and techniques described in this book to have considerable longevity.

As the title states, this is a book about *programming Java services using GT4*. More precisely, it describes how to use a key GT4 component, the *Java Web Services Core*, to create services that use conventions described in OASIS standards such as Web Services Resource Framework, Web Services Notification, and Web Services Security to create powerful Grid-enabled Web Services. There is, of course, much more to the Globus Toolkit than the Java Web Services Core: there are also Python and C implementations of the Web Services core functions, and numerous higher-level services for such things as execution management, data access, data management, authorization, accounting, and monitoring and discovery. There are also numerous complementary tools that build on GT4 mechanisms. Thus, we may hope that this book will be followed by other texts that address the use of both higher-level services and other languages. However, regardless of what other texts appear, this book will always be the one that provides the foundation.

In summary, we urge aspiring Grid developers to buy this book, download the Globus Toolkit, and start writing programs. We also encourage you to join the Globus community. Visit www.globus.org, participate in discussion groups, and consider contributing to the further development of this remarkable open source technology.

See you on the Grid!

Ian Foster and Carl Kesselman

Preface

Ok, I've installed the Globus Toolkit on my computer. Now how do I send my programs to run on the world's supercomputing Grid?

—Actual question sent by a Globus user

The Globus Toolkit is widely regarded as one of the key enablers of Grid computing. In fact, it has received rave reviews from the likes of The New York Times ("The Globus Toolkit is the de facto standard for Grid Computing"), the MIT Technology Review ("Globus Toolkit-based Grid computing is one of 'Ten Technologies That Will Change the World'"), and Ebert & Roeper ("Two thumbs way up!"). Ok, we made that last one up... our point, anyway, is that the Globus Toolkit 4 (GT4) is a really *groovy* piece of software!

However, because of all the buzz on the Globus Toolkit being this "great Grid enabler", many newcomers to the toolkit (like the one quoted above) tend to have a wrong idea about what the Globus Toolkit is. It is not a magical piece of software that instantly allows you to wield the awesome power of Grid computing. It is, in fact, a collection of software components which provide many of the building blocks necessary to create a Grid-based application.

Needless to say, those building blocks aren't going to piece themselves together on their own. You will have to integrate all the different software components, most of which are Web services-based and rely on an exciting new specification called WSRF (Web Services Resource Framework). So, you will have to be familiar with WSRF and with Web services programming using the Globus Toolkit. That is why we set out to write this book: to provide newcomers to Globus with a well-rounded introduction to the toolkit and, in particular, to the fundamental aspect of Java services programming with the toolkit. In fact, we like to think of this book as *"a practical guide for beginners"*. Let's take a closer look at what we mean...

- *A practical...:* The book teaches by example, and practically every chapter includes at least one example you can run on your computer, and later modify for your own evil purposes.

- *...guide...:* This book is not meant as a reference manual but, rather, as a text where new concepts and examples are explained step by step.

- *...for beginners:* This book is meant to help beginners take their first steps with Globus. To put it another way, the book is not meant as a comprehensive treatise on Java services programming, and some topics have been simplified (or even not included) to keep the book simple.

Scope of This Book

The Globus Toolkit 4 is *huge,* and if we had set out to write a book about the complete toolkit, you would now be staring at a 1500-page book. The scope of this book is limited to those GT4 components directly related to Java services programming. At the end of this book you will know how to program Java services using GT4, and this will enable you to progress towards using the other components included in the toolkit. It is very important to understand that *you cannot program Grid-based applications using only the components covered in this book.* This book should be approached as a stepping stone towards more powerful tooling, not as a definite guide on GT4 programming.

How This Book is Structured

The book is divided into four parts:

- **Key Concepts** (Chapters 1–5): This part introduces key concepts on Grid computing, WSRF, Web services, and GT4.

- **GT4 Java WS Core** (Chapters 6–14): In this part we will start to program basic services using the Java Web Services Core component of the toolkit. Each chapter includes a simple example you can run on your own computer.

- **GT4 Security** (Chapters 15–22): This part explores the security aspects of services in a Grid-based application. We will go through some of the security components included in the toolkit, providing more examples as we go along.

- **The FileBuy Application** (Chapters 23 and 24): The examples used in Parts II and III are used to illustrate certain key features, and are functionally trivial to keep them as simple as possible. Therefore, they are not representative of how a "real" GT4-based application would look. The FileBuy Application is a more elaborate example involving several services, and which illustrates design patterns usually found in GT4-based systems.

The book's conclusion provides useful pointers on "where to go next". As mentioned earlier, this book is intended to help you take your first steps with GT4. The conclusion will tell you where and how to take the next steps. Finally, the book's appendices complement the contents of the book by providing a simplified GT4 installation guide, an introduction to the WSDL language, and a summary of command-line client and examples seen throughout the book.

The Flow of the Book

Being a guide for beginners, the book is intended to be read more or less sequentially. As such, the first examples seen in the book are explained in excruciating detail, while the later ones glide through many concepts which we assume you are already familiar with from previous chapters.

However, there are a couple of chapters you can skip (and return to later) if you're really in a hurry. Figure 1, "Chapter precedence diagram" shows the book's chapter precedences. First of all, if you are already familiar with Grid computing, then you can safely skip Chapter 1. The rest of the Key Concepts should be read before you can advance to

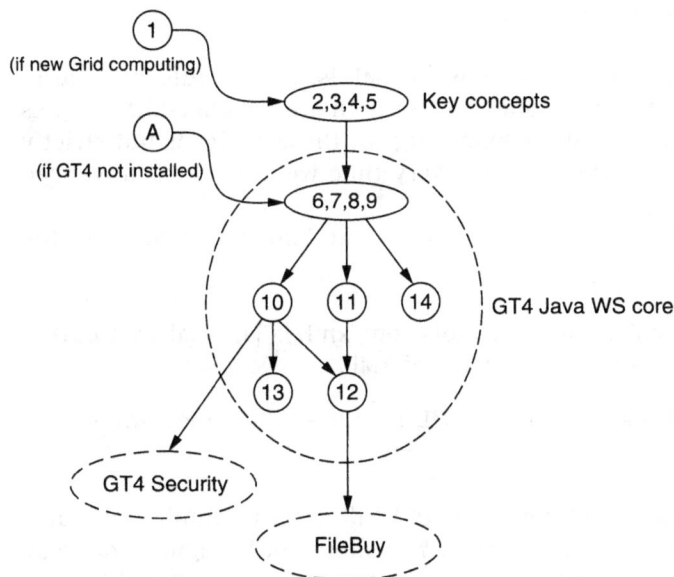

Figure 1: Chapter precedence diagram

programming simple services in Part II. Notice, however, that you will need to make a slight detour to Appendix A (the installation guide) if GT4 is not already installed in your system.

Next, you will need to read up to Chapter 10 before you can think of advancing to the security chapters. To read the FileBuy chapters, you will need to first read all the Java WS Core chapters. Reading the security chapters is not strictly necessary to understand the FileBuy application, but you will miss on some of the security-related discussion included in those chapters.

Prerequisites

We are assuming that you are already familiar (to some degree) with certain topics. Here is a list of prerequisites, including some pointers to useful websites in case you need a refresher in any of these topics:

- **Java Programming.** If you are new to Java, or want to brush up on Java programming, the following two websites might come in handy:

    The Java Tutorial (http://java.sun.com/docs/books/tutorial/): The official tutorial from Sun, the makers of Java. Very good if you know absolutely nothing about Java.

    The Coffee Break (http://www.javacoffeebreak.com/): Website with resources for Java programmers, including tutorials and FAQs.

- **Basic knowledge of XML.** You should know what XML is, and should be able to read XML documents. Although the book does delve into more advanced XML topics occasionally (XML Namespaces, DOM, etc.), knowledge of these topics is not strictly required, as we try to give a brief explanation every time we encounter 'advanced XML'.

    If you don't know XML, or simply want to further your knowledge of XML, the following websites are worth a look:

    W3Schools XML Tutorial (http://www.w3schools.com/xml/): Tutorial that covers both the basics and the more advanced aspects of XML.

    ZVON.org (http://www.zvon.org/): Tons of XML resources. Includes some very good reference guides.

- **UNIX** or **Windows.** This book is written mainly with UNIX users in mind, with notes on how to get the examples running on Windows. You should either know your way around a UNIX system or around a Windows system (specially the command-line).

On the other hand, you should be perfectly safe even if you have no knowledge of the following topics:

- **Grid Computing.** Although most of our readers will probably have a solid Grid Computing background, we realize that for many readers this will be their first contact with Grid programming. We have included a brief introduction to Grid Computing in the book to make sure we all stand on equal footing.

- **Web Services.** A brief introduction to Web Services is included in the book.

- **Previous versions of the Globus Toolkit.** The book is not written as a transition guide from previous Globus Toolkit versions. You have nothing to worry about if this is your very first contact with the Globus Toolkit.

The Book Website is Your Friend!

This book has a companion website (http://www.gt4book.com/) where you will find a lot of goodies:

- **Source code for the examples:** Throughout the book we will be working with a lot of examples. To run the examples in your computer, you will have to download the source code from the book website.

- **"Copy-pasteable" commands:** To run the examples, you will have to run a lot of command-line applications (such as **java**, **javac**, etc.). Manually typing these commands (and their often long list of parameters) can be cumbersome and error-prone so, for your convenience, the book website provides a text document with all the commands mentioned in the book. This way, you can easily copy-paste the commands to your command line, instead of manually typing them!

- **Updates to the book to track new releases of the Globus Toolkit:** This book was written using version 4.0.0 of the Globus Toolkit, and has also been tested with version 4.0.1, the latest version available when we finished the book. However, new versions of the toolkit will surely be released during this book's lifetime. Practically all the contents of this book will remain valid throughout all the 4.x releases but, of course, there might be minor issues or interesting new features that readers have to be aware of. We are committed to posting a document detailing such issues whenever a new version of GT4 is released. Updated example bundles will also be posted, in case a new GT4 release requires changes to the source code of the examples.

- **FAQs:** Readers are bound to come up with a lot of interesting questions that we did not foresee when writing the book. We will include a list of the questions most frequently asked by readers on the book website.

- **Errata:** A list of known typos and bugs can be found on the book website.

Other Important Web Resources

The Web offers countless resources on Grid Computing and the Globus Toolkit. However, there are three particular websites which you will probably need to refer to more than once while reading this book:

- **The official Globus documentation** (http://www.globus.org/toolkit/docs/): The official documentation includes vast amounts of information on the toolkit. Sometimes we will provide only a basic explanation of a feature or concept, and we will refer you to the documentation for all the nitty-gritty details. The official docs also deal with all the higher-level services not covered in this book.

- **The GT4 Java WS Core API documentation** (http://www-unix.globus.org/api/ javadoc-4.0/globus_java_ws_core/): Throughout the book we will use a considerable amount of Globus-supplied classes, but most of them won't be explained in full detail. The GT4 API documentation is the place to go when you want accurate and concise information about what a certain class does and what methods it provides.

- **The Globus Documentation Project (GDP)** (http://gdp.globus.org/): A documentation website with links to documentation resources produced by members of the Globus community.

Where to Get Help

Although we've tried to make the book as clear and straightforward as possible, we can't presume to have foreseen all the problems, questions, etc. that might arise while reading this book. If you find yourself in need of help, such as help with an example that refuses to run or a question about some concept you have trouble grasping, the first place to visit is the book website (http://www.gt4book.com/). The FAQs included in the website might provide an answer to your questions.

If the book website doesn't provide any relief, then a quick look at the official Globus documentation might prove beneficial, specially when dealing with conceptual questions. The official documentation usually provides a more in-depth and technical explanation of certain concepts.

If visiting the book website and the official documentation doesn't solve your problems, and you need to address your questions to a living, breathing human being, then you can send your questions to the *Globus-Discuss* mailing list, where all the Globus gurus hang out. You can find instructions on how to subscribe to this mailing list (you need to be subscribed to send messages) here: http://www.globus.org/toolkit/support.html (this website also lists other forms of Globus support you might find useful).

A word to the wise: if you're having trouble running an example, and are facing a baffling error message, then make a quick web search on that error message. It is quite possible that someone has already encountered that problem and posted a message to a Globus mailing list. Remember, Google is your friend!

Another word to the wise: if you post a question to Globus-Discuss please make sure to include as much information as possible about the problem you're facing. Short and vague e-mails that simply state *"I have a problem in example FOO, the error message says something about BAR. What am I doing wrong???"* will usually receive no response, or require several iterations to be solved. When available, send along stack traces, snippets of code related to your problem, etc. If you have time, take a moment to read the (excellent) *How To Ask Questions The Smart Way* (http://www.catb.org/~esr/faqs/smart-questions.html) by Eric S. Raymond, which explains how to ask questions in public forums, such as mailing lists.

Finally, we ask that you please do not send your questions directly to us (the authors). We are not saying this in a mean, unpleasant, green ogre-ish way. We simply believe that it is much more beneficial to the whole Globus community that questions be sent to a public forum, such as a mailing list. That way, more people will be able to help you out, and everyone benefits from the replies to your question. Besides, we monitor most of the Globus mailing lists and it is very possible that we will be the first to reply to any questions regarding the book.

Reporting Typos, Bugs, etc.

If you find a typo in the book's text, or a bug in any of the examples, please visit the book's website (http://www.gt4book.com/). There you will find instructions on how to report typos and bugs.

The Book's Kid Brother: The GT4 Programmer's Tutorial

This book is the evolution of a programming tutorial which has been freely available on the web since 2003 (back when the "bleeding edge" was GT3): http://gdp.globus.org/gt4-tutorial/. In fact, some portions of the book are directly based on material contained in the tutorial. But, what exactly sets the book apart from the tutorial? Allow us to elaborate...

- **More content:** The main difference is that the book is just plain and simply *bigger* than the tutorial! The tutorial is meant as a no-frills, quick introduction to GT4 programming, which leaves little room to explain certain concepts in detail. In the book, most of the chapters taken from the tutorial are greatly expanded. And, of course, the book includes quite a few chapters which are not included in the tutorial.

- **Reviewed, copyedited, proofread:** The tutorial does not undergo any formal review process. The book, on the other hand, has been reviewed by GT4 experts which provided invaluable suggestions on how to make the text as accurate and concise as possible.

- **It's a book!** Don't try to deny it... the soft touch of paper running through your fingers will always beat having to read from a computer screen for several hours.

The book, however, does not replace the tutorial, which will continue to be freely available on the web. Along with the book, it will be maintained and updated to track changes in the Globus Toolkit.

Acknowledgments

To Ian Foster and Carl Kesselman, our fearless leaders, for their pioneering work in Grid computing and the Globus Toolkit, and for their support in our efforts to make this book a reality.

To the Globus developers and contributors, for creating such an awesome piece of software, and sharing their knowledge with us. Without this talented group of people, we wouldn't have anything to write about.

To our amazing reviewers: Sebastien Barre, Jarek Gawor, and Sam Meder. Sebastien provided thorough and insightful comments from the point of view of a normal user, which helped keep the book more in touch with a user's needs. Jarek and Sam, as creators of much of the technology discussed in this book, provided invaluable corrections that only they (and a few others in the world) could notice.

To Rich Wellner, who provided many helpful comments on his own free time.

To our editors, Rick Adams, Rachel Roumeliotis, and Mona Buehler, for patiently guiding and supporting this pair of first-time authors.

We gratefully acknowledge the work of Leon Kuntz, to whom this book is dedicated in memoriam. Leon had a pivotal role in creating *The Globus Toolkit 3 Programmer's Tutorial*, the seed from which this book sprung. Without Leon's support and enthusiasm for producing quality documentation, this work might well have not been written.

Borja's Acknowledgments

On top of all the people mentioned above, I would like to extend my gratitude to...

- Rebeca Cortazar, my advisor when I was an engineering student at the University of Deusto (Bilbao, Spain). When I was searching high and low for an interesting topic for my engineering thesis, Rebeca is the one who, on a fateful day on November 2002, nudged me in the right direction by saying: "Have you heard about all this Grid stuff? Maybe you should look into it...".

- Jesús Marco, director of the Instituto de Física de Cantabria (Santander, Spain) and one of Spain's foremost Grid experts. Jesús very kindly helped me take my very first steps in the vast and complicated world of Grid computing.

- my former colleagues at the University of Deusto (both students and teachers), for their encouragement, their wise words, and *el buen rollo*. Special thanks to professor

Javier García Zubía, for all his guidance when I first started doing research under his tutelage in the BOOLE-DEUSTO project.

- my new colleagues at the University of Chicago, for making me feel welcome in a new city and school.

- Mike, for being such a great friend.

- y, finalmente, a mis padres, Eduardo y Ana (que no me entenderán si les escribo en inglés :-), por su incombustible apoyo y por aguantar día a día todas mis excentricidades informáticas.

Lisa's Acknowledgments

First and foremost, thanks go to my husband, Tom Brown, whose unwavering patience, kindness and support made this book possible. Thanks also to Cosmo and Dashiell for putting up with me and being so super. Thank you mom, dad and my entire family.

Thanks to Ben and Charles for being so cool, and to Gigi, my ultimate partner in crime. Thanks to Bill and Lee for their amazing efforts, and to my colleagues on the Globus Alliance Board. A big fat whuggle to everyone in the Globus Pub.

Aloha to David Lassner, who listened closely and gave me great advice.

Thanks to Mike Papka and Rick Stevens for bringing me in to the Argonne family and introducing me to Grid computing.

To my teachers past and present: Namaste.

Conventions

Finally, a note on the conventions observed throughout the book.

Code

```
public class HelloWorld
{
    public static final void main( String args[] )
    {
        ❶
        // Code in bold is important
        System.out.println("Hello World");
    }
}
```

❶ This is a callout, further explaining an important part of the code.

Note that, in some examples, the code shown in the book might not correspond *exactly* with the source code of the examples. Slight changes have been made to make the code more readable in the book.

Inlined Code

Whenever we refer to bits of code from the main text, it will be highlighted `like this`. For example:

The `HelloWorld` class has a single `main` method that prints out a "`Hello World`" string.

Shell Commands

```
javac HelloWorld.java
```

If a command is too long to fit in a single line, it will be wrapped into several lines using the backslash ("\") character. This way, on most UNIX shells (including BASH) you should be able to write the command in several lines, instead of one long line.

```
javac \

-classpath /usr/lib/java/Hello.jar \

HelloWorld.java \

HelloUniverse.java \

HelloEveryone.java
```

Note that we are using a UNIX shell syntax. Windows users must take care to use appropriate path separators (backslash instead of a regular slash).

Notes

You can find three types of notes in the text: complementary information, reminders, and warnings.

> ⓘ This is a complementary information block.
>   This kind of note contains interesting information that complements what is currently being discussed in the text.

> ☞ This is a reminder.
>   This kind of note is usually used after a block of code to remind you of where you can find the file that contains that particular code. It is also used to remind you of important concepts, and to suggest what sections of the book you should read again if you have a hard time understanding a particular section.

> ! This is a warning.
>   Warnings are used to emphatically point out something. They generally refer to common pitfalls or to things that you should take into account when writing your own code.

part I

Key Concepts

## chapter 1

Grid Computing

In this first chapter we will provide a brief introduction to Grid computing. This is not meant to be a comprehensive introduction, and our goal is for you to get a general feeling of what Grid computing is. This will allow you to better understand the relevance of OGSA and WSRF in the Grid universe (OGSA and WSRF are introduced in the following chapters). If you are already Grid-savvy, you can safely skip this chapter. If you are new to Grid computing and want to read more, we have included a list of "must-read" references at the end of the chapter. If you are a complete newcomer, then we highly recommend The Grid Café [7], a website that provides a gentle and didactic introduction to Grid computing.

1.1 A Problem

Although we *could* start by giving you a textbook definition, we find that it is usually easier to grasp what Grid computing is by first looking at a specific computational challenge and seeing how it can be solved using Grid computing. Don't worry, later on we will also give you a textbook definition to quote at conferences, papers, and dinner parties.

The example we have chosen is the Large Hadron Collider (LHC) being built in CERN (Geneva, Switzerland), the world's largest particle physics laboratory. The LHC is a particle accelerator and collider with a circumference of 27 kilometers (16.7 miles), which makes it the largest machine ever built by humans (Figure 1.1).

The reason why this gargantuan machine is a good example is because, when it starts to work in 2007, it will produce *huge* amounts of information. More exactly, it will generate about 10 Petabytes, or 10^7 Gigabytes, of information a year. Trust us, that is a pretty large amount of bytes. In fact, 10 Petabytes would account for roughly 10% of all the information produced on Planet Earth in a single year. And here's a nice "gee-whiz" statistic: if you

Figure 1.1: The Large Hadron Collider, at CERN, is the largest machine ever built

stored all the information produced by the LHC in CD-ROMs, the stack would be 20 km high!

Of course, all this information has to be processed and stored somewhere. The only problem is that, using current technology, processing and storing all that data in a single site is *impossible*. An estimated 100,000 high-tech processors would be needed to deal with the LHC's computational needs! Unfortunately, CERN 'only' has over 1,000 dual processor computers and 1 Petabyte of storage. So, how will we be able to deal with the computational and storage requirements of the LHC?

1.2   The Solution: Grid Computing

We've seen that a single site (CERN) is unable to deal with the requirements of the LHC. However, if we were somehow able to harness the computational power and storage space of *several* sites, their combined power might be enough. In fact, the EGEE Project (Enabling Grids for E-Science in Europe, [8]) will do exactly that: it will join the computational and storage resources from dozens of organizations all around Europe to meet the LHC's requirements.

In essence, this is what Grid computing is all about: achieving greater performance and throughput by pooling together resources from different organizations (we will refine this definition later on). Without Grid computing, an organization is stuck with using only the resources it has direct control over (Figure 1.2). Using Grid computing, resources from several different organizations are dynamically pooled into *virtual organizations* (or VO) to solve specific problems. Figure 1.3 shows how the resources from three 'real' organizations can be combined into two virtual organizations. Furthermore, although not shown in the figure, *users* also form part of virtual organizations. When a user forms part of a VO, he will generally have access to the resources pooled together in that VO.

Conceptually, all this might seems like a trivial notion. In fact, "using resources from several organizations" seems like a pretty intuitive course of action when a problem cannot be solved using the computational resources of a single organization. However, in practice, this is completely *non-trivial*. For example, ask yourself the following:

- How do we decide what resources are part of each virtual organization?
- Given a computational task, how do we decide what resources will be allocated to deal with that task? For how long? Surely, we don't want to give other organizations unfettered access to our resources!

● Computational resource
□ Organization

Figure 1.2: An organization and its resources

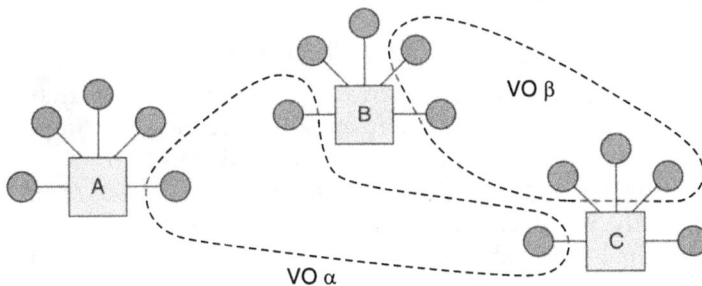

Figure 1.3: Virtual organizations

- How do we get the resources to communicate amongst themselves? Take into account that these are *heterogeneous* resources from *different* organizations!

- If I want to "split up" a task so that it can be performed in parallel by several computers in different organizations, how to I actually "split up" the program? Again, we're dealing with heterogeneous resources: each organization might be using a different operating system, or even a different computer architecture.

- Sharing your resources with other organizations might sound like a really cool idea on paper, but it entails a lot of security challenges. For example, how can an organization make sure its resources are only being used by trusted users and that they are not being abused by malicious users?

So, we could say that Grid computing, in general, enables us to access heterogeneous resources from different organizations by providing a set of protocols, technologies, and methodologies that provide an answer to these questions (and many more!). Before we actually take a closer look at the general architecture of Grid systems, let's take a look at a more concise definition of Grid computing.

1.3   The Textbook Definition

Unfortunately, definitions of Grid computing are just like resources on a Grid: numerous and heterogeneous. We think that one of the best definitions out there is Ian Foster's *What is the Grid? A Three Point Checklist* [4]. Although, as Ian himself points out in the paper, the checklist still leaves room for debate, it nonetheless provides a concise and straightforward definition. To quote directly from the checklist:

> **"A grid is a system that:**
>
> 1. **coordinates resources that are not subject to centralized control...**
> 2. **...using standard, open, general-purpose protocols and interfaces...**
> 3. **...to deliver nontrivial qualities of service"**

Let's take a closer look at the first two points:

1. Coordinates resources that are not subject to centralized control...

This alludes to the notion of "using resources from several organizations" that we've discussed earlier. To be more concise, we are actually referring to "integrating and coordinating resources and users that live within different *control domains*". We've talked about different organizations sharing resources, but these "control domains" could also be different administrative units inside a company. It is precisely when we have to deal with these different control domains that all the questions mentioned earlier will arise. Otherwise, you will be dealing with a problem that can be solved using *local management* solutions, not using a Grid system.

2. Uses standard, open, general-purpose protocols and interfaces...

We have mentioned several times that resources on a Grid are heterogeneous. On a Grid system, we somehow have to take a bunch of different resources (individuals computers, clusters, supercomputers, storage, etc.) that use a wide variety of operating systems and architectures, and somehow make them collaborate to solve computational tasks. The only way to do this is by using "standard, open, general-purpose protocols and interfaces" that provide a "common language" that everyone on the Grid can understand. The protocol-based approach allows for heterogeneity, and the fact that they are based on standards promotes interoperability. If you find that a problem can be solved using ad hoc protocols, then you are probably dealing with an "application-specific" system, not a Grid system.

Again, there is plenty of room for refinement, but this explanation provides a solid starting point. If you want to read about other definitions, the paper *Grid Characteristics and Uses: a Grid Definition* [3] provides a comparison of the most popular definitions out there.

☞ **Grid Computing? A Grid? The Grid?**

If you're new to Grid computing, you might be confused by the fact that there are three terms commonly used in a Grid context: "The Grid", "A Grid", and "Grid computing" itself. So what does each refer to?

- **Grid computing:** What we have defined above, strictly speaking, is not Grid computing but, rather "a Grid system". Grid computing, to put it simply, is the field of computer science which concerns itself with Grid systems ("systems that coordinate resources that...").

- **A Grid:** When we refer to "a Grid", we usually mean an actual, working Grid system.

- **The Grid:** Currently, Grid computing is used in a wide variety of different contexts, and there are a lot of "grids" (Grid systems) all around the world. However, there is no worldwide "The Grid" accessible to the general public (in the same sense that "The Internet" is a publicly accessible global internet). However, "The Grid" will ideally exist in the future.

  In case you're wondering, the word "grid" is used by analogy to the "electric grid". The same way we can plug an appliance into the electric grid to get electricity, "The Grid" would allow users to plug their computer to "The Grid" to obtain more computational power, more storage, etc.

1.4 The Grid Architecture

Creating a complete Grid system requires a wide variety of protocols, services, and software development kits. In the landmark paper *Anatomy of the Grid* [1], Foster, Kesselman,

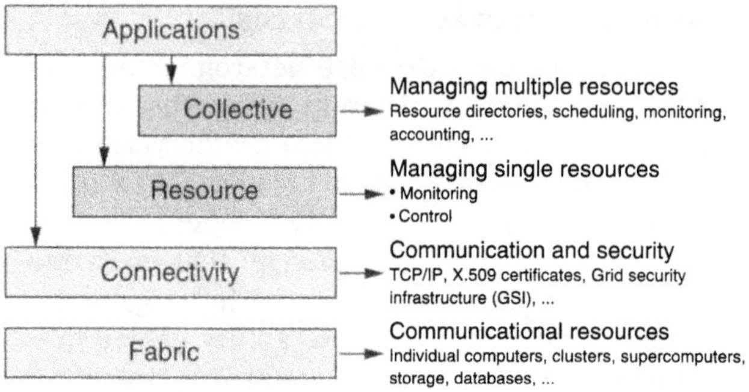

Figure 1.4: Grid architecture

and Tuecke defined a general *Grid architecture* in which all the different components that make up a Grid system are categorized according to their function and purpose. As we said in the Preface, this book covers only a fraction of what is needed to build a Grid system (Java services using the Globus Toolkit), so you should not expect this book to give you a working knowledge of how to work at every level of the Grid architecture. By going through the Grid architecture, we hope to give you a feel for the complexity of building a Grid system, and to show how a lot of different services are usually involved. In the book's conclusion, we will give you some useful pointers to other components of the Globus Toolkit and other software toolkits that will allow you to build complete Grid systems.

The Grid architecture can be expressed in terms of a layered diagram (Figure 1.4). We will describe each layer from the bottom-up.

1.4.1   Fabric

This layer refers to the resources which are actually going to be shared in our Grid system, such as individual computers, clusters, supercomputers, network storage, databases, etc.

1.4.2   Connectivity

Of course, our resources need to be able to communicate amongst themselves. The connectivity layer refers to all the protocols that will allow our resources to communicate. Fundamental Internet protocols, such as TCP/IP, HTTP, DNS, etc. fall into this layer. However, Grid systems also require *secure* communications, so this layer also includes a lot of protocols that have emerged from the Grid community in response to the peculiar security challenges faced in Grid systems. We will discuss these in detail in Part III, "GT4 Security".

1.4.3 Resource

This layer refers to all the services and protocols that enable us to manage resources individually. This management might include tasks such as initiating resources, monitoring them, and accounting them. At this layer, we are not concerned with the global interactions between resources in the Grid, only with individual resources. In particular, there are two primary classes of protocols in this layer:

- **Information protocols:** These protocols allow us to access a resource's information. For example, in the case of a computer, we might be interested in knowing it's CPU load, its available memory, the number of processes running in it, etc.

- **Management protocols:** These protocols actually allow us to control the resource to a certain degree. In a Grid system, we will usually not have complete control over a resource, so these services and protocols will generally also be in charge of checking that the type of operations we request in a resource are consistent with an organization's policies.

1.4.4 Collective

This layer encompasses the services and protocols that deal with managing multiple resources. Building on the services provided in the Resource layer, this layer will allow us to actually take a bunch of resources and make them work together to solve a common task. The following is just a sample of the type of services commonly found in this layer:

- **Resource registries:** Allow us to discover resources in a virtual organization and to query their properties.

- **Allocation and scheduling services:** When we want to run a program on a Grid system, we generally don't have to decide where exactly on the Grid it will run. An allocation service will use a resource directory to discover a resource (or resources) adequate for our program (usually called a *job*), and will allocate that resource for our job. A scheduling service will actually decide what jobs run where and when.

- **Monitoring services:** Allow us to monitor that all our resources are working properly.

- **Data management services:** Our jobs will generally require datasets to work with. Data management services keep track of these datasets and transfer them to the resource that needs them.

1.4.5 Applications

This layer refers to the actual applications that will be running on a Grid system. Notice how these applications are not required to interact directly with the Collective services.

They are also free to access the Resource and Connectivity services directly whenever required to.

1.5 Examples of Grid Systems

- **EGEE: Enabling Grids for E-Science in Europe** (http://public.eu-egee.org/): An ambitious Grid project that will give scientists access to computational resources across 27 countries. EGEE will also be responsible for providing the awesome computational power required by the LHC described above.

- **NEESit** (http://it.nees.org/): Provides an extensive infrastructure for the NEES (Network for Earthquake Engineering Simulation) Collaboratory by linking together earthquake research centers in the US.

- **TeraGrid** (http://www.teragrid.org/): A Grid system providing a powerful infrastructure for open scientific research. As of 2004, TeraGrid had 20 teraflops of computing power and 1 petabyte of distributed storage.

- **Access Grid** (http://www.accessgrid.org/): A Grid system used for "large-scale distributed meetings, collaborative work sessions, seminars, lectures, tutorials, and training".

- **eDiaMoND** (http://www.ediamond.ox.ac.uk/): The eDiaMoND project is an example of how Grid computing can be used for e-Health. This project "pools and distributes information on breast cancer treatment, enables early screening and diagnosis, and provides medical professionals with tools and information to treat the disease".

For a more complete list of Grid applications, please refer to [5], [6], and [7].

1.6 Summing Up...

As mentioned at the beginning of the chapter, we have provided a brief introduction to Grid computing, but only enough so you will understand how OGSA and WSRF (explained in the following chapters) are relevant to Grid computing. The two main ideas you should keep in mind are (a) that Grid systems involve heterogeneous resources from different organizations, and (b) that coordinating all these resources is non-trivial and involves a lot of different services such as job schedulers, resource managers, information services, etc.

Of course, Grid computing involves much more than these two simple ideas. For more details, and examples of other Grid applications, please refer to this chapter's list of references.

References

[1] I. Foster, C. Kesselman, and S. Tuecke. "The Anatomy of the Grid: Enabling Scalable Virtual Organizations". *International J. Supercomputer Applications* 15(3), 2001.

[2] I. Foster, C. Kesselman, J. Nick, and S. Tuecke. "The Physiology of the Grid: An Open Grid Services Architecture for Distributed Systems Integration". *Open Grid Service Infrastructure WG*. Global Grid Forum, June 22, 2002.

[3] Miguel L. Bote-Lorenzo, Yannis A. Dimitriadis, and Eduardo Gómez-Sánchez. "Grid Characteristics and Uses: a Grid Definition". *1st European Across Grids Conference*, February 13–14, 2003.

[4] I. Foster. "What is the Grid? A Three Point Checklist". *GRIDToday*, July 20, 2002.

[5] I. Foster and C. Kesselman. *The Grid 2: Blueprint for a New Computing Infrastructure.* Morgan Kaufmann, 2nd edition, November 18, 2003.

[6] Fran Berman, Geoffrey Fox, and Anthony J.G. Hey. *Grid Computing: Making The Global Infrastructure a Reality.* John Wiley & Sons, April 8, 2003.

[7] *Grid Café.* http://gridcafe.web.cern.ch/gridcafe/.

[8] *EGEE (Enabling Grids for E-Science in Europe) Website.* http://public.eu-egee.org/.

chapter **2**

OGSA, WSRF, and GT4

Two acronyms you will often see associated with GT4 and, in fact, with Grid computing itself, are OGSA and WSRF. But... what do they mean? How are they related to the Globus Toolkit 4? This chapter attempts to clarify these important concepts and how they are related.

2.1 OGSA and WSRF

First of all, we will start by taking a look at OGSA and WSRF *without* seeing (just yet) how they relate to GT4. Figure 2.1 summarizes the relationships between OGSA, WSRF, and Web Services which are explained in this section.

2.1.1 The Open Grid Services Architecture (OGSA)

A grid system will usually consist of several different components. For example, a typical grid system could have:

- **VO Management Service:** To manage what nodes and users are part of each Virtual Organization.

- **Resource Discovery and Management Service:** So applications on the grid can discover resources that suit their needs, and then manage them.

- **Job Management Service:** So users can submit tasks (in the form of "jobs") to the Grid.

- And a whole other bunch of services like security, data management, etc.

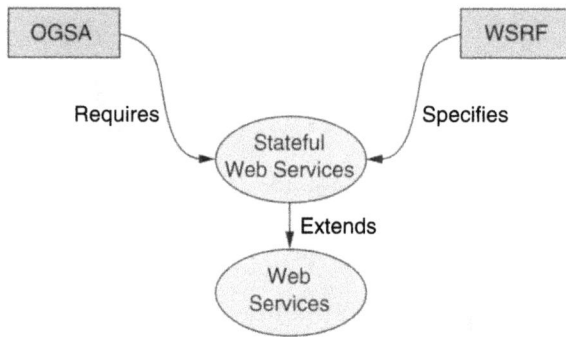

Figure 2.1: Relationship between OGSA, WSRF, and Web Services

Furthermore, all these services are interacting constantly. For example, the Job Management Service might consult the Resource Discovery Service to find computational resources that match the job's requirements. With so many services, and so many interactions between them, there exists the potential for chaos. What if every vendor out there decided to implement a Job Management Service in a completely different way, exposing not only different functionality but also different interfaces? It would be very difficult (or nearly impossible) to get all the different software pieces to work together.

The solution is *standardization:* define a common interface for each type of service. For example, take a look at the World Wide Web. One of the reasons why the Web is such a popular Internet application is because it is based on *standards* (HTML, HTTP, etc.) agreed upon by all the different major players (Microsoft, Netscape, etc.). Imagine, on the other hand, that you could only use a Microsoft browser to access websites implemented with Microsoft technology (ditto for Netscape, Opera, etc.) It would be definitely uncool. Thanks to standards, we can use our favorite browser (provided it follows standards, which most modern browsers do) to access most of the websites out there (regardless of what technology is used to implement the website). Why? Because a set of common languages was agreed upon for all the browsers and websites out there. Standardization is definitely a good thing.

The Open Grid Services Architecture (OGSA), developed by The Global Grid Forum [1], aims to define a common, standard, and open architecture for grid-based applications. The goal of OGSA is to standardize practically all the services one commonly finds in a grid system (job management services, resource management services, security services, etc.) by specifying a set of standard interfaces for these services. At the time of writing this book, this "set of standard interfaces" is still in the works. However, OGSA already defines a set of requirements that must be met by these standard interfaces. In other words, OGSA has already gone as far as identifying the most important services one encounters in Grid systems, and which most stand to benefit from standardization.

OGSA Requires 'Stateful Services'

However, when the powers-that-be undertook the task of creating this new architecture, they realized they needed to choose some sort of distributed middleware on which to *base* the architecture. In other words, if OGSA (for example) defines that the `JobSubmissionInterface` has a `submitJob` operation, there has to be a common and standard way to *invoke* that operation if we want the architecture to be adopted as an industry-wide standard. This *base* for the architecture could, in theory, be any distributed middleware (CORBA, RMI, or even traditional RPC). For reasons that will be explained further on, Web Services were chosen as the underlying technology.

However, although the Web Services Architecture was certainly the best option, it still didn't meet one of OGSA's most important requirements: the underlying middleware had to be *stateful* (don't worry if you don't know what a "stateful" service is, it is explained in the next chapter). Unfortunately, although Web services can in theory be either stateless or stateful, they are usually stateless and there is no standard way of making them stateful. So, clearly, something had to be done!

2.1.2 The Web Services Resource Framework (WSRF)

Enter the Web Services Resource Framework, a collection of specifications under the auspices of OASIS [2]. WSRF specifies how we can make our Web Services stateful, along with adding a lot of other cool features. It is important to note that WSRF is a joint effort by the Grid and Web Services communities, so it fits pretty nicely inside the whole Web Services Architecture (in the diagram: *WSRF extends Web Services*).

So what exactly is the relation between OGSA and WSRF? It's very simple: WSRF provides the stateful services that OGSA needs. In the diagram: **WSRF specifies stateful services** (as opposed to those services simply 'being required' by OGSA). Another way of expressing this relation is that, while OGSA is the *architecture*, WSRF is the *infrastructure* on which that architecture is built on.

> ☞ We provide an introduction to Web services in Chapter 3 and take a closer look at WSRF in Chapter 4.

2.2 How Does this Relate to GT4?

Now that we've cleared up what OGSA and WSRF are, we are ready to complete the above diagram to see how GT4 fits into the picture (Figure 2.2).

The Globus Toolkit 4

The Globus Toolkit is a software toolkit, developed by The Globus Alliance [4], which we can use to create Grid systems. The toolkit, first and foremost, includes quite a few

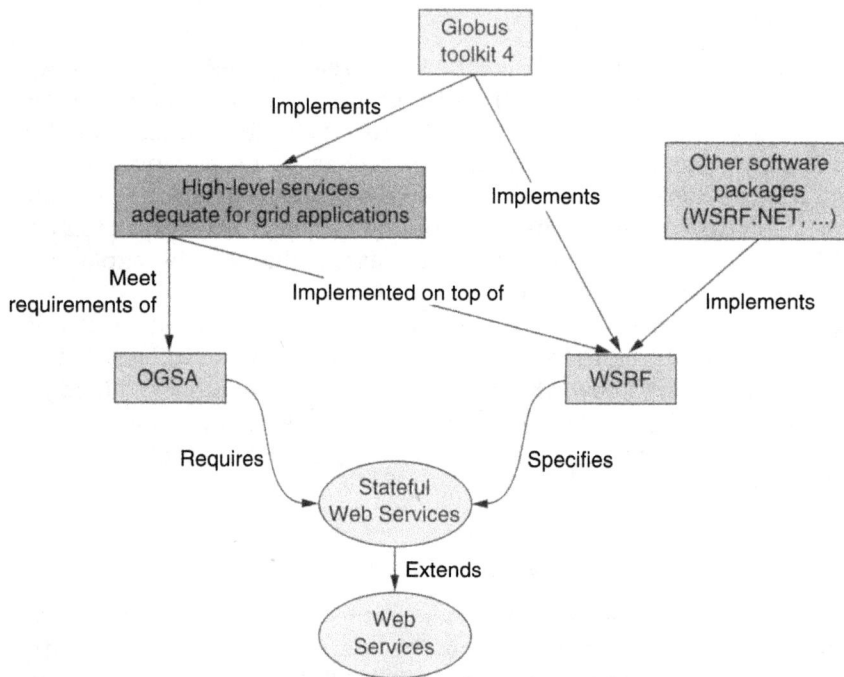

Figure 2.2: Relationship between OGSA, GT4, WSRF, and Web Services

high-level services that we can use to build Grid applications. These services, in fact, meet most of the abstract requirements set forth in OGSA. In other words, the Globus Toolkit includes a resource monitoring and discovery service, a job submission infrastructure, security infrastructure, and data management services (to name a few!). Since the working groups at GGF are still working on defining standard interfaces for these types of services, we can't say (at this point) that GT4 is an implementation of OGSA (although GT4 does implement a few specifications defined by GGF). However, it *is* a realization of the OGSA requirements and a sort of *de facto* standard for the Grid community while GGF works on standardizing all the different services.

Most of these services are implemented *on top of WSRF* (the toolkit also includes some services that are not implemented on top of WSRF and are called the *non-WS components*). The Globus Toolkit 4, in fact, includes a complete implementation of the WSRF specifications. This part of the toolkit (the WSRF implementation) is a very important part of the toolkit since so much is built on top of it. However, it's worth noting that it's also a *very small* part of the toolkit. At this point, we'll repeat something we said in the Preface:

> At the end of this book you will know how to program Java services using GT4, and this will enable you to progress towards using the other components included in the toolkit. It is very important to understand that *you cannot program Grid-based*

Standards in the works (GGF)
- VO management
- Security
- Resource management
- Job management
- Data services
- etc.

Grid applications are based
on high-level services
defined by OGSA
(i.e. not implemented from
scratch using WSRF)

Applications

OGSA

GT4 includes many of the services
required by OGSA

Standardized (OASIS)
and implemented (GT4)

WSRF

Web Services

Standardized (W3C, OASIS, IETF, ...)
and implemented (e.g. Apache axis)

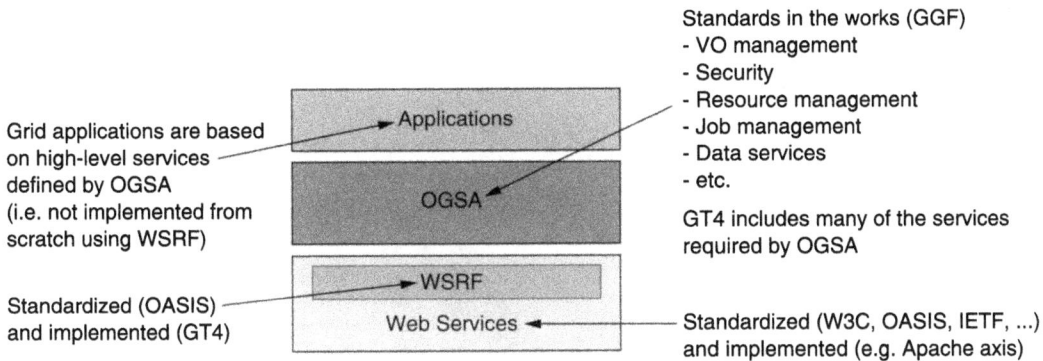

Figure 2.3: Layered diagram of OGSA, GT4, WSRF, and Web Services

applications using only the components covered in this book. This book should be approached as a stepping stone towards more powerful tooling, not as a definite guide on GT4 programming.

Sorry to have to hammer this in, but this really is a very important concept. Never forget that, on the long road towards true Grid Nirvana, WSRF is indeed a necessary step, but only the *first* step.

Finally, take into account that GT4 isn't the only WSRF implementation out there. For example, another complete implementation of WSRF is WSRF.NET [5].

⟨☞⟩ GT4 is discussed in more detail in Chapter 5, The Globus Toolkit 4.

The Mandatory Layered Diagram

If there's something we computer geeks like in documentation, it's layered diagrams! So, this chapter really wouldn't be complete without a diagram that explains the relationship between OGSA, WSRF, and GT4 using the wonderful language of layers (Figure 2.3).

References

[1] *Global Grid Forum (GGF)*. http://www.ggf.org/.

[2] *OASIS*. http://www.oasis-open.org/.

[3] *OASIS WSRF Technical Committee*. http://www.oasis-open.org/committees/tc_home. php?wg_abbrev=wsrf.

[4] *The Globus Alliance*. http://www.globus.org/.

[5] *WSRF.NET*. http://www.cs.virginia.edu/~gsw2c/wsrf.net.html.

## chapter 3

Web Services

Before we take a closer look at what the Web Services Resource Framework (WSRF) is, we need to have a basic understanding of how Web services work (so we can better appreciate how WSRF extends Web services). If you're already familiar with Web services, you can safely skip this section.

For quite a while now, there has been a lot of buzz about "Web Services," and many companies have begun to rely on them for their enterprise applications. So, what exactly are Web Services? To put it quite simply, they are *yet another* distributed computing technology (like CORBA, RMI, EJB, etc.). They allow us to create client/server applications.

For example, let's suppose I keep a database with up-to-date information about weather in the United States, and I want to distribute that information to anyone in the world. To do so, I could *publish* the weather information through a Web service that, given a ZIP code, will provide the weather information for that ZIP code.

ⓘ Don't mistake this with publishing something on a website. Information on a website is intended for humans, while information which is available through a Web service will *always* be accessed by software, *never* directly by a human (despite the fact that there might be a human using that software). Even though Web services rely heavily on existing Web technologies (such as HTTP, as we will see in a moment), they have no relation to web browsers and HTML.

As shown in Figure 3.1, the *client* (program that want to access the weather information) would contact the *Web service* (in the *server*), and send a *service request* asking for the weather information. The server would return the forecast through a *service response*. Of course, this is a very sketchy example of how a Web service works. We'll see all the details in a moment.

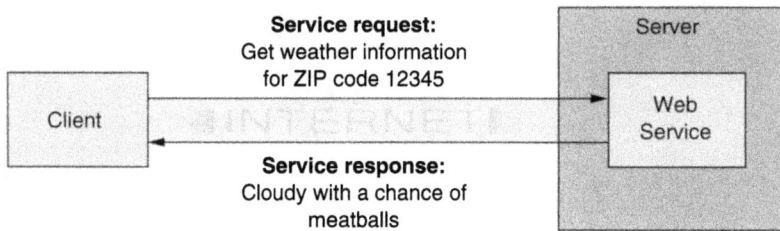

Figure 3.1: Web Services

However, you might be thinking: *"Hey! Wait a moment! I can do that with RMI, CORBA, EJBs, and countless other technologies!"* So, what makes Web services special? Well, Web services have certain advantages over other technologies:

■ Web Services are platform-independent and language-independent, since they use standard XML languages. This means that our client program can be developed in C++ and running under Windows, while the Web service is programmed in Java and running under Linux.

■ Most Web Services use HTTP for transmitting messages (such as the service request and response). This is a major advantage if you want to build an Internet-scale application, since most of the Internet's proxies and firewalls won't mess with HTTP traffic.

■ One of the oft-cited advantages of Web Services is the fact that they lend themselves naturally to build *loosely coupled* systems. These types of systems are more scalable than *strongly coupled* systems, and impose fewer architectural requirements on the actual implementation of the Web services. However, loose fewer coupling, in the context of software design, is a pretty abstract concept which is beyond the scope of the book (we recommend [1] for a detailed text on Web Services and loosely coupled systems). Suffice it to say that the reason why Web Services are ideal to build loosely coupled systems is because they are *message-oriented* and rely on language-neutral XML dialects to send messages, to specify interfaces, etc.

Of course, Web services also have some disadvantages:

■ Overhead. Transmitting all your data in XML is obviously not as efficient as using a proprietary binary code. What you win in portability, you lose in efficiency. Even so, this overhead is usually acceptable for most applications, but you will probably never find a critical real-time application that uses Web services.

■ Lack of maturity. Web Services are relatively new and, although the core specifications that deal with fundamental languages (XML, WSDL, ...) and protocols (HTTP, SOAP, ...) are pretty stable, the world of Web Services is still evolving at a fast pace. Standards dealing with more advanced capabilities expected from distributed systems, such as transactions, security, etc. are either very new or still in the works.

3.1   A Typical Web Service Invocation

So how does this all actually work? Let's take a look at all the steps involved in a complete Web service invocation (Figure 3.2). For now, don't worry about all the acronyms (SOAP, WSDL, ...). We'll explain them in detail in just a moment.

1. As we said before, a client may have no knowledge of what Web service it is going to invoke. So, our first step will be to *discover* a Web Service that meets our requirements. For example, we might be interested in locating a public Web service which can give us the weather forecast in US cities. We'll do this by contacting a *discovery service* (which is itself a Web service).

2. The discovery service will reply, telling us what servers can provide us the service we require.

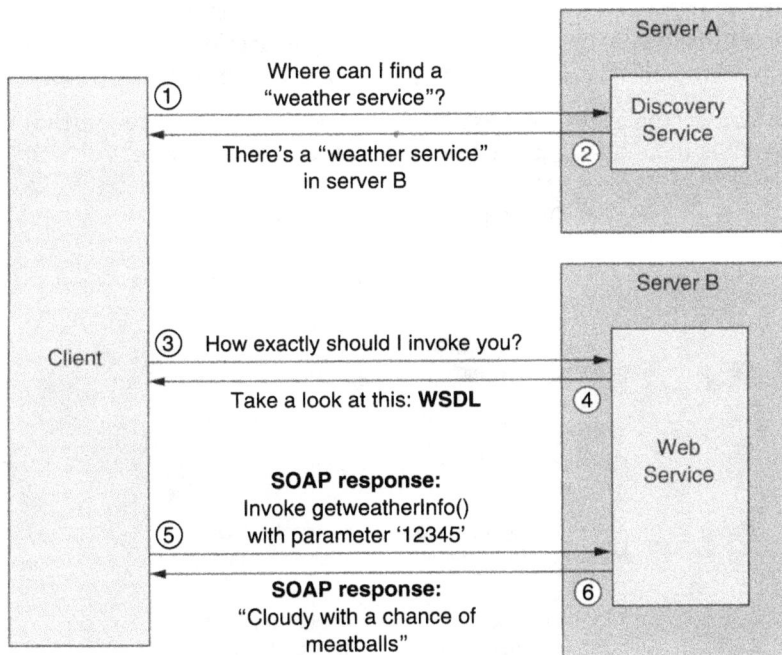

Figure 3.2: A typical Web Service invocation

3. We now know the location of a Web service, but we have no idea of how to actually invoke it. Sure, we know it can give me the forecast for a US city, but how do we perform the actual service invocation? The method I have to invoke might be called "`string getCityForecast(int CityPostalCode)`", but it could also be called "`string getUSCityWeather(string cityName, bool isFarenheit)`". We have to ask the Web service to *describe* itself (i.e. tell us exactly how we should invoke it).

4. The Web Service replies in a language called WSDL.

5. We finally know where the Web service is located and how to invoke it. The invocation itself is done in a language called SOAP. Therefore, we will first send a *SOAP request* asking for the weather forecast of a certain city.

6. The Web service will kindly reply with a *SOAP response* which includes the forecast we asked for, or maybe an error message if our SOAP request was incorrect.

3.2   Web Services Architecture

So, what exactly are SOAP and WSDL? They're essential parts of the Web Services Architecture, shown in Figure 3.3.

- **Service Processes:** This part of the architecture generally involves more than one Web service. For example, discovery belongs in this part of the architecture, since it allows us to locate one particular service from among a collection of Web services.

- **Service Description:** One of the most interesting features of Web Services is that they are *self-describing*. This means that, once you've located a Web service, you can ask it to 'describe itself' and tell you what operations it supports and how to invoke it. This is handled by the Web Services Description Language (WSDL).

Processes	→	Discovery, aggregation, choreography, etc.
Description	→	**WSDL** Web Services description language
Invocation	→	The most popular invocation protocol is **SOAP**, but we could, in theory, use other protocols.
Transport	→	The most popular transport protocol is **HTTP**, but we could, in theory, use other protocols.

Figure 3.3: The Web Services architecture

- **Service Invocation:** Invoking a Web Service (and, in general, any kind of distributed service such as a CORBA object or an Enterprise Java Bean) involves passing messages between the client and the server. SOAP (Simple Object Access Protocol) specifies how we should format requests to the server, and how the server should format its responses. In theory, we could use other service invocation languages (such as XML-RPC, or even some *ad hoc* XML language). However, SOAP is by far the most popular choice for Web services.

- **Transport:** Finally, all these messages must be transmitted somehow between the server and the client. The protocol of choice for this part of the architecture is HTTP (HyperText Transfer Protocol), the same protocol used to access conventional web pages on the Internet. Again, in theory we could be able to use other protocols, but HTTP is currently the most used one.

In case you're wondering, most of the Web Services Architecture is specified and standardized by the World Wide Web Consortium [2], the same organization responsible for XML, HTML, CSS, etc.

3.3 Web Services Addressing

We have just seen a simple Web service invocation. At one point, a discovery service 'told' the client *where* the Web service is located. But... how exactly are Web services addressed? The answer is very simple: just like web pages. We use plain and simple URIs (Uniform Resource Identifiers). If you're more familiar with the term URL (Uniform Resource Locator), don't worry: URI and URL are practically the same thing.

For example, the discovery registry might have replied with the following URI:

```
http://webservices.mysite.com/weather/us/WeatherService
```

This could easily be the address of a web page. However, remember that Web services are always used by software (never directly by humans). If you typed a Web service URI into your web browser, you would probably get an error message or some unintelligible code (some web servers *will* show you a nice graphical interface to the Web service, but that isn't very common). When you have a Web service URI, you will usually need to give that URI to a program. In fact, most of the client programs we will write later on in the book will expect to receive a Web service URI as a command-line argument.

ⓘ If you're anxious to see a real Web service working, then today's your lucky day! A "Weather Web Service" is probably one of the most typical examples of a simple Web service. You can find a real Weather Web Service here:

```
http://live.capescience.com/ccx/GlobalWeather
```

Wait a second... You didn't actually try to visit that URI, did you? Haven't you been paying attention? That's a Web service URI, so even though it may look and feel like the URIs you type in your browser when you want to visit your favorite website, this URI is meant only for software that "knows" how to invoke Web services.

Fortunately, the authors of that web service have been kind enough to provide a description (http://www.capescience.com/webservices/globalweather/index.shtml) of the Web service, along with a web interface (http://live.capescience.com/GlobalWeather) so you can actually invoke the service's methods. If you feel specially curious, you can even take a look at the Web service's WSDL (http://live.capescience.com/wsdl/GlobalWeather.wsdl).

For example, if you visit the web interface, you'll see that the Weather Web service offers a **getWeatherReport** operation that expects a single string parameter (an IATA airport designation, e.g. ORD for Chicago O'Hare and LHR for London Heathrow). If you invoke **getWeatherReport**, the Web service will return a **WeatherReport** structure with all sorts of interesting weather data. Fun!

3.4 How Does this Work in Practice?

OK, now that you have an idea of what Web services are, you are probably anxious to start programming Web services right away. Before you do that, you might want to know how Web Services-based applications are structured. If you've ever used CORBA or RMI, this structure will look pretty familiar.

First of all, you should know that despite having a lot of protocols and languages floating around, Web Services programmers usually only have to concentrate on writing code in their favorite programming language and, in some cases, in writing WSDL. SOAP code, on the other hand, is always generated and interpreted automatically for us. Once we've reached a point where our client application needs to invoke a Web service, we *delegate* that task to a piece of software called a *stub* which translates to our invocations to/from SOAP (Figure 3.4). The good news is that there are plenty of tools available that will generate stubs automatically for us, usually based on the WSDL description of the Web service.

Using stubs simplifies our applications considerably. We don't have to write a complex client program that dynamically generates SOAP requests and interprets SOAP responses (and similarly for the server side of our application). We can simply concentrate on writing the client and/or server code, and leave all the dirty work to the stubs (which, again, we don't even have to write ourselves... they can be generated automatically from the WSDL description of a web service).

☞ In practice, there are no tangible server stubs, unlike the client stubs which (as we will see in future chapters) we will generate and work with. The server is

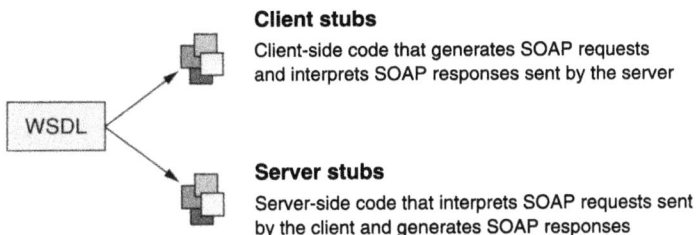

Client stubs
Client-side code that generates SOAP requests
and interprets SOAP responses sent by the server

Server stubs
Server-side code that interprets SOAP requests sent
by the client and generates SOAP responses

Figure 3.4: Client and server stubs are generated from the WSDL file

usually able to handle all incoming SOAP requests, without having to generate
any service-specific stubs.

The stubs are generally generated only once. In other words, you shouldn't interpret
Figure 3.2 as saying that we go through the discovery process every single time we want
to invoke a Web service, and generate the client stubs every time we want to invoke the
service. In general, we only go through the discovery step once, then generate the stubs
once (based on the WSDL of the service we've discovered) and then reuse the stubs as many
times as we want (unless the maintainers of the Web service decide to change the service's
interface and, thus, its WSDL description). Of course, there are more complex invocation
scenarios, but for now the one we've described is more than enough to understand how
Web services work.

3.4.1 A Typical Web Service Invocation (redux)

So, let's suppose that we've already located the Web service we want to use (either because
we consulted a discovery service, or because the Web service URI was given to us),
and we've generated the client stubs from the WSDL description. What exactly happens
when we want to invoke a Web service operation from a program? Figure 3.5 outlines the
steps involved.

1. Whenever the client application needs to invoke the Web service, it will really call
   the client stub. The client stub will turn this 'local invocation' into a proper SOAP
   request. This is often called the *marshaling* or *serializing* process.

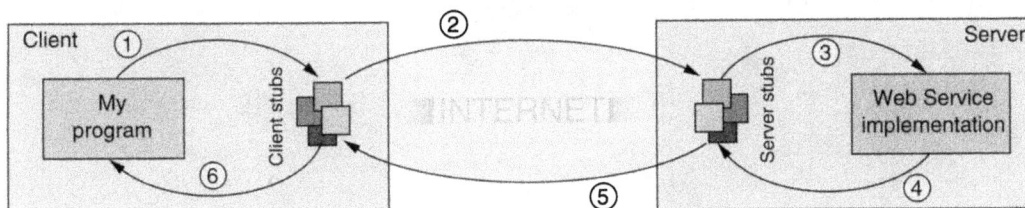

Figure 3.5: A typical Web service invocation (more detailed)

2. The SOAP request is sent over a network using the HTTP protocol. The server receives the SOAP requests and hands it to the server stub. The server stub will convert the SOAP request into something the service implementation can understand (this is usually called *unmarshaling* or *deserializing*).

3. Once the SOAP request has been deserialized, the server stub invokes the service implementation, which then carries out the work it has been asked to do.

4. The result of the requested operation is handed to the server stub, which will turn it into a SOAP response.

5. The SOAP response is sent over a network using the HTTP protocol. The client stub receives the SOAP response and turns it into something the client application can understand.

6. Finally the application receives the result of the Web Service invocation and uses it.

3.5 The Server Side, Up Close

Finally, let's take a close look at what the server looks like, specially what software we should expect to have to get Web services up and running on our server (Figure 3.6).

▪ **Web service:** First and foremost, we have our Web service. As we have seen, this is basically a piece of software that exposes a set of operations. For example, if we are

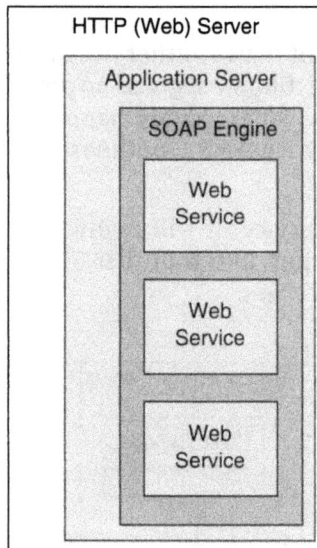

Figure 3.6: The server side in a Web Services application

implementing our Web service in Java, our service will be a Java class (and the operations will be implemented as Java methods). Obviously, we want a set of clients to be able to invoke those operations. However, our Web service implementation knows nothing about how to interpret SOAP requests and how to create SOAP responses. That's why we need a...

■ **SOAP engine:** This is a piece of software that knows how to handle SOAP requests and responses. In practice, it is more common to use a generic SOAP engine than to actually generate server stubs for each individual Web service (note, however, that we still need client stubs for the client). One good example of a SOAP engine is Apache Axis [3] (this is, in fact, the SOAP engine used by the Globus Toolkit). However, the functionality of the SOAP engine is usually limited to manipulating SOAP. To actually function as a server that can receive requests from different clients, the SOAP engine usually runs within an...

■ **Application server:** This is a piece of software that provides a 'living space' for applications that must be accessed by different clients. The SOAP engine runs as an application inside the application server. A good example is the Jakarta Tomcat [4] server, a Java Servlet and Java ServerPages container that is frequently used with Apache Axis and the Globus Toolkit. Note that, strictly speaking, it is more correct to say that Tomcat is simply a servlet container. IBM's WebSphere [5] is a better example of an application server.
Many application servers already include some HTTP functionality, so we can have Web services up and running by installing a SOAP engine and an application server. However, when an application server lacks HTTP functionality, we also need an...

■ **HTTP Server:** This is more commonly called a 'Web server'. It is a piece of software that knows how to handle HTTP messages. A good example is the Apache HTTP Server [6], one of the most popular Web servers in the Internet.

☞ Terminology in this area is still a bit inconsistent, so you might encounter different terms for the concepts we've just seen. In particular, it's very common to use the term *Web services container* as a catch-all term for the SOAP engine + application server + HTTP server.

References

[1] *Loosely Coupled: The Missing Pieces of Web Services*. Doug Kaye. RDS Press, 2003.

[2] *The World Wide Web Consortium (W3C)*. http://www.w3c.org/.

[3] *Apache Axis*. http://ws.apache.org/axis/.

[4] *Apache Jakarta Tomcat*. http://jakarta.apache.org/tomcat/.

[5] *IBM WebSphere Software*. http://www.ibm.com/websphere.

[6] *Apache HTTPD server.* http://httpd.apache.org/.

[7] Ethan Cerami. *Web Services Essentials.* O'Reilly, February, 2002.

[8] Eric van der Vlist. *XML Schema.* O'Reilly, June, 2002.

[9] *Building Web Services with Java.* Steve Graham. Sams, 2nd edition. June 28, 2004.

[10] *W3 Schools – WSDL Tutorial.* http://www.w3schools.com/wsdl/.

[11] *W3 Schools – XML Schema Tutorial.* http://www.w3schools.com/schema/.

chapter **4**

WSRF

In the previous chapter, we saw that Web services are the technology of choice for Internet-based applications with loosely coupled clients and servers. That makes them the natural choice for building the next generation of grid-based applications. However, remember Web Services do have certain limitations. In fact, plain Web services (as currently specified by the W3C) would be insufficient for building a grid application. Enter **WSRF**, which improves several aspects of Web services to make them more adequate for grid applications.

In this chapter we'll take a closer look at the WSRF specifications, concentrating on the main improvement introduced by WSRF: *statefulness*.

4.1 WSRF: It's All About State

Plain Web services are usually *stateless* (even though, in theory, there is nothing in the Web Services Architecture that says they can't be stateful). This means that the Web service can't "remember" information, or *keep state*, from one invocation to another. For example, imagine we want to program a very simple Web service which simply acts as an integer accumulator. This accumulator is initialized to zero, and we want to be able to add (accumulate) values in it. Suppose we have an **add** operation which receives the value to add and returns the current value of the accumulator. As shown in Figure 4.1 our first invocation of this operation might seem to work (we request that 5 be added, and we receive 5 in return). However, since a Web service is stateless, the following invocations have no idea of what was done in the previous invocations. So, in the second call to add we get back 6, instead of 11 (which would be the expected value if the Web service was able to keep state).

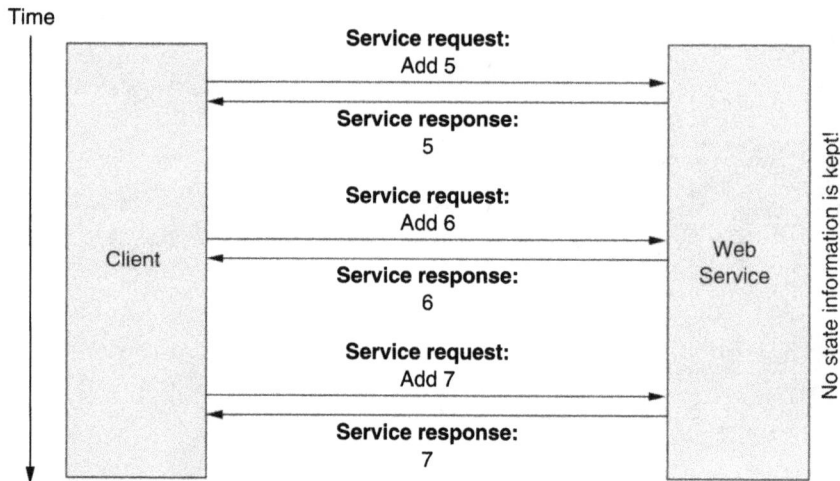

Figure 4.1: A stateless Web Service invocation

The fact that Web services don't keep state information is not necessarily a bad thing. There are plenty of applications which have no need whatsoever for statefulness. For example, the Weather Web service we saw in the previous chapter is a real, working Web service that has no need to know what happened in the previous invocations.

However, Grid applications *do* generally require statefulness. So, we would ideally like our Web service to somehow keep state information as shown in Figure 4.2. However, this is a pretty peculiar dilemma since, as mentioned above, a Web service is usually a stateless entity. In fact, some people might argue that a "stateful Web service" is a bit of a contradiction in terms! So, how do we get out of this jam?

4.2   The Resource Approach to Statefulness

Giving Web services the ability to keep state information while still keeping them stateless seems like a complex problem. Fortunately, it's a problem with a very simple solution: simply keep the Web service and the state information completely separate.

Instead of putting the state *in* the Web service (thus making it stateful, which is generally regarded as a bad thing) we will keep it in a separate entity called a *resource*, which will store all the state information. Each resource will have a unique *key*, so whenever we want a *stateful interaction* with a Web service we simply have to instruct the Web service to use a particular resource.

For example, take the accumulator example. As shown in Figure 4.3, our Web service could have three different resources (A, B, C) to choose from. If we want the integer value

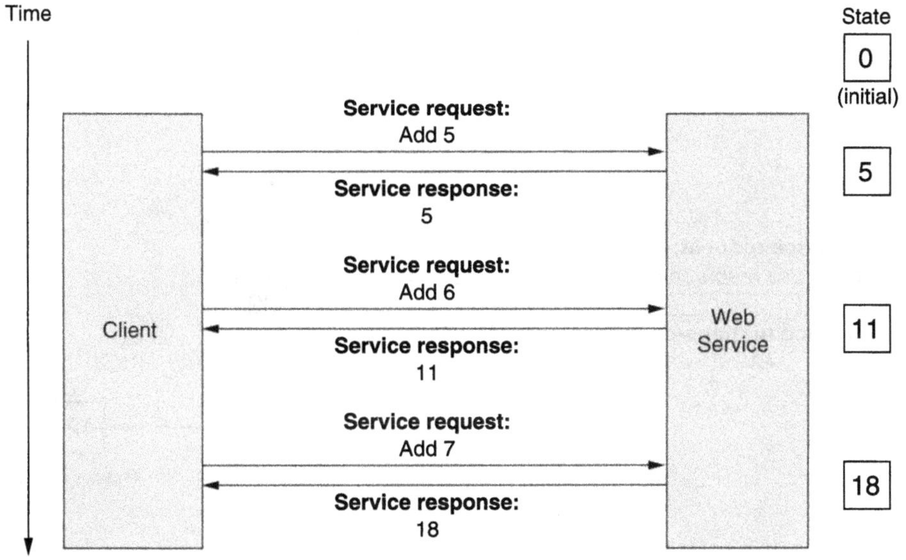

Time

State

Figure 4.2: A stateful Web Service invocation

to be 'remembered' from invocation to invocation, the client simply has to specify that he wants a method invoked *with* a certain resource.

In the figure we can see that the client wants the **add** operation invoked with resource C. When the Web service receives the **add** request, it will make sure to retrieve resource C so that **add** is actually performed on that resource. The resources themselves can be stored in memory, on secondary storage, or even in a database. Also, notice how a Web service can have access to more than one resource.

Of course, resources can come in all different shapes and sizes. A resource can keep multiple values (not just a simple integer value, as shown in the previous figure). For example, our resources could represent files as shown in Figure 4.4.

4.3 Addressing WS-Resources

Of course, you might be wondering: And how exactly does the client specify what resource must be used? A URI might be enough to address the Web service, but how do we specify the resource on top of that? In fact, the pairing of a Web service with a resource is called a *WS-Resource* (Figure 4.5). So, to be more specific, how do we address WS-Resources? There are actually several different ways of doing this. The preferred way of doing it is to use a relatively new specification called WS-Addressing which provides a more versatile way of addressing Web services (when compared to plain URIs).

Resources

24

Resource A

Service request:
Add 5, *use resource C*

Client → Web Service

Service response:
42

32

Resource B

37 → 42

Resource C   (new value)

Figure 4.3: The resource approach to statefulness

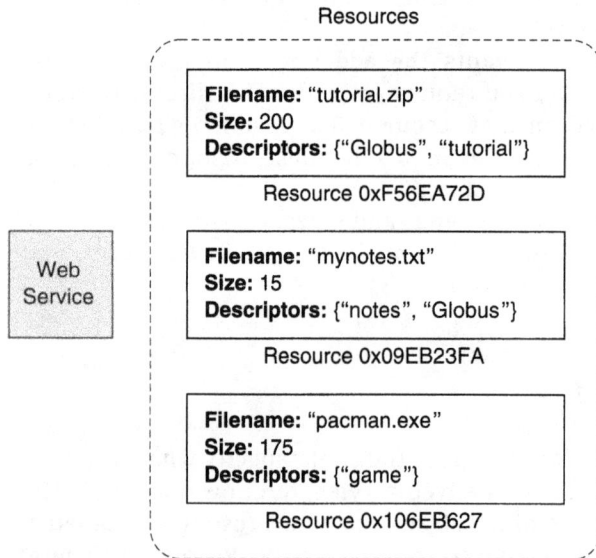

Resources

Web Service

Filename: "tutorial.zip"
Size: 200
Descriptors: {"Globus", "tutorial"}

Resource 0xF56EA72D

Filename: "mynotes.txt"
Size: 15
Descriptors: {"notes", "Globus"}

Resource 0x09EB23FA

Filename: "pacman.exe"
Size: 175
Descriptors: {"game"}

Resource 0x106EB627

Figure 4.4: A Web Service with several resources. Each resource represents a file

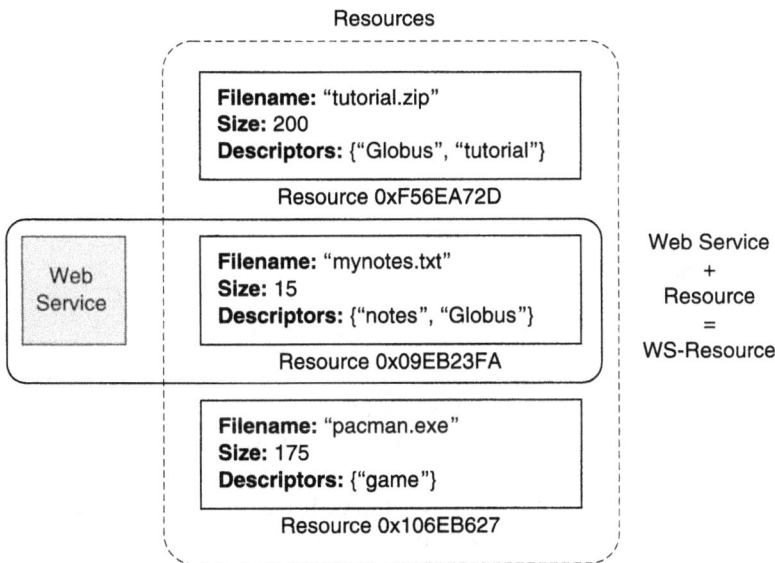

Resources

Filename: "tutorial.zip"
Size: 200
Descriptors: {"Globus", "tutorial"}

Resource 0xF56EA72D

Web Service

Filename: "mynotes.txt"
Size: 15
Descriptors: {"notes", "Globus"}

Resource 0x09EB23FA

Web Service
+
Resource
=
WS-Resource

Filename: "pacman.exe"
Size: 175
Descriptors: {"game"}

Resource 0x106EB627

Figure 4.5: WS-Resource

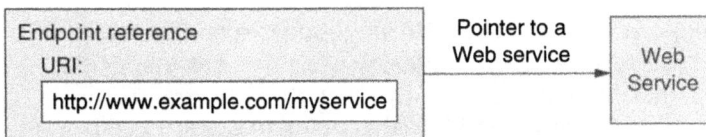

Endpoint reference
URI:
http://www.example.com/myservice

Pointer to a
Web service

Web
Service

Figure 4.6: Endpoint reference

> ☞ GT4.0, in particular, implements a *draft* of the WS-Addressing specification. However, GT4 will track future versions of WS-Addressing so the toolkit will work with other WS tooling.

WS-Addressing specifies a construct called an *endpoint reference* that allows us to address a Web services endpoint. Although the specification is full of nitty-gritty XML details, we can think of it simply as containing, at least, a URI pointing to a Web service, as shown in Figure 4.6.

However, this still doesn't answer our question: how do we address a WS-Resource? It turns out that an endpoint reference can include a lot more information besides a URI. One thing we can include in the endpoint reference is the resource identifier. In this case, the endpoint reference is known as a *WS-Resource-qualified endpoint reference* (Figure 4.7).

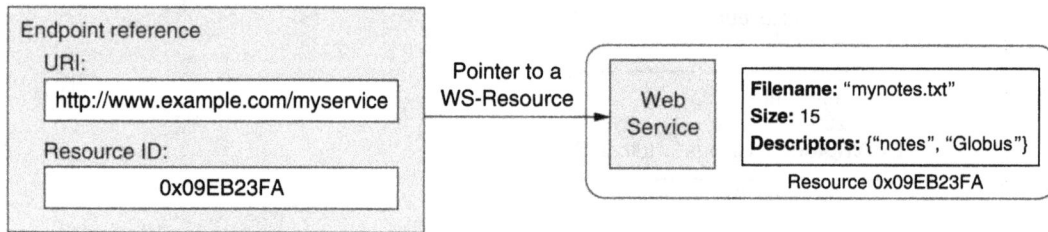

Figure 4.7: WS-Resource-qualified endpoint reference

So, in a sense, we can think of an endpoint reference (or EPR, for short), as a *pointer* to a WS-Resource. It is important to understand that this is an *opaque* pointer. As service implementors, we have to be aware of what is contained inside the EPR. However, client applications should use EPRs without modifying, or even looking at, the contents of the EPR. They should not worry about how the EPR is implemented internally. This might seem a bit odd: How, then, can a client specify the exact resource it wants to use if it can't modify the contents of the EPR? This will be cleared up in the first chapters of Part II, but, for now, suffice it to say that we will be using design patterns which allow the client to be unconcerned with the resource identifier part of the EPR.

ⓘ **Terminology, terminology, terminology**

Terminology surrounding EPRs can get a bit hairy. Throughout this book, unless otherwise noted, we will use the term *endpoint reference* to refer more specifically to a *WS-resource-qualified* EPR. This reflects the fact that, in practically all the examples in the book, we will be using EPRs that refer to some specific WS-Resource (not just a stateless Web service).

In some occasions, we will be using EPRs that do not include a resource identifier. This can be due to the fact that we are not accessing a WS-Resource (just a stateless Web service). Since the EPR will only contain a URI, throughout the book we will simply use the term "URI" instead of the more tongue-twisting *WS-Resource-non-qualified EPR* ("an EPR with a URI but no resource identifier"). Of course, you should remember that any URI we use in the examples, unless otherwise noted, will end up inside an EPR.

Again, don't worry if all this seems a bit odd. We will remind you about this when we start writing up our first examples.

4.4   Resource Properties

The actual data items in the resource are called the *resource properties*, which provide us a view on the current state of the resource. For example, in Figure 4.4 each resource has three resource properties: Filename, Size, and Descriptors.

Resource properties are generally used to store the following three types of information:

- **Service data values:** Provides information on the current state of the service, such as properties of the service, operation results, intermediate results, runtime information, etc. Filename, Size, and Descriptors could all be considered service data values.

- **Metadata about the value:** Information regarding the service data values themselves. For example, we could have a resource property called LastModifiedBy which specifies what user last modified the resource properties.

- **Information needed to manage the state:** This type of information is similar to metadata, but refers to the resource as a whole. For example, as we'll see in Chapter 11, we can add a TerminationTime resource property to specify a time when the resource must be destroyed.

As we'll see later on, when we start programming in Chapter 6, the resource properties are defined in the Web service's WSDL interface description. In Chapter 10, we will take a much closer look at resource properties, including the **resource properties document** (the XML representation of resource properties).

4.5 The WSRF Specification

The Web Services Resources Framework is a collection of four different specifications. Of course, they all relate (in some way or another) to the management of WS-Resources.

4.5.1 WS-ResourceProperties

This specification supplies a set of interfaces that will allow us to access, modify, and query resource properties.

4.5.2 WS-ResourceLifetime

Resources have non-trivial lifecycles. In other words, they're not a static entity that is created when our server starts and destroyed when our server stops. Resources can be created and destroyed at any time. The WS-ResourceLifetime supplies some basic mechanisms to manage the lifecycle of our resources.

4.5.3 WS-ServiceGroup

We will often be interested in managing *groups of Web Services* or *groups of WS-Resources*, and performing operations such as 'add new service to group', 'remove this service from group', and (more importantly) 'find a service in the group that meets condition FOOBAR'.

The WS-ServiceGroup specifies how exactly we should go about grouping services or WS-Resources together. Although the functionality provided by this specification is very basic, it is nonetheless the base of more powerful discovery services (such as GT4's IndexService) which allow us to group different services together and discover them through a single point of entry (the service group).

4.5.4   WS-BaseFaults

Finally, this specification aims to provide a standard way of representing faults when something goes wrong during a WS-Service invocation.

4.6   Related Specifications

4.6.1   WS-Notification

WS-Notification is another collection of specifications that, although not a part of WSRF, is closely related to it. This specification allows a Web service to be configured as a *notification producer*, and certain clients to be *notification consumers* (or subscribers). This means that if a change occurs in the Web service (or, more specifically, in one of the WS-Resources), that change is *notified* to all the subscribers (not *all* changes are notified, only the ones the Web services programmer wants to).

4.6.2   WS-Addressing

As mentioned before, the WS-Addressing specification provides us a mechanism to address Web services which is much more versatile than plain URIs. In particular, we can use WS-Addressing to address a Web service + resource pair (a WS-Resource).

References

[1] K. Czajkowski, D. Ferguson, I. Foster, J. Frey, S. Graham, T. Maguire, D. Snelling, and S. Tuecke. "From Open Grid Services Infrastructure to WS-Resource Framework: Refactoring & Evolution". March 5, 2004. http://www-106.ibm.com/developerworks/library/ws-resource/ogsi_to_wsrf_1.0.pdf.

[2] I. Foster, J. Frey, S. Graham, S. Tuecke, K. Czajkowski, D. Ferguson, F. Leymann, M. Nally, I. Sedukhin, D. Snelling, T. Storey, W. Vambenepe, and S. Weerawarana. "Modeling Stateful Resources with Web Services v.1.1". March 5, 2004. http://www-106.ibm.com/developerworks/library/ws-resource/ws-modelingresources.pdf.

[3] "WS-Resource specification". 1.2 Working Draft 03. *Web Services Resource Framework (WSRF) TC*. OASIS. March 8, 2005.

[4] "WS-ResourceProperties specification". 1.2 Working Draft 01. *Web Services Resource Framework (WSRF) TC.* OASIS. June, 2004.

[5] "WS-ResourceLifetime specification". 1.2 Working Draft 01. *Web Services Resource Framework (WSRF) TC.* OASIS. June, 2004.

[6] "WS-ServiceGroup specification". 1.2 Working Draft 01. *Web Services Resource Framework (WSRF) TC.* OASIS. June, 2004.

[7] "WS-BaseFaults specification". 1.2 Working Draft 01. *Web Services Resource Framework (WSRF) TC.* OASIS. June, 2004.

[8] "WS-BaseNotification specification". 1.2 Working Draft 01. *Web Services Notification (WSN) TC.* OASIS. June, 2004.

[9] "WS-Topics specification". 1.2 Working Draft 01. *Web Services Notification (WSN) TC.* OASIS. June, 2004.

[10] "WS-BrokeredNotification specification". 1.2 Working Draft 01. *Web Services Notification (WSN) TC.* OASIS. July, 2004.

chapter **5**

The Globus Toolkit 4

In Chapter 2 we saw how the Globus Toolkit 4, first and foremost, includes several high-level services for building Grid systems. The toolkit also includes an implementation of WSRF, on which many of the GT4 services are built. In this chapter we present a brief overview of GT4. For a more detailed look at GT4, we highly recommend reading Ian Foster's "GT4 Primer" [3].

5.1 GT4 Component Overview

The Globus Toolkit 4 is an open source toolkit organized as a collection of loosely coupled components. These components consist of services, programming libraries and development tools designed for building Grid-based applications. As shown in Figure 5.1, GT components fall into five broad domain areas: Security, Data Management, Execution Management, Information Services, and Common Runtime.

5.1.1 Security

The GT4 Security components, collectively referred to as *Grid Security Infrastructure* (GSI), facilitate secure communications and the application of uniform policies across distinct systems. A detailed discussion of some of the Security components can be found in Part III.

- **Authentication and Authorization:** Includes libraries and tools for controlling access to services and resources, along with a framework that enables the use of different authorization methods, including user-written methods.

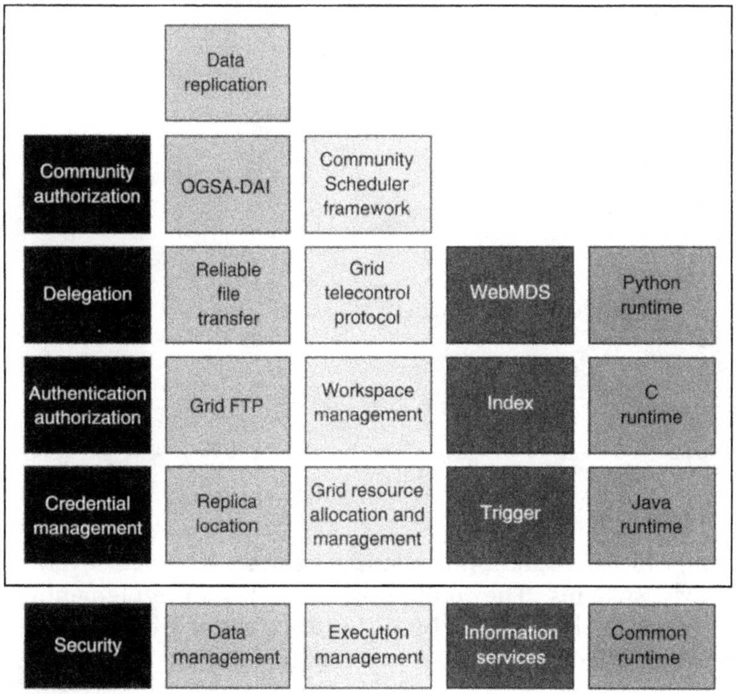

Figure 5.1: GT4 components

- **Delegation:** The toolkit includes a service that delegates credentials to a container. Although the delegation service itself is not covered in this book, a discussion on credential delegation can be found in Part III.

- **Community Authorization:** Virtual organizations can use the Community Authorization Service (CAS) to manage authorization policies for VO resources.

- **Credential Management:** This component includes SimpleCA, a simple Certificate Authority for users without access to a full-blown CA, and MyProxy, an online credential repository. SimpleCA is one of the CA alternatives discussed when installing the toolkit in Appendix A, Installing the Globus Toolkit 4.

5.1.2   Data Management

The Data Management components provide for the discovery, transfer and access of large data. These components are outside the scope of this book.

- **GridFTP:** This component includes a fully functional GridFTP server, and several client-side utilities. The GridFTP protocol is specially optimized to transfer large amounts of data between hosts.

- **RFT:** The Reliable File Transfer service is a WSRF-enabled service that uses GridFTP internally to move large amounts of data. It provides several interesting features over GridFTP, such as the possibility of resuming interrupted transfers.

- **Replica Location:** The Replica Location Service (RLS) allows users to keep track of where different replicas of a dataset are located in a virtual organization.

- **Data Replication:** The Data Replication Service (DRS) uses RLS and RFT to guarantee that local copies of replicas are available to the hosts that need them.

- **OGSA-DAI:** OGSA Data Access and Integration provides a framework to access and integrate datasets on a Grid which might be available in different formats (plain text files, databases, XML files, etc.). More details are available in the OGSA-DAI website [6].

5.1.3 Execution Management

Execution Management components deal with the deployment, scheduling and monitoring of executable programs, referred to as *jobs*. Execution Management components are outside the scope of this book.

- **Grid Resource Allocation & Management (GRAM):** GRAM is the heart of GT Execution Management, providing services to deploy and monitor jobs on a Grid.

- **Community Scheduler Framework (CSF):** This component provides a single interface to different resource schedulers such as PBS, Condor, LSF and SGE.

- **Workspace Management:** A new component in the toolkit that allows users to dynamically create and manage workspaces on remote hosts.

- **Grid Telecontrol Protocol:** This component provides a WSRF-enabled service interface for telecontrol (control of remote instruments).

5.1.4 Information Services

Information Services, commonly referred to as the Monitoring and Discovery System (MDS), includes a set of components to monitor and discover resources in a virtual organization. Though we touch briefly on the Index service in later chapters of the book, MDS is largely outside the book's scope.

- **Index Service:** This component is used to aggregate resources of interest to a VO.

- **Trigger Service:** Like the Index service, the Trigger service also collects data from resources, but is configured to perform certain actions based on that data.

- **WebMDS:** Provides a web browser-based view of data collected by GT4 aggregator services.

Note that GT4 also includes a pre-WS version of MDS (MDS2) for legacy purposes. This component is deprecated and will surely disappear in future releases of the toolkit.

5.1.5   Common Runtime

The Common Runtime components provide a set of fundamental libraries and tools for hosting existing services as well as developing new services. Components other than the Java runtime are outside the scope of this book.

- **C Runtime:** Includes tools, libraries and a WS hosting environment for C developers.

- **Python Runtime:** Includes tools, client libraries and a WS hosting environment for Python developers.

- **Java Runtime:** Includes tools, libraries and a service hosting environment for Java developers.

A Closer Look at the Java GT4 Container

Remember from Chapter 3, that a *Web services container* is a catch-all term for the combination of a SOAP engine and an application server, and possibly also an HTTP server. A container provides the runtime environment for a Web service. Many of the GT4 components are Web services, and need to run inside a Web services container in order to handle client requests.

GT4 includes a simple Java Web services container, based on Apache Axis [4], which is usually referred to as the *standalone container*. As shown in Figure 5.2, this container will allow us to run both the GT4-supplied WS services and our own custom WS services by using the toolkit's own WS implementation.

As we will see in the next chapter, the standalone container is very easy to work with. However, it is not as feature-rich as other Web services containers. As such, the Globus Toolkit offers the option of deploying the WS services into other application servers, such as Apache Jakarta Tomcat [5].

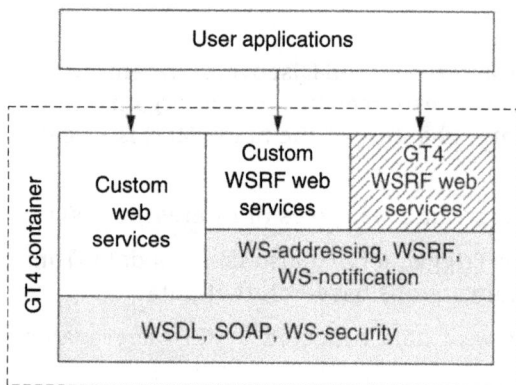

Figure 5.2: The Java GT4 container. Based on Figure 5 in Ian Foster's "GT4 Primer" [3]

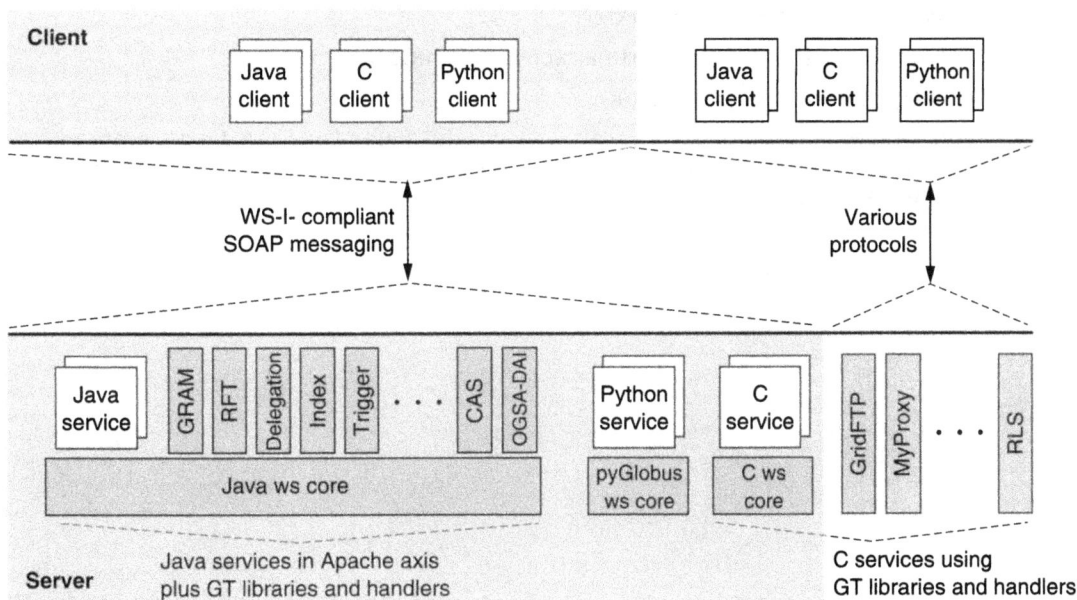

Figure 5.3: GT4 service overview

5.2 GT4 Service Overview

As mentioned in the Preface, this book highlights Java WS Core (a part of the Java Runtime) and some of the security components. Once again, it is important to realize that the Globus Toolkit includes *many* other services and libraries designed to help build Grids. Figure 5.3, provides a service-centric view of GT4, with WS components shown on the left and non-WS components on the right. Notice how all the Globus-supplied WS components (such as GRAM, RFT, etc.) are implemented on top of Java WS Core. Nonetheless, the toolkit also allows us to develop our services using Python or C using the Python WS Core and C WS Core components, respectively. After you've finished this book we suggest you further explore the many additional features included in GT4.

References

[1] *The Globus Alliance.* http://www.globus.org/.

[2] *The Globus Toolkit.* http://www.globus.org/toolkit/.

[3] Ian Foster. *A Globus Toolkit Primer.* (Draft). April 26, 2005. http://www.globus.org/toolkit/docs/4.0/key/GT4_Primer_0.6.pdf.

[4] *Apache Axis.* http://ws.apache.org/axis/.

[5] *Apache Jakarta Tomcat.* http://jakarta.apache.org/tomcat/.

[6] *OGSA-DAI.* http://www.ogsadai.org.uk/.

[7] Gregor von Laszewski, Ian Foster, Jarek Gawor, and Peter Lane. "A Java Commodity Grid Kit". *Concurrency and Computation: Practice and Experience.* 13. 8-9. 643–662. 2001. http:/www.cogkit.org/.

part **II**

GT4 Java WS Core

In this part of the book we will start programming basic stateful services using GT4's implementation of the WSRF specifications. Before reading these chapters, you need to have GT4 installed in your system. If it isn't, Appendix A will guide you through installing just the parts of the toolkit you need to work through the book's examples. Also, remember that the book assumes that the example files are installed in your system in a directory that we will call **$EXAMPLES_DIR**. If you have not done so, download the example files from the book's companion website at http://www.gt4book.com/.

## chapter 6

Writing Your First Stateful Web Service in 5 Simple Steps

MathService

In this chapter we are going to write and deploy a simple stateful web service that uses WSRF to keep state information. Our first web service is an extremely simple *Math Web Service*, which we'll refer to as *MathService*. It will allow users to perform the following operations:

- Addition
- Subtraction.

Furthermore, MathService will have the following resource properties (RPs for short):

- Value (integer)
- Last operation performed (string).

We will also add a "Get Value" operation to access the Value RP. In Chapter 10 we will see a better way of accessing resource properties, without having to add get/set operations.

MathService's internal logic is very simple. Once a new resource is created, the "value" RP is initialized to zero, and the "last operation" RP is initialized to "NONE". The addition and subtraction operations expect only *one integer parameter*. This parameter is added/subtracted to the "value" RP, and the "last operation" RP is changed to "ADDITION" or "SUBTRACTION" accordingly. Also, the addition and subtraction operations don't return anything.

Finally, this first example will be limited to having *one single resource*. In the following chapters we will see how we can write a service that has several resources associated to it, as seen in Section 4.2.

High-tech stuff, huh? Don't worry if this seems a bit lackluster. Since this is going to be our first stateful web service, it's better to start with a small didactic service which we'll gradually improve by adding more complex resource properties, notifications, etc. You should always bear in mind that MathService is, after all, just a means to get acquainted with GT4. Typical WSRF Web Services are generally much more complex and do more than expose trivial operations (such as addition and subtraction). At the end of the book, in Part IV, "The FileBuy Application" we present an example of a non-trivial, yet simple to understand, application based on WSRF Web Services.

The Five Steps

Writing and deploying a WSRF Web Service is easier than you might think. You just have to follow five simple steps.

1. **Define the service's interface.** This is done with the *WSDL* language.

2. **Implement the service.** This is done with *Java*.

3. **Define the deployment parameters.** This is done with the *WSDD* language and using a *JNDI* deployment file.

4. **Compile everything and generate a GAR file.** This is done with the *Ant* tool.

5. **Deploy service.** This is done with *a GT4* tool.

Don't worry if you don't understand these five steps or are baffled by terms such as WSDL, WSDD, and Ant. In this first example we're going to go through each step in great detail, explaining what each step accomplishes, and giving detailed instructions on how to perform each step. The rest of the examples in the book will also follow these five steps, but won't repeat the whole explanation of what that step is. So, if you ever find that you don't understand a particular step, you can always come back to this chapter to review the details of that step.

Before We Start...

Ready to start? Ok! Just hold your horses for a second. As mentioned in the Preface, we are assuming that you have the source code for all the examples installed in your machine. If you haven't done so yet, go to the book's companion website at http://www.gt4book.com/ and download the examples. The examples bundle includes the source code of all the examples, plus a couple of extra files we'll need to successfully build and deploy our service. Just create an empty directory on your file system and untar-gunzip the file there. From now on, we'll refer to that directory as **$EXAMPLES_DIR**.

Once you have the files, take into account that there are two ways of following the first chapters of the tutorial:

- **With the example source files:** You'll have all the source code (Java, WSDL, and WSDD) ready to use in **$EXAMPLES_DIR**, so there's no need to manually modify these files.

- **Without the examples source files:** Some people don't like getting all the source code ready to use out-of-the-box, but prefer to write the files themselves so they can have a better understanding of what they're doing at each point. In fact, we think this is probably the best way to follow this chapter (except for a few files which would take too long to write manually). Since this chapter includes complete code listings (which you can copy and paste to a file), you can easily write all the files yourself. However, you *do* need a set of auxiliary files included in the examples bundle that are needed to build and deploy the services. So, if you want to follow the examples without the source files, you still need to download the examples files. Once you're in **$EXAMPLES_DIR**, simply delete directory "**org**" to delete the source files, but *don't delete anything else*.

Ok, *now* we're ready to start :-)

6.1 Step 1: Defining the Interface in WSDL

The first step in writing a web service (including those that use WSRF to keep state) is to define the *service interface*. We need to specify what our service is going to provide to the outer world. At this point we're not concerned with the inner workings of that service (what algorithms it uses, other systems it interacts with, etc.). We just need to know what *operations* will be available to our users. In Web Services lingo, the service interface is usually called the *port type* (usually written *portType*).

As we saw in Chapter 3, there is a special XML language which can be used to specify what operations a web service offers: the Web Service Description Language (WSDL). So, what we need to do in this step is write a description of our MathService using WSDL.

At first sight, it might seem that starting with an interface language (such as a Java interface or an IDL interface) might be the best option, since (as you'll soon find out) it is more user-friendly than directly coding in WSDL. In fact, if we wanted to define our interface in Java, we could simply write the following:

```
public interface Math

{


    public void add(int a);
```

```
    public void subtract(int a);


    public int getValueRP();

}
```

...and we'd be nearly finished with step 1 (we would still need to specify the resource properties)! However, we are going to start with a WSDL description of the interface, even if it is a bit harder to understand than using a Java interface. The main reason for this is that, although Java interfaces might be easier to write and understand, in the long run it is better to write the interface directly in WSDL. Java-to-WSDL utilities tend to introduce language-specific features into the WSDL (thus introducing a "language bias" in an interface description language which is supposed to be language-neutral). Plus, we will generally be able to produce a much cleaner code than a WSDL generation tool. So, the sooner we start writing WSDL, the better!

However, the goal of this page is not to give a detailed explanation of how to write a WSDL file, but rather to present the WSDL file for this particular example. If you have no idea whatsoever of how to write WSDL, now is a good time to take a look at Appendix B, A WSDL Primer. Come on, go take a look at the appendix. We'll be waiting for you right here.

6.1.1   The WSDL Code

Ok, so supposing you either know WSDL or have visited the WSDL appendix, take a good thorough look at this WSDL code:

```
<?xml version="1.0" encoding="UTF-8"?>

<definitions name="MathService"

    targetNamespace="http://www.globus.org/namespaces/examples/

        MathService_instance"

xmlns="http://schemas.xmlsoap.org/wsdl/"

xmlns:tns="http://www.globus.org/namespaces/

    examples/MathService_instance"

xmlns:wsdl="http://schemas.xmlsoap.org/wsdl/"

xmlns:wsrp="http://docs.oasis-open.org/wsrf/2004/06/

    wsrf-WS-ResourceProperties-1.2-draft-01.xsd"

xmlns:xsd="http://www.w3.org/2001/XMLSchema">
```

```
<!--==============================================================

                    T Y P E S

==============================================================-->
<types>
<xsd:schema targetNamespace="http://www.globus.org/namespaces/examples/
    MathService_instance"
    xmlns:tns="http://www.globus.org/namespaces/examples/MathService_instance"
    xmlns:xsd="http://www.w3.org/2001/XMLSchema">

        <!-- REQUESTS AND RESPONSES -->

        <xsd:element name="add" type="xsd:int"/>
        <xsd:element name="addResponse">
                <xsd:complexType/>
        </xsd:element>

        <xsd:element name="subtract" type="xsd:int"/>
        <xsd:element name="subtractResponse">
                <xsd:complexType/>
        </xsd:element>

        <xsd:element name="getValueRP">
                <xsd:complexType/>
        </xsd:element>
        <xsd:element name="getValueRPResponse" type="xsd:int"/>


        <!-- RESOURCE PROPERTIES -->

        <xsd:element name="Value" type="xsd:int"/>
        <xsd:element name="LastOp" type="xsd:string"/>
```

```
        <xsd:element name="MathResourceProperties">
        <xsd:complexType>
                <xsd:sequence>
                        <xsd:element ref="tns:Value" minOccurs="1" maxOccurs="1"/>
                        <xsd:element ref="tns:LastOp" minOccurs="1" maxOccurs="1"/>
                </xsd:sequence>
        </xsd:complexType>
        </xsd:element>


</xsd:schema>
</types>



<!--==============================================================


                M E S S A G E S


==============================================================-->
<message name="AddInputMessage">
        <part name="parameters" element="tns:add"/>
</message>
<message name="AddOutputMessage">
        <part name="parameters" element="tns:addResponse"/>
</message>


<message name="SubtractInputMessage">
        <part name="parameters" element="tns:subtract"/>
</message>
<message name="SubtractOutputMessage">
        <part name="parameters" element="tns:subtractResponse"/>
</message>
```

```
<message name="GetValueRPInputMessage">
        <part name="parameters" element="tns:getValueRP"/>
</message>
<message name="GetValueRPOutputMessage">
        <part name="parameters" element="tns:getValueRPResponse"/>
</message>



<!--=============================================================

                        P O R T T Y P E

=============================================================-->
<portType name="MathPortType"
    wsrp:ResourceProperties="tns:MathResourceProperties">

        <operation name="add">
                <input message="tns:AddInputMessage"/>
                <output message="tns:AddOutputMessage"/>
        </operation>

        <operation name="subtract">
                <input message="tns:SubtractInputMessage"/>
                <output message="tns:SubtractOutputMessage"/>
        </operation>

        <operation name="getValueRP">
                <input message="tns:GetValueRPInputMessage"/>
                <output message="tns:GetValueRPOutputMessage"/>
        </operation>

</portType>

</definitions>
```

> ☞ This file is **$EXAMPLES_DIR/schema/examples/MathService_instance/Math.wsdl**.
> This file is located in that particular directory because of the tool we'll be using to
> build the service. You can find more details about the directory structure required
> by this tool in Appendix E, globus-build-service Script Reference.

If you know WSDL, you'll recognize this as a pretty straightforward WSDL file which defines
three operations: **add**, **subtract**, and **getValueRP** (along with all the necessary messages
and types). However, this WSDL file does have some peculiarities specific to WSRF and
Globus.

6.1.2   WSRF and Globus-Specific Features of WSDL

Resource Properties

We use the **wsrp:ResourceProperties** attribute of the **portType** element to specify what
our service's resource properties are. The resource properties must be declared in the
<types> section of the WSDL file. Remember that the resource properties are where we'll
keep all our state information.

> ⓘ **RPs have to be declared globally... it's the law!**
>
> If you're already familiar with WSDL, you will recognize that the two resource
> properties (**Value** and **LastOp**) are declared as *global elements*:
>
> ```
> <xsd:element name="Value" type="xsd:int"/>
>
> <xsd:element name="LastOp" type="xsd:string"/>
>
> <xsd:element name="MathResourceProperties">
>
> <xsd:complexType>
>
>         <xsd:sequence>
>
>             <xsd:element ref="tns:Value" minOccurs="1" maxOccurs="1"/>
>
>             <xsd:element ref="tns:LastOp" minOccurs="1" maxOccurs="1"/>
>
>         </xsd:sequence>
>
> </xsd:complexType>
>
> </xsd:element>
> ```
>
> A different coding style in XML Schema is to declare them locally. However, RPs
> *must* be declared globally. In other words, you cannot declare them like this:
>
> ```
> <xsd:element name="MathResourceProperties">
>
> <xsd:complexType>
> ```

```
        <xsd:sequence>

                <xsd:element name="Value" type="xsd:int"

                        minOccurs="1" maxOccurs="1"/>

                <xsd:element name="LastOp" type="xsd:string"

                        minOccurs="1" maxOccurs="1"/>

        </xsd:sequence>

    </xsd:complexType>

</xsd:element>
```

No Bindings

Bindings are an essential part of a normal WSDL file. They allow us to specify the nitty-gritty protocol details of our Web service. In our case, our bindings would need to specify that we want to use SOAP to encode the request and response messages. However, we don't have to write the bindings manually, since they are generated automatically for us by a GT4 tool. As we'll see later on, this tool is invoked when we build our service.

6.1.3 Namespace Mappings

One of the nice things about WSDL is that it's *language-neutral*. In other words, there is no mention of the language in which the service is going to be implemented, or of the language in which the client is going to be implemented.

However, there will of course come a moment when we'll want to refer to this interface from a specific language (in our case, Java). We do this through a set of *stub classes* (stubs were described in Chapter 3) which are generated from the WSDL file using a GT4 tool. The default behavior for this tool is to place the stub classes in a package whose name is derived from the namespace. Since this usually leads to very long (and messy) package names, we can override this default behavior and tell the stub generator in what Java package it should place the stub classes. We do this with a *mappings file*, which maps WSDL namespaces to Java packages:

```
http\://www.globus.org/namespaces/examples/MathService_instance=

    org.globus.examples.stubs.MathService_instance

http\://www.globus.org/namespaces/examples/MathService_instance/bindings=

    org.globus.examples.stubs.MathService_instance.bindings

http\://www.globus.org/namespaces/examples/MathService_instance/service=

    org.globus.examples.stubs.MathService_instance.service
```

> ☞ Each mapping must go in one line (i.e. the above file should have *three* lines). Also, take into account that the backslash before the colon is intentional. These three lines are a part of **$EXAMPLES_DIR/namespace2package.mappings**.

The first namespace is the target namespace of the WSDL file. The other two namespaces are automatically generated when a GT4 tool 'completes' the WSDL file (including the necessary bindings). Throughout the book, the stub classes for the examples will be placed in the following Java package:

> **org.globus.examples.stubs**

Since we're defining a service called **MathService_instance**, we're specifically mapping the WSDL file to the following package:

> **org.globus.examples.stubs.*MathService_instance***

However, take into account that the stubs classes are *generated* from the WSDL file, so they won't exist until we compile the service (which is when the stub classes are generated). In other words, don't look for the **org.globus.examples.stubs** package in **$EXAMPLES_DIR**, because you won't find them there. If you are of a curious disposition, don't worry: as soon as we generate the stub classes, we'll take a (very brief) look at the directory where they are generated.

6.2   Step 2: Implementing the Service in Java

After defining the service interface ("*what* the service does"), the next step is implementing that interface. The implementation is "*how* the service does what it says it does".

6.2.1   The QNames Interface

The first bit of code we need is a very simple Java interface that will make our life a bit easier. When we have to refer to just about anything related to a service, we will need to do so using its *qualified name*, or QName for short. This is a name which includes a namespace and a *local name*. For example, the QName of the **Value** RP is:

> **{http://www.globus.org/namespaces/examples/MathService_instance}Value**

> ☞ This is a common string representation of a QName. The namespace is placed between curly braces, and the local name is placed right after the namespace.

A qualified name is represented in Java using the **QName** class. Since we'll be referring to the service's qualified names frequently, it is a good practice to put them all in a separate interface:

```
package org.globus.examples.services.core.first.impl;

import javax.xml.namespace.QName;

public interface MathConstants {
        public static final String NS = "http://www.globus.org/
                    namespaces/examples/MathService_instance";

        public static final QName RP_VALUE = new QName(NS, "Value");

        public static final QName RP_LASTOP = new QName(NS, "LastOp");

        public static final QName RESOURCE_PROPERTIES = new QName(NS,
                    "MathResourceProperties");
}
```

☞ This file is **\$EXAMPLES_DIR/org/globus/examples/services/core/first/impl/ MathConstants.java**.

We are not really required to write this interface, but in the long run it's much better to have all the QNames in a single spot, so we can avoid making mistakes when manually writing QNames in our other classes.

6.2.2 The Service Implementation

In this first simple example, our service implementation will consist of a single Java class with the code for both the service *and* the resource. We will see in the following chapters that it is more common (in fact, desirable) to split the implementation into at least two classes: one for the service and another one for the resource. You should only use the approach described in this first example when coding very simple services.

Writing the code for the service is actually very mechanical. The only non-trivial piece of code is the method that will be in charge of initializing our service's single resource.

The bare bones of our resource class will be the following:

```
package org.globus.examples.services.core.first.impl;

import java.rmi.RemoteException;

import org.globus.examples.stubs.MathService_instance.AddResponse;
import org.globus.examples.stubs.MathService_instance.GetValueRP;
import org.globus.examples.stubs.MathService_instance.SubtractResponse;
import org.globus.wsrf.Resource;
import org.globus.wsrf.ResourceProperties;
import org.globus.wsrf.ResourceProperty;
import org.globus.wsrf.ResourcePropertySet;
import org.globus.wsrf.impl.ReflectionResourceProperty;
import org.globus.wsrf.impl.SimpleResourcePropertySet;

public class MathService implements Resource❶, ResourceProperties❷ {



}
```

❶ Since our Java class will implement both the service and the resource, we need to implement the **Resource** interface. However, this interface doesn't require any methods. It is simply a way of tagging a class as being a resource.

❷ By implementing the **ResourceProperties** interface we are indicating that our class has a set of resource properties which we want to make available. This interface requires that we add the following to our class:

```
    private ResourcePropertySet propSet;


    public ResourcePropertySet getResourcePropertySet() {

            return this.propSet;

    }
```

Now, remember that our resource has two resource properties: **Value** of type **xsd:int** and **LastOp** of type **xsd:string**. We need to add an attribute for each resource property along with a get/set method pair for each resource property:

```
package org.globus.examples.services.core.first.impl;


import java.rmi.RemoteException;


import org.globus.examples.stubs.MathService_instance.AddResponse;

import org.globus.examples.stubs.MathService_instance.GetValueRP;

import org.globus.examples.stubs.MathService_instance.SubtractResponse;

import org.globus.wsrf.Resource;

import org.globus.wsrf.ResourceProperties;

import org.globus.wsrf.ResourceProperty;

import org.globus.wsrf.ResourcePropertySet;

import org.globus.wsrf.impl.ReflectionResourceProperty;

import org.globus.wsrf.impl.SimpleResourcePropertySet;


public class MathService implements Resource, ResourceProperties {


        /* Resource Property set */
        private ResourcePropertySet propSet;


        /* Resource properties */
        private int value;
        private String lastOp;


        /* Get/Setters for the RPs */
        public int getValue() {
                return value;
        }
```

```
public synchronized void setValue(int value) {
        this.value = value;
}


public String getLastOp() {
        return lastOp;
}


public synchronized void setLastOp(String lastOp) {
        this.lastOp = lastOp;
}


/* Required by interface ResourceProperties */
public ResourcePropertySet getResourcePropertySet() {
        return this.propSet;
}
}
}
```

ⓘ **More state than meets the eye...**

In this example, we are exposing the **value** and **lastOp** attributes as resource properties. However, our resource can certainly have other stateful information that is not published in the service's interface. For example, our resource has a private **propSet** attribute which is not exposed as a resource property.

Bottom line: resource properties are not the *only* stateful properties in a resource, just those we want to publish through the service's WSDL.

⚠ For clarity, it is best for the attributes to have *the same name* that was given to the resource properties in the WSDL file (but with the first letter in lowercase). Remember:

```
<xsd:element name="Value" type="xsd:int"/>

<xsd:element name="LastOp" type="xsd:string"/>
```

This translates to:

```
private int value;

private String lastOp;
```

As for the get/set methods, we again use the same name used in the WSDL file (keeping the first letter in uppercase):

```
public int getValue() {...}

public void setValue(int value) {...}

public String getLastOp() {...}

public void setLastOp(String lastOp) {...}
```

Again, this is simply a recommended practice. The name of the Java attributes, the get/set methods, and the RPs (as specified in the WSDL file) need not match, but we can avoid potential errors by making sure we always use the same names in both the WSDL file and the Java code.

Next, we have to implement the constructor. Here we will initialize the resource properties.

```
/* Constructor. Initializes RPs */

public MathService() throws RemoteException {

        ❶

        this.propSet = new SimpleResourcePropertySet(
                MathConstants.RESOURCE_PROPERTIES);


        /* Initialize the RP's */

        try {

                ❷

                ResourceProperty valueRP = new ReflectionResourceProperty(
                        MathConstants.RP_VALUE, "Value", this);
                this.propSet.add(valueRP);
                setValue(0);


                ResourceProperty lastOpRP = new ReflectionResourceProperty(
                        MathConstants.RP_LASTOP, "LastOp", this);
                this.propSet.add(lastOpRP);
                setLastOp("NONE");
```

```
        } catch (Exception e) {

                throw new RemoteException(e.getMessage(), e);

        }

    }
```

❶ We create the resource property set. To do so, we need to provide the qualified name of the resource properties. In our case, that QName is:

      {http://www.globus.org/namespaces/examples/MathService_instance}

      MathResourceProperties

This was specified in the WSDL file. Remember that we put this QName in the **MathConstants** interface so we could access it with ease.

❷ We create the individual resource properties, and initialize them (again, notice how we're referring to each resource property's QName: **RP_VALUE** and **RP_LASTOP**).

ⓘ **ReflectionResourceProperty**

What we have just seen is the simplest type of resource creation: using **Reflec-tionResourceProperty** to represent each resource property. This makes the implementation much simpler, but also adds quite a bit of restrictions on our resource implementation (such as the need for get/set methods, as outlined in the caution box above). We will see another class, **SimpleResourceProperty**, in Chapter 10.

Finally, we need to provide the implementation of our remotely accessible methods (**add**, **subtract**, and **getValueRP**). These are pretty straightforward, except for some peculiarities in how the parameters and return types have to be declared. For example, take a look at the **add** method: (the **subtract** method is similar)

```
public synchronized AddResponse add(int a) throws RemoteException {

        value += a;

        lastOp = "ADDITION";


        return new AddResponse();

}
```

ⓘ **Thread safety issues**

Notice how the **add** method is declared using the **synchronized** keyword, to indicate that it must not be executed by two threads at the same time (i.e. by two clients at the same time). This is done to avoid a **value** or **lastOp** having incorrect values if two clients try to invoke the **add** operation at the same time.

It is entirely up to the service programmer to perform proper synchronization. Throughout the book, we use the **synchronized** keyword in any method that modifies a resource property. In this example, that includes the **add**, **subtract**, **setValue**, and **setLastOp** methods. In the next chapter, we will see how synchronization is done in a slightly different way.

You'll notice that, even though we defined the **add** operation as having no return type in the WSDL file, now the return type is **AddResponse**. A similar thing happens in the **getValueRP** method:

```
public int getValueRP(GetValueRP params) throws RemoteException {

        return value;

}
```

Even though **getValueRP** was defined as having no parameters, it turns out our method has a single "**GetValueRP params**" parameter. Don't get nervous... this all has a very logical explanation. This is due to the fact that WSRF uses *document/literal bindings*, which requires that the parameters be implemented in a very particular way.

ⓘ **How document/literal bindings affect our parameters**

Whenever we write an operation which is part of our WSDL interface (such as **add**, **subtract**, or **getValueRP**), the parameters and the return values will *in some cases* be "boxed" inside stub classes (which are generated automatically from the WSDL file). This is more evident when we have several parameters. For example, if we declared the following operation in our WSDL file:

```
void multiply(int a1, int a2);
```

The actual Java code would look like this:

```
public MultiplyResponse multiply(Multiply params) throws RemoteException

{

        int a1 = params.getA1()

        int a2 = params.getA2()


        // Do something


        return new MultiplyResponse();

}
```

Multiply and **MultiplyResponse** are stub classes. Notice how the two parameters (**a1** and **a2**) are 'boxed' inside a single **Multiply** parameter, and how we return a **MultiplyResponse** object, even though we don't really want to return anything.

The tricky thing about this is that, as mentioned earlier, this "boxing" process only happens in some cases:

- When the number of parameters is more than one. For example, our **add** method has a single parameter, so it is *not* "boxed".

- When the return type is void or a complex type. For example, our **getValueRP** method returns an **int** value, so it is not "boxed". On the other hand, both **add** and **subtract** return void, so what we really have to return is **AddResponse** and **SubtractResponse**.

- When there are no parameters. For example, the **getValueRP** operation expects no parameters, so we have to implement the method as having a single parameter of type **GetValueRP**.

The complete class would look like this:

```
/*
 * This file is licensed under the terms of the Globus Toolkit Public License
 * v3, found at http://www.globus.org/toolkit/legal/4.0/license-v3.html.
 *
 * This notice must appear in redistributions of this file, with or without
 * modification.
 */
package org.globus.examples.services.core.first.impl;


import java.rmi.RemoteException;


import org.globus.examples.stubs.MathService_instance.AddResponse;
import org.globus.examples.stubs.MathService_instance.GetValueRP;
import org.globus.examples.stubs.MathService_instance.SubtractResponse;
import org.globus.wsrf.Resource;
import org.globus.wsrf.ResourceProperties;
import org.globus.wsrf.ResourceProperty;
import org.globus.wsrf.ResourcePropertySet;
```

```java
import org.globus.wsrf.impl.ReflectionResourceProperty;
import org.globus.wsrf.impl.SimpleResourcePropertySet;

public class MathService implements Resource, ResourceProperties {

        /* Resource Property set */
        private ResourcePropertySet propSet;

        /* Resource properties */
        private int value;

        private String lastOp;

        /* Constructor. Initializes RPs */
        public MathService() throws RemoteException {
                /* Create RP set */
                this.propSet = new SimpleResourcePropertySet(
                                MathConstants.RESOURCE_PROPERTIES);

                /* Initialize the RP's */
                try {
                    ResourceProperty valueRP = new ReflectionResourceProperty(
                                MathConstants.RP_VALUE, "Value", this);
                    this.propSet.add(valueRP);
                    setValue(0);

                    ResourceProperty lastOpRP = new ReflectionResourceProperty(
                                MathConstants.RP_LASTOP, "LastOp", this);
                    this.propSet.add(lastOpRP);
                    setLastOp("NONE");
                } catch (Exception e) {
                        throw new RemoteException(e.getMessage(), e);
                }
        }
```

```java
/* Get/Setters for the RPs */
public int getValue() {
        return value;
}


public synchronized void setValue(int value) {
        this.value = value;
}


public String getLastOp() {
        return lastOp;
}


public synchronized void setLastOp(String lastOp) {
        this.lastOp = lastOp;
}


/* Remotely-accessible operations */

public synchronized AddResponse add(int a) throws RemoteException {
        value += a;
        lastOp = "ADDITION";

        return new AddResponse();
}

public synchronized SubtractResponse subtract(int a)
    throws RemoteException {
        value -= a;
        lastOp = "SUBTRACTION";

        return new SubtractResponse();
}
```

```
public int getValueRP(GetValueRP params) throws RemoteException {
        return value;
}


/* Required by interface ResourceProperties */
public ResourcePropertySet getResourcePropertySet() {
        return this.propSet;
}
}
```

> ☞ This file is **$EXAMPLE_DIR/org/globus/examples/services/core/first/impl/ MathService.java**.

6.3 Step 3: Configuring the Deployment in WSDD (and JNDI)

Up to this point, we have written the two most important parts of our stateful Web service: the service interface (WSDL) and the service implementation (Java). However, we still seem to be missing something... How do we actually make our Web service available to client connections? Does our Java class simply float around in some sort of mysterious ether? This next step will actually take all the loose pieces we have written up to this point and make them available through a *Web services container*. This step is called the *deployment* of the web service.

> ☞ Remember: The "Web Services container" is a catch-all term referring to all the software (SOAP Engine, Application Server, and HTTP Server) we need to make Web services available to clients. This might be a good moment to review Section 3.5, "The server side, up close".

6.3.1 The WSDD Deployment Descriptor

One of the key components of the deployment phase is a file called the *deployment descriptor*. It's the file that tells the Web Services container how it should publish our web service (for example, telling it what our service's URI will be). The deployment descriptor is written in WSDD format (Web Service Deployment Descriptor). The deployment descriptor for our Web service will look like this:

```
<?xml version="1.0" encoding="UTF-8"?>
<deployment name="defaultServerConfig"
```

```
    xmlns="http://xml.apache.org/axis/wsdd/"

    xmlns:java="http://xml.apache.org/axis/wsdd/providers/java"

    xmlns:xsd="http://www.w3.org/2001/XMLSchema">


    <service name="examples/core/first/MathService" provider="Handler"
            use="literal" style="document">

        <parameter name="className"
            value="org.globus.examples.services.core.first.impl.MathService"/>

        <wsdlFile>share/schema/examples/MathService_instance/Math_service.wsdl
            </wsdlFile>

        <parameter name="allowedMethods" value="*"/>

        <parameter name="handlerClass"
            value="org.globus.axis.providers.RPCProvider"/>

        <parameter name="scope" value="Application"/>

        <parameter name="loadOnStartup" value="true"/>

    </service>


</deployment>
```

> ☞ This file is **$EXAMPLES_DIR/org/globus/examples/services/core/first/
> deploy-server.wsdd.**

Let's take a close look at what all this means...

The 'service name'

```
<service name="examples/core/first/MathService" provider="Handler"

    use="literal" style="document">
```

This specifies the location where our web service will be found. If we combine this with the base address of our Web Services container, we will get the full URI of our web service. For example, if we are using the GT4 standalone container, the base URL will probably be **http://localhost:8080/wsrf/services**. Therefore, our service's URI would be:

http://localhost:8080/wsrf/services/examples/core/first/MathService

className

```
<parameter name="className"

    value="org.globus.examples.services.core.first.impl.MathService"/>
```

This parameter refers to the class which implements the service interface (in our case, **MathService** from the previous section).

The WSDL File

```
<wsdlFile>share/schema/examples/MathService_instance/Math_service.wsdl

    </wsdlFile>
```

The **wsdlFile** tag tells the Web Services container where the WSDL file for this service can be found. This path is relative to $GLOBUS_LOCATION. Take into account that, when our service is deployed, the WSDL file is copied into the **$GLOBUS_LOCATION/share/schema** directory.

Also, notice how there's a "**_service**" at the end of the filename. This is not a typo. This WSDL file (**Math_service.wsdl**) will be generated automatically by a GT4 tool when we compile the service.

Load on Startup

```
<parameter name="loadOnStartup" value="true"/>
```

This parameter allows us to control if we want the service to be loaded as soon as the container is started. In this special case where the service and the resource are implemented in the same class, the container needs to load the service on startup to make sure the resource is initialized correctly.

The Common Parameters

```
<parameter name="allowedMethods" value="*"/>

<parameter name="handlerClass" value="org.globus.axis.providers.RPCProvider"/>

<parameter name="scope" value="Application"/>
```

These are three parameters which we'll see in every web service we program and are better left untouched.

6.3.2 The JNDI Deployment File

This file barely comes into play in this example since we're implementing our service the simplest possible way. However, we still have to include this file, but we need you to take a little leap of faith at this point and just accept that we need the file "because we need it". In the next chapter we will introduce the concept of *resource homes* and we will explain this file in more detail (we will also revisit the file seen in this example). Also, in Section 8.7.2, "The JNDI deployment file" of Chapter 8, you can find more information about what JNDI actually is.

So, the JNDI deployment file looks like this:

```
<?xml version="1.0" encoding="UTF-8"?>

<jndiConfig xmlns="http://wsrf.globus.org/jndi/config">


<service name="examples/core/first/MathService">

        <resource name="home" type="org.globus.wsrf.impl.ServiceResourceHome">

        <resourceParams>


                <parameter>

                        <name>factory</name>

                        <value>org.globus.wsrf.jndi.BeanFactory</value>

                </parameter>


        </resourceParams>


        </resource>

</service>


</jndiConfig>
```

☞ This file is **$EXAMPLES_DIR/org/globus/examples/services/core/first/deploy-jndi-config.xml**.

6.4   Step 4: Create a GAR File With Ant

At this point we have (1) a service interface in WSDL, (2) a service implementation in Java, and (3) a deployment descriptor in WSDD and JNDI telling the Web Services container how to present (1) and (2) to the outer world. However, all this is a bunch of loose files. How are we supposed to place this in a Web services container? Do we have to copy these files to strategically located directories? And what about the Java files? We haven't compiled those yet!

Fear not, for this is the step when everything comes together in perfect harmony. Using those three files we wrote in the previous three pages we will generate a *Grid Archive*, or *GAR file*. This GAR file is a single file which contains all the files and information the Web services container needs to *deploy* our service and make it available to the whole world. In fact, in the next section we'll instruct the GT4 standalone container to take the GAR and deploy it.

However, creating a GAR file is a pretty complex task which involves the following:

- Processing the WSDL file to add missing pieces (such as bindings)

- Creating the stub classes from the WSDL

- Compiling the stubs classes

- Compiling the service implementation

- Organize all the files into a very specific directory structure.

Don't be scared by all this. Thanks to the hard work of the Globus guys and gals, we can do all this in a single step using a very useful tool called Ant.

6.4.1 Ant

Ant, an Apache Software Foundation (http://www.apache.org/) project, is a Java *build tool*. In concept, it is very similar to the classic UNIX **make** command. It allows programmers to forget about the individual steps involved in obtaining an executable from the source files, which will be taken care of by Ant. Each project is different, so the individual steps are described in a *buildfile* ('Makefile' in the make jargon). This buildfile directs Ant on what it should compile, how it should compile it, and in what order. This simplifies the whole process considerably. In fact, it reduces the number of steps to one! With Ant, all we have to worry about is writing the service interface, the service implementation, and the deployment descriptor. Ant takes care of the rest:

As you can see, Ant generates the GAR directly from the three sets of source files. Internally, it is carrying out all the steps listed earlier, sparing us the cumbersome task of doing them ourselves. In a GT4 project, Ant uses two sets of buildfiles: a couple of buildfiles which are a part of GT4, and a buildfile we'll have to write on our own. The GT4 buildfiles cover all the important steps (generating the WSDL code, generating the stubs,...). Our build file essentially has all the unique parameters of our web service, and a bunch of calls to the GT4 buildfiles.

Finally, if you want to learn more about Ant, take a look at the Ant Website (http://ant.apache.org/). It includes plenty of documentation, tutorials, etc.

Math.wsdl

Service interface
(WSDL)

MathService.java

Service implementation
(Java)

deploy-server.wsdd
deploy-jndi-config.xml

Deploment files
(WSDD and JNDI)

<APACHE ANT>

GT4 build
files

build.xml

Ant build file

GAR
file

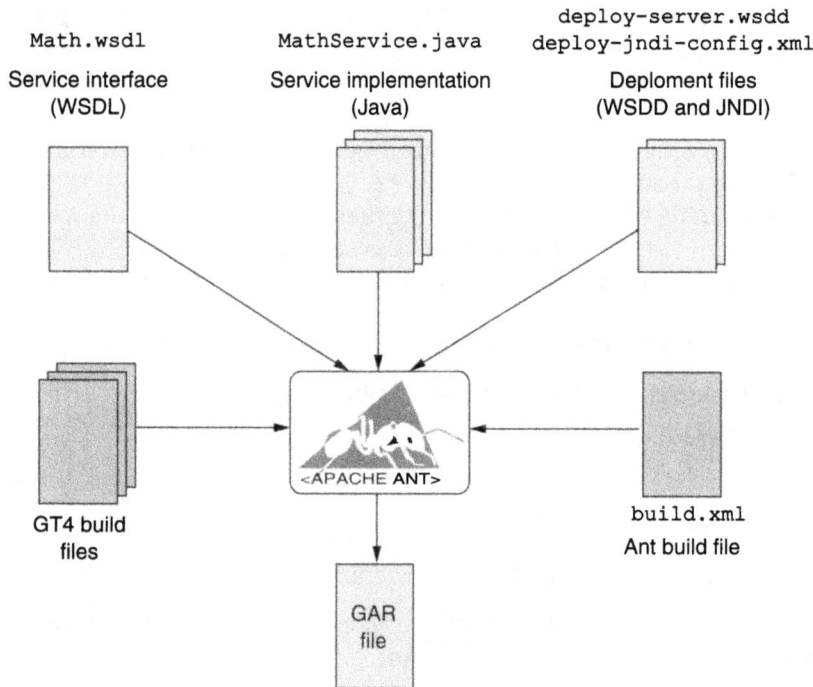

Figure 6.1: Generating a GAR file with Ant

6.4.2   The **globus-build-service** Script and buildfile

Throughout the book, we won't have to write a separate buildfile for each of our services. We will be relying on the **globus-build-service** script and buildfile, one of the tools developed as part of the Globus Service Build Tools (GSBT) project. This tool will allow us to create a GAR file with minimal effort, and without having to modify an Ant buildfile every time we move on to the next example. A copy of **globus-build-service** is included with the examples bundle, and more information on the tool can be found in Appendix E, globus-build-service Script Reference and on the GSBT website (http://gsbt.sourceforge.net/).

6.4.3   Creating the MathService GAR

Using the provided Ant buildfile and the handy script, building a web service is as simple as doing the following:

```
./globus-build-service.sh -d <service base directory> -s <service's WSDL file>
```

> ☞ Make sure you have an environment variable called GLOBUS_LOCATION pointed to your Globus Toolkit root (the script depends on this).

The "service base directory" is the directory where we placed the **deploy-server.wsdd** file, and where the Java files can be found (inside an **impl** directory). To build the first example we simply need to do the following:

```
./globus-build-service.sh \

    -d org/globus/examples/services/core/first/ \

    -s schema/examples/MathService_instance/Math.wsdl
```

globus-build-service also allows us to use a shorthand notation which is much easier (and faster) to use. For example, to build our first example and generate its GAR file, we simply need to do the following:

```
./globus-build-service.sh first
```

> ☞ Make sure you run this from **$EXAMPLES_DIR**. Also, if you are using a Windows machine, you will need to use the Python version of the script. For example:
>
> ```
> ./globus-build-service.py first
> ```
>
> Throughout the book, we will refer to the **.sh** script. You simply have to use **globus-build-service.py** instead.

We will be able to use this shorthand notation with all the examples included in the book. However, this shorthand notation will work because the examples bundle includes a file that maps an abbreviated name (like **first**) to a specific directory and schema file. To write your own mappings and use the shorthand notation in your own projects, refer to Appendix E, globus-build-service Script Reference. That appendix also includes more details on the **globus-build-service** script, such as where you can find the intermediate stub files generated by the script (in case you feel curious and want to take a peek).

If everything works fine, the GAR file will be placed in **$EXAMPLES_DIR**. To be exact, the GAR file generated for this example will be the following:

```
$EXAMPLES_DIR/org_globus_examples_services_core_first.gar
```

6.5 Step 5: Deploy the Service into a Web Services Container

The GAR file, as mentioned above, contains all the files and information the web server needs to deploy the web service. Deployment is done with a GT4 tool that, using Ant, unpacks the GAR file and copies the files within (WSDL, compiled stubs, compiled implementation, WSDD) into key locations in the GT4 directory tree.

This deployment command must be run with a user that has write permissions in $GLOBUS_LOCATION.

```
globus-deploy-gar $EXAMPLES_DIR/org_globus_examples_services_core_first.gar
```

> ☞ Note that, if the Globus standalone container is already running when you deploy the GAR file, you will need to stop it and start it again for the deployment to take effect.

There is also a command to *undeploy* a service:

```
globus-undeploy-gar org_globus_examples_services_core_first
```

Deployment is really as simple as that! That also concludes the five steps necessary to write and deploy a WSRF Web service. However, although you're probably beaming with pride because you've deployed your first WSRF web service, you'll certainly want to make sure that it works. We'll try out our recently deployed service using a very simple client application.

6.6 A Simple Client

We're going to test our web service with a command-line client which will invoke both the **add** and **subtract** operations and will also retrieve the **Value** resource property using the **getValueRP** operation. This client expects one argument from the command line, the service URI.

> ☞ This might be a good time to review Section 4.3, "Addressing WS-Resources". Remember that WS-Resources are addressed using endpoint references (EPRs). Back when we introduced EPRs, we specifically said that they are *opaque* pointers to WS-Resources, in the sense that the client shouldn't know what is contained in the EPR, even though, as service implementors, we are fully aware of what is contained inside the EPR. However, in many cases clients will need a URI to make their first contact with a web service. To put it another way, in many cases we will need a URI to *bootstrap* our interaction with a web service (or a collection of web services).
>
> In this chapter, and the next, our services will have a single resource, so we won't be able to see very fancy EPRs. So, we ask you to please suspend disbelief regarding EPRs until we reach Chapter 8, Multiple resources :-). In that chapter, it will be more clear how we use a URI to bootstrap our interaction with a set of web services, and then use only EPRs as opaque pointers to WS-Resources (without knowing, from a client's point of view, what is contained in them).

The client class will be called **Client** and we'll place it in the **$EXAMPLES_DIR/org/globus/ examples/clients/MathService_instance/Client.java** file. The full code for the client is the following:

```
package org.globus.examples.clients.MathService_instance;


import org.apache.axis.message.addressing.Address;

import org.apache.axis.message.addressing.EndpointReferenceType;

import org.globus.examples.stubs.MathService_instance.GetValueRP;

import org.globus.examples.stubs.MathService_instance.MathPortType;

import org.globus.examples.stubs.MathService_instance.service.

    MathServiceAddressingLocator;


public class Client {

        public static void main(String[] args) {
                MathServiceAddressingLocator locator =
                        new MathServiceAddressingLocator();

            try {
                String serviceURI=args[0];


                ❶

                EndpointReferenceType endpoint =
                        new EndpointReferenceType();
                endpoint.setAddress(new Address(serviceURI));


                ❷

                MathPortType math = locator.getMathPortTypePort(endpoint);


                ❸

                // Perform an addition
                math.add(10);
```

```
            // Perform another addition
            math.add(5);

            // Access value
            System.out.println("Current value:"
                + math.getValue(new GetValueRP()));

            // Perform a subtraction
            math.subtract(5);

            // Access value
            System.out.println("Current value:"
                + math.getValue(new GetValueRP()));
        } catch (Exception e) { ❹
            e.printStackTrace();
        }
    }
}
```

❶ First, we create an **EndpointReferenceType** object representing the endpoint reference of this service. Since our service has a single resource, our endpoint reference only needs the service's URI.

❷ Next, we obtain a reference to the service's portType. This is done with a stub class called **MathServiceAddressingLocator** that, given the service's endpoint, returns a **MathPortType** object that will allow us to contact the **Math** portType.

❸ Once we have that reference, we can work with the web service *as if it were a local object*. For example, to invoke the *remote* **add** operation, we simply have to use the **add** method in the **MathPortType** object.

❹ Finally, notice how all the code must be placed inside a try/catch block. We must always do this, since all the remote operations can throw **RemoteException**s (for example, if there is a network failure and we can't contact the service).

ⓘ **Exception handling, where art thou?**

Throughout this book, we have chosen to handle exceptions in a somewhat crude manner. For example, as you can see in the client application, we simply enclose the entire client in a try/catch block which captures a generic *Exception* and then prints a stack trace (seasoned Java programmers are probably shouting "Thy handling does sear mine eyeballs!" at the sight of this). Since we wanted the flow of our client and service code to be easily read on paper, we prefered not to overload the code with exception handling code.

It is up to you to use proper exception handling in your own code. The Globus API can be used to find out what exceptions are thrown by each class. On the client side you usually only have to worry about **RemoteExceptions**, but the server-side classes can usually throw a lot of different Globus-supplied exceptions.

We are now going to compile the client. Before running the compiler, you need to run a Globus-supplied script that takes care of putting all the Globus libraries into your CLASS-PATH. When compiling the service, Ant took care of this, but, since we're not using Ant to compile the client, we need to run the script. If you are using a BASH shell, you must run the following:

> source $GLOBUS_LOCATION/etc/globus-devel-env.sh

If you are using a CSH shell, then run this:

> source $GLOBUS_LOCATION/etc/globus-devel-env.csh

If you are a Windows user, run the following:

> $GLOBUS_LOCATION/etc/globus-devel-env.bat

To compile the client, do the following:

> javac \
>
> -classpath ./build/stubs/classes/:$CLASSPATH \
>
> org/globus/examples/clients/MathService_instance/Client.java

./build/classes is a directory generated by Ant where all the compiled stub classes are placed. We need to include this directory in the CLASSPATH so our client can access generated stub classes such as **MathServiceAddressingLocator**.

Now, before running the client, we need to start up the standalone container. Otherwise, our web service won't be available, and the client will crash.

> **globus-start-container -nosec**

> ! We are running the Globus standalone container without security (**-nosec**) to avoid having to deal with some of the messy security configuration at this point. In the security chapters we will see how this option only disables one type of security known as "transport-level security". If you've installed the toolkit following the instructions in Appendix A, Installing the Globus Toolkit 4, then you will have to use the **-nosec** option if you have not set up your user certificates.

> Take into account that you still have to set up the host and container certificates, even if you use the **-nosec** option (the installation appendix explains how to set up these certificates).
>
> Finally, take into account that 'real' Grid applications will almost *always* require security. We will see how to make our services secure in Part III, "GT4 Security".

When the container starts up, you'll see a list with the URIs of all the deployed services. One quick way of checking if MathService has been correctly deployed is to check if the following line appears in the list of services:

```
http://127.0.0.1:8080/wsrf/services/examples/core/first/MathService
```

> ☞ This is the service as it would appear in a default GT4 installation, with the standalone container located in **http://localhost:8080/wsrf/services**. The URI might be different if you've changed the location of the container.

If the service is correctly deployed, we can now run the client:

```
java \
-classpath ./build/stubs/classes/:$CLASSPATH \
org.globus.examples.clients.MathService_instance.Client \
http://127.0.0.1:8080/wsrf/services/examples/core/first/MathService
```

If all goes well, you should see the following:

```
Current value: 15
Current value: 10
```

Now, remember that our service is, at the same time, the resource itself. So, if we invoke the service repeatedly, we will access the same stateful information. If you run the client a couple more times, you should see the value increase with each run:

```
Current value: 25
Current value: 20

Current value: 35
Current value: 30
```

> ⓘ **Stopping the container**
>
> To stop the container, you can use the **globus-stop-container**, which is described in Section C.5.2, "globus-stop-container". As you'll see there, stopping

the container can be a bit messy because of certain security issues. If you're just trying out examples on your computer, the simplest way of stopping your container is simply by killing the container's process (by pressing "Control-C" on most systems). However, on production systems, you should *always* use **globus-stop-container**, as this will guarantee that the container cleanly releases any system resources it might be holding.

chapter **7**

Singleton Resources

In the previous chapter, we saw how to implement a single-resource stateful web service. We did this the simplest possible way: implementing the service *and* the resource in the same class. In this chapter, although we will continue to have a single resource, we will learn more about the preferred way of implementing web services in GT4: using a separate class for the service and the resource. To do this, we will learn more about *resource homes.*

7.1 Splitting Up the Implementation

7.1.1 The Resource, the Home, and the Service

In this chapter, we will split our implementation into three files. We will see that, for the most part, we will simply take code from the previous chapter and divide it among the three files.

- The resource: **$EXAMPLES_DIR/org/globus/examples/services/core/singleton/ impl/MathResource.java**

- The resource home: **$EXAMPLES_DIR/org/globus/examples/services/core/ singleton/impl/MathResourceHome.java**

- The service itself: **$EXAMPLES_DIR/org/globus/examples/services/core/ singleton/impl/MathService.java**

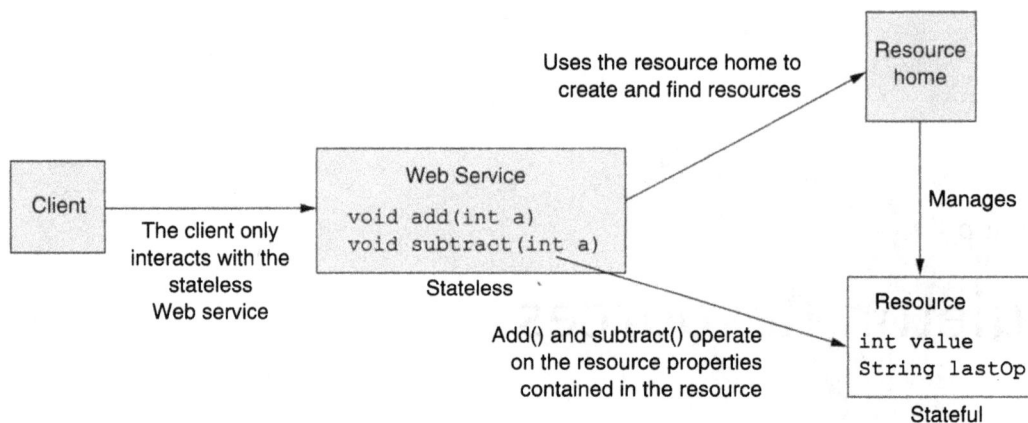

Figure 7.1: Relationships between the Service, the Resource Home, and the Resource

Before looking at the actual Java code, let's make sure we understand how these three implementation files are related.

- The **service** is the *stateless* frontend (the client only interacts with this class, even if there are more classes lurking around in the background). Remember from Chapter 4, WSRF section that, since we're following a "resource approach" to statefulness, the web service will *always* be stateless. However, we can give the impression of being stateful by retrieving a *stateful resource* whenever we want to access state information.

- The **resource** is the *stateful* class where we keep all our information.

- The **resource home** is in charge of *managing* the resources. For example, the (stateless) service will use the resource home to retrieve the (stateful) resource. In this chapter, the resource home will be very simple since it will only deal with a single (or *singleton*) resource. In the next chapter, we will see how to set up a resource home that can manage several resources.

ⓘ **ServiceResourceHome**

You might be wondering how this related to the example we saw in the previous chapter. Even though we did not implement a resource home, there *was* a resource home lurking around in the background. Remember the following line from the JNDI config file?

```
<resource name="home" type="org.globus.wsrf.impl.ServiceResourceHome">
```

We used a Globus-supplied resource home called **ServiceResourceHome**. As the following figure shows, the **ServiceResourceHome** is a special type of resource home that always returns the service object when asked for a resource. This allows us to implement our resource and service in the same class.

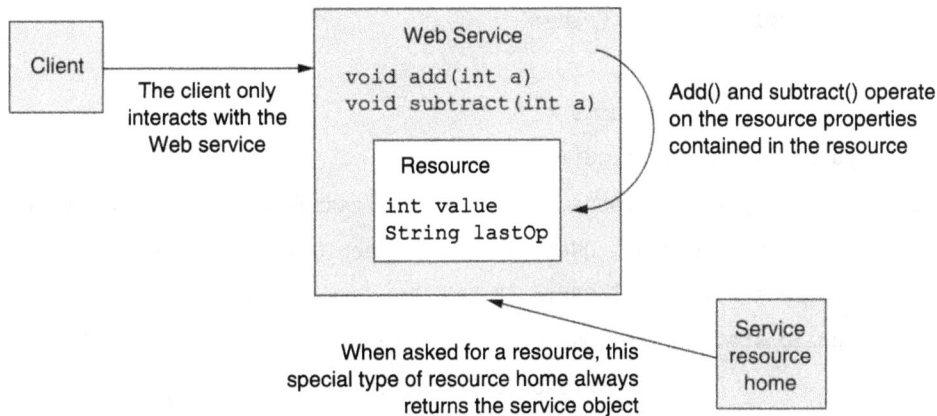

For simplicity, we will use **ServiceResourceHome** in other examples in the book, as it will spare us a lot of code. However, remember that the preferred way of implementing services is by splitting up the implementation, as we will do in this chapter. When you start writing your own services, you should only use **ServiceResourceHome** for very simple services.

7.1.2 The WSDL File

In this chapter, we are only changing the *implementation* of our service. The interface is still the same, so there's no need to modify the WSDL file. We can reuse the one from the previous chapter.

☞ The WSDL file is **$EXAMPLES_DIR/schema/examples/MathService_instance/Math.wsdl**

7.1.3 The Constants Interface

Once again, the first bit of code we are going to write is the namespaces interface. Again, since we are reusing the WSDL file from the previous chapter, there's no big changes to the **MathConstants** interface, except for the fact that we are now placing our Java classes in a new package.

```
package org.globus.examples.services.core.singleton.impl;


import javax.xml.namespace.QName;


public interface MathConstants {
        public static final String NS =
            "http://www.globus.org/namespaces/examples/MathService_instance";
        public static final QName RP_VALUE = new QName(NS, "Value");
        public static final QName RP_LASTOP = new QName(NS, "LastOp");
        public static final QName RESOURCE_PROPERTIES = new QName(NS,
                "MathResourceProperties");

}
```

> ☞ This file is **$EXAMPLES_DIR/org/globus/examples/services/core/singleton/impl/**
> **MathConstants.java**.

In the following chapters, we won't see the complete code of each new **MathConstants** interface. As you see, it is pretty straightforward to write it from the WSDL file. From now on, we will simply point you to the location of the file in the examples bundle.

7.1.4   The Resource Implementation

The first big class we will see is the resource implementation. You will be (pleasantly) surprised to see that it is practically identical to the **MathService** class from the previous chapter. The only thing missing is the **add**, **subtract**, and **getValueRP** methods, which we will now place in the service implementation.

Also, notice how all the RP initialization code is no longer in the constructor, but in an **initialize** method. This is not required and, in fact, we could continue to have all the initialization code in the constructor. However, when we start seeing how to manage multiple resources (next chapter) and persistent resources (Chapter 12), having the initialization code in a separate method (instead of the constructor) will come in handy.

```
package org.globus.examples.services.core.singleton.impl;


import org.globus.wsrf.Resource;
```

```java
import org.globus.wsrf.ResourceProperties;
import org.globus.wsrf.ResourceProperty;
import org.globus.wsrf.ResourcePropertySet;
import org.globus.wsrf.impl.ReflectionResourceProperty;
import org.globus.wsrf.impl.SimpleResourcePropertySet;

public class MathResource implements Resource, ResourceProperties {

        /* Resource Property set */
        private ResourcePropertySet propSet;

        /* Resource properties */
        private int value;

        private String lastOp;

        /* Initializes RPs */
        public void initialize() throws Exception {
                this.propSet = new SimpleResourcePropertySet(
                                MathConstants.RESOURCE_PROPERTIES);

                try {
                    ResourceProperty valueRP = new ReflectionResourceProperty(
                                MathConstants.RP_VALUE, "Value", this);
                    this.propSet.add(valueRP);
                    setValue(0);

                    ResourceProperty lastOpRP = new ReflectionResourceProperty(
                                MathConstants.RP_LASTOP, "LastOp", this);
                    this.propSet.add(lastOpRP);
                    setLastOp("NONE");
```

```
            } catch (Exception e) {
                throw new RuntimeException(e.getMessage());
            }
    }


    /* Get/Setters for the RPs */
    public int getValue() {
        return value;
    }


    public synchronized void setValue(int value) {
        this.value = value;
    }


    public String getLastOp() {
        return lastOp;
    }


    public synchronized void setLastOp(String lastOp) {
        this.lastOp = lastOp;
    }


    /* Required by interface ResourceProperties */
    public ResourcePropertySet getResourcePropertySet() {
        return this.propSet;
    }
}
```

☞ This file is **$EXAMPLES_DIR/org/globus/examples/services/core/singleton/impl/**
MathResource.java.

As you can see, this class contains all the code required to implement the resource and its resource properties (**Value** and **LastOp**). Remember that this is the *stateful* component.

7.1.5 The Service Implementation

This class, on the other hand, will contain the **add**, **subtract**, and **getValueRP** methods the client will interact with. However, we can't reuse the code from the previous chapter. Remember, for example, how we implemented the **add** operation:

```
public AddResponse add(int a) throws RemoteException {

        value += a;

        lastOp = "ADDITION";


        return new AddResponse();

}
```

Now that we're splitting up the implementation, the stateful information is no longer in the service class itself, so we don't have a **value** or **lastOp** variable we can interact with. Any operation that requires working with stateful information will have to work with a **MathResource** object. So, our **add** method will look something like this:

```
public AddResponse add(int a) throws RemoteException {

        MathResource mathResource = getResource(); ❶

        mathResource.setValue(mathResource.getValue() + a); ❷

        mathResource.setLastOp("ADDITION"); ❸


        return new AddResponse();

}
```

❶ First of all, we have to get a reference to the resource. The **getResource** method is described shortly.

❷ Now that we have a hold of the resource, we can work with its stateful information. In this step, we simply retrieve the value (using the **getValue** method in the **MathResource** object), add parameter **a**, and set the new value with **setValue**.

❸ Finally, we set the last operation to be "ADDITION".

ⓘ **Thread safety issues**

Unlike the previous chapter, the **add** and **subtract** are *not* declared with the **synchronized** keyword. Since we have split up the implementation, **add** and **subtract** no longer interact directly with the **value** and **lastOp** attributes, but use get/set methods which *are* declared with the **synchronized** keyword.

Of course, you can still choose to declare **add** and **subtract** with **synchronized**, but this would probably affect your performance.

The **getResource** method used above is a private method that retrieves this service's singleton resource. As you can see, this method simply uses **ResourceContext** (a Globus class) to obtain the resource.

```
private MathResource getResource() throws RemoteException {
        Object resource = null;
        try {
                resource = ResourceContext.getResourceContext().getResource();
        } catch (NoSuchResourceException e) {
                throw new RemoteException("Specified resource does not exist", e);
        } catch (ResourceContextException e) {
                throw new RemoteException("Error during resource lookup", e);
        } catch (Exception e) {
                throw new RemoteException("", e);
        }


        MathResource mathResource = (MathResource) resource;
        return mathResource;
}
```

The complete source code for the service implementation is:

```
/*
 * This file is licensed under the terms of the Globus Toolkit Public License
 * v3, found at http://www.globus.org/toolkit/legal/4.0/license-v3.html.
 *
 * This notice must appear in redistributions of this file, with or without
 * modification.
 */
package org.globus.examples.services.core.singleton.impl;


import java.rmi.RemoteException;


import org.globus.examples.stubs.MathService_instance.AddResponse;
import org.globus.examples.stubs.MathService_instance.GetValueRP;
```

```java
import org.globus.examples.stubs.MathService_instance.SubtractResponse;
import org.globus.wsrf.NoSuchResourceException;
import org.globus.wsrf.ResourceContext;
import org.globus.wsrf.ResourceContextException;

public class MathService {

    /*
     * Private method that gets a reference to the resource specified
     * in the endpoint reference.
     */
    private MathResource getResource() throws RemoteException {
        Object resource = null;
        try {
            resource = ResourceContext.getResourceContext().
                getResource();
        } catch (NoSuchResourceException e) {
            throw new RemoteException("Specified resource does
                not exist", e);
        } catch (ResourceContextException e) {
            throw new RemoteException("Error during resource
                lookup", e);
        } catch (Exception e) {
            throw new RemoteException("", e);
        }

        MathResource mathResource = (MathResource) resource;
        return mathResource;
    }
```

```
        /* Implementation of add, subtract, and getValue operations */

        public AddResponse add(int a) throws RemoteException {
                MathResource mathResource = getResource();
                mathResource.setValue(mathResource.getValue() + a);
                mathResource.setLastOp("ADDITION");

                return new AddResponse();
        }


        public SubtractResponse subtract(int a) throws RemoteException {
                MathResource mathResource = getResource();
                mathResource.setValue(mathResource.getValue() - a);
                mathResource.setLastOp("SUBTRACTION");

                return new SubtractResponse();
        }


        public int getValueRP(GetValueRP params) throws RemoteException {
                MathResource mathResource = getResource();

                return mathResource.getValue();
        }

}
```

☞ This file is **$EXAMPLES_DIR/org/globus/examples/services/core/singleton/impl/**
MathService.java.

7.1.6 The Resource Home

The implementation of the resource home is extremely simple since we're extending from an existing class included in the toolkit, **SingletonResourceHome**. That base class provides practically all the functionality our resource home needs to manage a single resource. The only thing we have to do is implement the **findSingleton** method, which is called internally by the **ResourceContext** class when we first request the resource. The **findSingleton** method creates a new **MathResource** object, initializes it, and returns it. The base class **SingletonResourceHome** keeps a copy of that resource, which is returned each time the resource is requested.

The complete source code would be:

```
package org.globus.examples.services.core.singleton.impl;


import org.globus.wsrf.Resource;

import org.globus.wsrf.impl.SingletonResourceHome;


public class MathResourceHome extends SingletonResourceHome {

        public Resource findSingleton() {

                try {

                        // Create a resource and initialize it.

                        MathResource mathResource = new MathResource();

                        mathResource.initialize();

                        return mathResource;

                } catch (Exception e) {

                        e.printStackTrace();

                        return null;

                }


        }

}
```

☞ This file is **$EXAMPLES_DIR/org/globus/examples/services/core/singleton/impl/ MathResourceHome.java**.

The usefulness of having a resource home might not be apparent in this simple case (when we have a singleton resource). However, a resource home adds a lot of versatility to our implementation, specially when we have to deal with multiple resources. For example, a resource home can be used to perform special actions when a resource is created and later destroyed (adding an entry in a database, writing out a log message, etc.). In the next chapter, we will see how we modify the implementation of the resource home to accomodate multiple resources.

7.2   Build, Deploy, and Try it Out... With the Same Client

After splitting up the implementation, we are now ready to build and deploy our new service. First off, the WSDD file has only two small changes: a new service name, and a new service class name. Since we are reusing the WSDL file from the previous chapter, we don't have to change anything else in the WSDD file.

```xml
<?xml version="1.0" encoding="UTF-8"?>
<deployment name="defaultServerConfig"
    xmlns="http://xml.apache.org/axis/wsdd/"
    xmlns:java="http://xml.apache.org/axis/wsdd/providers/java"
    xmlns:xsd="http://www.w3.org/2001/XMLSchema">


    <service name="examples/core/singleton/MathService" provider="Handler"
        use="literal" style="document">
            <parameter name="className" value="org.globus.examples.services.
                core.singleton.impl.MathService"/>
            <wsdlFile>share/schema/examples/MathService_instance/
                Math_service.wsdl</wsdlFile>
            <parameter name="allowedMethods" value="*"/>
            <parameter name="handlerClass"
                value="org.globus.axis.providers.RPCProvider"/>
            <parameter name="scope" value="Application"/>
    </service>


</deployment>
```

> ☞ This file is **$EXAMPLES_DIR/org/globus/examples/services/core/singleton/
> deploy-server.wsdd**.

Now, let's take a closer look at the JNDI deployment file. In the previous chapter we asked you to please take a leap of faith and accept that we needed this file "because we need it".

Now, we can explain what this file does. It is responsible for specifying what resource home our service has to use to get a hold of resources. In this file we will also specify parameters related to how the resource home manages those resources. However, since at this point we are only managing a single resource, our JNDI deployment file will be pretty simple.

```xml
<?xml version="1.0" encoding="UTF-8"?>

<jndiConfig xmlns="http://wsrf.globus.org/jndi/config">


<service name="examples/core/singleton/MathService">

        <resource name="home" type="org.globus.examples.services.core.

            singleton.impl.MathResourceHome">

        <resourceParams>


                <parameter>

                        <name>factory</name>

                        <value>org.globus.wsrf.jndi.BeanFactory</value>

                </parameter>


        </resourceParams>


        </resource>

</service>


</jndiConfig>
```

> ☞ This file is **$EXAMPLES_DIR/org/globus/examples/services/core/singleton/ deploy-jndi-config.xml**.

In a nutshell, the root element **jndiConfig** of the file can contain several **service** elements (one for each service we're configuring...since we're only configuring one service, we'll have a single **service** element). This element has a **name** attribute whose value *must match* the service name specified in the WSDD file (this is basically the "glue" between the WSDD file and the JNDI file).

The **service** element contains a **resource** element which we'll use to specify the resource home for our service. Notice that we do so using the **type** attribute. The **resource** element can contain several resource parameters. In this example we have a single parameter, which will be common to all the services we deploy.

> ☞ If you look back on the JNDI deployment file from the previous chapter, you'll see that it is the same as the one shown above, except that the resource home we specify is **ServiceResourceHome**.

Now, we can build the service:

./globus-build-service.sh singleton

And deploy it:

globus-deploy-gar EXAMPLES_DIR/org_globus_examples_services_wsrf_core_

singleton.gar

> ☞ You will need to restart the Globus standalone container for the deployment to take effect.

Finally, we're going to make sure the service works. Another nice perk of reusing the WSDL file is that we can also reuse the client described in the previous chapter. Remember that we've only changed the implementation of the service; as long as we don't change the WSDL interface, there's no need to write a new client.

So, remember you have to run the client like so:

**java **

**-classpath ./build/stubs/classes/:$CLASSPATH **

**org.globus.examples.clients.MathService_instance.Client **

http://127.0.0.1:8080/wsrf/services/examples/core/singleton/MathService

If all goes well, you should see the following:

Current value: 15

Current value: 10

If you run the client another time, since our service is tied to a singleton resource, you should see the value increase with each run of the client.

Current value: 25

Current value: 20

Current value: 35

Current value: 30

Multiple Resources

In the previous two chapters we implemented a simple stateful web service that used a single resource to keep stateful information. First, we used the **ServiceResourceHome** so we could implement the service and the resource in the same class, and then we split up the implementation into a service class, a resource class, and a resource home class.

In this chapter we will learn how to write a service that, using a design pattern known as the *factory/instance* pattern, will be able to manage *multiple* resources.

8.1   The WS-Resource Factory Pattern

The factory/instance pattern is a well-known design pattern in software design, and specially in object-oriented languages. In this pattern, we are not allowed to create instances of objects directly, but must do so through a *factory* that will provide a **create** operation.

When dealing with multiple resources, the WSRF specs recommend that we follow this pattern, having one service in charge of creating the resources (*"the factory service"*) and another one to actually access the information contained in the resources (*"the instance service"*).

Figure 8.1 summarizes the relationship between these two services, the resources, and the client. Whenever the client wants to create a new resource, it will contact the factory service, who will take care of creating and initializing a new resource. It is important to see that, in this case, the resource is also assigned *a unique key*. Since we are no longer dealing with a single resource, we need some way of telling each resource apart. The factory service will return an *endpoint reference* to a WS-Resource composed of the instance service and the recently created resource. Using the EPR returned by the factory, the client can now interact with the WS-Resource.

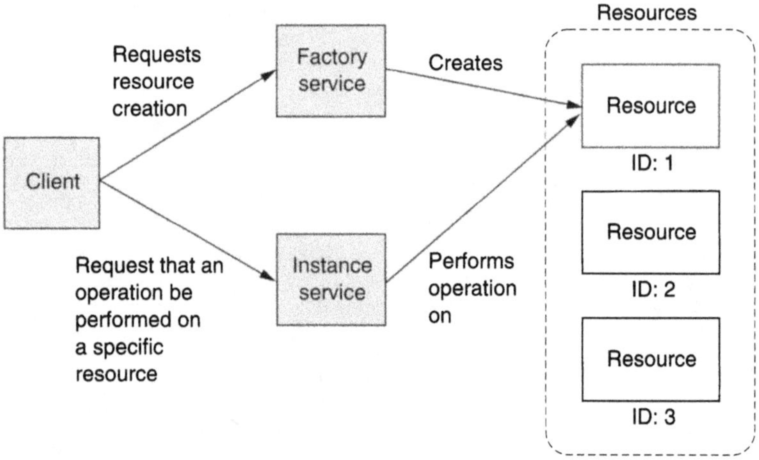

Figure 8.1: The WS-Resource factory pattern

ⓘ **Not your typical factory/instance...**

It would be more correct to say that the factory pattern described in this book is "inspired" by the textbook factory pattern, which usually deals with objects, not services. In particular, the "instance service" can be a source of confusion, and merits further discussion.

The factory service provides clients with an interface to request the creation of new WS-Resources. However, as we saw in Section 4.3, a WS-Resource is the pairing of a web service with a resource. So, the factory service has to return the address of a web service, and a resource identifier (both encapsulated in an EPR). To do so, it must first *create* a new resource. In a sense, we could say the resources are the instances.

On the other hand, it is important to understand that the "instance service" is *not* created. It is simply another service deployed in the container, along with the factory service. The EPR returned by the factory service includes the instance service's URI because we want clients to interact with the resources through that particular service (and not the factory service, which is *only* responsible for creating new resources). So, it would be more correct for us to refer to the "instance service" as "the service that allows us to access the resources ("the instances") created by the factory service". Of course, we prefer the shorter version :-).

Finally, a word of caution to those of you with an OGSI/GT3 mindset. The "instance service" we talk about in this book has nothing to do with OGSI instance services. OGSI did, in fact, allow you to *create* new services dynamically. Once more, in GT4 we will *not* create new services, only new resources which get accessed through a separate service (the "instance service").

8.2 Implementing the WS-Resource Factory Pattern in GT4

Implementing this design pattern in GT4 is actually not too complicated. In fact, it is very similar to the example seen in the previous chapter, with two main differences, highlighted in Figure 8.2, (compare with Figure 7.1).

- **Factory service and instance service.** To handle multiple resources, we will now need to deploy two services: a factory service and an instance service. The factory service provides a **createResource** operation that returns an EPR to the new WS-Resource. The instance service provides the operations we have been working with in the previous chapters: **add**, **subtract**, and **getValueRP**.

- **Non-trivial resource home.** The resource home no longer deals with a single resource. In this case, it must keep track of several resources at the same time. However, notice how we have a single resource home, shared by the factory and instance services. The factory service will use the resource home to *create* new resources, while the instance service will use it to *find* a resource with a given key.

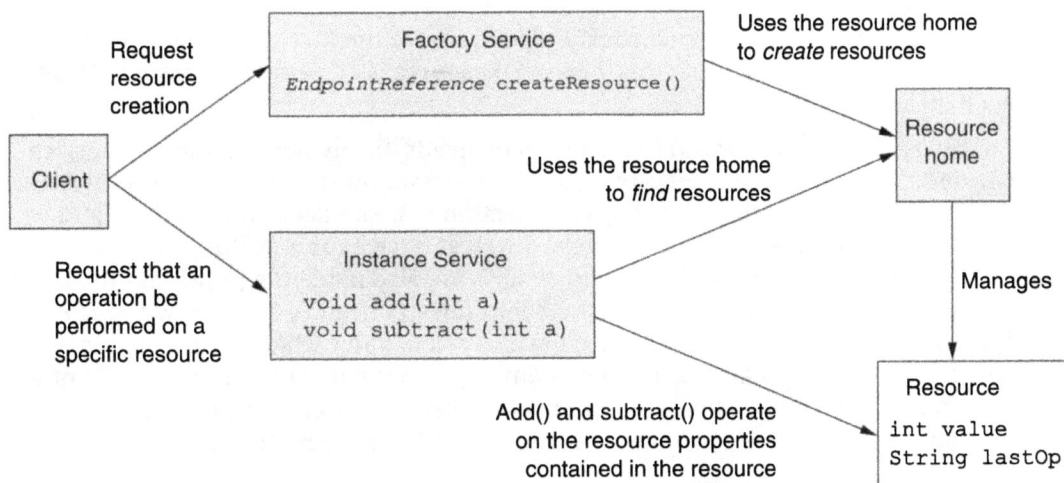

Figure 8.2: Relationships between the Factory Service, the Instance Service, the Resource Home, and the Resource.

> ☞ To be more precise, the resource home is primarily associated with the instance service. The factory service can access that resource home to request the creation of new resources (in fact, this will be reflected in our JNDI deployment file). The factory service could have its own resource home (separate from the instance's resource home) to maintain its own resources. However, we will not explore that scenario in this book. Conceptually, it is safe to think of the resource home as being "shared" by the factory service and instance service.

So, for this example, we will have four Java classes (plus the **MathConstants** interface):

- The factory service: **$EXAMPLES_DIR/org/globus/examples/services/core/ factory/impl/MathFactoryService.java**
- The instance service: **$EXAMPLES_DIR/org/globus/examples/services/core/ factory/impl/MathService.java**
- The resource: **$EXAMPLES_DIR/org/globus/examples/services/core/factory/ impl/MathResource.java**
- The resource home: **$EXAMPLES_DIR/org/globus/examples/services/core/ factory/impl/MathResourceHome.java**

Before seeing the actual code, a good way of seeing what role each class plays is to see how they interact. For now, don't worry about all the deployment details. Just imagine that we actually have our two services (factory and instance) up and ready to accept invocations from a client class, and that the service class has access to the resource home and that the resource home, in turn, has access to a bunch of resource objects. Let's start with the creation of a new resource, shown in Figure 8.3.

1. The client invokes the **createResource** operation on the factory service. This will return the *endpoint reference* to a new WS-Resource. Let's analyze this step from the client's point of view:

    - **Invoking createResource:** The client needs to invoke the factory service and, to do so, it will need to know its address. As we have said in previous chapters (you might want to review Section 4.3, and Section 6.6), the client is supposed to use an EPR to address a web service endpoint (furthermore, this EPR can be WS-Resource-qualified or not). We also made the point that the EPR is an *opaque* pointer, and that the client doesn't need to know how the EPR is implemented (and, in fact, doesn't even need to know what is contained inside it). However, in many cases, the client will usually need to know the URI of a service to bootstrap his interaction with a service, or collection of services. In our case, the client *only* needs to know the URI of the factory service.

    - **Returning an EPR:** The **createResource** operation returns an EPR. This is where the opaqueness of the EPR is most apparent. The client doesn't need to know what URI or what resource identifier is contained inside the EPR

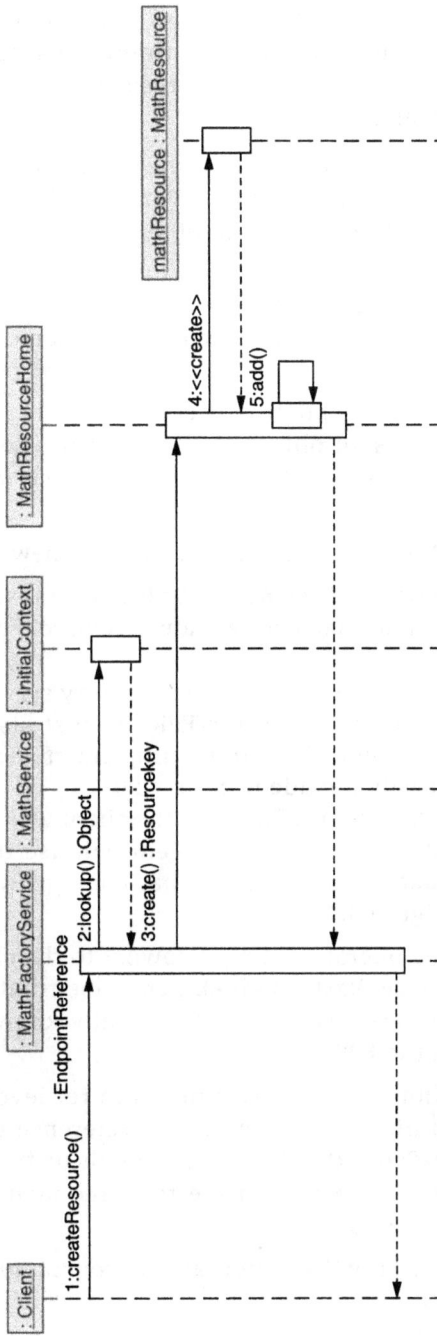

Figure 8.3: Sequence diagram for resource creation

(although, as service implementors, we know what the contents of the EPR are). In fact, the client doesn't even need to know that his interactions with the newly created resource will be done through a separate "instance service"! The client simply receives an EPR, and sees it as an atomic (as an "indivisible") pointer to a WS-Resource.

Of course, from the implementor's point of view, we *do* know what URI and what resource identifier will be placed inside the EPR. The following steps deal with how the EPR (which the client will receive) is created.

2. First of all, the factory service has to create a new resource. This necessarily has to be done through the resource home, which is in charge of managing all the resources. However, we have to locate our resource home first. We do this using the JNDI *InitialContext* class.

3. Now that we have the resource home, we can ask it to create the new resource. The creation method returns an object of type **ResourceKey**. This is the resource identifier which we need to create the endpoint reference we'll be returning to the client.

4. The resource home will take care of actually creating a new **MathResource** instance.

5. Next, the resource home will add the new **MathResource** instance to its internal list of resources. This list will allow us to access any resource if we know that resource's identifier.

   Although not shown in the diagram, once the factory service has created the new resource and included its identifier in the EPR, it must also include the instance service's URI in the EPR. As we will see in the implementation, the factory "knows" what the URI is and can easily include it in the EPR.

   Once the **createResource** call has finished, the client will have the WS-Resource's endpoint reference. In all future calls, the client will use the EPR to interact with the WS-Resource. Let's take a close look at what happens when we invoke the **add** operation, as shown in Figure 8.4.

6. The client invokes the **add** operation. Unbeknownst to the client, this invocation is done on the instance service (**MathService**). Remember that the client simply uses the EPR to address a WS-Resource, but doesn't really know what URI or resource identifier is contained in the EPR.

7. However, the **add** operation is stateless. It needs to retrieve a resource to actually work. The resource identifier is in the endpoint reference used in the invocation. Fortunately, the **ResourceContext** helper class shields us from all the potential nastiness. It will be in charge of extracting the resource identifier from the EPR and finding the resource it refers to.

8. However, it's interesting to note that, internally, *ResourceContext* uses the *ResourceHome* to find the resource.

9. Once we have the resource, the instance service can access all its state information, such as the "Value" and the "LastOp" resource properties. First of all, we will access

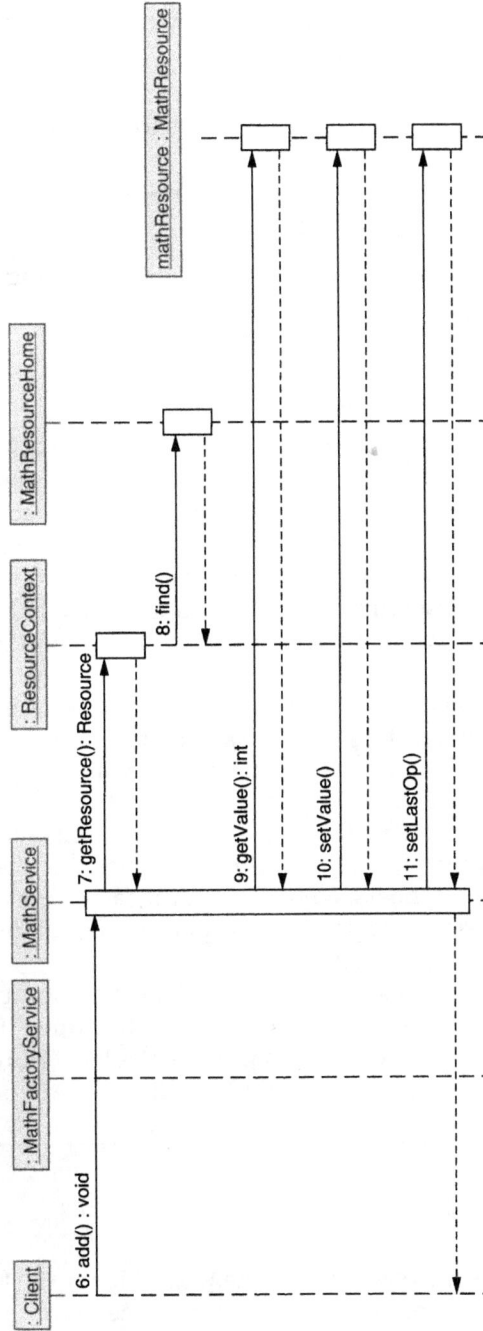

Figure 8.4: Sequence diagram for WS-Resource invocation

the "Value" resource property. As in the example seen in the previous chapter, our resource (**MathResource**) will allow us to modify the RP's using get/set methods (in this case, with a simple **getValue()** method).

10. Once we've modified the value, we have to make sure we commit the change in the resource (in our case, using **setValue()**). Otherwise, that bit of state information won't be remembered.

11. Finally, we use the **setLastOp()** method in the resource to modify the **LastOp** resource property to equal "**ADDITION**".

Don't worry if you're a bit confused. When we actually start coding all this, it'll probably seem clearer (even so, you might want to review these diagrams once we've coded the full example).

ⓘ **This design isn't written in stone!**

What we have shown here is just one possible way of implementing the WS-Resource factory pattern. One of the limitations of our implementation is that it requires that the factory service and instance service be deployed in the same container. This is not really a big limitation, as it is usually sensible to have the factory service and instance service deployed on the same container (in fact, a lot of the GT4 higher-level services are deployed like this). Our point is that you can certainly improve the design to accomodate other scenarios. As a more elaborate example, consider if our resources actually resided in a database server accessible by several hosts, each with the instance service deployed in them. Furthermore, the instance services would always retrieve the resources from this database server (let's assume that the resource identifier is the primary key of the resource in some database table).

The factory service could choose from this pool of instance services (in different hosts) when creating a WS-Resource to make sure that the load of requests is distributed among several hosts. For example, the factory service could choose between 10 instance service URIs, and choose one at random (or in a round-robin fashion) to balance the load of requests.

We will not explore these scenarios in this book. Our point is that the implementation of the factory/instance pattern is completely open (i.e. not mandated by any specification). Our implementation, in particular, follows best practices observed by the Globus team, so it should be able to meet your needs in most cases.

8.3 The Factory Service

We begin by implementing the factory service. The WSDL file for the factory service is very simple, as we only have a single operation **createResource** with no parameters and that returns an endpoint reference.

☞ You should be able to read the file and recognize that there is, indeed, a single operation **createResource** with no parameters and returning an endpoint reference. If not, this might be a good time to review Appendix B, A WSDL Primer.

```xml
<?xml version="1.0" encoding="UTF-8"?>
<definitions name="FactoryService"
    targetNamespace="http://www.globus.org/namespaces/examples/
        FactoryService" ❶
    xmlns="http://schemas.xmlsoap.org/wsdl/"
    xmlns:tns="http://www.globus.org/namespaces/examples/FactoryService"
    xmlns:wsa="http://schemas.xmlsoap.org/ws/2004/03/addressing" ❷
    xmlns:wsdl="http://schemas.xmlsoap.org/wsdl/"
    xmlns:xsd="http://www.w3.org/2001/XMLSchema">



<!--============================================================


                              T Y P E S


    ===========================================================-->
<types>
<xsd:schema targetNamespace="http://www.globus.org/namespaces/examples/
    FactoryService"
    xmlns:tns="http://www.globus.org/namespaces/examples/FactoryService"
    xmlns:xsd="http://www.w3.org/2001/XMLSchema">


        ❸
        <xsd:import
            namespace="http://schemas.xmlsoap.org/ws/2004/03/addressing"
            schemaLocation="../../ws/addressing/WS-Addressing.xsd" />
```

```
<!-- REQUESTS AND RESPONSES -->


<xsd:element name="createResource">
        <xsd:complexType/>
</xsd:element>
<xsd:element name="createResourceResponse">
<xsd:complexType>
        <xsd:sequence>
                <xsd:element ref="wsa:EndpointReference"/>
        </xsd:sequence>
</xsd:complexType>
</xsd:element>


</xsd:schema>
</types>



<!--===========================================================


                M E S S A G E S



===========================================================-->
<message name="CreateResourceRequest">
        <part name="request" element="tns:createResource"/>
</message>
<message name="CreateResourceResponse">
        <part name="response" element="tns:createResourceResponse"/>
</message>
```

```
<!--==============================================================



                    P O R T T Y P E



============================================================-->
❹
<portType name="FactoryPortType">

        <operation name="createResource">
                <input message="tns:CreateResourceRequest"/>
                <output message="tns:CreateResourceResponse"/>
        </operation>


</portType>


</definitions>
```

> ☞ This file is **$EXAMPLES_DIR/schema/FactoryService/Factory.wsdl**.

- ❶ The factory service's target namespace is **http://www.globus.org/namespaces/examples/FactoryService**.
- ❷ The service's **createResource** operation returns an endpoint reference, a structure that is part of the WS-Addressing specification. We need to declare the WS-Addressing namespace.
- ❸ We also need to import the WS-Addressing Schema file, which contains the definition of the endpoint reference structure (**wsa:EndpointReference**)
- ❹ Our portType, **FactoryPortType**, has a single operation **createResource**.

Since we have added a new interface, we need to map the new WSDL namespaces to Java packages (as described in Section 6.1.3).

```
http\://www.globus.org/namespaces/examples/FactoryService=
                                org.globus.examples.stubs.Factory
http\://www.globus.org/namespaces/examples/FactoryService/bindings=
                                org.globus.examples.stubs.Factory.bindings
```

```
http\://www.globus.org/namespaces/examples/FactoryService/service=
                              org.globus.examples.stubs.Factory.service
```

> ☞ These three lines must be present in **$EXAMPLES_DIR/namespace2package.mappings**.

Now, we have to write the Java implementation of the factory service. This will be a single Java class, with a single **createResource** method:

```
public class MathFactoryService {


        /* Implementation of createResource Operation */
        public CreateResourceResponse createResource(CreateResource request)
                        throws RemoteException {

        }


}
```

> ☞ This is part of file **$EXAMPLES_DIR/org/globus/examples/services/core/factory/impl/MathFactoryService.java**.

Inside this method, we will perform three steps:

1. Retrieve the resource home.
2. Use the resource home to create a new resource.
3. Create the endpoint reference we will return to the client. This EPR must contain the instance service's URI and the new resource's key.

In the following snippet of code we perform steps 1 and 2:

```
try {
        home = (MathResourceHome) this.getInstanceResourceHome(); ❶
        key = home.create();
} catch (Exception e) {
        throw new RemoteException(e.getMessage(), e);
}
```

❶ **getInstanceResourceHome** is a private method which retrieves a reference to the resource home. This method relies on the JNDI deployment file, so we will defer explaining how this method really works until we see the JNDI file for this example.

If we succeed in retrieving the resource home, then the **key** variable will contain the resource's identifier, which we'll use to construct the endpoint reference:

```
EndpointReferenceType epr = null;


try {
        URL baseURL = ServiceHost.getBaseURL();

        String instanceService = home.getInstanceServicePath();

        String instanceURI = baseURL.toString() + instanceService;

        // The endpoint reference includes the instance's URI and the

        // resource key

        epr = AddressingUtils.createEndpointReference(instanceURI, key);

} catch (Exception e) {

        throw new RemoteException(e.getMessage(), e);

}
```

Notice how we have to create a new endpoint reference (of type **EndpointReferenceType**) using the instance server's URI (**instanceURI**) and the resource's identifier (**key**). The path of the instance service is obtained from the **MathResourceHome**. Finally, the only thing left to do is to 'box' the EPR inside a **CreateResourceResponse** object and return it.

```
CreateResourceResponse response = new CreateResourceResponse();

response.setEndpointReference(epr);

return response;
```

> ☞ Remember from the information box how document/literal bindings affect our parameters in Section 6.2, "Step 2: Implementing the service in Java" that whenever one of our operations returns a complex type (such as an endpoint reference), it is 'boxed' inside a stub class.

> ☞ Now is a good moment to review Figure 8.3.

8.4 The Instance Service

Implementing the instance service is going to be very simple, since we can reuse both the WSDL file and practically all the Java implementation from the previous chapter (with only minor changes to the resource class).

> ☞ The implementation of the instance service is **$EXAMPLES_DIR/org/globus/ examples/services/core/factory/impl/MathService.java**.

But let's not leave it at that: this is a good moment to ask ourselves: why exactly can we reuse both the WSDL file and the Java implementation of the service and the resource? Well, take into account that what we are doing in this chapter, in a sense, is a *generalization* of the singleton service. In the previous chapter, we were interested in having a service with operations **add**, **subtract**, and **getValueRP** that interacted with a single (or *singleton*) resource. Interacting with *multiple* resources doesn't fundamentally affect the implementation of the service that will be accessing the resources; it only affects those parts of our application that are in charge of *managing* the resource. We've added a new factory service and, as we shall see right now, we have to modify the resource home. But the instance service is unaffected because it doesn't really care whether it has access to one or a million resources.

Even so, this doesn't mean that there isn't more stuff happening in the "background" in the instance service. For example, in the **add** operation:

```
public AddResponse add(int a) throws RemoteException {

        MathResource mathResource = getResource();

        mathResource.setValue(mathResource.getValue() + a);

        mathResource.setLastOp("ADDITION");


        return new AddResponse();

}
```

We are still calling the **getResource**, which is still implemented as in the previous chapter:

```
private MathResource getResource() throws RemoteException {

        Object resource = null;

        try {

                resource = ResourceContext.getResourceContext().getResource();
        } catch (NoSuchResourceException e) {

                throw new RemoteException("Specified resource does not exist", e);
        } catch (ResourceContextException e) {

                throw new RemoteException("Error during resource lookup", e);
```

```
        } catch (Exception e) {
                throw new RemoteException("", e);
        }


        MathResource mathResource = (MathResource) resource;
        return mathResource;
    }
```

However, this time the Globus-supplied **ResourceContext** will do more than simply look up a singleton resource. It will look inside the endpoint reference that is used to invoke **add**, extract the resource key, and lookup the corresponding resource through the resource home. One of the nice things about using endpoint references, instead of plain URIs, is that the resource key is passed to the service *transparently* (inside the EPR), so our methods can be declared simply as **add(int a)**, instead of something like **add(int a, int resourceID)**.

> ☞ Now is a good moment to review Figure 8.4.

8.5 The Resource

The resource implementation requires only minimal changes. Remember that each resource will now have a unique key identifying it. We will need to reflect this in our resource by implementing the *ResourceIdentifier* interface:

```
    public class MathResource implements Resource, ResourceIdentifier,
                    ResourceProperties {
    }
```

This interface requires us to implement a *getID* method returning the resource's identifier. Notice that the identifier is of type **Object**. In other words, our unique identifier can be of any type we wish (throughout the book we will use a key of type **String**). Later on we will see that we will need to specify the type of the resource identifier in the JNDI deployment file.

```
    /* Resource key. This uniquely identifies this resource. */
    private Object key;


    /* Required by interface ResourceIdentifier */
    public Object getID() {
            return this.key;
    }
```

The initialization of the resource identifier takes place in the **initialize** method of the resource class. To guarantee that the key is unique, we will use the Axis **UUIDGen** class included with the toolkit:

```
import org.apache.axis.components.uuid.UUIDGen;

import org.apache.axis.components.uuid.UUIDGenFactory;
```

To use this class, we need to add a new static attribute of type **UUIDGen** (which is created using the **UUIDGenFactory** class):

```
private static final UUIDGen uuidGen = UUIDGenFactory.getUUIDGen();
```

Now, we create the key in the **initialize** method. Notice how this method now returns the resource identifier.

```
/* Initializes RPs and returns a unique identifier for this resource */

public Object initialize() throws Exception {
        this.key = uuidGen.nextUUID();


        // Initialize the resource properties


        return key;

}
```

☞ This is part of file **$EXAMPLES_DIR/org/globus/examples/services/core/factory/ impl/MathResource.java**.

! In Java, every object has a hash code which can be accessed using the **hashCode** method. Although this can be used for simple applications, you should avoid using it as a resource identifier, as the hash code is not guaranteed to be unique. Identifiers generated with **UUIDGen**, on the other hand, are always unique.

8.6 The Resource Home

The resource home has to be modified, but still remains relatively simple because, as in the previous chapter, our resource class extends from a Globus-supplied class. In the previous chapter, we extended from **SingletonResourceHome**, a Globus-supplied class that provided most of the functionality of a resource home for a single resource. Now we will extend from **ResourceHomeImpl**, another Globus-supplied class for resource homes that manage several resources.

The only method we have to implement is the **create** method, where we will create a new resource and return its identifier. All the other methods we would expect in a resource home (such as a **find** method to retrieve a resource given a certain key) are already implemented for us in **ResourceHomeImpl**.

```
package org.globus.examples.services.core.factory.impl;

import org.globus.wsrf.ResourceKey;
import org.globus.wsrf.impl.ResourceHomeImpl;
import org.globus.wsrf.impl.SimpleResourceKey;

public class MathResourceHome extends ResourceHomeImpl {

        public ResourceKey create() throws Exception {
                // Create a resource and initialize it
                MathResource mathResource = (MathResource)
                            this.createNewInstance(); ❶
                mathResource.initialize(); ❷
                // Get key
                ResourceKey key = new SimpleResourceKey(this.getKeyTypeName(),
                            mathResource.getID()); ❸
                // Add the resource to the list of resources in this home
                this.add(key, mathResource);❹
                return key; ❺
        }


        ❻
        private String instanceServicePath;

        public String getInstanceServicePath() {
                return instanceServicePath;
        }

        public void setInstanceServicePath(String instanceServicePath) {
                this.instanceServicePath = instanceServicePath;
        }
}
```

> ☞ This file is **$EXAMPLES_DIR/org/globus/examples/services/core/factory/ impl/MathResourceHome.java**.

❶ We create a new instance of the resource. Notice that this *must* be done using the private **createNewInstance** method, *not* by using the **new** operator. Also, since **createNewInstance** returns a **Resource** object, we must cast it to our specific resource type: **MathResourceType**

❷ We initialize the resource.

❸ We obtain the resource identifier using the **getID** method implemented earlier, and use it to create a **SimpleResourceKey** object. When creating the **SimpleResourceKey**, **keyTypeName** is a protected attribute of **ResourceHomeImpl** containing the key's type.

❹ We add the recently created resource and its key to the resource home's internal list of resources. **add** is a protected method of **ResourceHomeImpl**.

❺ Finally, we return the resource's key.

❻ When implementing the factory service, we said that the factory service obtains the instance service's path from the resource home. As you can see, our resource home includes an **instanceServicePath** attribute, and a get/set pair of methods for that attribute, but the attribute is not initialized anywhere. As we will see in a moment, this attribute will be initialized using JNDI.

> ☞ Now is *another* good moment to review Figure 8.3.

> ⓘ **There's more to the resource home than meets the eye...**
>
> The resource home shown above, along with the one seen in the previous chapter, covers the simplest possible case of resources: *in-memory resources*, or resources which reside in main memory while the container is running. However, resource homes can also be used to manage *persistent resources*, or resources that are stored in disk so they can survive container restarts. We will take a close look at persistent resources in Chapter 12.
>
> Another thing we can do to a resource home is to override its **add** and **remove** methods, to control exactly what happens when a resource is added or removed from the resource home. For example, we might want to write to a log, or register our resource with an index service.

8.7 Build and Deploy

8.7.1 The Deployment Descriptor

The WSDD file must now reflect that we have two services: the factory service and the instance service.

```xml
<?xml version="1.0" encoding="UTF-8"?>
<deployment name="defaultServerConfig"
    xmlns="http://xml.apache.org/axis/wsdd/"
    xmlns:java="http://xml.apache.org/axis/wsdd/providers/java"
    xmlns:xsd="http://www.w3.org/2001/XMLSchema">


❶
<!-- Instance service -->
<service name="examples/core/factory/MathService" provider="Handler"
        use="literal" style="document">
    <parameter name="className" value="org.globus.examples.services.core
            .factory.impl.MathService"/>
    <wsdlFile>share/schema/examples/MathService_instance/Math_service.wsdl
            </wsdlFile>
    <parameter name="allowedMethods" value="*"/>
    <parameter name="handlerClass"
            value="org.globus.axis.providers.RPCProvider"/>
    <parameter name="scope" value="Application"/>
    <parameter name="providers" value="GetRPProvider"/>
    </service>


❷
<!-- Factory service -->
<service name="examples/core/factory/MathFactoryService"
            provider="Handler" use="literal" style="document">
    <parameter name="className" value="org.globus.examples.services.core
            .factory.impl.MathFactoryService"/>
    <wsdlFile>share/schema/examples/FactoryService/Factory_service.wsdl
            </wsdlFile>
    <parameter name="allowedMethods" value="*"/>
```

```
<parameter name="handlerClass"
            value="org.globus.axis.providers.RPCProvider"/>
<parameter name="scope" value="Application"/>
</service>


</deployment>
```

☞ This file is **$EXAMPLES_DIR/org/globus/examples/services/core/factory/deploy-server.wsdd**.

---

❶ The parameters for the instance service are the same as the ones used in the previous chapter.

❷ The deployment parameters of the factory are pretty straightforward. We simply specify the factory service's class (**MathFactoryService**) and WSDL file.

8.7.2 The JNDI Deployment File

In the previous chapter we saw that this file specifies what resource home must be used by each service. When managing just one resource, this file was very simple. Now, however, we will need to specify more parameters to manage multiple resources. Furthermore, our JNDI deployment file must include two **<service>** tags (one for the instance service, and one for the factory service).

```
<?xml version="1.0" encoding="UTF-8"?>

<jndiConfig xmlns="http://wsrf.globus.org/jndi/config">


<!-- Instance service -->

<service name="examples/core/factory/MathService">

        <resource name="home" type="org.globus.examples.services.core
                .factory.impl.MathResourceHome">❶
        <resourceParams>


                ❷

                <parameter>

                        <name>resourceClass</name>
```

```
                  <value>org.globus.examples.services.core.factory.
                      impl.MathResource</value>
          </parameter>


  ❸
  <parameter>
          <name>resourceKeyType</name>
          <value>java.lang.String</value>
  </parameter>


  ❹
  <parameter>
          <name>resourceKeyName</name>
  <value>http://www.globus.org/namespaces/examples/
          MathService_instanceMathResourceKey</value>
  </parameter>


  ❺
  <parameter>
          <name>instanceServicePath</name>
          <value>examples/core/factory/MathService</value>
  <parameter>


  ❻
  <parameter>
          <name>factory</name>
          <value>org.globus.wsrf.jndi.BeanFactory</value>
  </parameter>


      </resourceParams>
      </resource>
</service>
```

```
<!-- Factory service -->
<service name="examples/core/factory/MathFactoryService">

        ❼

        <resourceLink name="instanceHome" target="java:comp/env/services/
                examples/core/factory/MathService/home"/>

</service>


</jndiConfig>
```

> ☞ This file is **$EXAMPLES_DIR/org/globus/examples/services/core/factory/ deploy-jndi-config.xml**.

❶ We use the **<resource>** tag to specify what resource home will be used by the instance service.

❷ The **resourceClass** parameter specifies the type of our resources.

❸ The value we put in the **resourceKeyType** parameter must match the type used in the implementation when creating the key. Remember that we used the resource's hash code, which is of type **java.lang.Integer**. Thus, we have to include that type in the JNDI configuration.

❹ The **resourceKeyName** parameter must be a qualified name. Notice that we're using a name that is not mentioned in our WSDL file. This is Ok and, in fact, we could use any QName we wanted. However, for clarity we should choose a QName that is in the same namespace as the service.

❺ Using the **instanceServicePath** parameter we specify the path of the instance service. When JNDI initializes the resource home, it will set the value of the **instance-ServicePath** attribute in **MathResourceHome** to the value of this parameter. The value of this parameter must be set to the **name** of the instance service (as written in its **<service>** tag).
Yes, this is a bit redundant, and there is a cleaner way of doing this. However, this requires more code than is probably necessary in a simple example like this. Later on, we will briefly mention the "cleaner way" of doing this.

❻ Remember from the previous chapter that this is a common parameter which we will find in all our JNDI deployment files. However, it is important to note that, even though this parameter is called **factory**, it has nothing to do with the factory/ instance pattern we are seeing in this chapter. It refers to a completely different factory within the Globus code.

❼ The factory service accesses *the same resource home* as the instance service. So, we do not need to repeat all the parameters of the instance service. We simply have to include a `<resourceLink>` tag linking to the previously specified resource home. Note that we cannot use the name **home**, as this would refer to factory service's *own* resource home. Remember that we mentioned earlier that it was possible for the factory and instance service to each have its own resource home. However, we will not be considering that scenario. To emphasize that the factory service simply accesses the resource home containing the **MathResource**s, instead of having its own resource home, we use the name **instanceHome**. Also, notice that we must do so using a special path.

ⓘ **JNDI**

Our JNDI deployment file is growing with each example, and so far the only thing we know about it is that it magically allows us to glue the service and the resource together through a resource home. So, what exactly is JNDI?

The *Java Naming and Directory Interface* is a Java API that provides a standard interface to directories. In a nutshell, a directory-enabled application will have a lot of *named* objects which will be easily accessibly through a *directory* (as long as we know the name of the object we're interested in).

In our case, a service (identified by its path, as given by the **name** attribute in the WSDD file) will want to locate its resource home (with the same name as the service). For example, when we use the **getResource** method of the **ResourceContext** class (when retrieving the current resource), JNDI is used in the background to locate the service's resource home (and the home is then used to retrieve the resource).

Also, note that JNDI is an API that can be used to interact with a wide variety of directories (such as LDAP). GT4 uses a basic in-memory directory, meaning that all the objects in the directory are stored in the container's memory space. More details on JNDI can be found at http://java.sun.com/products/jndi/.

Finally, we can now explain how the factory service retrieves the resource home. The following is the code of the **getInstanceResourceHome** method:

```
protected ResourceHome getInstanceResourceHome()
            throws NoResourceHomeException, ResourceContextException {
    ResourceHome home;

    ResourceContext ctx;


❶
    ctx = ResourceContext.getResourceContext();
    String homeLoc = Constants.JNDI_SERVICES_BASE_NAME + ctx.getService()
            + "/instanceHome";
```

```
        try {

                ❷

                Context initialContext = new InitialContext();

                home = (ResourceHome) initialContext.lookup(homeLoc);

        } catch (NameNotFoundException e) {

                throw new NoResourceHomeException();

        } catch (NamingException e) {

                throw new ResourceContextException("", e);

        }


                ❸

        return home;

}
```

❶ We are going to use JNDI to retrieve the resource home. To do this, we need to specify the JNDI location of the resource home object. The convention followed in GT4 is that this location starts with **java:comp/env/services/**, followed by the service's name, and followed by the actual JNDI object we want to retrieve (in our case, **instanceHome**, which is a link to the resource home defined in the instance service). Note that the beginning of the location path is conveniently located in a Globus-supplied **Constants** class. Also, the service's path can be obtained using the **ResourceContext** class.

❷ We use the JNDI **InitialContext** class to perform the lookup.

❸ If all goes well (if no exceptions are thrown), we return the resource home.

8.7.3   Build and Deploy

We are finally ready to build and deploy our service:

> **./globus-build-service.sh factory**

> **globus-deploy-gar $$EXAMPLES_DIR/org_globus_examples_services**
> **_wsrf_core_factory.gar**

8.8 A Simple Client

We will try out our service first with a simple client that creates a new resource and performs a couple operation on it. This client expects only one argument from the command line, the factory service's URI

```
package org.globus.examples.clients.FactoryService_Math;


import org.apache.axis.message.addressing.Address;

import org.apache.axis.message.addressing.EndpointReferenceType;

import org.globus.examples.stubs.Factory.CreateResource;

import org.globus.examples.stubs.Factory.CreateResourceResponse;

import org.globus.examples.stubs.Factory.FactoryPortType;

import org.globus.examples.stubs.Factory.service
    .FactoryServiceAddressingLocator;

import org.globus.examples.stubs.MathService_instance.GetValueRP;

import org.globus.examples.stubs.MathService_instance.MathPortType;

import org.globus.examples.stubs.MathService_instance.service
    .MathServiceAddressingLocator;


/*

* This client creates a new WS-Resource through a FactoryService. This client

* expects one parameter: the factory URI.

*/

public class Client {


        public static void main(String[] args) {
                FactoryServiceAddressingLocator factoryLocator =
                    new FactoryServiceAddressingLocator();
                MathServiceAddressingLocator instanceLocator =
                    new MathServiceAddressingLocator();
```

```
try {
        String factoryURI = args[0];
        EndpointReferenceType factoryEPR, instanceEPR;
        FactoryPortType mathFactory;
        MathPortType math;

    ❶
        factoryEPR = new EndpointReferenceType();
        factoryEPR.setAddress(new Address(factoryURI));
        mathFactory = factoryLocator.getFactoryPortTypePort
            (factoryEPR);
    ❷
        CreateResourceResponse createResponse = mathFactory
                    .createResource(new CreateResource());

        System.out.println("Created WS-Resource.");

    ❸
        instanceEPR = createResponse.getEndpointReference();
        math = instanceLocator.getMathPortTypePort(instanceEPR);

        System.out.println("Created instance.");

    ❹
        // Perform an addition
        math.add(10);

        // Perform another addition
        math.add(5);

        // Access value
        System.out.println("Current value:" +
            math.getValueRP(new GetValueRP()));
```

```
                  // Perform a subtraction
                  math.subtract(5);


                  // Access value
                  System.out.println("Current value:" +
                        math.getValueRP(new GetValueRP()));
          } catch (Exception e) {
                  e.printStackTrace();
          }

      }


  }
```

☞ This file is **$EXAMPLES_DIR/org/globus/examples/clients/FactoryService_Math/
Client.java**.

❶ Here we obtain a reference to the factory's portType. Notice how we only need the
factory's URI to do this.

❷ Once we have the factory's portType, we use it to invoke the **createResource**
operation. This operation returns an endpoint reference, "boxed" inside a
CreateResourceResponse object. This endpoint reference includes both the instance
service's URI *and* the new resource's identifier. In the next client we will take a peek
inside the endpoint reference.

❸ Using the instance EPR, we obtain a reference to the **MathPortType** in the instance
service. Notice how the client uses the EPR as a pointer to the WS-Resource, without
accessing the contents of the EPR. Once again, remember that the client handles EPRs
as opaque pointers.

❹ We now use the **MathPortType** to invoke **add**, **subtract**, and **getValueRP**.

Compile and run the client:

```
javac \
-classpath ./build/stubs/classes/:$CLASSPATH \
org/globus/examples/clients/FactoryService_Math/Client.java


java \
-classpath ./build/stubs/classes/:$CLASSPATH \
```

```
org.globus.examples.clients.FactoryService_Math.Client \
http://127.0.0.1:8080/wsrf/services/examples/core/factory/MathFactoryService
```

If all goes well, you should see the following:

```
Created instance.
Current value:15
Current value:10
```

If you run it again, you will get the exact same result. This is because we are creating a new resource every time we run the client.

```
Created instance.
Current value:15
Current value:10
```

8.9   A Slightly Less Simple Client

We will now split the previous client into two client applications: a client in charge of creating the resource, and a client in charge of invoking the **add** operation in the instance service. The first client writes the endpoint reference of the new WS-Resource to a file, which will later be read by the second client.

8.9.1   The Creating Client

The first client expects at least one parameter from the command line: the factory service's URI. A second parameter, with the name of the file where the EPR must be written to, can also be specified. If it isn't, then it will be saved to a file called **epr.txt**.

```
package org.globus.examples.clients.FactoryService_Math;


import java.io.BufferedWriter;
import java.io.FileWriter;


import org.apache.axis.message.addressing.Address;
import org.apache.axis.message.addressing.EndpointReferenceType;
import org.globus.examples.services.core.factory.impl.MathConstants;
import org.globus.examples.stubs.Factory.CreateResource;
import org.globus.examples.stubs.Factory.CreateResourceResponse;
```

```
import org.globus.examples.stubs.Factory.FactoryPortType;
import org.globus.examples.stubs.Factory.service.
    FactoryServiceAddressingLocator;
import org.globus.wsrf.encoding.ObjectSerializer;


public class ClientCreate {

        static final String EPR_FILENAME = "epr.txt";


        public static void main(String[] args) {
                FactoryServiceAddressingLocator factoryLocator =
                        new FactoryServiceAddressingLocator();


                try {
                        String factoryURI = args[0];
                        String eprFilename;

                        if (args.length == 2)
                                eprFilename = args[1];
                        else
                                eprFilename = EPR_FILENAME;


                        EndpointReferenceType factoryEPR, instanceEPR;
                        FactoryPortType mathFactory;


                        ❶
                        factoryEPR = new EndpointReferenceType();
                        factoryEPR.setAddress(new Address(factoryURI));
                        mathFactory = factoryLocator.getFactoryPortTypePort
                                (factoryEPR);
```

```
                         CreateResourceResponse createResponse = mathFactory
                                  .createResource(new CreateResource());
                         instanceEPR = createResponse.getEndpointReference();


                       ❷
                         String endpointString = ObjectSerializer.toString(
                                  instanceEPR, MathConstants.RESOURCE_REFERENCE);
                         FileWriter fileWriter = new FileWriter(eprFilename);
                         BufferedWriter bfWriter=new BufferedWriter(fileWriter);
                         bfWriter.write(endpointString);
                         bfWriter.close();
                         System.out.println("Endpoint reference written to file "
                                  + eprFilename);
                 } catch (Exception e) {
                         e.printStackTrace();
                 }
         }


     }
```

☞ This file is **$EXAMPLES_DIR/org/globus/examples/clients/FactoryService_Math/
ClientCreate.java**.

---

❶ As in the previous client, here we obtain a reference to the factory's portType and
use it to invoke the **createResource** operation, that returns an endpoint reference
to the new WS-Resource.

❷ This block of code writes the endpoint reference to a file. We use the Globus-supplied
class **ObjectSerializer**, which creates an XML representation of the EPR. Note that
we need to specify the QName of the root element of the XML file. We can choose
any name we want but, for clarity, it is best to choose a QName inside our service's
namespace. The QName we're using is declared in the MathConstants interface:

```
        public static final QName RESOURCE_REFERENCE = new QName(NS,

                "MathResourceReference");
```

Now compile the client:

```
javac \
-classpath ./build/stubs/classes/:$CLASSPATH \
org/globus/examples/clients/FactoryService_Math/ClientCreate.java


java \
-classpath ./build/stubs/classes/:$CLASSPATH \
org.globus.examples.clients.FactoryService_Math.ClientCreate \
http://127.0.0.1:8080/wsrf/services/examples/core/factory/MathFactoryService
```

If all goes well, you should see the following:

Endpoint reference written to file epr.txt

Let's take a look inside the **epr.txt** file:

```
<ns1:MathResourceReference xsi:type="ns2:EndpointReferenceType"
    xmlns:ns1="http://www.globus.org/namespaces/examples/MathService_instance"
    xmlns:xsi="http://www.w3.org/2001/XMLSchema-instance"
    xmlns:ns2="http://schemas.xmlsoap.org/ws/2004/03/addressing">


    <ns2:Address xsi:type="ns2:AttributedURI">
    http://127.0.0.1:8080/wsrf/services/examples/core/factory/MathService
    </ns2:Address>


    <ns2:ReferenceProperties xsi:type="ns2:ReferencePropertiesType">
        <ns1:MathResourceKey>1137a200-c41b-11d9-ae21-cb47209ff11a
            </ns1:MathResourceKey>
    </ns2:ReferenceProperties>


    <ns2:ReferenceParameters xsi:type="ns2:ReferenceParametersType"/>


</ns1:MathResourceReference>
```

Notice how the endpoint reference does, in fact, include the instance service's URI and the resource's key. Note that you will almost certainly get a different key in your resource.

8.9.2   The Adding Client

This client expects two arguments from the command line. The first argument is a service's URI or the name of a file containing and endpoint reference. The client is implemented to recognize both formats since, in the next chapters, we will use this client again to interact with singleton services (where we only need the service's URI, without a resource key, to address the service). The second argument is the value we wish to add.

```
package org.globus.examples.clients.MathService_instance;

import java.io.FileInputStream;

import org.apache.axis.message.addressing.Address;
import org.apache.axis.message.addressing.EndpointReferenceType;
import org.globus.examples.stubs.MathService_instance.GetValueRP;
import org.globus.examples.stubs.MathService_instance.MathPortType;
import org.globus.examples.stubs.MathService_instance.service
     .MathServiceAddressingLocator;
import org.globus.wsrf.encoding.ObjectDeserializer;
import org.xml.sax.InputSource;

public class ClientAdd {

        public static void main(String[] args) {
                MathServiceAddressingLocator instanceLocator =
                            new MathServiceAddressingLocator();

                try {
                        int value = Integer.parseInt(args[1]);
                        EndpointReferenceType instanceEPR;

                        if (args[0].startsWith("http")) {
                            ❶
                                // First argument contains a URI
                                String serviceURI = args[0];
```

```
                        // Create endpoint reference to service
                        instanceEPR = new EndpointReferenceType();
                        instanceEPR.setAddress(new Address(serviceURI));
                } else {
                        ❷
                        // First argument contains an EPR file name
                        String eprFile = args[0];
                        // Get endpoint reference of WS-Resource from file
                        FileInputStream fis = new FileInputStream(eprFile);
                        instanceEPR = (EndpointReferenceType)
                            ObjectDeserializer.deserialize(
                                    new InputSource(fis),
                                            EndpointReferenceType.class);
                        fis.close();
                }


                ❸
                // Get PortType
                MathPortType math = instanceLocator
                                .getMathPortTypePort(instanceEPR);

                // Perform addition
                math.add(value);

                // Access value
                System.out.println("Current value: "
                            + math.getValueRP(new GetValueRP()));
        } catch (Exception e) {
                e.printStackTrace();
        }
    }
}
```

> ☞ This file is **$EXAMPLES_DIR/org/globus/examples/clients/MathService_instance/ ClientAdd.java**.

❶ If the user specifies a URI, then we create the instance's EPR simply by creating a new **EndpointReferenceType** object and setting its URI to the one passed as a parameter. Remember that we will only use this option when interacting with singleton services, where the client must supply a URI.

❷ If the user specifies a file, then we create the instance's EPR by reading the XML file using the Globus-supplied **ObjectDeserializer** class.

❸ Finally, we use the instance EPR to obtain a reference to the **MathPortType**. We use this portType to invoke the **add** operation with the value specified in the second parameter of the client.

Now, compile and run the client:

```
javac \
-classpath ./build/stubs/classes/:$CLASSPATH \
org/globus/examples/clients/MathService_instance/ClientAdd.java


java \
-classpath ./build/stubs/classes/:$CLASSPATH \
org.globus.examples.clients.MathService_instance.ClientAdd
epr.txt
10
```

If all goes well, you should see the following:

```
Current value: 10
```

If you run the adder client several times using the same EPR file, you will be able to observe how the value in the resource keeps getting bigger and bigger.

```
Current value: 20
```

```
Current value: 30
```

chapter **9**

Logging

This chapter introduces an interesting utility included with GT4 Java WS Core which we will use in many of the examples in the rest of the book. Using the Apache Jakarta Commons Logging (http://jakarta.apache.org/commons/logging/) component and the Log4j Logging Engine (http://logging.apache.org/log4j/), we will be able to print a log of interesting events (warnings, error, debug information, etc.) to the console or to a file. In this short chapter we will see how to add logginig to our first example. You can find a modified version of the first example (with logging added) in the following directory of the examples bundle:

    $EXAMPLES_DIR/org/globus/examples/services/core/logging/

9.1 The Jakarta Commons Logging Architecture

The goal of the Apache Jakarta Commons Project (http://jakarta.apache.org/commons/) is the development of reusable Java components, such as validation classes, command line option parsers, etc. One of the components in this project is the Commons Logging component, which allows us to easily produce a log from our Java class.

The Commons Logging component has 6 levels of logging. This means that we are not limited to just one type of log message, but 6 types of messages with varying degree of "severity". This allows us to filter the types of messages, so we have a log with only the information we want. For example, at one point we might be interested in producing a log with all the debugging information, but later on we will probably only want a log with errors and warnings produced by our program.

The six levels of log messages are:

- **Debug**
- **Trace**
- **Info**
- **Warn**
- **Error**
- **Fatal**.

What messages go into each category is entirely up to the programmer, as we'll see later on.

> ☞ A more detailed discussion of these logging levels, and what kinds of messages should be placed in each level, can be found in the Jakarta Commons Logging guide (http://jakarta.apache.org/commons/logging/guide.html).

Finally, note that the Commons Logging only provides an abstract logging API, and we will require a *logging engine* that implements this abstract API. The Globus Toolkit uses the Log4j Logging Engine (http://logging.apache.org/log4j/). To perform basic logging, you will not need to know how Log4j actually works. However, to use logging to its full potential, you will probably have to modify the Log4j configuration files included with the toolkit. To do so, you should refer to the official Log4j documentation.

9.2 Adding Logging to MathService

Enabling logging in MathService is very easy. The following code shows all the necessary changes in bold.

```
// ...

import org.apache.commons.logging.Log;
import org.apache.commons.logging.LogFactory; ❶

// ...

public class MathService implements Resource, ResourceProperties
{

        /* Added for logging */
        static final Log logger = LogFactory.getLog(MathService.class); ❷
```

```
// ...

public AddResponse add(int a) throws RemoteException {
        logger.info("Addition invoked with parameter a="
                + String.valueOf(a)); ❸
        if (a == 0)
                logger.warn("Adding zero doesn't modify the
                        internal value!"); ❹

        value += a;
        lastOp = "ADDITION";

        return new AddResponse();
}

public SubtractResponse subtract(int a) throws RemoteException {
        logger.info("Subtraction invoked with parameter a="
                + String.valueOf(a));
        if (a == 0)
                logger.warn("Subtracting zero doesn't modify
                        the internal value!");

        value -= a;
        lastOp = "SUBTRACTION";

        return new SubtractResponse();
}

public int getValueRP(GetValueRP params) throws RemoteException {
        logger.info("getValueRP() invoked");
        return value;
}

}
```

> ☞ This file is **$EXAMPLES_DIR/org/globus/examples/services/core/logging/impl/ MathService.java**

❶ First of all, we need to import two packages from the Commons Logging component.

❷ After that, we need to create a static **Log** attribute. This attribute is created using a **LogFactory**. Notice how we have to pass the name of our class to the **getLog** method.
 Note that the logger isn't required to be static. However, having a static **Log** object makes it easier to log messages, as we won't have to call **LogFactory.getLog** every time we wanted to use the logger.

❸ After these two modifications, our **MathService** class is ready to do some serious logging. First, we're going to generate an Info message each time **add** is invoked. This is as simple as calling the **info** method in the **logger** static attribute. The only necessary parameter is the message we want to write in the log.

❹ Now, we are going to write out a message in a different logging level. We will write a Warn message whenever the parameter received by **add** is equal to zero (we want to warn the user that this has no effect whatsoever on the internal value). Again, this is as simple as calling the **warn** method in the **logger** static attribute.

Of course, you can generate messages in any of the other levels by calling:

- **logger.debug("Message")**
- **logger.trace("Message")**
- **logger.error("Message")**
- **logger.fatal("Message").**

That's basically all you need to add logging to your service. Now, simply build and deploy as you normally would.

```
./globus-build-service.sh logging
```

```
globus-deploy-gar $EXAMPLES_DIR/org_globus_examples_services_wsrf_core_logging.gar
```

> ☞ If you've modified the first example, then remember that the commands to build and deploy are the following:
>
> ```
> ./globus-build-service.sh first
> ```
>
> ```
> globus-deploy-gar $EXAMPLES_DIR/org_globus_examples_services_wsrf_core_
> first.gar
> ```

9.3 Viewing Log Output

Our MathService class is now ready to generate logs. But, where do all those log messages end up? Well, we can either write them to the console output of the GT4 container, or write them in a file. This is specified in this file: **$GLOBUS_LOCATION/container-log4j.properties**. Just add the following line at the end of that file:

```
log4j.logger.org.globus.examples.services.core.logging.impl.MathService=INFO
```

Each line of that file specifies how logging must be handled in classes that are logging-enabled. In our case, the class where we've enabled logging is **org.globus.examples. services.core.logging.impl.MathService**. The option after the equals sign (=) tell the logger how to filter the log messages (according to their level).

The filtering option can take any of the following values:

- **ALL** or **DEBUG**
- **TRACE**
- **INFO**
- **WARN**
- **ERROR**
- **FATAL**
- **OFF**.

Each of these corresponds to the logging levels we saw earlier. We can also ask for all or none of the messages to be displayed. Take into account that you can only specify *one* level of filtering. For example, if you select the **WARN** level, you will get all the messages generated at that level and at 'more severe' levels (**ERROR** and **FATAL**). The logic behind this is that usually you don't want the log message from one specific level, but all the messages which have *at least* a certain severity (if you're interested in the warnings, you're probably also interested in the errors and the fatal exceptions).

☞ Take into account that all classes inside the **org.globus** package have **INFO** logging activated by default. So, strictly speaking, you would not need to add the following line to **$GLOBUS_LOCATION/container-log4j.properties**:

```
log4j.logger.org.globus.examples.services.core.logging.impl.
```

```
MathService=INFO
```

You *do* need to modify **$GLOBUS_LOCATION/container-log4j.properties** if you want to specify a different logging level (other than INFO) for a specific **org.globus** class, or for your own classes (assuming they are not in the **org.globus** package).

> Throughout the book, we will not need to modify the **$GLOBUS_LOCATION/
> container-log4j.properties** file, since all the examples are in the **org.globus**
> package.

Let's put all this to the test. Since we haven't changed the interface of the service we can, once again, reuse the MathService client we've used in previous examples.

```
java
-classpath ./build/stubs/classes/:$CLASSPATH \
org.globus.examples.clients.MathService_instance.Client \
http://127.0.0.1:8080/wsrf/services/examples/core/logging/MathService
```

Since we've set the log level to INFO, we should get both Info and Warn messages. You should see this in the console output of the services container:

```
DATE TIME INFO CLASS_NAME [Thread-1,add:70] Addition invoked with parameter a=10
DATE TIME INFO CLASS_NAME [Thread-2,add:70] Addition invoked with parameter a=5
DATE TIME INFO CLASS_NAME [Thread-2,getValueRP:92] getValue() invoked
DATE TIME INFO CLASS_NAME [Thread-3,subtract:81] Subtraction invoked with
    parameter a=5
DATE TIME INFO CLASS_NAME [Thread-2,getValueRP:92] getValue() invoked
```

Each log entry includes the date and time of the entry, plus the abbreviated name of the class which produced the log entry (in our case you should see "**impl.MathService**"). We didn't get any Warn message because we need to invoke the **add** method with the value zero. Let's try to do that with the **ClientAdd** client seen in the previous chapter:

```
java
-classpath ./build/stubs/classes/:$CLASSPATH \
org.globus.examples.clients.MathService_instance.ClientAdd \
http://127.0.0.1:8080/wsrf/services/examples/core/logging/MathService \
0
```

You should see this in the console:

```
DATE TIME INFO CLASS_NAME [Thread-1,add:70] Addition invoked with parameter a=0
DATE TIME WARN CLASS_NAME [Thread-1,add:72] Adding zero doesn't modify
    the internal value!
DATE TIME INFO CLASS_NAME [Thread-2,getValueRP:92] getValue() invoked
```

Finally, let's try changing the log level in the **$GLOBUS_LOCATION/container-log4j. properties**:

```
log4j.logger.org.globus.examples.services.core.logging.impl.MathService=WARN
```

You will need to restart the container for this change to have effect. Once you've done so, try running the client again (passing a zero as the value to add). You should see this in the console:

```
DATE TIME WARN CLASS_NAME [Thread-1,add:72] Adding zero doesn't modify
    the internal value!
```

Since the log level is WARN, this means that the logger will only output messages which are "at least as severe as a warning". Since an Info message is not as severe as a Warn message, it will not pass the filter.

## chapter 10

Resource Properties

In the previous chapters we have seen how state information in the service is stored inside a resource and, more specifically, in *resource properties*. However, our interaction with resource properties was very limited: our service could modify their values, and we could only access one particular resource property (**Value**) using the **GetValueRP** operation. In this chapter we will see all the tools that will allow us to work with resource properties. We will also see how we can declare resource properties more complex than the ones seen in the previous examples.

10.1 A Closer Look at Resource Properties

Before we begin, we need to take a closer look at how resource properties are represented and handled internally in our service. First of all, let's recall how our resource properties are declared in all the examples we've seen so far:

```
<types>
<xsd:schema targetNamespace="http://www.globus.org/namespaces/examples/
                              MathService_instance"
    xmlns:tns="http://www.globus.org/namespaces/examples/MathService_instance"
    xmlns:xsd="http://www.w3.org/2001/XMLSchema">

        <!-- REQUESTS AND RESPONSES -->


        <!-- ... -->
```

```
<!-- RESOURCE PROPERTIES -->


<xsd:element name="Value" type="xsd:int"/>
<xsd:element name="LastOp" type="xsd:string"/>


<xsd:element name="MathResourceProperties">
<xsd:complexType>
        <xsd:sequence>
                <xsd:element ref="tns:Value" minOccurs="1" maxOccurs="1" \>
                <xsd:element ref="tns:LastOp" minOccurs="1" maxOccurs="1" \>
        </xsd:sequence>
</xsd:complexType>
</xsd:element>


</xsd:schema>

</types>
```

Notice how we're using XML Schema to declare an element named **MathResource-Properties** that must contain a **Value** element and a **LastOp** element. The **Value** element, in turn, is declared to contain an integer (**xsd:int**) and the **LastOp** element, a string (**xsd:string**).

> ☞ Remember that the individual resource properties (such as **Value** and **LastOp** must be declared as global elements. This was explained in Section 6.1.2, "WSRF and Globus-specific features of WSDL".

In the previous examples, we have simply interpreted this as meaning "Our service has two resource properties, **Value** of type integer and **LastOp** of type string". In our Java implementation of the resource, this simply meant that our resource class had attributes representing each of the resource properties, and that we used special Globus classes (**ReflectionResourceProperty** and **ResourcePropertySet**) to manage those resource properties.

However, the reason why our resource properties are declared in XML Schema, and in that particular way, is because even though they can be implemented internally in different ways (not only in GT4, but in other WSRF implementations), they *must* be exchanged with other entities (clients, other services, etc.) as an XML document. This XML representation is called the *resource property document*. For example, the following is an example of how our service's RP document might look like at a given point:

```
<MathResourceProperties xmlns:tns="http://www.globus.org/namespaces/examples/
                                    MathService_instance">
        <tns:Value>50</tns:Value>
        <tns:LastOp>ADDITION</tns:LastOp>
</MathResourceProperties>
```

It is important to be familiar with this representation because many operations related with resource properties are better explained in terms of how that operation modifies the RP document. For example, let's suppose our resource properties are declared the following way:

```
<!-- RESOURCE PROPERTIES -->


<xsd:element name="Value" type="xsd:int"/>
<xsd:element name="LastOp" type="xsd:string"/>


<xsd:element name="MathResourceProperties">
<xsd:complexType>
        <xsd:sequence>
                <xsd:element ref="tns:Value" minOccurs="1" maxOccurs="unbounded" />
                <xsd:element ref="tns:LastOp" minOccurs="1" maxOccurs="unbounded" />
        </xsd:sequence>
</xsd:complexType>
</xsd:element>
```

Notice how we are allowing **Value** and **LastOp** to occur at least one time, with no other limit (**unbounded**). Although internally this will be implemented as an array of integers and an array of strings, the RP document could look like this at a given point:

```
<MathResourceProperties xmlns:tns="http://www.globus.org/namespaces/examples/
                                    MathService_instance">
        <tns:Value>10</tns:Value>
        <tns:Value>30</tns:Value>
        <tns:Value>50</tns:Value>
        <tns:Value>40</tns:Value>
```

```
        <tns:LastOp>ADDITION</tns:LastOp>

        <tns:LastOp>ADDITION</tns:LastOp>

        <tns:LastOp>ADDITION</tns:LastOp>

        <tns:LastOp>SUBTRACTION</tns:LastOp>

    </MathResourceProperties>
```

Later on, for example, we will talk about "inserting a new resource property **LastOp** with value **ADDITION**". This doesn't mean that we are *declaring* a new RP but, rather, that we are inserting a new element **LastOp** inside our resource property document. Again, it is useful to be aware of how resource properties are represented in XML.

ⓘ **Accessing the resource properties document**

There is a quick way of accessing a service's RP document using one of the Globus-supplied command-line clients, **wsrf-query** (this command is described in more detail at the end of the chapter). Simply write the following from the command line:

> **wsrf-query -s** *service_URI*

However, to be able to use this command, the service must expose the standard WSRF **QueryResourceProperties** portType, described below. Although you won't be able to access the RP document in the examples seen in the previous chapters, you will be able to do so in the example described in this chapter.

10.2   Using Standard WSRF portTypes

One of the important new concepts we introduce in this chapter is how we can expose standard WSRF portTypes to improve the functionality of our services. In particular, we will be interested in exposing portTypes that allow us to deal with resource properties.

First of all, let's clarify what we mean by "exposing a portType". Up to this point, our services only exposed a single portType, **MathPortType**, with operations of particular interest to us. WSRF specifies a lot of portTypes with operations of *general* interest, such as operations to read RPs, to manage a WS-Resource's lifetime, etc. By having these fundamental operations standardized, we can be sure that any WSRF client library can access a service that exposes a standard WSRF portType.

So, how do we expose these WSRF portTypes in our own services? For example, let's suppose we're interested in exposing the **GetResourceProperty** portType, which includes an operation by the same name that allows us to access individual RPs in our WS-Resource. If we were writing strict WSDL, the only way of including operations and portTypes from

WSRF specifications would be to actually copy and paste those definitions from the spec's WSDL file into our own WSDL file. Our portType would look something like this:

```
<portType name="MathPortType"
    wsrp:ResourceProperties="tns:MathResourceProperties">


    <operation name="add">
            <input message="tns:AddInputMessage"/>
            <output message="tns:AddOutputMessage"/>
    </operation>


    <operation name="subtract">
            <input message="tns:SubtractInputMessage"/>
            <output message="tns:SubtractOutputMessage"/>
    </operation>


    <!-- Copied from the official GetResourceProperty WSDL file -->
    <operation name="GetResourceProperty">
        <input name="GetResourcePropertyRequest"
            message="wsrpw:GetResourcePropertyRequest"
        wsa:Action="http://docs.oasis-open.org/
            wsrf/2004/06/wsrf-WS-ResourceProperties/GetResourceProperty"/>
        <output name="GetResourcePropertyResponse"
            message="wsrpw:GetResourcePropertyResponse"
        wsa:Action="http://docs.oasis-open.org/wsrf/2004/06/
            wsrf-WS-ResourceProperties/GetResourcePropertyResponse"/>
        <fault name="InvalidResourcePropertyQNameFault"
            message="wsrpw:InvalidResourcePropertyQNameFault"/>
        <fault name="ResourceUnknownFault"
            message="wsrpw:ResourceUnknownFault"/>
    </operation>


</portType>
```

And, furthermore, we would need to copy all the necessary **<message>**s and XML Schema type definitions. This, of course, is very error-prone. Worry not... for our convenience, GT4 includes a WSDL Preprocessor tool that does that automatically for us. Let's take a look at the changes we would need to make to our WSDL file to use the GetResourceProperty portType in our own service:

```
<?xml version="1.0" encoding="UTF-8"?>

<definitions name="MathService"

targetNamespace="http://www.globus.org/namespaces/examples/
                MathService_instance_rp" ❶

    xmlns="http://schemas.xmlsoap.org/wsdl/"

    xmlns:tns="http://www.globus.org/namespaces/examples/MathService_instance"

    xmlns:wsdl="http://schemas.xmlsoap.org/wsdl/"

    xmlns:wsrp="http://docs.oasis-open.org/wsrf/2004/06/wsrf-WS-
                ResourceProperties-1.2-draft-01.xsd"

    xmlns:wsrpw="http://docs.oasis-open.org/wsrf/2004/06/wsrf-WS-
                ResourceProperties-1.2-draft-01.wsdl"

    xmlns:wsdlpp="http://www.globus.org/namespaces/2004/10/WSDLPreprocessor" ❷

    xmlns:xsd="http://www.w3.org/2001/XMLSchema">


        ❸

<wsdl:import

    namespace=

    "http://docs.oasis-open.org/wsrf/2004/06/wsrf-WS-ResourceProperties-1.2-
      draft-01.wsdl"

    location="../../wsrf/properties/WS-ResourceProperties.wsdl" />


<-- ... -->


<portType name="MathPortType"

    wsdlpp:extends="wsrpw:GetResourceProperty" ❹

    wsrp:ResourceProperties="tns:MathResourceProperties">
```

```
<operation name="add">

        <input message="tns:AddInputMessage"/>

        <output message="tns:AddOutputMessage"/>

</operation>


<operation name="subtract">

        <input message="tns:SubtractInputMessage"/>

        <output message="tns:SubtractOutputMessage"/>

</operation>


                ❺


</portType>


</definitions>
```

❶ Notice how we declare a new target namespace for our new WSDL interface.

❷ We need to declare the WS-ResourceProperties WSDL namespace (**wsrpw**) if we want to use the portTypes defined in that specification. In previous examples, we only declared a **wsrp** namespace which referred only to the WS-ResourceProperties XML Schema type definitions. This allowed us to use the **wsrp:ResourceProperties** attribute in our portType (to specify the service's RPs).
We also declare the WSDL Preprocessor namespace (**wsdlpp**), which we'll use later on.

❸ Furthermore, we have to make sure we import the WS-ResourceProperties WSDL file, where the portTypes are actually defined. This file (**WS-ResourceProperties.wsdl**) is a part of the WS-ResourceProperties spec, and is included with GT4. The path given is relative to the location of our WSDL when it is deployed. More specifically, our WSDL file will be deployed in the following directory:

$GLOBUS_LOCATION/share/schema/examples/MathService_instance_rp/

The WS-ResourceProperties file can be found in the following directory:

$GLOBUS_LOCATION/share/schema/wsrf/properties/

❹ We use the **wsdlpp:extends** attribute to tell the WSDL Preprocessor that we want it to take the **GetResourceProperty** portType and merge it into our own portType.

❺ Finally, notice how we've eliminated the **GetValueRP** operation (although not shown above, the WSDL file also lacks the corresponding **GetValueRP** messages and elements). Since we are now going to use the **GetResourceProperty** portType, there is no need to expose an explicit **GetValueRP** operation.

ⓘ **The WSDL Preprocessor**

The WSDL Preprocessor (the **wsdlpp:extends** attribute in the **portType** element) is provided in GT4 as a *convenience*. Conceptually, it is very important to understand that WSDL files using **wsdlpp:extends** will always be converted to standard WSDL before they are actually used. In other words, **wsdlpp:extends** doesn't affect GT4's interoperability with other WSRF implementations because the **extends** attribute is *always* "purged" from our WSDL file before the service is deployed. This process is usually called "flattening" because we take several WSDL files (our file plus any WSRF WSDL files we extend from) and then merge them into a single (flattened) file. GT4 will always publish the *flattened* version of our WSDL file.

Also, take into account that you are not *required* to use **wsdlpp:extends**. If you choose to, you can write the flattened version directly (as shown earlier). However, this involves a fair amount of copy-pasting that can be very error-prone. The book examples all use **wsdlpp:extends**.

Bottom line: GT4 doesn't require that other Web Services implementations or other WSRF implementations use **wsdlpp:extends** because WSDL files are *always* exchanged in their flattened versions. It is a purely internal feature of the toolkit.

10.3 WS-ResourceProperties portTypes

The WS-ResourceProperties specification includes other portTypes besides **GetResource-Property**. Each of the four portTypes included in the spec exposes a single operation, with the same name as the portType. In this chapter's example we will use all of these portTypes.

10.3.1 GetResourceProperty

This portType allows us to access the value of any resource property given its QName. This portType provides a general way of accessing RPs without the need of an individual **get** operation for each RP (recall that, in previous chapters, we used the **GetValueRP** operation to access the **Value** resource property).

10.3.2 GetMultipleResourceProperties

This portType allows us to access the value of several resource properties at once, given each of their QNames.

10.3.3   SetResourceProperties

This portType allows us to request one or several modifications on a service's RPs. In particular we can perform the following operations:

- Update: Change the value of a RP with a new value.
- Insert: Add a new RP with a given value.
- Delete: Eliminate all occurrences of a certain RP.

Again, note that the **SetResourceProperties** portType has a single operation (not three separate ones). We will use the parameters of the **SetResourceProperties** to specify what action (update, insert, or delete) we want to carry out. Also note that we can perform multiple actions at the same time (such as several updates and several inserts at the same time.

> ☞ The **SetResourceProperties** portTypes provides us a uniform way to modify a service's RP. However, as you will see in this chapter's examples, using this portType requires quite a bit of code (unlike the **GetResourceProperty** portType, which is very simple to use). In general, it is usually better to simply write setter methods for your RPs (such as writing a **setValue** method for the **Value** RP), unless there's some specific reason to use **SetResourceProperties**.

10.3.4   QueryResourceProperties

This portType allows us to perform complex queries on the RP document. Currently, the query language used is XPath.

10.4   Accessing Resource Properties the Right Way

We will now write and deploy a new service that exposes all the WS-ResourceProperty portTypes. Our client application will, in turn, make a call to each of these portTypes. For simplicity, our service will be based on the example presented in Chapter 6, Writing your first stateful web service in 5 simple steps (the example that uses **ServiceResourceHome** to confine our implementation to a single class). However, the steps described in this chapter are equally valid for the other two types of implementations we have seen in the previous two chapters (singleton resource homes, and factory/instance services).

10.4.1   The WSDL File

In the previous chapters, we were always able to reuse our original WSDL file because we were only modifying implementation details (for example, changing the implementation from a singleton resource home to a factory/service approach). However, in this chapter we *do* have to use a new WSDL file because we want to extend from new portTypes, which necessarily changes our service's interface. The changes we require to extend from a port-Type have been explained above. The only change with respect to the code shown earlier is that we want to extend from the four WS-ResourceProperty portTypes:

```
<?xml version="1.0" encoding="UTF-8"?>

<definitions name="MathService" ...>


<portType name="MathPortType"

    wsdlpp:extends="wsrpw:GetResourceProperty

                wsrpw:GetMultipleResourceProperties

                wsrpw:SetResourceProperties

                wsrpw:QueryResourceProperties"

    wsrp:ResourceProperties="tns:MathResourceProperties">


        <!-- ... -->


</portType>


</definitions>
```

☞ This is part of file **$EXAMPLES_DIR/schema/examples/MathService_instance_rp/Math.wsdl**.

Since we have added a new interface, we need to map the new WSDL namespaces to Java packages (as described in Section 6.1.3).

```
http\://www.globus.org/namespaces/examples/MathService_instance_rp=

            org.globus.examples.stubs.MathService_instance_rp

http\://www.globus.org/namespaces/examples/MathService_instance_rp/bindings=

            org.globus.examples.stubs.MathService_instance_rp.bindings

http\://www.globus.org/namespaces/examples/MathService_instance_rp/service=

            org.globus.examples.stubs.MathService_instance_rp.service
```

☞ These three lines must be present in **$EXAMPLES_DIR/namespace2package.mappings**.

10.4.2 The Java Files

The implementation files only require minimal changes. The only noteworthy change is that we no longer need to implement the **getValueRP** operation. In general, using the WS-ResourceProperties portTypes doesn't require that we add any extra code to our Java files. Wait a second... no extra Java code? If our service will include a bunch of new WS-ResourceProperties operations, then where are they implemented? As we'll see shortly, we will be able to rely on *operation providers* included with GT4 that provide an implementation for the WS-ResourceProperties operations (and many others).

☞ The service class for this example is **$EXAMPLES_DIR/org/globus/examples/ services/core/rp/impl/MathService.java**.

10.4.3 Operation Providers

Java WS Core uses a design pattern called *operation providers* that will make our lives as programmers much easier. Right now, we are going to see how we can *use* the operation providers already included with GT4; in Chapter 14, we will see how to actually implement our own operation providers.

To put it quite simply, an operation provider is a Java class, providing a set of operations, that we can easily plug into our service. For example, remember our WSDL file includes the following:

```
<portType name="MathPortType"

    wsdlpp:extends="wsrpw:GetResourceProperty

                    wsrpw:GetMultipleResourceProperties

                    wsrpw:SetResourceProperties

                    wsrpw:QueryResourceProperties"

    wsrp:ResourceProperties="tns:MathResourceProperties">
```

Remember that we are using **wsdlpp:extends** to specify that our service will implement four standard WSRF portTypes: **GetResourceProperty**, **GetMultipleResourceProperties**, **SetResourceProperties**, and **QueryResourceProperties**. This means our service class would need to implement the operations in those portTypes. However, instead of having to implement them ourselves, we can rely on the operation providers included with GT4 that *provide* an implementation of all the WSRF portTypes. To specify we want to use an operation provider in our service, we simply add the following parameter to our WSDD file:

```
<parameter name="providers" value="GetRPProvider GetMRPProvider SetRPProvider

    QueryRPProvider"/>
```

> ☞ **GetRPProvider**, **GetMRPProvider**, **SetRPProvider**, and **QueryRPProvider** is a shorthand notation for actual Java classes included with the toolkit.

In the following chapters, each time we want our service to provide standard functionality specified in the WSRF specs, we will simply make our service extend from a standard WSRF portType and then 'plug in' a Globus operation provider that implements that portType.

10.4.4 The Deployment Files

So, as we have just seen, to be able to use the WS-ResourceProperties portTypes we need to modify our WSDD file to make sure that our service relies on the Globus-supplied operation providers for those portTypes.

```xml
<?xml version="1.0" encoding="UTF-8"?>

<deployment name="defaultServerConfig"
    xmlns="http://xml.apache.org/axis/wsdd/"
    xmlns:java="http://xml.apache.org/axis/wsdd/providers/java"
    xmlns:xsd="http://www.w3.org/2001/XMLSchema">


    <service name="examples/core/rp/MathService" provider="Handler"
        use="literal" style="document">
        <parameter name="className" value="org.globus.examples.services.core.
                                            rp.impl.MathService"/>
        <wsdlFile>share/schema/examples/MathService_instance_rp/
         Math_service.wsdl</wsdlFile>
        <parameter name="allowedMethods" value="*"/>
        <parameter name="handlerClass" value="org.globus.axis.providers.
                                            RPCProvider"/>
        <parameter name="scope" value="Application"/>
        <parameter name="providers" value="GetRPProvider GetMRPProvider
                                            SetRPProvider QueryRPProvider"/>
        <parameter name="loadOnStartup" value="true"/>
    </service>


</deployment>
```

> ✍ This is file **$EXAMPLES_DIR/org/globus/examples/services/core/rp/deploy-server.wsdd**.

The JNDI deployment file, on the other hand, doesn't require any changes.

10.4.5 Build and Deploy

Build the service:

```
./globus-build-service.sh rp
```

And deploy it:

```
globus-deploy-gar $EXAMPLES_DIR/org_globus_examples_services_wsrf_core_rp.gar
```

10.4.6 Client Code

Our client application will make calls to some of the WS-ResourceProperties portTypes. The next example will use more complex resource properties and then we will see how to invoke the rest of the portTypes.

The code for this client is rather lengthy, so instead of seeing all the code all at once, we are going to run the client first, and then take a close look at what happens at each moment.

> ✍ This source code for the client is **$EXAMPLES_DIR/org/globus/examples/clients/MathService_instance_rp/Client.java**

Compile the client:

```
javac \
-classpath ./build/stubs/classes/:$CLASSPATH \
org/globus/examples/clients/MathService_instance_rp/Client.java
```

And run it:

```
java \
-classpath ./build/stubs/classes/:$CLASSPATH \
org.globus.examples.clients.MathService_instance_rp.Client \
http://127.0.0.1:8080/wsrf/services/examples/core/rp/MathService
```

The full output of the client should be the following:

```
Value RP: 0
LastOp RP: NONE
```

```
Value RP: 10
LastOp RP: ADDITION


Value RP: 100
LastOp RP: ADDITION


Value: 100
LastOp: ADDITION
```

Let's take a close look at what happens in each of these three blocks.

Invoking getResourceProperty

```
Value RP: 0
LastOp RP: NONE
Value RP: 10
LastOp RP: ADDITION
```

The first block of code prints out the initial values of the **Value** and **LastOp** RPs using the **getResourceProperty** operation, performs an addition, and then prints out the RPs again. All the **getResourceProperty** code is placed inside a **printResourceProperties** method.

```
printResourceProperties(math);
math.add(10);
printResourceProperties(math);
```

Let's take a close look at what happens in the **printResourceProperties** method:

```
/*
 * This method prints out MathService's resource properties by using the
 * GetResourceProperty operation.
 */
private void printResourceProperties(MathPortType math) throws Exception {
        GetResourcePropertyResponse valueRP, lastOpRP, lastLogRP;
        String value, lastOp, lastLog;


        ❶
        valueRP = math.getResourceProperty(MathConstants.RP_VALUE);
        lastOpRP = math.getResourceProperty(MathConstants.RP_LASTOP);
```

❷

```
value = valueRP.get_any()[0].getValue();
lastOp = lastOpRP.get_any()[0].getValue();
```

❸

```
System.out.println("Value RP: " + value);
System.out.println("LastOp RP: " + lastOp);
}
```

❶ We first invoke the **getResourceProperty** operation on our portType. Take into account that, since our **MathPortType** portType *extends* from the standard **GetResourceProperty** portType, our portType also includes a **getResourceProperty** operation. The only parameter we have to include is the QName of the RP we want to retrieve. Notice how the return value is of type **GetResourcePropertyResponse**, a Globus-supplied stub class.

❷ We must now extract the actual value of the RPs from the **GetResourceProperty-Response** return value. This is when knowing about the *resource property document* (explained at the beginning of the chapter) comes in really handy. The **GetResource-PropertyResponse** object will contain zero, one, or many RPs in XML format (i.e. the same way they are represented in the RP document). To access these RPs, we need to use the **get_any** method, which returns an array of *elements* (in the XML sense of the word). In our case, the **GetResourcePropertyResponse** from requesting the **Value** RP will contain the following:

```
<ns1:Value xmlns:ns1="http://www.globus.org/namespaces/examples/

          MathService_instance_rp">0</ns1:Value>
```

To obtain the value **0** contained in that element, we simply need to access the first position of the array of elements (**get_value()[0]**) and get its value (**getValue**).

❸ Finally, we print out the values.

Invoking SetResourceProperties to Update

```
Value RP: 100

LastOp RP: ADDITION
```

The second block of code updates the value of the **Value** RP using the **SetResource-Properties** operation and requesting an **Update** action. All the update code is placed inside a **updateRP** method.

```
updateRP(endpoint, MathConstants.RP_VALUE, "100");

printResourceProperties(math);
```

Now, let's see how the update operation is actually carried out:

```
/*
 * This method updates resource property "rpQName" in the WS-Resource
 * pointed at by the endpoint reference "epr" with the new value "value".
 */
private void updateRP(EndpointReferenceType epr, QName rpQName, String value)
                throws Exception {
            ❶

            WSResourcePropertiesServiceAddressingLocator locator =
                new WSResourcePropertiesServiceAddressingLocator();
            SetResourceProperties_PortType port = locator
                            .getSetResourcePropertiesPort(epr);


            ❷

            UpdateType update = new UpdateType();
            MessageElement msg = new MessageElement(rpQName, value);
            update.set_any(new MessageElement[] { msg });


            ❸

            SetResourceProperties_Element request =
                new SetResourceProperties_Element();
            request.setUpdate(update);


            ❹

            port.setResourceProperties(request);
}
```

❶ First of all, we obtain a reference to a generic **SetResourceProperties** port-Type. This approach is different from the one used in the previous block of code, where we simply used our own **MathPortType**. Take into account that we *could* use our **MathPortType** to invoke the **setResourceProperties** operation. However, the approach followed here can come in handy when all we want to access is the standard WSRF operations, without having to get a reference to the full portType (in our case, **MathPortType**). In particular, we can use the **WSResourcePropertiesServiceAddressingLocator** class to obtain a reference to any WS-ResourceProperty portType. More details can be found in the official Globus API documentation.

❷ Since we are going to perform an update action through the **SetResourceProperties** operation, we first need to create an **UpdateType** object where we specify the update to carry out. Take into account that an **UpdateType** object can contain *several* update requests. We encapsulate each of these requests inside a **MessageElement** object. Then, we create an array of **MessageElement**s and include that array in our **UpdateType** object (using the **set_any** method).

❸ Now, we create a **SetResourceProperties_Element** object which will represent our **SetResourceProperties** request. This object can contain insert, update, and delete actions. In our case, we add the recently created **UpdateType** object to the request using the **setUpdate** method.

❹ Finally, we invoke **SetResourceProperties**.

Invoking GetMultipleResourceProperties

```
Value: 100
```

```
LastOp: ADDITION
```

The third, and last, block of code prints out the values of the **Value** and **LastOp** RPs using the **GetMultipleResourceProperties** operation. All the **GetMultipleResourceProperties** code is placed inside a **printResourceProperties** method.

```
printMultipleResourceProperties(math);

/*
 * This method prints out MathService's resource properties by using the
 * GetMultipleResourceProperties operation.
 */
private void printMultipleResourceProperties(MathPortType math)
            throws Exception {
    GetMultipleResourceProperties_Element request;
    GetMultipleResourcePropertiesResponse response;


    ❶
    QName[] resourceProperties = new QName[] { MathConstants.RP_VALUE,
                    MathConstants.RP_LASTOP };
    request = new GetMultipleResourceProperties_Element(resourceProperties);
```

❷

```
response = math.getMultipleResourceProperties(request);
```

❸

```
for(int i=0; i<response.get_any().length;i++)
{
        String name = response.get_any()[i].getLocalName();
        String value = response.get_any()[i].getValue();
        System.out.println(name +": " + value);
}
}
```

❶ First, we need to create a **GetMultipleResourceProperties_Element** object that represents the request to **getMultipleResourceProperties**. The constructor expects an array of QNames. In our case, we specify the QNames for the **Value** and **LastOp** RPs.

❷ Next, we invoke the **getMultipleResourceProperties**. Notice how the return value is of type **GetMultipleResourcePropertiesResponse**.

❸ As in **getResourceProperty**, the return of **getMultipleResourceProperties** encapsulates zero, one, or many RPs in XML format. In this case, the **GetMultipleResource-PropertiesResponse** will contain the following:

```
<ns1:Value xmlns:ns1="http://www.globus.org/namespaces/examples/

MathService_instance_rp">100</ns1:Value>

<ns2:LastOp xmlns:ns2="http://www.globus.org/namespaces/examples/

MathService_instance_rp">ADDITION</ns2:LastOp>
```

To extract the value of the RPs, we once again rely on the **get_any** method, which returns an array of elements. We simply have to iterate through this array, and write the value of each element using the **getValue** method. Here we are also printing out the name of the property using the **getLocalName** method.

10.5   A More Elaborate Example

Now we will take a look at a service similar to the previous one, but with more complex resource properties. This, in turn, will allow us to experiment with the WS-ResourceProperties portTypes we didn't use in the previous example.

10.5.1   The WSDL File

We will change the definition of our resource properties document by adding the following RPs:

- **RecentValues**: An array containing the most recent values passed as to either the **add** or **subtract** operations.

- **RecentOps**: An array with the most recent values of the **LastOp** RP.

- **SystemStats**: A resource property with a complex data type, containing some information about the system the service is running on.

The changes to the WSDL file are highlighted in bold.

```
<xsd:element name="Value" type="xsd:int"/>

<xsd:element name="LastOp" type="xsd:string"/>

<xsd:element name="RecentValues" type="xsd:int"/>

<xsd:element name="RecentOps" type="xsd:string"/>

<xsd:element name="SystemStats">

    <xsd:complexType>

    <xsd:sequence>

    <xsd:element name="CpuSpeed" type="xsd:float"/>

        <xsd:element name="Mem" type="xsd:int"/>

        <xsd:element name="Status" type="xsd:string"/>

    </xsd:sequence>

    </xsd:complexType>

</xsd:element>


<xsd:element name="MathResourceProperties">

<xsd:complexType>

    <xsd:sequence>

            <xsd:element ref="tns:Value" minOccurs="1" maxOccurs="1"/>

            <xsd:element ref="tns:LastOp" minOccurs="1" maxOccurs="1"/>

            <xsd:element ref="tns:RecentValues" minOccurs="0" maxOccurs="unbounded"/>

            <xsd:element ref="tns:RecentOps" minOccurs="0" maxOccurs="unbounded"/>

            <xsd:element ref="tns:SystemStats" minOccurs="1" maxOccurs="1"/>

    </xsd:sequence>

</xsd:complexType>

</xsd:element>
```

> ☞ This is part of file **$EXAMPLES_DIR/schema/examples/MathService_instance_rp_complex/Math.wsdl**.

First, notice how we use the **unbounded** keyword to indicate that **RecentValues** and **RecentOps** will be array values.

Next, take into account that, since **SystemStats** has a complex data type, a stub class will be generated for it. It will look something like this:

```
package org.globus.examples.stubs.MathService_instance_rp_complex;

public class SystemStats implements java.io.Serializable {

    private float cpuSpeed;

    private int mem;

    private java.lang.String status;

    // ...

}
```

> ☞ If you want to see the complete source code of this file, it will be generated when you build the service and placed it in:
> **$EXAMPLES_DIR/build/stubs/src/org/globus/examples/stubs/MathService_instance_rp_complex/SystemStats.java**.

Finally, since we have added a new interface, we need to map the new WSDL namespaces to Java packages (as described in Section 6.1.3).

```
http\://www.globus.org/namespaces/examples/MathService_instance_rp_complex=
    org.globus.examples.stubs.MathService_instance_rp_complex

http\://www.globus.org/namespaces/examples/MathService_instance_rp_complex/
    bindings=org.globus.examples.stubs.MathService_instance_rp_complex.bindings

http\://www.globus.org/namespaces/examples/MathService_instance_rp_complex/
    service=org.globus.examples.stubs.MathService_instance_rp_complex.service
```

> ☞ These three lines must be present in **$EXAMPLES_DIR/namespace2package.properties**.

10.5.2 The Resource Implementation

The resource class must be modified to reflect the new resource properties. Remember that, since we're using **ServiceResourceHome** as our resource home, the service and the resource are implemented in the same class. In general, new resource properties will always be implemented in the resource class (not the service class).

First of all, we need to add attributes representing the new resource properties. Array resource properties can be implemented using Java **Vector** objects. The **SystemStats** RP is represented by an attribute of type **SystemStats** (the stub class described earlier), so we need to remember to include an import statement for that class.

```
import org.globus.examples.stubs.MathService_instance_rp_complex.SystemStats;

/* Resource properties */
private int value;
private String lastOp;
private SystemStats systemStats;


/* Vectors to support unbounded resource properties */
private Vector recentValues;
private Vector recentOps;
```

Next, we need to initialize the resource properties.

```
ResourceProperty valueRP = new ReflectionResourceProperty(
            MathConstants.RP_VALUE, "Value", this);
this.propSet.add(valueRP);
setValue(0);


ResourceProperty lastOpRP = new ReflectionResourceProperty(
            MathConstants.RP_LASTOP, "LastOp", this);
this.propSet.add(lastOpRP);
setLastOp("NONE");


ResourceProperty recentValuesRP = new ReflectionResourceProperty(
            MathConstants.RP_RECENTVALUES, "RecentValues", this);
this.propSet.add(recentValuesRP);
recentValues = new Vector();


ResourceProperty recentOpsRP = new ReflectionResourceProperty(
            MathConstants.RP_RECENTOPS, "RecentOps", this);
```

```
this.propSet.add(recentOpsRP);
recentOps = new Vector();


ResourceProperty sysStatsRP = new ReflectionResourceProperty(
            MathConstants.RP_SYSTEMSTATS, "SystemStats", this);
this.propSet.add(sysStatsRP);
setSystemStats(new SystemStats(1333.3f,512,"RUNNING"));
```

☞ Remember we're using the special **ReflectionResourceProperty** to represent our resource properties. This means that we also need to include get/set methods for each of the attributes representing the resource properties. Implementing these get/set methods is pretty straightforward (you can see them in the full source code for this example). If you need more information on how **ReflectionResourceProperty** works, then this would be a good moment to review ReflectionResourceProperty.

Finally, we need to update the **RecentValues** and **RecentOps** RPs whenever **add** and **subtract** are invoked.

```
public AddResponse add(int a) throws RemoteException {
        value += a;
        lastOp = "ADDITION";
        recentValues.add(new Integer(a));
        recentOps.add(lastOp);
        return new AddResponse();
}
```

☞ All the code shown above is part of **$EXAMPLES_DIR/org/globus/examples/ services/core/rp_complex/impl/MathService.java**.

☞ The QNames of the new resource properties must also be added to the MathConstants interface. The updated MathConstants is **$EXAMPLES_DIR/org/ globus/examples/services/core/rp_complex/impl/MathConstants.java**.

ⓘ The changes explained above are necessary because we are adding new resource properties to our service. As explained in the previous example, using the WS-ResourceProperties portTypes does not, in general, require that we modify any of our Java files.

10.5.3 The Deployment Files

The WSDD and JNDI deployment files require no changes, except those already explained in the previous example (adding the required operation providers to the **providers** parameter in the WSDD file).

10.5.4 Build and Deploy

Build the service:

```
./globus-build-service.sh rp_complex
```

And deploy it:

```
globus-deploy-gar $EXAMPLES_DIR/
org_globus_examples_services_wsrf_core_rp_complex.gar
```

10.5.5 Client Code

As in the previous example, the code for the client is rather long, so instead of seeing all the code all at once, we are going to first run the client, and then take a close look at what happens at each moment.

> ☞ This source code for the client is **$EXAMPLES_DIR/org/globus/examples/clients/ MathService_instance_rp_complex/Client.java**

Compile the client:

```
javac \
-classpath ./build/stubs/classes/:$CLASSPATH \
org/globus/examples/clients/MathService_instance_rp_complex/Client.java
```

And run it:

```
java \
-classpath ./build/stubs/classes/:$CLASSPATH \
org.globus.examples.clients.MathService_instance_rp_complex.Client \
http://127.0.0.1:8080/wsrf/services/examples/core/rp_complex/MathService
```

You should see the following:

```
Value RP: 45
RecentValues RP: 10 20 30 15
LastOp RP: SUBTRACTION
```

```
RecentOps RP: ADDITION ADDITION ADDITION SUBTRACTION


RecentValues RP: 10 20 30 15 4242


LastOp RP: SUBTRACTION

RecentOps RP: Empty list

[Sys Stats] Speed: 1333.3, Memory: 512, Status: RUNNING
```

Let's take a close look at what exactly happens in each of these four blocks.

Invoking getResourceProperty with Unbounded RPs

```
Value RP: 45

RecentValues RP: 10 20 30 15

LastOp RP: SUBTRACTION

RecentOps RP: ADDITION ADDITION ADDITION SUBTRACTION
```

The first block of code prints out the values of the **Value**, **RecentValues**, **LastOp**, and **RecentOps** RPs after performing some **add** and **subtract** calls on the service. All the **getResourceProperty** code is placed inside a **printValues** and a **printLastOps** method.

```
math.add(10);
math.add(20);
math.add(30);
math.subtract(15);
printValues(math);
printLastOps(math);
```

Let's take a close look at what happens in the **printValues** method: (the **printLastOps** is similar)

```
private void printValues(MathPortType math) throws Exception {
        GetResourcePropertyResponse valueRP, recentValuesRP;
        String value, recentValues;


        ❶

        valueRP = math.getResourceProperty(MathConstants.RP_VALUE);
        recentValuesRP = math.getResourceProperty(MathConstants.
                                        RP_RECENTVALUES);
```

❷

```
value = valueRP.get_any()[0].getValue();


if (recentValuesRP.get_any() == null) ❸
        recentValues = "Empty list";
else {
        recentValues = "";
        for (int i = 0; i < recentValuesRP.get_any().length; i++) ❹
                recentValues += recentValuesRP.get_any()[i].
                                getValue() + " ";
}
System.out.println("Value RP: " + value);

System.out.println("RecentValues RP: " + recentValues);
```

}

❶ As in the previous example, we first invoke the **getResourceProperty** operation to obtain the **Value** RP and the **RecentValues** RP.

❷ We extract the value of the **Value** RP the same way we did in the previous example.

❸ Now, extracting the *values* in the **RecentValues** RP is not that simple. Remember how the **GetResourcePropertyResponse** object (returned by **GetResourceProperty**) will contain zero, one, or many RPs in XML format. To access these RPs, we use the **get_any** method, which returns an array of elements. First of all, we need to check if the array is equal to **null**, in which case the number of RPs returned is zero.

❹ Otherwise, we can iterate through the RPs and create a string **recentValues** with a list of the recent values. In our case, the **GetResourcePropertyResponse** returned for the **RecentValues** RP will contain the following elements:

```
<ns1:RecentValues xmlns:ns1="http://www.globus.org/namespaces/examples/

    MathService_instance_rp_complex">10</ns1:RecentValues>

<ns1:RecentValues xmlns:ns1="http://www.globus.org/namespaces/examples/

    MathService_instance_rp_complex">20</ns1:RecentValues>

<ns1:RecentValues xmlns:ns1="http://www.globus.org/namespaces/examples/

    MathService_instance_rp_complex">30</ns1:RecentValues>

<ns1:RecentValues xmlns:ns1="http://www.globus.org/namespaces/examples/

    MathService_instance_rp_complex">15</ns1:RecentValues>
```

For each element in the array of elements returned by **get_value**, we obtain the value using the **getValue** method.

Invoking SetResourceProperties **to Insert**

```
RecentValues RP: 10 20 30 15 4242
```

The second block of code inserts a new **RecentValues** RP. Remember that this means a new **RecentValues** element will be added to the resource property document, which is perfectly valid in this case because **RecentValues** can occur an **unbounded** number of times in the RP document. This insertion is done with the **SetResourceProperties** operation and requesting an **Insert** action. All the update code is placed inside a **insertRP** method.

```
insertRP(endpoint, MathConstants.RP_RECENTVALUES, "4242");

printValues(math);
```

The code to perform the insertion is very similar to the code we used to perform an RP update in the previous example. The difference is that, instead of creating an **UpdateType** to specify an update, we will use an **InsertType** to specify an insertion.

```
/*
 * This method inserts resource property "rpQName" in the WS-Resource
 * pointed at by the endpoint reference "epr" with value "value".
 */
private void insertRP(EndpointReferenceType epr, QName rpQName, String value)
            throws Exception {
    /* Get a SetResourceProperties port type */
    WSResourcePropertiesServiceAddressingLocator locator =
        new WSResourcePropertiesServiceAddressingLocator();
    SetResourceProperties_PortType port = locator
                    .getSetResourcePropertiesPort(epr);


    ❶
    InsertType insert = new InsertType();
    MessageElement msg = new MessageElement(rpQName, value);
    insert.set_any(new MessageElement[] { msg });
```

❷

```
SetResourceProperties_Element request =
    new SetResourceProperties_Element();
request.setInsert(insert);


/* Invoke SetResourceProperties */
port.setResourceProperties(request);
```

}

❶ We create a **InsertType** object where we specify the insertion. Like an **UpdateType** object, and **InsertType** object can contain *several* insertion requests. We encapsulate each of these requests inside a **MessageElement** object. Then, we create an array of **MessageElement**s and include that array in our **InsertType** object (using the **set_any** method).

❷ In this example, the **SetResourceProperties_Element** object (representing our request to the **SetResourceProperties** operation) will carry the **InsertType** object we just created.

Invoking SetResourceProperties **to Delete**

LastOp RP: SUBTRACTION

RecentOps RP: Empty list

The second block of code deletes all occurrences of the **RecentOps** in the RP document. This is done using the **SetResourceProperties** operation and requesting a **Delete** action.

```
deleteRP(endpoint, MathConstants.RP_RECENTOPS);

printLastOps(math);
```

Once again, the code to perform the deletion (inside a **deleteRP** method) is very similar to the code we used in the previous **SetResourceProperties** examples. However, now not only will we be creating a **DeleteType** to specify the deletion, we will be limited to specifying a single RP. This makes the code a bit simpler, since we don't have to deal with an array of **MessageElement**s.

```
/*
 * This method deletes resource property "rpQName" from the WS-Resource
 * pointed at by the endpoint reference "epr".
 */
private void deleteRP(EndpointReferenceType epr, QName rpQName)
            throws Exception {
```

```
                    /* Get a SetResourceProperties port type */
                    WSResourcePropertiesServiceAddressingLocator locator =
                    new WSResourcePropertiesServiceAddressingLocator();
                    SetResourceProperties_PortType port = locator
                                    .getSetResourcePropertiesPort(epr);


                    /* We will be invoking SetResourceProperties with a single Delete */
                    ❶
                    DeleteType delete = new DeleteType(rpQName);


                    ❷
                    SetResourceProperties_Element request =
                        new SetResourceProperties_Element();
                    request.setDelete(delete);


                    /* Invoke SetResourceProperties */
                    port.setResourceProperties(request);
            }
```

❶ We create a **DeleteType** object. The parameter to the constructor is the QName of the RP we want to delete. Remember that this means that *all* the RP's with that QName will be deleted.

❷ We create **SetResourceProperties_Element** and include the **DeleteType** object we just created.

Invoking GetResourceProperty **with a Complex RP**

> **[Sys Stats] Speed: 1333.3, Memory: 512, Status: RUNNING**

This final block of code prints out the values contained in the **SystemStats** RP using the **getResourceProperty** operation. The tricky thing about this is that, unlike the previous times we've used **getResourceProperty**, the type of the RP is not a primitive type (integer, string, etc.) but a *complex* type. For example, remember that requesting the **Value** RP yielded the following:

```
<ns1:Value xmlns:ns1="http://www.globus.org/namespaces/examples/
    MathService_instance_rp">0</ns1:Value>
```

Extracting the value is simple because we just have to retrieve the content of the **ns1:Value**
element. Even though the XML API used to do this returns a **String** representation of
the value, we can easily cast it to an integer using the Java API. However, requesting the
SystemsStats RP yields the following:

```
<ns1:SystemStats xmlns:ns1="http://www.globus.org/namespaces/examples/
MathService_instance_rp_complex">
<CpuSpeed>1333.3</CpuSpeed>
<Mem>512</Mem>
<Status>RUNNING</Status>
</ns1:SystemStats>
```

Although we can certainly navigate through this XML document (if we feel comfortable
enough with an XML API like DOM), we would ideally want this XML representation to be cast
to the **SystemStats** stub class described earlier. Fortunately, we will be able to do just that.

```
/*
 * This method prints out MathService's SystemStats resource property by
 * using the GetResourceProperty operation.
 */
private void printSystemStats(MathPortType math) throws Exception {
        GetResourcePropertyResponse systemStatsRP;


        ❶
        systemStatsRP = math.getResourceProperty(MathConstants.RP_SYSTEMSTATS);


        ❷
        MessageElement msg = systemStatsRP.get_any()[0];


        ❸
        SystemStats stats = (SystemStats)
            ObjectDeserializer.toObject(msg, SystemStats.class);

        System.out.print("[Sys Stats] ");
        System.out.print("Speed: " + stats.getCpuSpeed() + ", ");
        System.out.print("Memory: " + stats.getMem() + ", ");
        System.out.println("Status: " + stats.getStatus());
}
```

❶ We retrieve the **SystemsStats** RP using the **getResourceProperty** operation.

❷ We extract the first (and only) element contained in the returned **GetResource-PropertyResponse** object.

❸ If we used the **getValue** method on the **MessageElement** object (**msg**), we would get the **String** representation of everything that is inside the **SystemStats** element. Instead, we use the Globus-supplied **ObjectDeserializer** class, which will cast the **System-Stats** element into the **SystemStats** stub class. We simply have to provide the **MessageElement** that contains the **SystemStats** RP, and the class we want to cast it into.

10.6   SimpleResourceProperty

So far, we have used a special Globus-supplied class called **ReflectionResourceProperty** to implement our RPs. This class had a number of benefits, described in ReflectionResourceProperty, the main one being that it greatly simplified our implementation since we could use the RPs as if they were normal Java variables.

However, we can also use a different Globus-supplied class to represent our RPs: **SimpleResourceProperty**. This class, makes the implementation a little bit more complicated, but it shouldn't be too hard to understand now that we know what the *resource property document* is. In this section we will simply highlight what code is necessary to use **SimpleResourceProperty**. No example is provided, but we will see **SimpleResourceProperty**'s in action in Chapter 13.

First of all, remember how in all the previous examples, our RPs were implemented simply as two attributes in the resource class:

```
private int value;

private String lastOp;
```

Now, this will be replaced by the following:

```
/* Resource properties */

private ResourceProperty valueRP;

private ResourceProperty lastOpRP;
```

> ☞ **ResourceProperty** is a Globus-supplied interface that all resource properties must implement. Both **ReflectionResourceProperty** and **SimpleResourceProperty**, for example, implement it.

Furthermore, we are not *required* to implement get/set methods for the RPs, as we did when using **ReflectionResourceProperty**. However, as will be explained later on, it will nonetheless be convenient to do so, as it will make working with the RPs easier, specially if we split our implementation into a service, a resource, and a resource home.

Next, we need to initialize the resource properties.

```
public MathService() throws RemoteException {
        this.propSet = new SimpleResourcePropertySet(
                    MathConstants.RESOURCE_PROPERTIES); ❶
        try {
                valueRP = new SimpleResourceProperty(MathConstants.RP_VALUE); ❷
                valueRP.add(new Integer(0)); ❸
                ❹
                lastOpRP = new SimpleResourceProperty(MathConstants.RP_LASTOP);
                lastOpRP.add("NONE");
        } catch (Exception e) {
                throw new RuntimeException(e.getMessage());
        }


        ❺
        this.propSet.add(valueRP);
        this.propSet.add(lastOpRP);
}
```

❶ First, we create the RP set. This, in effect, creates an empty RP document. In our case, this would be something like this:

```
<MathResourceProperties xmlns:tns="http://www.globus.org/namespaces/

    examples/MathService_instance_rp">

</MathResourceProperties>
```

❷ Next, we create a **SimpleResourceProperty**. If you compare with the previous examples, you'll notice that the constructor for **SimpleResourceProperty** only requires the QName of the RP (whereas **ReflectionResourceProperty** required more parameters).

❸ Now, we set the initial value of the RP. When using **ReflectionResourceProperty**, we simply had to modify the **value** attribute. Now, however, we have to use **SimpleResourceProperty** method to do this. By adding **new Integer(0)**, we are creating a new **Value** RP with value 0:

```
<tns:Value>0</tns:Value>
```

Note that, if the RP were unbounded, we could keep on invoking **valueRP.add** to create more **Value** RPs:

```
<tns:Value>0</tns:Value>

<tns:Value>0</tns:Value>

<tns:Value>0</tns:Value>
```

However, we cannot do this because **Value** is declared to occur once (and only once) in the RP document.

❹ We perform the previous two steps again to add a new **LastOp** RP.

❺ Finally, we add the RPs to the RP set. Now, our RP document will look something like this:

```
<MathResourceProperties xmlns:tns="http://www.globus.org/namespaces/examples/

    MathService_notif">

<tns:Value>0</tns:Value>

<tns:LastOp>NONE</tns:LastOp>

</MathResourceProperties>
```

Next, we need to modify the code that actually accesses the values in the RPs. When using **ReflectionResourceProperty**, our **add** method was as simple as this:

```
public AddResponse add(int a) throws RemoteException {

        value += a;

        lastOp = "ADDITION";


        return new AddResponse();

    }
```

Now, however, the code will look something like this:

```
public AddResponse add(int a) throws RemoteException {

        Integer value = (Integer) valueRP.get(0); ❶

        value = new Integer(value.intValue()+a); ❷

        valueRP.set(0, value); ❸

        lastOpRP.set(0,"ADDITION"); ❹


        return new AddResponse();

    }
```

❶ We retrieve the current value of the **Value** RP. Since this RP can have one (and only one) value, we have to access the value in position **0** using the **get** method. Since **get** returns an **Object**, we need to cast this into an **Integer** object.

❷ Next, we perform the actual addition.

❸ Next, we modify the value of the **Value** RP using the **set** method. Again, since this RP can hold a single value, the new value is placed in the first position of the RP (position 0).

❹ Finally, we modify the value of the **LastOp** RP using, once again, the **set** method.

Accessing the RPs if we Split Up the Implementation

Remember that, in this chapter, we are using the **ServiceResourceHome** which allows us to implement the service and the resource in the same class. This means that our **add** and **subtract** methods have direct access to the **ResourceProperty** objects representing our RPs.

However, this will not be so if we split up the implementation as seen in Chapter 7 and Chapter 8. In these cases, we will need to use our resource's **ResourceProperties** interface to access the RP set and then the RPs themselves. This means that our code could end up looking something like this:

```
public AddResponse add(int a) throws RemoteException {

    MathResource mathResource = getResource();


    ResourceProperty valueRP = mathResource.propSet.
        get(MathConstants.RP_VALUE);
    Integer value = (Integer) valueRP.get(0);
    value = new Integer(value.intValue()+a);
    valueRP.set(0, value);


    ResourceProperty lastOpRP = mathResource.propSet.
        get(MathConstants.RP_LASTOP);
    lastOpRP.set(0,"ADDITION");


    return new AddResponse();

}
```

Of course, this doesn't make things any nicer. This is why it is usually a good idea to include get/set methods for our RPs in the resource implementation, even if they are not required by **SimpleResourceProperty**. In other words, we could add the following to our resource:

```
public int getValue() {
        Integer value_obj = (Integer) valueRP.get(0);
        return value_obj.intValue();
}


public synchronized void setValue(int value) {
        Integer value_obj = new Integer(a);
        valueRP.set(0, value_obj);
}


public String getLastOp() {
        String lastOp_obj = (String) lastOpRP.get(0);
        return lastOp_obj;
}


public synchronized void setLastOp(String lastOp) {
        valueRP.set(0, lastOp);
}
```

With these get/set methods, our **add** method could be implemented like this:

```
public AddResponse add(int a) throws RemoteException {
        MathResource mathResource = getResource();

        mathResource.setValue(mathResource.getValue() + a);
        mathResource.setLastOp("ADDITION");

        return new AddResponse();
}
```

This, of course, looks much nicer. In fact, it is very similar to the way we were able to implement **add** and **subtract** in Chapter 7 and Chapter 8.

10.7 Command-line Clients

GT4 includes a set of command-line clients we can use to access and modify a service's resource properties without having to write a client specifically for that service. All the GT4 command-line clients have a set of common options which are described in Appendix C, Command-line clients.

10.7.1 wsrf-get-property

This command uses the **GetResourceProperty** portType to access the value of a resource property. The resource property must be specified using its QName.

Usage

```
wsrf-get-property [common options] <resource property>
```

Example

```
wsrf-get-property \
   -s http://127.0.0.1:8080/wsrf/services/examples/core/rp/MathService \
   {http://www.globus.org/namespaces/examples/MathService_instance_rp}Value
```

Expected output:

```
<ns1:Value xmlns:ns1="http://www.globus.org/namespaces/examples/
MathService_instance_rp">0</ns1:Value>
```

10.7.2 wsrf-get-properties

This command uses the **GetResourceProperties** portType to access the value of several resource properties at once. The resource properties must be specified using their QNames.

Usage

```
wsrf-get-properties [common options] <resource property 1> [<rp 2> ... <rp N>]
```

Example

```
wsrf-get-properties \
   -s http://127.0.0.1:8080/wsrf/services/examples/core/rp/MathService \
   {http://www.globus.org/namespaces/examples/MathService_instance_rp}Value \
   {http://www.globus.org/namespaces/examples/MathService_instance_rp}LastOp
```

Expected output:

```
<ns1:Value xmlns:ns1="http://www.globus.org/namespaces/examples/
    MathService_instance_rp">0</ns1:Value>
<ns2:LastOp xmlns:ns2="http://www.globus.org/namespaces/examples/
    MathService_instance_rp">NONE</ns2:LastOp>
```

10.7.3   wsrf-update-property

This command uses the **SetResourceProperties** portType to update the value of one or several resource properties.

Usage

```
wsrf-update-property [common options] <updateFile>
```

Where **updateFile** must be a file with the following format:

```
<updateFile>

    <tns:ResourcePropertyName xmlns:tns="namespace">

    new_value

    </tns:ResourcePropertyName>

</updateFile>
```

Note that several resource property updates can be included inside the **updateFile** element.

Example

We will update the **Value** RP and change its value to 100. Our **updateFile** would look like this.

```
<updateFile>

    <tns:Value xmlns:tns="http://www.globus.org/namespaces/examples/
        MathService_instance_rp">

    100

    </tns:Value>

</updateFile>
```

Assuming we've saved the file with the name **update.xml**:

```
wsrf-update-property \

    -s http://127.0.0.1:8080/wsrf/services/examples/core/rp/MathService \

    update.xml
```

You should not expect any output if the command is successful. To see that the update has been performed, you can use **wsrf-get-property** to access the **Value** RP. You should get the following:

```
<ns1:Value xmlns:ns1="http://www.globus.org/namespaces/examples/

MathService_instance_rp">100</ns1:Value>
```

10.7.4   wsrf-insert-property

This command uses the **SetResourceProperties** portType to insert one or several new resource properties.

Usage

```
wsrf-insert-property [common options] <insertFile>
```

Where **insertFile** must be a file with the following format:

```
<insertFile>

    <tns:ResourcePropertyName xmlns:tns="namespace">

    new_value

    </tns:ResourcePropertyName>

</insertFile>
```

Note that several resource property updates can be included inside the **insertFile** element.

Example

We will insert two new **RecentOps** RPs. Our **insertFile** would look like this:

```
<insertFile>

    <tns:RecentOps xmlns:tns="http://www.globus.org/namespaces/examples/

        MathService_instance_rp_complex">

    ADDITION

    </tns:RecentOps>
```

```
<tns:RecentOps xmlns:tns="http://www.globus.org/namespaces/examples/
    MathService_instance_rp_complex">
SUBTRACTION
</tns:RecentOps>
</insertFile>
```

Assuming we've saved the file with the name **insert.xml**:

wsrf-insert-property \
    -s http://127.0.0.1:8080/wsrf/services/examples/core/rp_complex/MathService \
    insert.xml

You should not expect any output if the command is successful. To see that the update has been performed, you can use **wsrf-get-property** to access the **RecentOps** RP. You should get the following:

```
<tns:RecentOps xmlns:tns="http://www.globus.org/namespaces/examples/
    MathService_instance_rp_complex">
ADDITION
</tns:RecentOps>
<tns:RecentOps xmlns:tns="http://www.globus.org/namespaces/examples/
    MathService_instance_rp_complex">
SUBTRACTION
</tns:RecentOps>
```

10.7.5   wsrf-delete-property

This command uses the **SetResourceProperties** portType to delete all occurrences of a resource property. The resource property must be specified using its QName.

Usage

    wsrf-delete-property [common options] <resource property>

Example

    wsrf-delete-property \
        -s http://127.0.0.1:8080/wsrf/services/examples/core/rp_complex/MathService \

```
{http://www.globus.org/namespaces/examples/MathService_instance_rp_complex}
    RecentOps
```

You should not expect any output if the command is successful. To test that the deletion has been performed, you can use the **wsrf-get-property** to access the **RecentOps** RP. The command should simply output the following, indicating that there are no **RecentOps** RPs:

```
null
```

10.7.6 wsrf-query

This command uses the **QueryResourceProperties** portType to query the resource properties document. Currently, the only query dialect supported (and, therefore, the default) is XPath.

Usage

```
wsrf-query [common options] [query] [query dialect]
```

Example

The following query retrieves all the **RecentOps** RPs with a value greater than or equal to 20:

```
wsrf-query \
-s http://127.0.0.1:8080/wsrf/services/examples/core/rp_complex/MathService \
"/*/*[local-name()='RecentValues'][text()>=20]"
```

Expected output:

```
<ns1:RecentValues xmlns:ns1="http://www.globus.org/namespaces/examples/
    MathService_instance_rp_complex">
        20
</ns1:RecentValues>
<ns1:RecentValues xmlns:ns1="http://www.globus.org/namespaces/examples/
    MathService_instance_rp_complex">
        30
</ns1:RecentValues>
```

```
<ns1:RecentValues xmlns:ns1="http://www.globus.org/namespaces/examples/
    MathService_instance_rp_complex">
        4242
</ns1:RecentValues>
```

Reference

[1] "WS-ResourceProperties specification". 1.2 Working Draft 01. *Web Services Resource Framework (WSRF) TC*. OASIS, June, 2004.

## chapter 11

Lifecycle Management

In this chapter we will see the two lifecycle management solutions offered by the WS-ResourceLifetime specification. Since lifecycle management mainly makes sense when we have several resources, the examples will focus on explaining what modifications are necessary to the example seen in Chapter 8 (the factory/instance example). The version of that example with the lifecycle modifications can be found in directory **EXAMPLES_DIR/org/globus/examples/services/core/rl/**

11.1 Immediate Destruction

Immediate destruction is the simplest type of lifecycle management. It allows us to request that a resource be destroyed immediately by invoking a **destroy** operation in the *instance* service. Notice how, even though the *factory* service is responsible for creating the resources, destruction must be requested to each individual resource through the instance service.

To add immediate destruction to our service, we simply need to extend from the standard WSRF **ImmediateResourceTermination** portType. This portType adds a **destroy** operation to our portType that will instruct the current resource to terminate itself immediately.

```
<portType name="MathPortType"

    wsdlpp:extends="wsrpw:GetResourceProperty

                    wsrlw:ImmediateResourceTermination"

    wsrp:ResourceProperties="tns:MathResourceProperties">
```

```
<operation name="add">
            <input message="tns:AddInputMessage"/>
            <output message="tns:AddOutputMessage"/>
</operation>


<operation name="subtract">
            <input message="tns:SubtractInputMessage"/>
            <output message="tns:SubtractOutputMessage"/>
</operation>


</portType>
```

To be able to do this, we must remember to declare the WS-ResourceLifetime namespace, and import its WSDL file:

```
<definitions name="MathService"
    targetNamespace="http://www.globus.org/namespaces/examples/
        MathService_instance_rl"
    xmlns="http://schemas.xmlsoap.org/wsdl/"
    xmlns:tns="http://www.globus.org/namespaces/examples/
        MathService_instance_rl"
    xmlns:wsdl="http://schemas.xmlsoap.org/wsdl/"
    xmlns:wsrlw="http://docs.oasis-open.org/wsrf/2004/06/
        wsrf-WS-ResourceLifetime-1.2-draft-01.wsdl"
    xmlns:wsrp="http://docs.oasis-open.org/wsrf/2004/06/
        wsrf-WS-ResourceProperties-1.2-draft-01.xsd"
    xmlns:wsrpw="http://docs.oasis-open.org/wsrf/2004/06/
        wsrf-WS-ResourceProperties-1.2-draft-01.wsdl"
    xmlns:wsdlpp="http://www.globus.org/namespaces/2004/10/WSDLPreprocessor"
    xmlns:xsd="http://www.w3.org/2001/XMLSchema">

<wsdl:import
    namespace=
    "http://docs.oasis-open.org/wsrf/2004/06/
        wsrf-WS-ResourceLifetime-1.2-draft-01.wsdl"
    location="../../wsrf/lifetime/WS-ResourceLifetime.wsdl" />
```

☞ This is part of file **$EXAMPLES_DIR/schema/MathService_instance_rl/Math.wsdl**

Next, we need to add the Globus-supplied **DestroyProvider** operation provider to the instance service. This provider implements the **destroy** operation mentioned above.

```xml
<?xml version="1.0" encoding="UTF-8"?>
<deployment name="defaultServerConfig"
    xmlns="http://xml.apache.org/axis/wsdd/"
    xmlns:java="http://xml.apache.org/axis/wsdd/providers/java"
    xmlns:xsd="http://www.w3.org/2001/XMLSchema">


    <!-- Instance service -->
    <service name="examples/core/rl/MathService" provider="Handler"
            use="literal" style="document">
        <parameter name="className" value="org.globus.examples.services.
            core.rl.impl.MathService"/>
        <wsdlFile>share/schema/examples/MathService_instance_rl/Math_
            service.wsdl</wsdlFile>
        <parameter name="allowedMethods" value="*"/>
        <parameter name="handlerClass" value="org.globus.axis.providers.
            RPCProvider"/>
        <parameter name="scope" value="Application"/>
        <parameter name="providers" value="GetRPProvider DestroyProvider"/>
    </service>


    <!-- Factory service -->
    <service name="examples/core/rl/MathFactoryService" provider="Handler"
            use="literal" style="document">
        <parameter name="className" value="org.globus.examples.services.
            core.rl.impl.MathFactoryService"/>
```

```
        <wsdlFile>share/schema/examples/FactoryService/Factory_
            service.wsdl</wsdlFile>

        <parameter name="allowedMethods" value="*"/>

        <parameter name="handlerClass" value="org.globus.axis.providers.
            RPCProvider"/>

        <parameter name="scope" value="Application"/>

    </service>

</deployment>
```

☞ This file is **$EXAMPLES_DIR/org/globus/examples/services/core/rl/deploy-server.wsdd**.

Now, we can compile the service:

> **./globus-build-service.sh rl**

And deploy it:

> **globus-deploy-gar $EXAMPLES_DIR/org_globus_examples_services_wsrf_core_rl.gar**

To try out resource destruction, we will use a client that is identical to the simple client seen in Chapter 8. The only difference is that, at the end of the client we will add a call to the **destroy** operation.

```
package org.globus.examples.clients.FactoryService_Math_rl;


import org.apache.axis.message.addressing.Address;

import org.apache.axis.message.addressing.EndpointReferenceType;

import org.globus.examples.stubs.Factory.CreateResource;

import org.globus.examples.stubs.Factory.CreateResourceResponse;

import org.globus.examples.stubs.Factory.FactoryPortType;

import org.globus.examples.stubs.Factory.service.
        FactoryServiceAddressingLocator;

import org.globus.examples.stubs.MathService_instance_rl.MathPortType;

import org.globus.examples.stubs.MathService_instance_rl.service.
        MathServiceAddressingLocator;

import org.oasis.wsrf.lifetime.Destroy;
```

```
/* This client creates a new MathService instance through a FactoryService.
         This client
 * expects one parameter: the factory URI.
 */
public class Client_immed {

        public static void main(String[] args) {
                FactoryServiceAddressingLocator factoryLocator = new
                        FactoryServiceAddressingLocator();
                MathServiceAddressingLocator instanceLocator = new
                        MathServiceAddressingLocator();

                try {
                        String factoryURI = args[0];
                        EndpointReferenceType factoryEPR, instanceEPR;
                        FactoryPortType mathFactory;
                        MathPortType math;

                        // Get factory portType
                        factoryEPR = new EndpointReferenceType();
                        factoryEPR.setAddress(new Address(factoryURI));
                        mathFactory = factoryLocator.getFactoryPortTypePort
                                (factoryEPR);

                        // Create resource and get endpoint reference of
                                WS-Resource.
                        CreateResourceResponse createResponse = mathFactory.
                                createResource(new CreateResource());
                        instanceEPR = createResponse.getEndpointReference();

                        System.out.println("Created WS-Resource.");
```

```
                        // Get instance service PortType
                        math = instanceLocator.getMathPortTypePort
                                (instanceEPR);

                        // Perform an addition
                        math.add(10);
                        // Perform another addition
                        math.add(5);

                        // Perform a subtraction
                        math.subtract(5);

                        math.destroy(new Destroy());
                        System.out.println("Destroyed WS-Resource.");
                } catch (Exception e) {
                        e.printStackTrace();
                }
        }
}
```

☞ This file is **$EXAMPLES_DIR/org/globus/examples/clients/**
FactoryService_Math_rl/Client_immed.java

Compile the client:

**javac **

**-classpath ./build/stubs/classes/:$CLASSPATH **

org/globus/examples/clients/FactoryService_Math_rl/Client_immed.java

And run it:

**java **

**-classpath ./build/stubs/classes/:$CLASSPATH **

org.globus.examples.clients.FactoryService_Math_rl.Client_immed

http://127.0.0.1:8080/wsrf/services/examples/core/rl/MathFactoryService

If all goes well, you should see the following:

> **Created WS-Resource.**
>
> **Destroyed WS-Resource.**

Well, that wasn't too exciting, was it? How do we really know that resource destruction is actually happening? Well, there's a simple way of testing it. Modify the last lines of the client so they will look like so:

```
math.destroy(new Destroy());

System.out.println("Destroyed WS-Resource.");


// Perform another addition

math.add(5);
```

As you can see, we are going to try to invoke an operation *after* destroying the resource that operation is supposed to use. As you can probably imagine, no good will come of this. If you recompile the client and run it again, you should again see the following:

> **Created WS-Resource.**
>
> **Destroyed WS-Resource.**

And, then, the following error message:

> **ERROR: java.rmi.RemoteException: Specified resource does not exist; nested**
>
> **exception is:**
>
> **org.globus.wsrf.NoSuchResourceException**

What has just happened is that the **add** has been invoked as normal. However, the endpoint reference that is being passed in the call refers to a resource that no longer exists. So, when **add** tries to retrieve the resource, a **NoSuchResourceException** is thrown.

11.2 Scheduled Destruction

Scheduled destruction is a more elaborate form of resource lifecycle management, as it allows us to specify exactly when we want the resource to be destroyed. The main application of scheduled destruction is to perform *lease-based lifecycle management*, where we initially set the destruction time of a resource some time in the future (for example, 5 minutes). This is called the *lease*. Our application must periodically *renew the lease* (setting the destruction time another 5 minutes in the future), or the resource will eventually be destroyed. This will allow our application to purge resources from services that for some reason (network failure, programmer errors, etc.) have become unavailable (and therefore can't receive the lease renewal).

Using scheduled destruction requires adding more code that immediate destruction because the standard WSRF portType that provides scheduled destruction not only adds a new operation (**SetTerminationTime**) but also two new resource properties: **Termination-Time** and **CurrentTime**. **TerminationTime** specifies when the resource is set to be destroyed, and the value of **CurrentTime** must always be the time in the machine that hosts the resource. This means that, not only will we have to modify the WSDL file, we will also have to make sure those two new resource properties are properly implemented in our resource class.

11.2.1   The WSDL File

So, let's start with the easy part. To use scheduled resource termination, our portType must extend from the **ScheduledResourceTermination** portType:

```
<portType name="MathPortType"

    wsdlpp:extends="wsrpw:GetResourceProperty

            wsrlw:ScheduledResourceTermination"

    wsrp:ResourceProperties="tns:MathResourceProperties">


        <operation name="add">

            <input message="tns:AddInputMessage"/>

            <output message="tns:AddOutputMessage"/>

        </operation>


        <operation name="subtract">

            <input message="tns:SubtractInputMessage"/>

            <output message="tns:SubtractOutputMessage"/>

        </operation>


</portType>
```

> ☞ As seen in immediate destruction, we mustn't forget to declare the WS-ResourceLifetime namespace (**wsrlw**), and import its WSDL file.

11.2.2   The Resource Implementation

Next, we have to implement the **ResourceLifetime** interface in our resource class. This interface requires that we provide get/set methods for the **TerminationTime** and **CurrentTime** RPs.

```
public class MathResource implements Resource, ResourceIdentifier,

            ResourceProperties, ResourceLifetime
```

So, we'll start by adding a **terminationTime** attribute of type **Calendar** to our class to represent the resource's termination time. We don't need to add a **currentTime** attribute because that RP's get method will always return the system's time (which, as we'll see, we can easily obtain using the Java API).

```
/* Resource properties */

private int value;

private String lastOp;

private Calendar terminationTime;
```

Now, we have to make sure we add the two RPs to our resource's RP set:

```
/* Initializes RPs and returns a unique identifier for this resource */

public Object initialize() throws Exception {

        this.key = uuidGen.nextUUID();

        this.propSet = new SimpleResourcePropertySet(
                    MathConstants.RESOURCE_PROPERTIES);


        ResourceProperty valueRP = new ReflectionResourceProperty(
                    MathConstants.RP_VALUE, "Value", this);
        this.propSet.add(valueRP);
        setValue(0);


        ResourceProperty lastOpRP = new ReflectionResourceProperty(
                    MathConstants.RP_LASTOP, "LastOp", this);
        this.propSet.add(lastOpRP);
        setLastOp("NONE");
```

```
        ResourceProperty termTimeRP = new ReflectionResourceProperty(
                    SimpleResourcePropertyMetaData.TERMINATION_TIME, this);
        this.propSet.add(termTimeRP);


        ResourceProperty currTimeRP = new ReflectionResourceProperty(
                    SimpleResourcePropertyMetaData.CURRENT_TIME, this);
        this.propSet.add(currTimeRP);


        return key;
    }
```

Notice we use a Globus-supplied **SimpleResourcePropertyMetaData** class which includes information on the **TerminationTime** and **CurrentTime** RPs. We must make sure we import this class:

```
    import org.globus.wsrf.impl.SimpleResourcePropertyMetaData;
```

Finally, the last thing needed in the resource implementation is to add a **get** and **set** method for the **TerminationTime** RP, and a **get** method for the **CurrentTime** RP (we can't "set" the current time). Take into account that having only a **get** method for this RP works fine with **ReflectionResourceProperty**, which will realize that this is a read-only RP.

```
    /* Required by interface ResourceLifetime */
    public Calendar getCurrentTime() {
        return Calendar.getInstance();
    }


    public Calendar getTerminationTime() {
        return this.terminationTime;
    }


    public void setTerminationTime(Calendar terminationTime) {
        this.terminationTime=terminationTime;
    }
```

⌖ This is part of file **EXAMPLES_DIR/org/globus/examples/services/core/rl/impl/ MathResource.java**

11.2.3 Deployment

As we did in immediate destruction, we need to add a Globus-supplied operation provider, **SetTerminationTimeProvider**, to the instance service. This provider implements the **set-TerminationTime** operation that will allow us to set the resource's termination time. Note that we *cannot* set the termination time by directly modifying the **TerminationTime** RP (using, for example, the **SetResourceProperties** operation). We must use the **setTerminationTime** operation (this operation, as implemented in the Globus-supplied operation provider, does more than just update the RP).

```
<parameter name="providers" value="GetRPProvider SetTerminationTimeProvider"/>
```

☞ This is part of file **EXAMPLES_DIR/org/globus/examples/services/core/rl/deploy-server.wsdd**.

We can also modify the JNDI deploy file to control how often the container will check if a resource is past its termination time. This is done with the **sweeperDelay** parameter, specified in milliseconds. The default value is to check every one minute (60,000 milliseconds). We will change this value to one second (1000 milliseconds) so our client will be able to observe how the resource does, in fact, expire.

```
<parameter>

        <name>sweeperDelay</name>

        <value>1000</value>

</parameter>
```

☞ This is part of file **EXAMPLES_DIR/org/globus/examples/services/core/rl/deploy-jndi-config.xml**.

Finally, build and deploy:

```
./globus-build-service.sh rl

globus-deploy-gar EXAMPLES_DIR/org_globus_examples_services_wsrf_core_rl.gar
```

11.2.4 The Client

We will test our service by creating a new resource, setting its termination 10 seconds in the future, and then checking every second to see if the resource is still "alive." When the resource is terminated, any call to the resource will produce an exception. Like the immediate destruction client, this client is similar to the simple client seen in Chapter 8.

The following is the code that we will run after the resource has been created:

❶

```
Calendar termination = Calendar.getInstance();
termination.add(Calendar.SECOND, 10);
```

❷

```
SetTerminationTime request;
SetTerminationTimeResponse response;
request = new SetTerminationTime(termination);
response = math.setTerminationTime(request);
```

❸

```
System.out.println("Current time          "
            + response.getCurrentTime().getTime());
System.out.println("Requested termination time "
            + termination.getTime());
System.out.println("Scheduled termination time "
            + response.getNewTerminationTime().getTime());

boolean terminated = false;
int seconds = 0;
while (!terminated) { ❹
      try {
            System.out.println("Second " + seconds);
            math.add(10);
            Thread.sleep(1000);
            seconds++;
      } catch (RemoteException e) {
            System.out.println("Resource has been destroyed");
            terminated = true;
      }
}
```

> ☞ This is part of file **EXAMPLES_DIR/org/globus/examples/clients/**
> **FactoryService_Math_rl/Client_sched.java**

❶ We get an instance of the **Calendar** class, which contains the current time. We add 10 seconds to it. This will be the termination time of our resource.

❷ We make a call to the **SetTerminationTime** operation, sending the new termination time.

❸ The response from the **SetTerminationTime** operation returns interesting information: the resource's current time and the *scheduled* termination, which might differ from the requested termination time (in simple scenarios like the one we are trying out now, this will not happen).

❹ Finally, this loop makes a call to the **add** operation every second. When the resource is finally destroyed, and an exception is thrown, we exit the loop.

Compile and run the client:

```
javac \
-classpath ./build/stubs/classes/:$CLASSPATH \
org/globus/examples/clients/FactoryService_Math_rl/Client_sched.java
```

```
java \
-classpath ./build/stubs/classes/:$CLASSPATH \
org.globus.examples.clients.FactoryService_Math_rl.Client_sched \
http://127.0.0.1:8080/wsrf/services/examples/core/rl/MathFactoryService
```

If all goes well, you should see the following:

```
Created WS-Resource.
Current time              Sun Apr 03 00:54:29 CST 2005
Requested termination time Sun Apr 03 00:54:39 CST 2005
Scheduled termination time Sun Apr 03 00:54:39 CST 2005
Second 0
Second 1
Second 2
Second 3
Second 4
Second 5
```

Second 6

Second 7

Second 8

Second 9

Second 10

Resource has been destroyed

11.3 Performing an Action When a Resource is Destroyed

Java WS Core includes an interface called **RemoveCallback** that, when implemented by a resource class, will allow us to perform an action when the resource is going to be destroyed. This method requires that we implement a **remove** method, where we can include any code we want. Usually, we will want to release any system resources (database connections, network connections, etc.) which might be held by our resource class. In the next chapter, in fact, we will use **RemoveCallback** when managing persistent resources.

For example:

```
public class MathResource implements Resource, ResourceIdentifier,
                ResourceProperties, ResourceLifetime, RemoveCallback {

    // Other methods
    /* Required by interface RemoveCallback */
    public void remove()
    {
            logger.info("Resource is going to be removed.");
    }
}
```

☞ If you take a look at the source code of the example seen throughout this chapter, you will notice that this snippet of code is already included. If you look back at the server logs, you will see that a "Resource id going to be removed" message is printed before a resource is destroyed.

11.4 Command-Line Clients

GT4 includes a set of command-line clients we can use to destroy a resource or modify its termination time without having to write a client specifically for a certain service. All the GT4 command-line clients have a set of common options which are described in Appendix C, Command-line clients.

11.4.1 wsrf-destroy

This command uses the **ImmediateResourceTermination** portType to destroy a resource.

Usage

```
wsrf-destroy [common options]
```

Note: This command has no specific parameters. The common options must be used to specify what resource has to be destroyed.

Example

To try this client, we must first create a new resource. However, the clients we have seen in this chapter create a resource and then destroy it themselves. So, we will have to use a new client that creates a resource and returns its endpoint reference. This client is identical to the one seen in Section 8.9.1, "The creating client."

> ☞ The client that creates a new resource in the service described in this chapter is:
> **$EXAMPLES_DIR/org/globus/examples/clients/FactoryService_Math_rl/**
> **ClientCreate.java**

Compile the client:

```
javac \
-classpath ./build/stubs/classes/:$CLASSPATH \
org/globus/examples/clients/FactoryService_Math_rl/ClientCreate.java
```

And run it:

```
java \
-classpath ./build/stubs/classes/:$CLASSPATH \
org.globus.examples.clients.FactoryService_Math_rl.ClientCreate \
http://127.0.0.1:8080/wsrf/services/examples/core/rl/MathFactoryService
```

An endpoint reference will we written to file **epr.txt**. We can now use this file as a parameter to **wsrf-destroy**.

```
wsrf-destroy -e epr.txt
```

11.4.2 wsrf-set-termination-time

This command uses the **ScheduledResourceTermination** portType to schedule the destruction of a resource.

Usage

```
wsrf-set-termination-time [common options] ( <seconds> | "infinity" )
```

If **seconds** are specified, then the resource is scheduled to be destroyed that many seconds in the future. If **infinity** is specified, any scheduled destruction is canceled (the resource must now be explicitly destroyed, or another termination time must be scheduled).

Example

Once again, we must use the **ClientCreate** client described above to create a new resource. The following command sets its termination time 100 seconds in the future:

```
wsrf-set-termination-time -e epr.txt 100
```

The expected output is:

requested: DATE TIME

scheduled: DATE TIME

☞ In this case, the scheduled time should be 100 seconds in the future, relative to the current system time. Note that the requested and scheduled termination times will usually be the same.

To cancel the scheduled destruction:

```
wsrf-set-termination-time -e epr.txt infinity
```

Expected output:

requested: infinity

scheduled: infinity

References

[1] "WS-ResourceLifetime specification". 1.2 Working Draft 01. *Web Services Resource Framework (WSRF) TC*. OASIS, June, 2004.

chapter **12**

Persistent Resources

Up to this point in the book, all our resources have been *in-memory resources*. In other words, the objects representing our resources were stored in main memory (RAM). In some cases, however, it is preferable for our resources to be *persistent*, or stored in secondary storage (disk, database, etc.). In this chapter we will explain how to add persistence to our resources. We will start by providing comparison of in-memory and persistent resources. Next, we provide an overview of the **PersistentResource** interface which must be implemented by persistent resources. Then, we show how we can add persistence to our MathService example. Finally, we conclude by briefly discussing how we can use *resource caches* to improve our application's performance.

12.1 In-Memory vs. Persistent

Having our resources stored in memory can work fine in many cases, but there are also many cases where in-memory resources are not a good option. This type of resource has two main disadvantages:

- **They don't survive container restarts:** When a container is stopped, all its in-memory information is lost. In some cases, this might be perfectly OK for us but, in many cases, we will want our resources to survive container restarts.

- **They consume main memory:** Main memory (RAM) is limited and, if we need to manage large amounts of resources, our system's performance could be impacted.

Persistent resources, on the other hand, reside in secondary storage, such as files on a disk or a database. Whenever the container needs to use a particular resource, it will bring it into memory, and will write it again into secondary storage whenever the resource is modified. This helps persistent resources overcome the two disadvantages of in-memory resources:

- **They survive container restarts:** A container restart does not affect persistent resources, which are not stored in main memory but in secondary storage. Next time the container starts, it simply has to retrieve the resource from disk.

- **They consume secondary storage:** Secondary storage (such as a hard drive) is much larger than main memory, so it is harder to exhaust system resources by having too many resources.

Of course, persistent resources sound really nifty, but they're not the panacea. Their main disadvantage is *performance*. Reading a resource from secondary storage is much slower than reading it from main memory. Although caching strategies can be used to improve performance, it's difficult to outperform a pure in-memory implementation. In your applications, you will have to balance the benefits of persistent resources against their cost (performance) to decide if they're really worth your while. In fact, in Part IV, we will face exactly that decision when designing a GT4-based application.

12.2   The PersistentResource Interface

To make our resources persistent, our resource class must implement the **Persistent-Resource** interface. Furthermore, our resource home must be able to handle this type of resource. The Globus-supplied **ResourceHomeImpl** (used in the previous chapters) is already capable of handling persistent resources so, unless we are implementing our own resource home from scratch (i.e. not extending from **ResourceHomeImpl**), we only have to worry about implementing the **PersistentResource** interface. This interface is, in fact, an extension of three interfaces we have already seen and a new interface called **PersistenceCallback**.

```
package org.globus.wsrf;


public interface PersistentResource
        extends Resource, ResourceIdentifier, PersistenceCallback,
            RemoveCallback {
}
```

Remember that **Resource** is an interface that "tags" our class as representing a resource. **ResourceIdentifier** (seen in Chapter 8) requires that we implement the **getID** method returning a unique identifier for the resource. Although you can conceivably add persistence to a singleton resource, it makes sense mostly for services with multiple resource (as described in Chapter 8). Finally, the **RemoveCallback** interface (seen in the previous chapter) requires that we implement a **remove** method, which gets called right before the resource is destroyed.

The **PersistenceCallback** interface requires that we implement two methods, **load** and **store**, which handle the resource's persistence.

```
public interface PersistenceCallback {

        void load(ResourceKey key) throws ResourceException,

                                          NoSuchResourceException,

                                          InvalidResourceKeyException;

        void store() throws ResourceException;

}
```

12.2.1 The **load** Method

The **load** method is responsible for loading a resource, given its key, from secondary storage into memory. When using **ResourceHomeImpl**, the resource home automatically calls **load** when a resource has to be retrieved from disk.

In general, we will need to perform the following actions inside the **load** method:

1. Validate that the *key* parameter is correct. In other words, we need to check whether a resource with that key exists in secondary storage (a file, a row in a database, etc.).

2. Initialize the resource. As seen in previous examples (in the **initialize** method), this involves creating a resource property set and initializing each individual resource property (which must be added to the resource property set).

3. Read the RP values from secondary storage, and place them in our in-memory RPs.

12.2.2 The **store** Method

The **store** method is responsible for storing a resource into secondary storage. **Resource-HomeImpl** does not call **store** at any point, so we alone are responsible for calling **store** whenever a resource has to be persisted. In general, we will need to invoke **store** every time we modify the value of an RP.

In general, the only thing we need to do in the **store** method is to take the values of our RPs and write them to secondary storage. This might involve, for example, writing a file or updating a row in a database.

12.2.3 Cleaning Up

The reason why the **PersistentResource** interface requires that we implement the **RemoveCallback** interface (seen in Section 11.3) is because, when dealing with persistent resources, we will generally want to make sure we "clean up" after a resource is destroyed.

For example, if our resource is persisted to a database, we want to make sure we delete the row representing that resource when the resource is destroyed.

So, remember that we will need to implement the **remove** method, which gets called when the resource is destroyed:

```
/* Required by interface RemoveCallback */

public void remove()

{

        // Remove resource from secondary storage (file, database, etc.)

}
```

12.3   Adding Persistence to MathService

We will now make the resources in MathService persistent using a Globus-supplied **FilePersistenceHelper** that allows us to persist resources to files. The example in this chapter is based on the one seen in the previous chapter, which will allow us to invoke the **Destroy** operation to observe what happens when we destroy a persistent resource. All major changes are confined to the **MathResource** class, which will now implement the **PersistentResource** interface:

```
public class MathResource implements PersistentResource, ResourceProperties,

    ResourceLifetime {

        // ...

}
```

Of course, there will also be minor changes to the deployment files to reflect a new service path.

☞ The code for this example can be found in **$EXAMPLES_DIR/org/globus/ examples/services/core/persistent/**

The resource class is **$EXAMPLES_DIR/org/globus/examples/services/core/ persistent/impl/MathResource**.java

The factory service path is now **examples/core/persistent/MathFactoryService**. The instance service path is now **examples/core/persistent/MathService**.

12.3.1   Tweaking the `initialize` Method

Before we actually start implementing the **PersistentResource** interface, we need to tweak the *initialize* method. Remember that, in previous chapters, this method created a unique identifier for the resource, initialized the resource properties, and returned the resource identifier:

```
/* Initializes RPs and returns a unique identifier for this resource */
public Object initialize() throws Exception {
        this.key = uuidGen.nextUUID();
        this.propSet = new SimpleResourcePropertySet(
                    MathConstants.RESOURCE_PROPERTIES);


        // Initialize resource properties


        return key;
    }
```

This **initialize** method was only called from our **MathResourceHome**. However, now we will need to initialize a resource from two different places. The resource home will continue to initialize new resources, but the **load** method will also need to initialize methods for which the resource identifier is already known (when it needs to initialize a resource whose RPs are going to be retrieved from secondary storage).

So, we now need two **initialize** methods: one that creates a key for the resource, and one that initializes a resource given its key. The latter is just like the **initialize** method used in previous chapters, except that the key is passed as a parameter to the method:

```
/* Initializes resource with a given key */
public void initialize(Object key) throws Exception {
        this.key = key;
        this.propSet = new SimpleResourcePropertySet(
                    MathConstants.RESOURCE_PROPERTIES);
        // Initialize resource properties
    }
```

The other **initialize** method (the one invoked by the resource home) creates a new key, and then calls the **initialize** method above. Notice how we also call the **store** method to make sure we persist the recently created resource.

```
/* Initializes resource and returns a unique identifier for this resource */
public Object initialize() throws Exception {
        String key = uuidGen.nextUUID();
```

```
    initialize(key);

    store();

    return key;

}
```

12.3.2   Using FilePersistenceHelper

The Globus-supplied **FilePersistenceHelper** allows us to easily persist a resource to a file sparing most (but not all) of the I/O code. When using this handy little class, we will be mostly responsible for actually writing the RPs to the file. **FilePersistenceHelper** will take care of creating (and later deleting) the file representation of the resource. The name of each file will be composed of the resource identifier along with an extension chosen by us. For example, if we had a resource whose identifier is **89b89cb2cfda**, it would be saved to a file called **89b89cb2cfda.data** (assuming we chose the **.data** extension). By default, these files are stored in the following directory:

/home/globus/.globus/persisted/*hostname*/*resource_class*

This path assumes that user **globus** is running the container. Furthermore, it is possible to use a non-default directory (we'll see how to do this later on).

> ✍ In GT4.0.1, the default directory is different, and includes the IP of the machine and the port the container is listening on:
>
> /home/globus/.globus/persisted/*ip-port*/*resource_class*
>
> This was changed to accommodate multiple containers running in a single machine. For example, assuming that you are running the container with IP 123.231.132.213 and using port 8080, the directory would be:
>
> /home/globus/.globus/persisted/123.231.132.213-8080/*resource_class*

To use **FilePersistenceHelper**, we will add a **persistenceHelper** attribute to our resource class. We will also include a protected **get** method that first checks if the **persistenceHelper** attribute has been created (if it hasn't, the **get** method will create it).

```
public class MathResource implements PersistentResource, ResourceProperties,
        ResourceLifetime {


    /* Persistence helper class */
    private FilePersistenceHelper persistenceHelper;
```

```
// Other attributes

/* Returns this resource's FilePersistenceHelper object */
protected synchronized FilePersistenceHelper getPersistenceHelper() {
    /* If the persistenceHelper has not been created, create it */
    if (this.persistenceHelper == null) {
        try {
                this.persistenceHelper =
                    new FilePersistenceHelper(this
                        .getClass(), ".data");}
        } catch (Exception e) {
            throw new RuntimeException(e.getMessage());
        }
    }
    /* Return the persistenceHelper */
    return this.persistenceHelper;
}


    // Other methods
}
```

Notice how the **FilePersistenceHelper** constructors expects two parameters: the **Class** of our resource class, and the extension of the resource file. **FilePersistenceHelper** has an additional constructor which allows us to specify the directory where the files must be placed:

```
FilePersistenceHelper(Class resourceCLass, String storageDir, String extension)
```

Note that **FilePersistenceHelper** will create the file in a *hostname/resource_class* directory inside the storage directory we specify.

Next, we also include a private **getKeyAsFile** method that invokes the method of the same name in our **FilePersistenceHelper** attribute. This method simply checks, as an added precaution, that the key we specify is a **String**.

```
private File getKeyAsFile(Object key) throws InvalidResourceKeyException {
    /*
     * If the key is a String, we use the FilePersistenceHelper to
     * retrieve the resource
     */
```

```
            if (key instanceof String) {
                    return getPersistenceHelper().getKeyAsFile(key);
                    /* Otherwise, an exception is thrown */
            } else {
                    throw new InvalidResourceKeyException();
            }
    }
```

12.3.3   The **store** Method

Now, let's take a look at what goes on in the **store** method. Instead of directly writing to the resource file, we will first create a temporary file, and then rename it to the resource file. This will make it easier to recover from errors during the writing process.

```
    public synchronized void store() throws ResourceException {
            ❶
            FileOutputStream fos = null;
            File tmpFile = null;

            logger.info("Attempting to store resource " + this.getID());
            try {
                    ❷
                    tmpFile = File.createTempFile("math", ".tmp",
                                    getPersistenceHelper().getStorageDirectory());
                    ❸
                    fos = new FileOutputStream(tmpFile);
                    ObjectOutputStream oos = new ObjectOutputStream(fos);
                    ❹
                    oos.writeInt(this.value);
                    oos.writeUTF(this.lastOp);
                    oos.writeObject(this.terminationTime);
                    oos.flush();
                    logger.info("Successfully stored resource with Value=" + value
                                    + " and LastOp=" + lastOp);
```

```
        } catch (Exception e) {
                ❺
                tmpFile.delete();
                throw new ResourceException("Failed to store resource", e);
        } finally {
                ❻
                if (fos != null) {
                    try {
                                fos.close();
                    } catch (Exception ee) {
                    }
                }
        }
        ❼


        File file = getKeyAsFile(this.key);
        if (file.exists()) {
                file.delete();
        }
        if (!tmpFile.renameTo(file)) {
                tmpFile.delete();
                throw new ResourceException("Failed to store resource");
        }
    }
```

❶ We will use the Java **FileOutputStream** class to write to disk. The **tmpFile** variable (of type **File**) will represent the temporary file.

❷ We start by creating the temporary file.

❸ We open the file for writing, and create an **ObjectOutputStream** that will allow us to easily write our RPs to the file.

❹ We write the RPs in the file. For writing other data types, take a look at **ObjectOutputStream** in the Java API.

❺ If an exception is thrown at any point, we delete the temporary file and throw a **ResourceException**.

❻ Regardless of whether the file is successfully created, we make sure we close the **FileOutputStream**.

❼ At this point, we have successfully created a temporary file with our resource's RPs. Now, if there is a previous copy of our resource on disk, we first have to delete it. Next, we rename the temporary file to the file representing our resource.

Don't forget that it is our responsibility to invoke **store** whenever it makes sense to persist the resource. As mentioned earlier, we will generally want to do this whenever we modify the value of an RP. So, we will need to modify the **set** methods for our RPs. For example, this is how the **get/set** methods for the **Value** RP would look like:

```
public int getValue() {
        return value;
}


public synchronized void setValue(int value) {
        this.value = value;
        try {
                store();
        } catch (Exception e) {
                throw new RuntimeException(e.getMessage());
        }
}
```

12.3.4   The **load** Method

Now, let's see what happens in the **load** method:

```
public void load(ResourceKey key) throws ResourceException {
        ❶
        File file = getKeyAsFile(key.getValue());
        if (!file.exists()) {
                throw new NoSuchResourceException();
        }


        ❷
        try {
                initialize(key.getValue());
```

```
} catch (Exception e) {
        throw new ResourceException("Failed to initialize resource", e);
}

logger.info("Attempting to load resource " + key.getValue());

❸
FileInputStream fis = null;
int value;
String lastOp;
Calendar terminationTime;

try {
        ❹
        fis = new FileInputStream(file);
        ObjectInputStream ois = new ObjectInputStream(fis);

        ❺
        value = ois.readInt();
        lastOp = ois.readUTF();
        terminationTime = (Calendar) ois.readObject();

        logger.info("Successfully loaded resource with Value=" + value
                        + " and LastOp=" + lastOp);

        ❻
        this.value = value;
        this.lastOp = lastOp;
        this.terminationTime = terminationTime;
} catch (Exception e) {
```

```
        ❼
                throw new ResourceException("Failed to load resource", e);
        } finally {
            ❽
            if (fis != null) {
                try {
                        fis.close();
                } catch (Exception ee) {
                }
            }
        }

    }
```

❶ First of all, we try to retrieve the persisted resource from disk. We do this using the **getKeyAsFile** method explained earlier. Notice that a **File** object is returned regardless of whether a resource with that key has been persisted or not. So, we need to check if the file exists or not. If the file does not exist, no resource with that key was ever persisted, so we obviously can't load it.

❷ We try to initialize the resource using the **initialize** method described earlier. Remember that this initializes the RPs, but places default values in them. We still have to load the values of the RPs from disk.

❸ We declare a couple of variables. We will use the Java **FileInputStream** class to read from the file. **value**, **lastOp**, and **terminationTime** will be used to store the values retrieved from the file.

❹ We open the file for reading and create an **ObjectInputStream** object that will allow us to easily read the RPs from the file.

❺ We read the RPs from the file. To read other data types, refer to the **ObjectInput-Stream** documentation on the official Java API.

❻ We assign the RPs to the resource class's attributes.

❼ If an exception is thrown at any point, we throw a **ResourceException**.

❽ Finally, we make sure we close the resource file, whether the load succeeds or not.

12.3.5   Cleaning Up

Finally, we have to make sure that once a resource is destroyed, its corresponding file is also deleted. We will do this using the **remove** method required by the **RemoveCallback** interface. To delete the file, we simply need to use the **remove** method in our **FilePersistenceHelper** attribute.

```
public void remove() throws ResourceException {

        logger.info("Resource " + this.getID() + " is going to be removed.");

        getPersistenceHelper().remove(this.key);

}
```

12.3.6 Trying it Out

After writing all that code, let's make sure that this actually works. We will create a new WS-Resource and see how it survives container restarts. First of all, let's build the service:

./globus-build-service.sh persistent

And deploy it:

globus-deploy-gar $EXAMPLES_DIR/org_globus_examples_services

_core_persistent.gar

To try out the service, we will use two clients: a client to create new WS-Resources and a client that will invoke the **add** operation on those WS-Resources. These clients are nearly identical to the ones seen in Section 8.9.

☞ The creation client is: **$EXAMPLES_DIR/org/globus/examples/clients/ FactoryService_Math_rl/ClientCreate.java**

The addition client is: **$EXAMPLES_DIR/org/globus/examples/clients/ MathService_instance_rl/ClientAdd.java**

Let's start by creating a new WS-Resource. Compile the creation client:

**javac **

**-classpath ./build/stubs/classes/:$CLASSPATH **

org/globus/examples/clients/FactoryService_Math_rl/ClientCreate.java

And run it:

**java **

**-classpath ./build/stubs/classes/:$CLASSPATH **

**org.globus.examples.clients.FactoryService_Math_rl.ClientCreate **

http://127.0.0.1:8080/wsrf/services/examples/core/persistent/MathFactoryService

The EPR of the WS-Resource will be written to an **epr.txt** file. If you take a look at the container's output, you will notice the following log messages:

```
Attempting to store resource f2f58050-d14e-11d9-931e-89b89cb2cfda
```

```
Successfully stored resource with Value=0 and LastOp=NONE
```

> ☞ Take into account that the key you will see in your log message will be different.

Remember that when initializing a new resource, we called the **store** method to make sure the new resource was immediately persisted to secondary storage. But, just in case you're skeptical about this whole persistence thingamajig, let's see how the resource has, in fact, been stored to a file.

Assuming you're running the container with the **globus** user, take a peek at the following directory:

/home/globus/.globus/persisted/127.0.0.1/MathResource

You should see the following file:

f2f58050-d14e-11d9-931e-89b89cb2cfda.data

Notice how the key matches the one shown in the log message. In case you're very curious, the file is binary, so you shouldn't try to open it and read it (unless you're fluent in reading hexadecimal dumps).

Now, let's try to modify the RPs of the resource and see how, thanks to resource persistence, the changes survive a container restart. Start by compiling the addition client:

```
javac \
-classpath ./build/stubs/classes/:$CLASSPATH \
org/globus/examples/clients/MathService_instance_rl/ClientAdd.java
```

And run it:

```
java \
-classpath ./build/stubs/classes/:$CLASSPATH \
org.globus.examples.clients.MathService_instance_rl.ClientAdd \
epr.txt \
10
```

You should see the following:

```
Value RP: 10
LastOp RP: ADDITION
```

Now run it again:

```
Value RP: 20

LastOp RP: ADDITION
```

If you take a look at the container's output, you should see the following:

```
Attempting to store resource f2f58050-d14e-11d9-931e-89b89cb2cfda
Successfully stored resource with Value=10 and LastOp=NONE


Attempting to store resource f2f58050-d14e-11d9-931e-89b89cb2cfda
Successfully stored resource with Value=10 and LastOp=ADDITION


Attempting to store resource f2f58050-d14e-11d9-931e-89b89cb2cfda
Successfully stored resource with Value=20 and LastOp=ADDITION


Attempting to store resource f2f58050-d14e-11d9-931e-89b89cb2cfda
Successfully stored resource with Value=20 and LastOp=ADDITION
```

Since invoking **add** involves modifying the **Value** RP and then the **LastOp** RP. So, you should see two pairs of messages each time you invoke **add**.

Now, stop the container and start it again. If we were using in-memory resources, our resource would disappear, never to be seen again. However, thanks to resource persistence, we can now laugh in the face of container restarts! Don't believe us? Try running the addition client again, exactly as instructed above (i.e. make sure you use the **epr.txt** of the WS-Resource we created before you restarted the container). You should see the following:

```
Value RP: 30

LastOp RP: ADDITION
```

This means that the container successfully retrieved the resource from disk (where the **Value** RP was saved with a value of 20) and then performed the **add** operation. This is confirmed by looking at the container's output, where you will see how the resource is loaded and then stored twice while invoking the **add** operation.

```
Attempting to load resource f2f58050-d14e-11d9-931e-89b89cb2cfda
Successfully loaded resource with Value=20 and LastOp=ADDITION


Attempting to store resource f2f58050-d14e-11d9-931e-89b89cb2cfda
Successfully stored resource with Value=30 and LastOp=ADDITION
```

```
Attempting to store resource f2f58050-d14e-11d9-931e-89b89cb2cfda
```

```
Successfully stored resource with Value=30 and LastOp=ADDITION
```

You have to admit, that was pretty cool, huh? Finally, let's take a look at what happens if we destroy the resource:

```
wsrf-destroy -e epr.txt
```

You should see the following message:

```
Destroy operation was successful
```

If you check the container's output, you will see the following:

```
Resource f2f58050-d14e-11d9-931e-89b89cb2cfda is going to be removed.
```

Furthermore, if you check the directory where the persisted resources are stored, you will see how the resource's file has been deleted.

12.4 The Resource Cache

At the beginning of the chapter we mentioned that the main disadvantage of using persistent resources was performance, for a very simple reason: secondary storage (files, databases, etc.) is slower than main memory. However, we can improve performance by using a *resource cache*. A cache keeps some of the resources in-memory so that we won't have to access the disk every time we want to use a resource. The resources that get to stay in the cache depends on our caching strategy and, more specifically, on the replacement algorithm we use to determine when a resource has to be removed from the cache to make room for other resources.

If you've studied operating systems, or computer architecture, this will probably sound pretty familiar. Caching strategies and replacement algorithms are a big part of improving the performance of memory chips. However, they are way outside the scope of this book, and we will simply explain how you can use a Globus-supplied cache to improve the performance of your persistent resources, without giving an in-depth explanation of how the cache actually works. If you *do* want to learn more about caches and replacement algorithms, a good starting point could be [1] and [2].

GT4 includes a resource cache that uses the LRU (Least Recently Used) replacement algorithm. To use it, we will need to modify out JNDI deployment file to (1) include a new **<resource>** called **cache** with the configuration options of the cache, and (2) tell our service to use that cache.

```
<service name="examples/core/persistent/MathService">

    <resource name="home" type="org.globus.examples.services.core

        .persistent.impl.MathResourceHome">
```

```
<resourceParams>

        <!-- Other resource parameters -->

        ❶
        <parameter>
                <name>cacheLocation</name>
                <value>java:comp/env/services/examples/core/persistent/
                        MathService/cache</value>
        </parameter>


</resourceParams>
</resource>

        ❷
<resource name="cache" type="org.globus.wsrf.utils.cache.LRUCache">
<resourceParams>
        <parameter>
                <name>factory</name>
                <value>org.globus.wsrf.jndi.BeanFactory</value>
        </parameter>
        <parameter>
                <name>timeout</name>
                <value> 120000 </value>
        </parameter>
</resourceParams>
</resource>
</service>
```

☞ This is part of file **EXAMPLES_DIR/org/globus/examples/services/core/persistent/**
deploy-jndi-config.xml

❶ We use the **cacheLocation** parameter in our resource home to specify what cache we want to use.

❷ Using a new **<resource>** (named **cache**), we specify what class will act as cache (the Globus-supplied **LRUCache**) and we supply some parameters. The **timeout** parameter refers to the time (in milliseconds) a resource must remain idle before it is removed from the cache.

The code above was already included in the example we ran earlier. This is the reason why, when accessing the resource several times in a row (for example, when invoking **add** repeatedly) the resource was not being loaded from disk every single time. The resource home retrieved it from the cache instead of reading it from disk.

☞ GT4 only includes the **LRUCache** class. However, if you have some performance requirements and need to implement your own resource cache, you can do so by implementing the **Cache** interface. More details on this interface are found in the Globus API.

References

[1] "Cache". *Wikipedia*. http://en.wikipedia.org/wiki/Cache.

[2] "Cache algorithms". *Wikipedia*. http://en.wikipedia.org/wiki/Cache_algorithms.

chapter **13**

Notifications

In this chapter we will introduce the concept of *notification*, a common design pattern that allows clients to be notified when interesting events happen in a server. In particular, we will focus on WS-Notifications, a family of specification that allow us to use this design pattern with Web Services. Then, we will see two examples of how we can use notifications in our services.

13.1   What Are Notifications?

Notifications are nothing new. It's a very popular software design pattern, although you might know it with a different name, such as Observer/Observable. Let's suppose that our software had several distinct parts (e.g. a GUI and the application logic, a client and a server, etc.) and that one of the parts of the software needs to be aware of the changes that happen in one of the other parts. For example, the GUI might need to know when a value is changed in a database, so that the new value is immediately displayed to the user. Taking this to the client/server world is easy: suppose a client needs to know when the server reaches a certain state, so the client can perform a certain action.

The most crude approach to keep the client informed is a *polling* approach (Figure13.1). The client periodically *polls* the server (asks if there are any changes). For example, let's suppose a client applications wants to know when the load of a server drops below 50%. The server is called the *producer* of events (in this case, the event is a drop in the server load). The client, on the other hand, is called the *consumer* of events. The polling approach would go like this:

1. The consumer asks the producer if there are any changes. The producer replies "No", so the consumer waits a while before making another call.

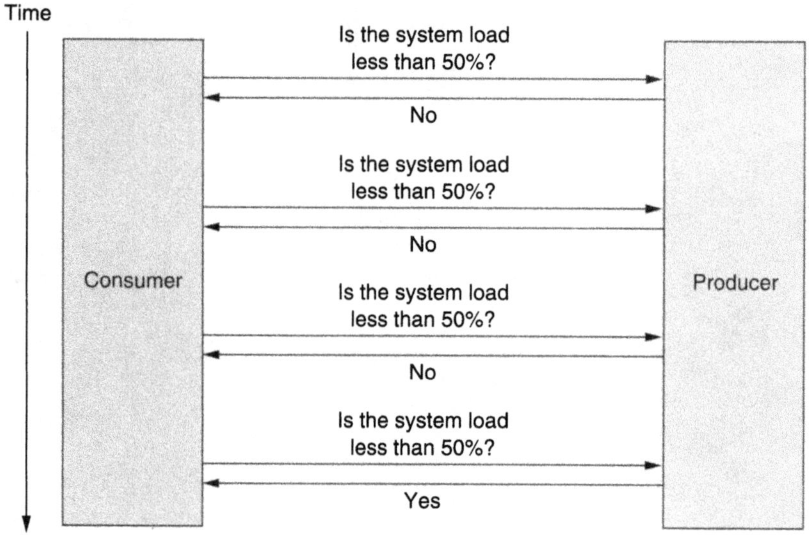

Time

Figure 13.1: Keeping track of changes using polling

2. Once again, the consumer asks the producer if there are any changes. The producer replies "No", so the consumer waits a while before making another call.

3. As you can see, this step can be repeated *ad nauseam* until the server finally replies that there has been a change.

This approach isn't very efficient, specially if you consider the following:

- If the time between calls is very small, the amount of network traffic and CPU use increases.

- There can be more than one consumer. If we have dozens of consumers, waiting for an event to happen, then the producer could get saturated with calls asking it if there are any changes.

The answer to this problem is actually terribly simple (and common sense). Instead of periodically asking the producer if there are any changes, we make an initial call asking the producer to *notify* the consumer whenever a certain event occurs. This is the *notification* approach (Figure 13.2).

1. The consumer asks the producer to notify him as soon as the server load drops below 50%. The producer keeps a list of all its registered consumers. This step is normally called the *subscription* or *registration* step.

2. The consumer and the producer go about their business until the server load drops below 50%.

Time

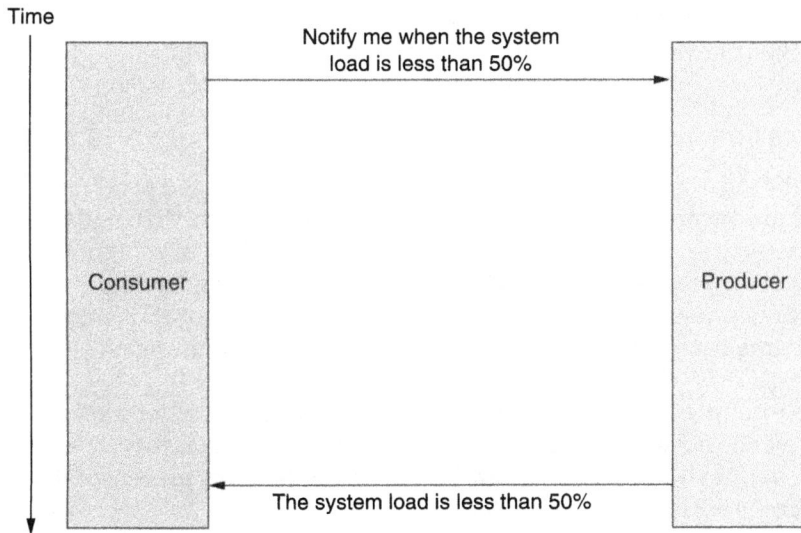

Figure 13.2: Keeping track of changes using notifications

3. Once the server load drops below 50%, the producer *notifies* all its consumers (remember, there can be more than one) of that event.

As you can see, this approach is much more efficient (in this simple example, network traffic has been sliced in half with respect to the polling approach).

13.2 WS-Notifications

The WS-Notifications family of specifications, although not a part of WSRF, has strong ties to it. It provides a set of standard interfaces to use the notification design pattern with Web Services. WS-Notifications is divided into three specifications: WS-Topics, WS-BaseNotification, and WS-BrokeredNotification.

13.2.1 WS-Topics

First of all, we have *topics*, which are used by the other two specifications in WS-Notifications to present a set of "items of interest for subscription". As we will see next, a service can publish a set of topics that clients can subscribe to, and receive a notification whenever the topic changes. Topics are very versatile, as they even allow us to create *topic trees*, where a topic can have a set of *child topics*. One possible use of this feature is for a client to subscribe to a topic and then have it automatically receive notifications from all the descendent topics (without having to manually subscribe to each of them).

13.2.2   WS-BaseNotification

This specification defines the standard interfaces of notification consumers and producers. In a nutshell, notification producers have to expose a *subscribe* operation that notification consumers can use to request a subscription. Consumers, in turn, have to expose a *notify* operation that producers can use to deliver the notification. Furthermore, the client actually requesting the subscription need not necessarily be the consumer of those notifications. In other words, clients can perform subscriptions "on behalf of other notification consumers".

Figure 13.3 shows an example interaction between a notification consumer and producer, in the simple case when the subscriber and consumer are the same entity. In this example we have a single notification consumer, and a single notification producer that publishes two topics: **SystemLoadHigh** and **SystemFault**.

1. First of all, the notification consumer subscribes himself to the **SystemLoadHigh** topic. It is interesting to note that, internally, a **Subscription** resource is created with information regarding the subscription (not shown in the figure).

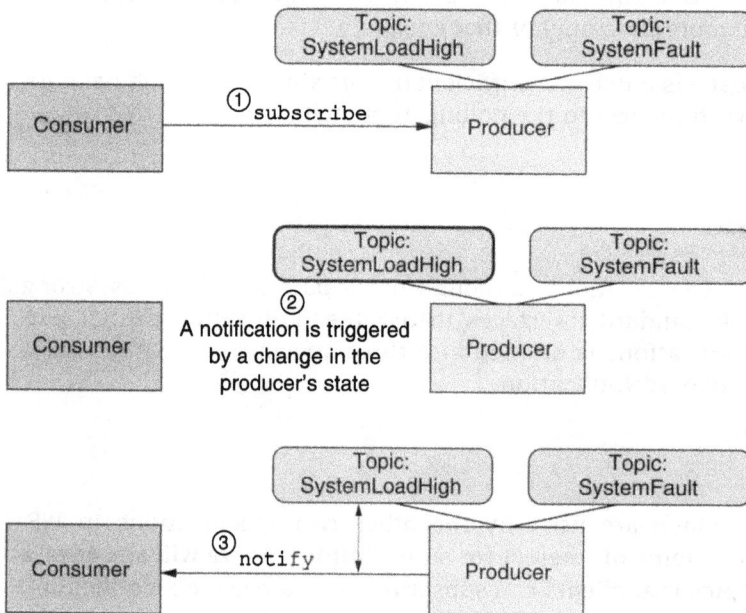

Figure 13.3: A typical WS-Notification interaction

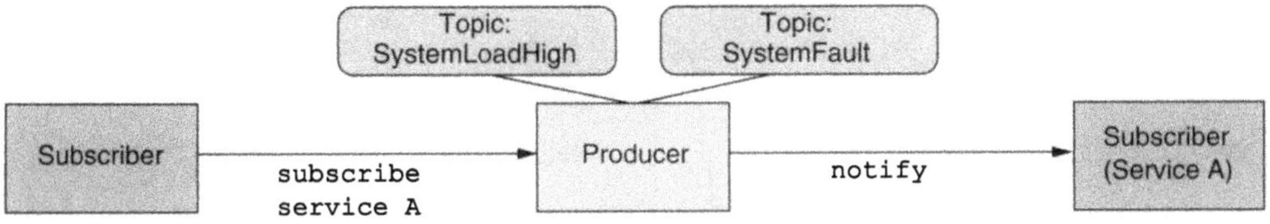

Figure 13.4: A WS-Notification interaction where the subscriber and the consumer are different entities

2. Next, at some point in time, something happens in the notification producer that must trigger a notification from the **SystemLoadHigh** topic. For example, we might have implemented our service to send out a notification every time the system load passes from "more than 50%" to "less than 50%".

3. The notification producer delivers the notification to the consumer by invoking the **notify** operation in the consumer. As shown in the figure, this notification delivery is tied to the topic that triggered the notification.

Figure 13.4 on the other hand, shows how the subscriber and the consumer need not be the same entity. In the figure, the subscriber requests the producer that Service A be subscribed to the **SystemLoadHigh** topic. When a notification is triggered, the notification is sent to Service A (the consumer) not to the subscriber.

13.2.3 WS-BrokeredNotification

In brokered notifications we consider the case when notifications are delivered from the producer to the consumer through an intermediate entity called the *broker*. The WS-BrokeredNotification defines the standard interfaces for the notification broker.

As shown in Figure 13.5 in the presence of a notification broker, the producer must register with the broker and publish its topics there. The subscriber (separate from the consumer in this case), must also subscribe through the broker, not directly with the producer. Finally, when a notification is produced, it is delivered to the consumer through the broker.

13.3 Notifications in GT4

GT4 currently doesn't implement the WS-Notifications family of specifications completely. For example, no support for brokered notifications is included. However, GT4 does allow us to perform effective topic-based notifications. One of the more interesting parts of the GT4 implementation of WS-Notifications is that it will allow us to effortlessly expose a resource property as a topic, triggering a notification each time the value of the RP changes. We will also be able to define our own topics, which need not trigger a notification every

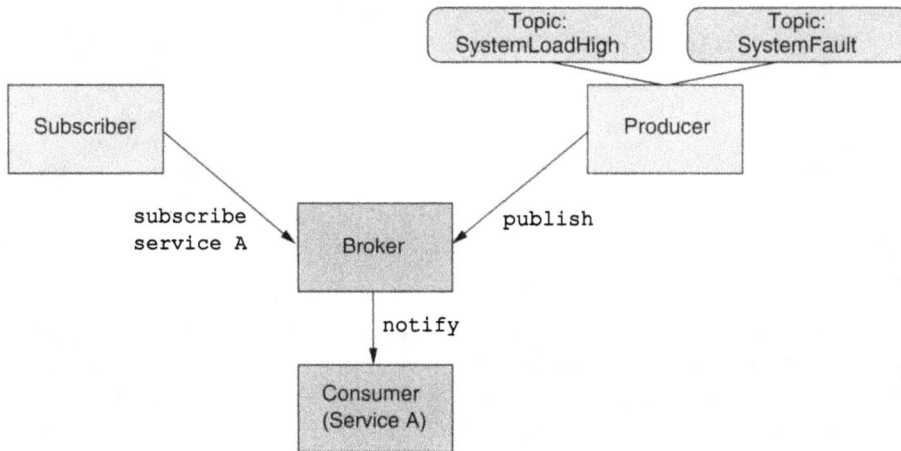

Figure 13.5: A typical brokered WS-Notification interaction

single time the value of an RP changes. In the remainder of the chapter, we will see how we can add both types of topics to our service.

13.4   Notifying Changes in a Resource Property

We will see how we can add notifications to a service so clients can be notified each time a certain RP is modified. As we did in Chapter 6 and Chapter 10 our example will be based, for simplicity, on the **ServiceResourceHome** resource home.

13.4.1   The WSDL File

Our portType will need to extend from a standard WS-Notifications portType called **NotificationProducer**, which exposes a **Subscribe** operation that consumers can use to subscribe themselves to a particular topic. We also need to extend from the **Subscription-Manager** portType, which exposes operations that allow us to manage a subscription. As mentioned earlier, a subscription results in the creation of a **Subscription** WS-Resource with stateful information on the subscription. The **SubscriptionManager** portType will allow us to access that information (**SubscriptionManager** also exposes the **GetResource-Property** operation), and to pause and resume subscriptions. Finally, **SubscriptionManager** also exposes the **Destroy** operation to allow us to destroy the **Subscription** resource when we want to cancel the subscription.

First of all, we need to declare the WS-Notifications namespace, and import its WSDL file.

```
<?xml version="1.0" encoding="UTF-8"?>
<definitions name="MathService"
    targetNamespace="http://www.globus.org/namespaces/examples/
        MathService_instance_notif"
    xmlns="http://schemas.xmlsoap.org/wsdl/"
    xmlns:tns="http://www.globus.org/namespaces/examples/
        MathService_instance_notif"
    xmlns:wsdl="http://schemas.xmlsoap.org/wsdl/"
    xmlns:wsrp="http://docs.oasis-open.org/wsrf/2004/06/
        wsrf-WS-ResourceProperties-1.2-draft-01.xsd"
    xmlns:wsrpw="http://docs.oasis-open.org/wsrf/2004/06/
        wsrf-WS-ResourceProperties-1.2-draft-01.wsdl"
    xmlns:wsntw="http://docs.oasis-open.org/wsn/2004/06/
        wsn-WS-BaseNotification-1.2-draft-01.wsdl"
    xmlns:wsrlw="http://docs.oasis-open.org/wsrf/2004/06/
        wsrf-WS-ResourceLifetime-1.2-draft-01.wsdl"
    xmlns:wsdlpp="http://www.globus.org/namespaces/2004/10/WSDLPreprocessor"
    xmlns:xsd="http://www.w3.org/2001/XMLSchema">

<wsdl:import
    namespace=
    "http://docs.oasis-open.org/wsrf/2004/06/wsrf-WS-ResourceProperties-
        1.2-draft-01.wsdl"
    location="../../wsrf/properties/WS-ResourceProperties.wsdl" />

<wsdl:import
    namespace=
    "http://docs.oasis-open.org/wsn/2004/06/wsn-WS-BaseNotification-
        1.2-draft-01.wsdl"
    location="../../wsrf/notification/WS-BaseN.wsdl"/>
```

```
<wsdl:import

    namespace=

    "http://docs.oasis-open.org/wsrf/2004/06/

        wsrf-WS-ResourceLifetime-1.2-draft-01.wsdl"

    location="../../wsrf/lifetime/WS-ResourceLifetime.wsdl" />

    <!-- ... -->



</definitions>
```

Then, we need to extend from the **NotificationProducer** and **SubscriptionManager** portTypes.

```
<portType name="MathPortType"

    wsdlpp:extends="wsntw:NotificationProducer

                    wsntw:SubscriptionManager"

    wsrp:ResourceProperties="tns:MathResourceProperties">


    <!-- <operation>s -->

</portType>
```

☞ This is part of file **$EXAMPLES_DIR/schema/examples/MathService_instance_ notif/Math.wsdl**.

Finally, since these modifications create a new interface, we need to map the new WSDL namespaces to Java packages.

```
http\://www.globus.org/namespaces/examples/MathService

    _instance_notif=org.globus.examples.stubs.MathService_instance_notif

http\://www.globus.org/namespaces/examples/MathService_instance_notif/bindings

    =org.globus.examples.stubs.MathService_instance_notif.bindings

http\://www.globus.org/namespaces/examples/MathService_instance_notif/service

    =org.globus.examples.stubs.MathService_instance_notif.service
```

> ✍ These three lines must be present in $EXAMPLES_DIR/namespace2package.
> **mappings.**

13.4.2 The Resource Implementation

For our resource, we will assume that the RPs are implemented using **SimpleResourceProperty**, as explained in Section 10.6, "SimpleResourceProperty". The reason we are using this class instead of **ReflectionResourceProperty** is because it will allow us to send a notification automatically whenever an RP is modified. Later on, we will see that using notifications with **ReflectionResourceProperty** requires us to add some code in the service implementation to manually trigger the notification.

Besides using **SimpleResourceProperty**, we will use a Globus-supplied class called **ResourcePropertyTopic** which is both a resource property *and* a topic (more precisely, it implements both the **ResourceProperty** and *Topic* interfaces). As we will see, the only thing we need to do is create new **ResourcePropertyTopic** objects and "wrap them around" our **SimpleResourceProperty** objects. Then, the **ResourcePropertyTopic** objects are added both to the resource's list of RPs (the RP set) and the list of topics.

First of all, our resource class must implement the **TopicListAccessor** interface, which requires that we implement a **getTopicList** method returning a **TopicList**. A **TopicList** attribute must therefore be added to our resource class to keep track of all the topics published by our resource.

```
import org.globus.wsrf.TopicListAccessor;

public class MathService implements Resource, ResourceProperties,
        TopicListAccessor {


    private TopicList topicList;


    // ...


    /* Required by interface TopicListAccessor */
    public TopicList getTopicList() {
        return topicList;
    }

}
```

Next, we initialize the topic list, create the **ResourcePropertyTopic** objects, and add them to the RP set and the topic list:

```java
public MathService() throws RemoteException {
        /* Create RP set */
        this.propSet = new SimpleResourcePropertySet(
                        MathConstants.RESOURCE_PROPERTIES);


        /* Initialize the RP's */
        try {
                valueRP = new SimpleResourceProperty(MathConstants.RP_VALUE);
                valueRP.add(new Integer(0));


                lastOpRP= new SimpleResourceProperty(MathConstants.RP_LASTOP);
                lastOpRP.add("NONE");
        } catch (Exception e) {
                throw new RuntimeException(e.getMessage());
        }


        ❶
        this.topicList = new SimpleTopicList(this);


        ❷
        valueRP = new ResourcePropertyTopic(valueRP);
        ((ResourcePropertyTopic) valueRP).setSendOldValue(true);


        lastOpRP = new ResourcePropertyTopic(lastOpRP);
        ((ResourcePropertyTopic) lastOpRP).setSendOldValue(true);


        ❸
        this.topicList.addTopic((Topic) valueRP);
        this.topicList.addTopic((Topic) lastOpRP);
```

```
        this.propSet.add(valueRP);

        this.propSet.add(lastOpRP);

    }
```

❶ We initialize the topic list using the Globus-supplied **SimpleTopicList** class.

❷ We take the previously created **SimpleResourceProperty** objects and put them "inside" **ResourcePropertyTopic** objects. Notice how the **valueRP** and **lastOpRP** attributes (of type **ResourceProperty**) are set to the **ResourcePropertyTopic** objects, *not* the original **SimpleResourceProperty** objects.
Next, we will activate a nice feature included in **ResourcePropertyTopic**s. We can ask that the notification include not only the new value (whenever an RP is modified), but also the old value.

❸ Finally, we add the **ResourcePropertyTopic** objects to the topic list.

☞ The code shown above is part of **$EXAMPLES_DIR/org/globus/examples/services/core/notifications/impl/MathService.java**.

13.4.3 The Service Implementation

When using **ResourcePropertyTopic**s with **SimpleResourceProperty**, the notification is sent out *automatically* whenever we modify the value of an RP. We do not need to add any code to trigger the notification.

☞ If you take a look at the source code for this example, you'll notice several references to a "BigValue" notification. You can safely ignore this for now, as it will be explained in the next section.

13.4.4 Deployment Descriptor

To be able to use the WS-Notifications portTypes we need to modify our WSDD file to make sure that our service relies on the Globus-supplied operation providers for those portTypes.

```xml
<?xml version="1.0" encoding="UTF-8"?>

<deployment name="defaultServerConfig"

    xmlns="http://xml.apache.org/axis/wsdd/"

    xmlns:java="http://xml.apache.org/axis/wsdd/providers/java"

    xmlns:xsd="http://www.w3.org/2001/XMLSchema">
```

```
<service name="examples/core/notifications/MathService" provider="Handler"
    use="literal" style="document">
    <parameter name="className" value="org.globus.examples.services.
        core.notifications.impl.MathService"/>
    <wsdlFile>share/schema/examples/MathService_instance_notif/
        Math_service.wsdl</wsdlFile>
    <parameter name="allowedMethods" value="*"/>
    <parameter name="handlerClass" value="org.globus.axis.providers.
        RPCProvider"/>
    <parameter name="scope" value="Application"/>
    <parameter name="providers" value="
            ❶ SubscribeProvider GetCurrentMessageProvider
            ❷ PauseSubscriptionProvider ResumeSubscriptionProvider
        GetRPProvider DestroyProvider SetTerminationTimeProvider"/>
    <parameter name="loadOnStartup" value="true"/>
</service>

</deployment>
```

❶ **SubscribeProvider GetCurrentMessageProvider** are required to implement the operations in the **NotificationProducer** portType.

❷ **PauseSubscriptionProvider**, **ResumeSubscriptionProvider**, **GetRPProvider**, **DestroyProvider**, and **SetTerminationTimeProvider** are required to implement the operations in the **SubscriptionManager** interface. Even though we are not going to use the **Pause** and **Resume** operations, we need to include an implementation for them nonetheless (otherwise, the container will refuse to start up the service).

> ☞ This file is **$EXAMPLES_DIR/org/globus/examples/services/core/notifications /deploy-server.wsdd**.

13.4.5   Compile and Deploy

Let's build the service:

> **./globus-build-service.sh notifications**

And deploy it:

```
globus-deploy-gar $EXAMPLES_DIR/org_globus_examples_services_wsrf_core
    _notifications.gar
```

13.4.6 Client Code

To try out this service, we will need two clients. The first client will be in charge of *listening* for notifications, and includes a lot of new code. The second client is a very simple client that invokes the **add** operation. This will allow us to test if a change in the **Value** RP (triggered by the **add** operation) is indeed notified to the listener client.

Listener Client

This client is composed of two important parts:

1. **Subscription**: This block of code will be in charge of setting up the subscription with the **Value** RP (which, remember, is also published as a topic). Once the subscription is set up, this block of code simply loops indefinitely until we press a key. Then, the subscription is cancelled.

2. **Delivery**: Once the subscription has been set up, and the main thread of the program is looping indefinitely, the delivery code gets invoked any time a notification arrives at the client. In fact, the listener must implement the **NotifyCallback** interface, which requires that we implement a **deliver** method that will be in charge of handling incoming notifications.

```
public class ValueListener implements NotifyCallback {

}
```

First off, let's take a look at the code that sets up the subscription. This code is inside a method called **run** that expects the notification producer's URI as its only parameter.

```
public void run(String serviceURI) {
        try {

                ❶

                NotificationConsumerManager consumer;


                ❷

                consumer = NotificationConsumerManager.getInstance();
                consumer.startListening();
                EndpointReferenceType consumerEPR = consumer
                            .createNotificationConsumer(this);
```

❸

```
Subscribe request = new Subscribe();
request.setUseNotify(Boolean.TRUE);
request.setConsumerReference(consumerEPR);
```

❹

```
TopicExpressionType topicExpression = new
    TopicExpressionType();
topicExpression.setDialect(WSNConstants.SIMPLE_TOPIC_DIALECT);
topicExpression.setValue(MathConstants.RP_VALUE);
request.setTopicExpression(topicExpression);
```

❺

```
WSBaseNotificationServiceAddressingLocator notifLocator =
    new WSBaseNotificationServiceAddressingLocator();
EndpointReferenceType endpoint = new
    EndpointReferenceType();
endpoint.setAddress(new Address(serviceURI));
NotificationProducer producerPort = notifLocator
    .getNotificationProducerPort(endpoint);
```

❻

```
SubscribeResponse response = producerPort.subscribe(request);
```

❼

```
EndpointReferenceType subscriptionEPR = response
    .getSubscriptionReference();
SubscriptionManagerServiceAddressingLocator subscripLocator =
    new SubscriptionManagerServiceAddressingLocator();
    SubscriptionManager subscripPort = subscripLocator
            .getSubscriptionManagerPort(subscriptionEPR);
```

❽

```
System.out.println("Waiting for notification. Press any key
    to stop.");
System.in.read();
```

❾

```
subscripPort.destroy(new Destroy());
consumer.stopListening();
System.out.println("Not listening anymore!");
} catch (Exception e) {
    e.printStackTrace();
}
}
```

❶ Our client is going to act as a notification consumer. This means that our client will have to expose a **Notify** operation that will be invoked by the notification producer. For this to happen, our client has to act as both a client and a server. Fortunately, thanks to a Globus-supplied class called **NotificationConsumerManager**, we are shielded from all the potential nastiness involved in doing this.

❷ Once we invoke the **startListening** method in the **NotificationConsumerManager**, our client becomes a server hosting a service that implements the standard **NotificationConsumer** portType. As such, this service will have an endpoint reference. We need to keep track of this EPR, since it will be used by the **NotificationProducer** to deliver the notifications.

❸ We create the request to the remote **Subscribe** call. There are two properties we must set: whether the producer must use the standard **Notify** operation to deliver notifications (in general, we will always want this to be true), and the consumer's EPR.

❹ Next, we create a **TopicExpressionType** object representing the topic we want to subscribe to. Notice how we're subscribing to the **Value** RP.

❺ A this point, the **Subscribe** request is ready to be sent to the notification producer. To do this, we need to obtain a reference to the standard **NotificationProducer** portType in the remote service.

❻ We are finally ready to send the subscription request. Notice how we store the response in a variable of type **SubscribeResponse**.

❼ We obtain the EPR of the **Subscription** WS-Resource and, through that EPR, a reference to a **SubscriptionManager** portType. We need this portType to destroy the **Subscription** resource once we cancel the subscription.

❽ Finally, we block our client until a key is pressed. This doesn't affect the client's ability to receive notifications, as it will be woken up whenever a notification is delivered.

❾ Once a key is pressed, we need to cancel the notification. To do this, we need to destroy the **Subscription** resource using the **SubscriptionManager** portType obtained previously. It is important to understand that we are *not* destroying a **Math-Resource**, but a different resource used internally to keep track of subscription information. After we've destroyed it, we need to tell the **NotificationConsumerManager** object to stop listening for notifications.

Now, let's take a look at the code that handles incoming notifications. Remember that the **deliver** method is required by the **NotifyCallback** interface. If we do not implement it, our client will be unable to receive notifications.

```
public void deliver(List topicPath, EndpointReferenceType producer, ❶
            Object message) {
        ResourcePropertyValueChangeNotificationElementType notif_elem;
        ResourcePropertyValueChangeNotificationType notif;


        ❷
        try {
                notif_elem = (ResourcePropertyValueChangeNotification
                    ElementType) message;
                notif = notif_elem.getResourcePropertyValueChange
                    Notification();
        } catch(Exception e)
        {
                System.out.println("Error when casting notification
                    message.");
                System.out.println("Message: " + e.getMessage());
        }
```

```
            if (notif != null) {
                    System.out.println("A notification has been delivered");

                    ❸
                    if (notif.getOldValue() != null)
                    {
                            System.out.print("Old value: ");
                            System.out.println(notif.getOldValue().get_any()[0].
                                getValue());
                    }
                    System.out.print("New value: ");
                    System.out.println(notif.getNewValue().get_any()[0].
                        getValue());
            }
    }
```

❶ The **deliver** method has three parameters:

1. **topicPath**: the topic that produced the notification.
2. **producer**: the EPR of the notification producer.
3. **message**: the actual notification. Notice how it is of type **Object**, so we will need to cast it to a more useful type.

❷ When using **ResourcePropertyTopic**s to notify changes in RPs, the notification message is of type **ResourcePropertyValueChangeNotificationElementType**. This type, in turn, contains an object of type **ResourcePropertyValueChangeNotificationType**. This object is the one that contains the new value of the RP. Remember that, in this example, we've also asked that the notification include the old value too.

❸ Finally, we print out the old and new values of the RP. Checking if the old value is null (i.e. checking if no "old value" is sent with the notification) will come in handy later on when we see how to use **ReflectionResourceProperty** in our implementation.

> ☞ The code shown above is part of **$EXAMPLES_DIR/org/globus/examples/clients/ MathService_instance_notif/ValueListener.java**

Adding Client

The adding client requires no explanation, as it is identical to the ones seen in previous chapters.

> ☞ The source code for the adding client is **$EXAMPLES_DIR/org/globus/examples/clients/MathService_instance_notif/ClientAdder.java**
>
> If you're not sure about how the client works, this might be a good time to review Section 8.9.2, "The adding client".

Compile and Run

First of all, let's compile the listener client:

```
javac \
-classpath $CLASSPATH:build/stubs/classes/ \
org/globus/examples/clients/MathService_instance_notif/ValueListener.java
```

Since we are going to use two clients, you should run the listener in a separate console.

```
java \
-DGLOBUS_LOCATION= $GLOBUS_LOCATION \
-classpath $CLASSPATH:build/stubs/classes/ \
org/globus/examples/clients/MathService_instance_notif/ValueListener \
http://127.0.0.1:8080/wsrf/services/examples/core/notifications/MathService
```

> ☞ Notice how we have to define a property called **GLOBUS_LOCATION**. This should be set to the directory where GT4 is installed. We need to define this property because, as mentioned earlier, our client is also going to act as a server. Therefore, it needs to know where all the Globus files are located (some of which are necessary for it to work as a server).

If all goes well, you should see the following:

```
Waiting for notification. Ctrl-C to end.
```

Now, let's compile the adder client:

```
javac \
-classpath $CLASSPATH:build/stubs/classes/ \
org/globus/examples/clients/MathService_instance_notif/ClientAdd.java
```

And run it:

```
java \
-classpath $CLASSPATH:build/stubs/classes/ \
org/globus/examples/clients/MathService_instance_notif/ClientAdd \
http://127.0.0.1:8080/wsrf/services/examples/core/notifications/MathService \
10
```

If all goes well, you should see the following:

```
Value RP: 10
LastOp RP: ADDITION
```

Now, if you check the console where the listener client is running, you should see the following:

```
A notification has been delivered
Old value:0
New value:10
```

You can try to run the adder client once more:

```
Value RP: 20
LastOp RP: ADDITION
```

And the following will be output by the listener.

```
A notification has been delivered
Old value:10
New value:20
```

13.5 Using ReflectionResourceProperty Instead of SimpleResourceProperty

We can also use **ReflectionResourceProperty** to implement our RPs, instead of using **SimpleResourceProperty**, but that means that we will have to manually trigger the notification. For example, the **add** method would look like this:

```
public synchronized AddResponse add(int a) throws RemoteException {
        value += a;
        lastOp = "ADDITION";


        /* Send notification */
        ResourcePropertyTopic valueTopic = (ResourcePropertyTopic) this.
            valueRP;
        ResourcePropertyTopic lastOpTopic = (ResourcePropertyTopic) this.
            lastOpRP;


        try {
                valueTopic.notify(null);
                lastOpTopic.notify(null);
        } catch (Exception e) {
                throw new RemoteException(
                                "Exception when notifying Value and LastOp
                                        subscribers",
                                e);
        }


        return new AddResponse();
}
```

☞ The code shown above is part of **$EXAMPLES_DIR/org/globus/examples/services/ core/notifications/impl/MathServiceRefl.java**.

As you can see, we have to manually invoke the **notify** method in the **ResourceProperty-Topic** object wrapping around our **ReflectionResourceProperty**.

The examples bundle includes an implementation of the notifications example using **ReflectionResourceProperty** instead of **SimpleResourceProperty**. It is deployed along with the example already seen. You can reuse all the clients, but will need to use the following URL:

http://127.0.0.1:8080/wsrf/services/examples/core/notifications/

MathServiceRefl

Note that, when running the listener client, you will not receive the old value. One drawback of using **ReflectionResourceProperty** with notifications is that only the new value is sent in the notification.

13.6 Custom Notification Messages

In the previous example, we saw how we could easily create a new topic based on an existing resource property (provided it was implemented with **SimpleResourceProperty**). We can also create topics that are bound to an RP but, rather, that are triggered whenever we choose to. Furthermore, we can control exactly what information is sent in the notification message.

In this example, we will create a new topic called **BigValueChange** that sends out notifications only when **add** or **subtract** are invoked with a value larger than 100. The notification message will include the value that triggered the notification, the new value of the **Value** RP, and the operation that was invoked (addition or subtraction). This example will build on top of the previous example, so we will only highlight the new code that is necessary.

13.6.1 The WSDL File

To send out a custom notification message, we need to define that new message in our WSDL file's **<types>** section.

```
<types>
<xsd:schema targetNamespace="http://www.globus.org/namespaces/examples/
       MathService_instance_notif"
    xmlns:tns="http://www.globus.org/namespaces/examples/MathService_
       instance_notif"
    xmlns:xsd="http://www.w3.org/2001/XMLSchema">


    <!-- Requests and responses -->


    <!-- Resource properties -->
```

```
<!-- Custom Notification Messages -->
❶
<xsd:element name="BigValueChangeNotificationMessage"
    type="tns:BigValueChangeNotificationMessageType"/>


<xsd:element name="BigValue" type="xsd:int"/>
<xsd:element name="NewValue" type="xsd:int"/>
<xsd:element name="Op" type="xsd:string"/>


<xsd:complexType name="BigValueChangeNotificationMessageType">
        <xsd:sequence>
                <xsd:element ref="tns:BigValue" minOccurs="1"
                    maxOccurs="1"/>
                <xsd:element ref="tns:NewValue" minOccurs="1"
                    maxOccurs="1"/>
                <xsd:element ref="tns:Op" minOccurs="1" maxOccurs="1"/>
        </xsd:sequence>
</xsd:complexType>


❷
<xsd:complexType name="BigValueChangeNotificationMessageWrapperType">
    <xsd:sequence>
                <xsd:element ref="tns:
                    BigValueChangeNotificationMessage"/>
        </xsd:sequence>
    </xsd:complexType>
</xsd:schema>
</types>
```

☞ This is part of file **$EXAMPLES_DIR/schema/examples/MathService_instance_notif/Math.wsdl**.

❶ First of all, we define the actual message element, which we will call **BigValueChangeNotificationMessage**. Notice that this element is of type **BigValueChangeNotificationMessageType**, which in turn contains the new value, the value that triggered the notification, and the operation invoked.

❷ When we define a custom notification message, we also need to define a *message wrapper* complex type, whose sole purpose is to contain a single notification element. In our case, we declare a type called **BigValueChangeNotification-MessageWrapperType** that contains a single **BigValueChangeNotificationMessage** element.

13.6.2   Resource Implementation

Our resource class must now reflect the fact that we have a new topic. First of all, we need to include the following attribute in our resource class:

```
private SimpleTopic BigValueChangeTopic;
```

Next, we have to add code to initialize that topic and add it to the list of topics published by the resource:

```
/* Configure the Topics */

this.topicList = new SimpleTopicList(this);


valueRP = new ResourcePropertyTopic(valueRP);

((ResourcePropertyTopic) valueRP).setSendOldValue(true);


lastOpRP = new ResourcePropertyTopic(lastOpRP);

((ResourcePropertyTopic) lastOpRP).setSendOldValue(true);


this.BigValueChangeTopic = new SimpleTopic(MathConstants.TOPIC_
    BIGVALUECHANGE); ❶


this.topicList.addTopic((Topic) valueRP);

this.topicList.addTopic((Topic) lastOpRP);

this.topicList.addTopic(BigValueChangeTopic); ❷

this.propSet.add(valueRP);

this.propSet.add(lastOpRP);
```

❶ We create a new topic. Notice that, when creating the new topic, we need to specify its QName. For convenience, we have specified it in the MathConstants interface:

```
public static final QName TOPIC_BIGVALUECHANGE = new

QName(NS,"BigValueChange");
```

❷ We add the topic to the topic list.

13.6.3   Service Implementation

When using **ResourcePropertyTopic**, the service implementation didn't require any changes (except, in our case, we had to modify it because we switched to using **SimpleResourceProperty**). When using custom notifications, in general, we *will* have to modify the service implementation because we have to manually trigger the notification.

```
public AddResponse add(int a) throws RemoteException {
        Integer value = (Integer) valueRP.get(0);
        value = new Integer(value.intValue()+a);
        valueRP.set(0, value);
        lastOpRP.set(0,"ADDITION");

        try {   ❶
            if (a >= 100) {
                    ❷
                BigValueChangeNotificationMessageType message = new
                    BigValueChangeNotificationMessageType(
                        a, value.intValue(), "ADDITION");
                    ❸
                BigValueChangeNotificationMessageWrapperType
                    msgWrapper = new BigValueChangeNotificationMessage
                        WrapperType(message);
                    ❹
                BigValueChangeTopic.notify(msgWrapper);
            }
```

```
        } catch (Exception e) {
                throw new RemoteException(
                                "Exception when notifying BigValueChangeTopic
                                subscribers",
                                e);
        }
        return new AddResponse();
}
```

❶ We will trigger the notification if the value received is greater than or equal to 100.

❷ We create the notification message. Remember that, in the WSDL file, we declared this to be of type **BigValueChangeNotificationMessageType**, so a stub class for that type will be generated.

❸ Next, we create a message wrapper and add the message object to it.

❹ Finally, we trigger the notification sending out the message wrapper.

13.6.4 Compile and Deploy

Build the service:

./globus-build-service.sh notifications

And deploy it:

**globus-deploy-gar EXAMPLES_DIR/org_globus_examples_services_wsrf_core_
notifications.gar**

13.6.5 Listening for Notifications

To try out this service, we will be able to reuse the adder client, and the listener client will be very similar to the one seen earlier. We only need to change two things. First of all, when setting up the subscription, we need to specify that we are subscribing to the **BigValueChange** topic:

```
topicExpression.setValue(MathConstants.TOPIC_BIGVALUECHANGE);
```

Next, we have to modify the **delivery** method, which will now be receiving our custom notification message. Notice that, since our notification message is a stub class, we can easily cast the **message** parameter into an object of type **BigValueChangeNotificationMessageType** using the Globus-supplied **ObjectDeserializer** class.

```
public void deliver(List topicPath, EndpointReferenceType producer,
                Object message) {
        try {

                BigValueChangeNotificationMessageType notif;
                notif = (BigValueChangeNotificationMessageType)
                    ObjectDeserializer
                                .toObject((Element) message,
                                        BigValueChangeNotification
                                        MessageType.class);


                if (notif != null) {
                        System.out.println("A notification has been
                                delivered");

                        System.out.print("New value: ");
                        System.out.println(notif.getNewValue());
                        System.out.print("Big value: ");
                        System.out.println(notif.getBigValue());
                        System.out.print("Operation: ");
                        System.out.println(notif.getOp());
                }
        } catch (Exception e) {
                e.printStackTrace();
        }
}
```

☞ This is part of **$EXAMPLES_DIR/org/globus/examples/clients/MathService_ instance_notif/BigValueListener.java**.

Now, we can compile the client:

```
javac \
-classpath $CLASSPATH:build/stubs/classes/ \
org/globus/examples/clients/MathService_instance_notif/BigValueListener.java
```

And run it:

```
java \
-DGLOBUS_LOCATION= $GLOBUS_LOCATION \
-classpath $CLASSPATH:build/stubs/classes/ \
org/globus/examples/clients/MathService_instance_notif/BigValueListener \
http://127.0.0.1:8080/wsrf/services/examples/core/notifications/MathService
```

If you run the adder client, specifying a "small" value (for example, 10), the adder client will output the following:

```
Value RP: 10
LastOp RP: ADDITION
```

However, no notification will be received by the **BigValueChange** listener because 10 is not big enough to trigger a notification. On the other hand, if we invoke the adder client with a "big" value (1000), we will see the following:

```
Value RP: 1010
LastOp RP: ADDITION
```

And a notification will be delivered to the listener client:

```
A notification has been delivered
New value: 1010
Big value: 1000
Operation: ADDITION
```

Parameter	Description
-b, - -subEpr <file>	Saves the EPR of the **Subscription** resource to **file**

Table 13.1: Parameters specific to **wsn-subscribe**

13.7 Command-Line Clients

GT4 includes a set of command-line clients we can use to test notifications in a service without having to implement a listener client for a specific service.

13.7.1 wsn-subscribe

This client allows us to subscribe to a topic and see the raw XML sent in the notification, without having to write a client for a specific service. The topic must be specified using its QName.

Usage

```
wsn-subscribe [common options] <topic>
```

Example

```
wsn-subscribe \
-s http://127.0.0.1:8080/wsrf/services/examples/core/notifications/
    MathService \
"{http://www.globus.org/namespaces/examples/MathService_instance_notif}Value"
```

Expected output:

```
Subscription successful
Address: http://127.0.0.1:8080/wsrf/services/SubscriptionManagerService
Reference property[0]:
<ns1:SubscriptionKey xmlns:ns1="http://www.globus.org/
    namespaces/2004/06/core">
3135e260-a4ae-11d9-ad9d-a9c044fad770
</ns1:SubscriptionKey>
```

When the **Value** RP is modified, the following will be output by **wsn-subscribe**:

> Received:
>
> <ns5:Value xmlns:ns5="http://www.globus.org/namespaces/examples/MathService_
>   instance_notif"> 10 </ns5:Value>

13.7.2 wsn-get-current-message

This client allows us to inspect the latest message sent out to the subscribers of a topic. The topic must be specified using its QName.

Usage

> wsn-get-current-message [common options] <topic>

Example

> wsn-get-current-message \
>
> -s http://127.0.0.1:8080/wsrf/services/examples/core/notifications/
>   MathService \
>
> "{http://www.globus.org/namespaces/examples/MathService_instance_notif}Value"

Expected output:

> <ns1:ResourcePropertyValueChangeNotificationType xmlns:ns1="http://docs.oasis
>   -open.org/wsrf/2004/06/wsrf-WS-ResourceProperties-1.2-draft-01.xsd">
>
> <ns1:OldValue>
>
> <ns2:Value xmlns:ns2="http://www.globus.org/namespaces/examples/MathService
>   _instance_notif"> 0 </ns2:Value>
>
> </ns1:OldValue>
>
> <ns1:NewValue>
>
> <ns3:Value xmlns:ns3="http://www.globus.org/namespaces/examples/MathService
>   _instance_notif"> 10 </ns3:Value>
>
> </ns1:NewValue>
>
> </ns1:ResourcePropertyValueChangeNotificationType>

References

[1] "WS-BaseNotification specification". 1.2 Working Draft 01. *Web Services Notification (WSN) TC*. OASIS, June, 2004.

[2] "WS-Topics specification". 1.2 Working Draft 01. *Web Services Notification (WSN) TC*. OASIS, June, 2004.

[3] "WS-BrokeredNotification specification". 1.2 Working Draft 01. *Web Services Notification (WSN) TC*. OASIS, July, 2004.

Implementing Your Own Operation Providers

In the previous chapter we have been using Globus-supplied operation providers to avoid having to implement the operations required by the standard WSRF portTypes. However, operation providers can be used for more than just that. You can implement your own operation providers to implement some functionality that you easily want to plug into your services. In this chapter we will learn how to do just that.

14.1 The RemoteLogging Provider

Let's suppose that you are programming an application composed of several services deployed in different containers. Furthermore, suppose you want the client applications to be able to instruct the services to write certain log messages in their containers. It would be as simple as having each service expose a **writeLog(String msg)** operation, and have that operation use the logging infrastructure seen in Chapter 9, Logging to write string **msg** to the container's log.

This is very simple in concept but, in practice, we would have to add the **writeLog(String msg)** operation to the WSDL file and Java implementation of each service. A better solution is to take that code and put it in an operation provider that we will be able to easily "plug into" our services, the same way we "plugged in" operation provider **GetRPProvider** whenever we wanted to use the **GetResourceProperty** operation to access our service's RPs.

So, we will write an operation provider called **RemoteLogging**. In general, writing our own operation providers requires three simple steps:

1. Write the WSDL file for our operation provider.

2. Write the Java implementation of our provider's operations.

3. Plug the operation provider into our service.

241

14.2   The Operation Provider's WSDL File

The WSDL file for our operation provider is pretty straightforward. We will define a new portType called **RemoteLogging** with a single operation called **log** that expects a single parameter of type **string** and doesn't return anything. Our portType will also include a single resource property **LastLog** (of type **string**) with the value of the last log written.

```xml
<?xml version="1.0" encoding="UTF-8"?>

<wsdl:definitions name="RemoteLogging"

    targetNamespace="http://www.globus.org/namespaces/examples/utils/
        RemoteLogging"

xmlns="http://schemas.xmlsoap.org/wsdl/"

xmlns:utils="http://www.globus.org/namespaces/examples/utils/
        RemoteLogging"

xmlns:wsrp="http://docs.oasis-open.org/wsrf/2004/06/
        wsrf-WS-ResourceProperties-1.2-draft-01.xsd"

xmlns:wsdl="http://schemas.xmlsoap.org/wsdl/"

xmlns:xsd="http://www.w3.org/2001/XMLSchema">




<!--============================================================



                            T Y P E S



============================================================-->


<wsdl:types>


<xsd:schema targetNamespace="http://www.globus.org/namespaces/examples/utils/
        RemoteLogging"

    xmlns:utils="http://www.globus.org/namespaces/examples/utils/
        RemoteLogging"

    xmlns:xsd="http://www.w3.org/2001/XMLSchema">
```

```
<!-- Requests and responses -->

<xsd:element name="log" type="xsd:string"/>
<xsd:element name="logResponse">
        <xsd:complexType/>
</xsd:element>

<!-- Resource properties -->

<xsd:element name="LastLog" type="xsd:string"/>

<xsd:element name="RemoteLoggingResourceProperties">
<xsd:complexType>
     <xsd:sequence>
        <xsd:element ref="utils:LastLog" minOccurs="1" maxOccurs="1"/>
     </xsd:sequence>
</xsd:complexType>
</xsd:element>

</xsd:schema>

</wsdl:types>


<!--=============================================================

                    M E S S A G E S

=============================================================-->

<wsdl:message name="LogInputMessage">
      <wsdl:part name="LogInputMessage" element="utils:log"/>
</wsdl:message>
```

```
<wsdl:message name="LogOutputMessage">
        <wsdl:part name="LogOutputMessage" element="utils:logResponse"/>
</wsdl:message>



<!--================================================================



                        P O R T T Y P E



================================================================-->


<wsdl:portType name="RemoteLogging"
    wsrp:ResourceProperties="utils:RemoteLoggingResourceProperties">


        <wsdl:operation name="log">
                <wsdl:input message="utils:LogInputMessage"/>
                <wsdl:output message="utils:LogOutputMessage"/>


        </wsdl:operation>


</wsdl:portType>


</wsdl:definitions>
```

☞ This file is **$EXAMPLES_DIR/schema/examples/MathService_instance_remotelog/
Math.wsdl**.

14.3   The Operation Provider Implementation

First off, let's suppose that the portType we just defined *doesn't* have any resource
properties. In that case, the implementation would be extremely simple:

```
package org.globus.examples.services.core.providers.impl;


import java.rmi.RemoteException;
```

```
import org.apache.commons.logging.Log;

import org.apache.commons.logging.LogFactory;


import org.globus.examples.stubs.utils.RemoteLogging.LogResponse;


public class RemoteLoggingProvider {


    /* Added for logging */

    static final Log logger = LogFactory.getLog(RemoteLoggingProvider.class);


    public LogResponse log(String message) throws RemoteException

    {

        // Write log message

        logger.info(message);


        return new LogResponse();

    }

}
```

So, if you write an operation provider that doesn't add any RPs (like, for example, **GetRP-Provider**), then you just have to focus on implementing the provider's operations in a single Java class, and you would be done with the implementation step.

However, we are going to see a special case, where our operation provider *does* add its own resource properties (like, for example, **SetTerminationTimeProvider** which added two RPs: **CurrentTime** and **TerminationTime**). In this case, our operation provider needs to access the current resource, and modify the **LastLog** RP. To be able to do this, we first need to define the following interface:

```
package org.globus.examples.services.core.providers.impl;


public interface RemoteLogging {

        public abstract String getLastLog();


        public abstract void setLastLog(String lastLog);

}
```

☞ This file is **$EXAMPLES_DIR/org/globus/examples/services/core/providers/impl/RemoteLogging.java**.

Then, in the implementation of our operation provider, we will cast the **Resource** returned by **ResourceContext** into the **RemoteLogging** interface, which will allow us to modify the **LastLog** RP (as we will see shortly, we will have to modify the resource class so it will implement the **RemoteLogging** interface, in the same way we had to implement the **ResourceLifetime** interface when we wanted to use the **SetTerminationTimeProvider** provider).

So, the operation provider would look like this:

```java
package org.globus.examples.services.core.providers.impl;


import java.rmi.RemoteException;


import org.apache.commons.logging.Log;

import org.apache.commons.logging.LogFactory;

import org.globus.examples.stubs.utils.RemoteLogging.LogResponse;

import org.globus.wsrf.ResourceContext;


public class RemoteLoggingProvider {


        /* Added for logging */
        static final Log logger = LogFactory.getLog(RemoteLoggingProvider.class);


        public LogResponse log(String message) throws RemoteException
        {
                // Write log message
                logger.info(message);


                /* Update LastLog resource property*/


                // Get current resource
                Object resource = ResourceContext.getResourceContext().
                    getResource();
```

```
        // Just in case, check that the Resource implements the
           RemoteLogging interface
        if (! (resource instanceof RemoteLogging))
               throw new RemoteException();


        // Set last log message
        RemoteLogging loggingResource = (RemoteLogging) resource;

        loggingResource.setLastLog(message);


        return new LogResponse();
    }
}
```

☞ This file is **$EXAMPLES_DIR/org/globus/examples/services/core/providers/**
impl/RemoteLoggingProvider.java.

14.4 Plugging Our Operation Provider into MathService

Finally, we will plug **RemoteLoggingProvider** into MathService. In general, we have to
perform the following steps:

1. Modify our service's WSDL file so it will extend from our operation provider's
   portType.
2. [Only if our operation provider adds new RP's] Modify our resource's implementation so it will include the new RPs.
3. Add the operation provider to our WSDD file.

14.4.1 The WSDL File

The WSDL file requires two simple changes:

```
<?xml version="1.0" encoding="UTF-8"?>
<definitions name="MathService"
    targetNamespace="http://www.globus.org/namespaces/examples/
        MathService_instance_remotelog"
    xmlns="http://schemas.xmlsoap.org/wsdl/"
```

```
        xmlns:tns="http://www.globus.org/namespaces/examples/
            MathService_instance_remotelog"
    xmlns:utils="http://www.globus.org/namespaces/examples/utils/
            RemoteLogging"❶
        xmlns:wsdl="http://schemas.xmlsoap.org/wsdl/"
        xmlns:wsrp="http://docs.oasis-open.org/wsrf/2004/06/
            wsrf-WS-ResourceProperties-1.2-draft-01.xsd"
        xmlns:wsrpw="http://docs.oasis-open.org/wsrf/2004/06/
            wsrf-WS-ResourceProperties-1.2-draft-01.wsdl"
        xmlns:wsdlpp="http://www.globus.org/namespaces/2004/10/WSDLPreprocessor"
        xmlns:xsd="http://www.w3.org/2001/XMLSchema">

<wsdl:import
    namespace=
    "http://docs.oasis-open.org/wsrf/2004/06/
            wsrf-WS-ResourceProperties-1.2-draft-01.wsdl"
    location="../../wsrf/properties/WS-ResourceProperties.wsdl" />

<wsdl:import
    namespace=
    "http://www.globus.org/namespaces/examples/utils/RemoteLogging"
    location="RemoteLogging.wsdl" />❷

    <!--...-->

<portType name="MathPortType"
    wsdlpp:extends="wsrpw:GetResourceProperty utils:RemoteLogging"
    wsrp:ResourceProperties="tns:MathResourceProperties"> ❸

    <!--...-->

</portType>

</definitions>
```

> ☞ This is part of file **$EXAMPLES_DIR/schema/examples/
> MathService_instance_remotelog/Math.wsdl.**

❶ We need to declare our operation provider's namespace. We declare it with the name **utils**.

❷ We need to import our operation provider's WSDL file.

❸ We need to specify that our portType extends from the operation provider's portType (**utils:RemoteLogging**). Remember that the **wsdlpp:extends** attribute is a Globus-specific feature. This means that the WSDL Preprocessor will take both WSDL files (**Math.wsdl** and **RemoteLogging.wsdl**) and will *merge* their RPs into a single resource properties element (**MathResourceProperties**) and all the operations into a single portType (**MathPortType**). If we were writing plain vanilla WSDL, we would have to manually add the **LastLog** RP to **MathResourceProperties** and the **log** operation to **MathPortType**.

14.4.2 The Resource Implementation

Since our operation provider adds a new RP, we need to make sure that our resource implements the **RemoteLogging** interface described above.

```
public class MathService implements Resource, ResourceProperties, RemoteLogging{

}
```

> ☞ Remember we are modifying the first MathService, which uses **Service-ResourceHome**. So, the resource is implemented by the service class. However, in general, you will have to modify the *resource implementation*.

To implement this interface, our resource will have to include a **LastLog** resource property:

```
/* Resource properties */
private int value;
private String lastOp;
private String lastLog;
```

We mustn't forget to initialize this new resource property:

```
ResourceProperty lastLogRP = new ReflectionResourceProperty(
            MathConstants.RP_LASTLOG ❶, "LastLog", this);
this.propSet.add(lastLogRP);
setLastLog("NONE");
```

❶ We have to add the new RP to the **MathConstants** interface. You can find the modified version at **$EXAMPLES_DIR/org/globus/examples/services/core/providers/ impl/MathConstants.java**.

Finally, we add the get/set methods for the **LastLog** resource property:

```
public void setLastOp(String lastOp) {
        this.lastOp = lastOp;
}


public String getLastLog() {
    return lastLog;
}
```

☞ This is part of file **$EXAMPLES_DIR/org/globus/examples/services/core/ providers/impl/MathService.java**.

14.4.3 The Deployment Descriptor

The very last step, before we actually try this new service out, is to modify the WSDD file to reflect that we want our service to rely on our operation provider for the new **log** operation.

```
<?xml version="1.0" encoding="UTF-8"?>
<deployment name="defaultServerConfig"
    xmlns="http://xml.apache.org/axis/wsdd/"
    xmlns:java="http://xml.apache.org/axis/wsdd/providers/java"
    xmlns:xsd="http://www.w3.org/2001/XMLSchema">

    <service name="examples/core/providers/MathService" provider="Handler"
        use="literal" style="document">
            <parameter name="className"
                value="org.globus.examples.services.core.providers.
                    impl.MathService"/>
            <wsdlFile>share/schema/examples/MathService_instance_remotelog/
                Math_service.wsdl</wsdlFile>
```

```
<parameter name="allowedMethods" value="*"/>
<parameter name="handlerClass"
        value="org.globus.axis.providers.RPCProvider"/>
<parameter name="scope" value="Application"/>
<parameter name="providers" value="GetRPProvider
    org.globus.examples.services.core.providers.
        impl.RemoteLoggingProvider"/>
<parameter name="loadOnStartup" value="true"/>
</service>


</deployment>
```

☞ This file is **$EXAMPLES_DIR/org/globus/examples/services/core/providers/
deploy-server.wsdd**.

ⓘ **Using shorthand notation for the operation providers**

Our WSDD file refers to the complete class name of our operation provider. However, every time we've used a Globus-supplied operation provider, we've been able to use a shorthand notation (like **GetRPProvider** or **SetTerminationTime-Provider**). If you find yourself using one of your operation providers over and over again, this shorthand notation might come in handy. To use it, you simply have to modify the file **$GLOBUS_LOCATION/etc/globus_wsrf_core/server-config.wsdd**. Inside the **<globalConfiguration>** element, add the following tag:

```
<parameter
            name="short_name"
            value="full_name"/>
```

In our case, we could add the following:

```
<parameter
            name="RemoteLoggingProvider"
            value="org.globus.examples.services.core.providers.impl.
                RemoteLoggingProvider"/>
```

14.5 Trying It Out

First of all, since the whole purpose of our operation provider is to write log messages, we have to remember to activate logging for our operation provider's class:

```
log4j.logger.org.globus.examples.services.core.providers.impl.
    RemoteLoggingProvider=INFO
```

> ☞ Add at the end of **$GLOBUS_LOCATION/container-log4j.properties**.

Now, let's compile the service:

```
./globus-build-service.sh remote_logging
```

And deploy it:

```
globus-deploy-gar $EXAMPLES_DIR/org_globus_examples_services_wsrf_core
    _providers.gar
```

Since we have modified the service's WSDL file, we need to use a new client. This new client is practically the same as all the client's we've seen in previous chapters, except we will now be invoking the **log** operation:

```
printResourceProperties(math);
math.add(10);
math.log("Added 10");
printResourceProperties(math);
math.add(5);
math.log("Added 5");
printResourceProperties(math);
math.subtract(10);
math.log("Subtracted 10");
printResourceProperties(math);
```

> ☞ This is part of **$EXAMPLES_DIR/org/globus/examples/clients/
> MathService_instance_remotelog/Client.java**.

Compile the client:

```
javac \
-classpath ./build/stubs/classes/:$CLASSPATH \
org/globus/examples/clients/MathService_instance_remotelog/Client.java
```

And run it:

```
java \
-classpath ./build/stubs/classes/:$CLASSPATH \
org.globus.examples.clients.MathService_instance_remotelog.Client \
http://127.0.0.1:8080/wsrf/services/examples/core/providers/MathService
```

On the client side, you should see the following:

```
Value RP: 0
LastOp RP: NONE
LastLog RP: NONE


Value RP: 10
LastOp RP: ADDITION
LastLog RP: Added 10


Value RP: 15
LastOp RP: ADDITION
LastLog RP: Added 5


Value RP: 5
LastOp RP: SUBTRACTION
LastLog RP: Subtracted 10
```

And, on the server side, you should see the following log messages:

```
DATE TIME INFO impl.RemoteLoggingProvider [Thread-2,log:19] Added 10
DATE TIME INFO impl.RemoteLoggingProvider [Thread-2,log:19] Added 5
DATE TIME INFO impl.RemoteLoggingProvider [Thread-4,log:19] Subtracted 10
```

part **III**

GT4 Security

We are now entering the next major part of the book: **GT4 Security**. This part of the book assumes that the reader knows his way around GT4 Java WS Core and all the fundamental concepts (how to compile a service, how to deploy it, etc.). This means some explanations won't be as detailed as before (to avoid being repetitious). One of the first things you'll notice is that, since the examples are starting to be quite long, complete code listings will be less frequent. Instead, relevant code sections will be described, usually describing what must be added to a typical service to enable a certain security feature. So, if you want to run the examples, don't forget to download the example files from the book's companion website at http://www.gt4book.com/.

## chapter 15

Fundamental Security Concepts

Working with the security components of GT4 requires, of course, a basic knowledge of certain fundamental computer security concepts. If you are already familiar with concepts such as authentication, authorization, public key cryptography, and certificate authorities, then you can safely skip this chapter. If you've never dealt with secure communications, or feel your knowledge of these concepts might be a bit rusty, then you should definitely read this chapter. However, take into account that this chapter is meant as an *overview* of these concepts. Some readers, specially complete newcomers, should consider reading some material that deals specifically with computer security, such as [1] or [2].

15.1 What is a Secure Communication?

The first thing we have to ask ourselves is: Well, just what is a secure communication? Newcomers to the field of computer security tend to think that a 'secure communication' is simply any communication where data are encrypted. However, security encompasses much more than simply encrypting and decrypting data.

15.1.1 The Three Pillars of a Secure Communication

Most authors consider the three pillars of a secure communication (or 'secure conversation') to be *privacy*, *integrity*, and *authentication*. Ideally, a secure conversation should feature all three pillars, but this is not always so (sometimes it might not even be desirable). Different security scenarios might require different combination of features (e.g. "only privacy", "privacy and integrity, but no authentication", "only integrity", etc.).

> ☞ You might stumble upon books and URLs which also talk about "non-repudiation", a feature which some authors consider the "fourth pillar" of secure conversations. Since non-repudiation never comes up in Globus literature, and because most authors tend to simply consider it a part of 'authentication', we've chosen not to include it in this chapter.

Privacy

A secure conversation should be *private*. In other words, only the sender and the receiver should be able to understand the conversation. If someone eavesdrops on the communication, the eavesdropper should be unable to make any sense out of it. This is generally achieved by encryption/decryption algorithms.

For example, imagine we want to transmit the message "INVOKE METHOD ADD", and we want to make sure that, if a third party intercepts that message (e.g. using a network sniffer), they won't be able to understand that message. We could use a trivial encryption algorithm which simply changes each letter for the next one in the alphabet. The encrypted message would be "JOWPLFANFUIPEABEE" (let's suppose 'A' comes after the whitespace character). Unless the third party knew the encryption algorithm we're using, the message would sound like complete gibberish. On the other hand, the receiving end would know the decryption algorithm beforehand (change each letter for the *previous* one in the alphabet) and would therefore be able to understand the message. Of course, this method is trivial, and encryption algorithms nowadays are much more sophisticated. We'll look at some of those algorithms in the next section.

Integrity

A secure communication should ensure the *integrity* of the transmitted message. This means that the receiving end must be able to know *for sure* that the message he is receiving is exactly the one that the transmitting end sent him. Take into account that a malicious user could intercept a communication with the intent of modifying its contents, not with the intent of eavesdropping.

"Traditional" encryption algorithms don't protect against these kind of attacks. For example, consider the simple algorithm we've just seen. If a third party used a network sniffer to change the encrypted message to "JAMJAMJAMJAMJAMJA", the receiving end would apply the decryption algorithm and think the message is "I LI LI LI LI LI ". Although the malicious third party might have no idea what the message contains, he is nonetheless able to modify it (this is relatively easy to do with certain network sniffing tools). This confuses the receiving end, which would think there has been an error in the communication. Public-key encryption algorithms (which we'll see shortly) *do* protect against this kind of attack (the receiving end has a way of knowing if the message it received is, in fact, the one the transmitting end sent and, therefore, not modified).

Authentication

A secure communication should ensure that the parties involved in the communication are who they claim to be. In other words, we should be protected from malicious users who try to *impersonate* one of the parties in the secure conversation. Again, this is relatively easy to do with some network sniffing tools. However, modern encryption algorithms also protect against this kind of attack.

15.1.2 Authorization

Another important concept in computer security, although not generally considered a 'pillar' of secure communications, is the concept of *authorization*. Simply put, authorization refers to mechanisms that decide when a user is *authorized* to perform a certain task. Authorization is related to authentication because we generally need to make sure that a user is who he claims to be (authentication) before we can make a decision on whether he can (or cannot) perform a certain task (authorization).

For example, once we've ascertained that a user is a member of the Mathematics Department, we would then allow him to access all the MathServices. However, we might deny him access to other services that are not related to his department (BiologyService, ChemistryService, etc.)

ⓘ **Authorization vs. Authentication**

It is very easy to confuse *authentication* and *authorization*, not so much because they are related (you generally need to perform authentication on a user to make authorization decisions on that user), but because they sound alike ("auth...a-tion")! This is somewhat aggravated by the fact that many people tend to shorten both words as "auth" (especially in programming code). At this point, you might be saying to yourself: "That's pretty silly, they're different concepts...I'm not going to confuse them just because they sound alike!" Well, believe me, it happens, and quite a lot :-). When in doubt, remember that *authentication* refers to finding out if someone's identity is *authentic* (if they really are who they claim to be) and that *authorization* refers to finding out if someone is *authorized* to perform a certain task.

15.2 Introduction to Cryptography

Cryptography is "the art of writing in secret characters". *Encrypting* is the act of translating a "normal message" to a message written with "secret characters" (also known as the *encrypted message*). Decrypting is the act of translating a message written with "secret characters" into a readable message (the *unencrypted message*). It is, by far, one of the most important areas in computer security, since modern encryption algorithms can ensure all three pillars of a secure conversation: privacy, integrity, and authentication.

15.2.1 Key-based Algorithms

In the previous page we saw a rather simple encryption algorithm which simply substituted each letter in a message by the next one in the alphabet. The decryption algorithm was, of course, substituting each letter in the encrypted message with the *previous* letter in the alphabet. This kind of algorithm, based on the *substitution* of letters, is easily broken. Most modern algorithms, however, are *key-based.*

A *key-based algorithm* uses an *encryption key* to encrypt the message. This means that the encrypted message is generated using not only the message, but also using a "key" (Figure 15.1).

The receiver can then use a *decryption key* to decrypt the message. Again, this means that the decryption algorithm doesn't rely only on the encrypted message. It also needs a "key" (Figure 15.2)

Some algorithms use the same key to encrypt and decrypt, and some do not. However, we'll look into this in more detail below.

Let's take a look at a simple example. To make things simpler, let's suppose we're not transmitting alphanumerical characters, only numerical characters. For example, we might be interested in transmitting the following message:

```
1 2 3 4 5 6 5 4 3 2 1
```

We will now choose a key which will be used to encrypt the message. Let's suppose the key is "4232". To encrypt the message, we'll repeat the key as many times as necessary to 'cover' the whole message:

```
1 2 3 4 5 6 5 4 3 2 1
4 2 3 2 4 2 3 2 4 2 3
```

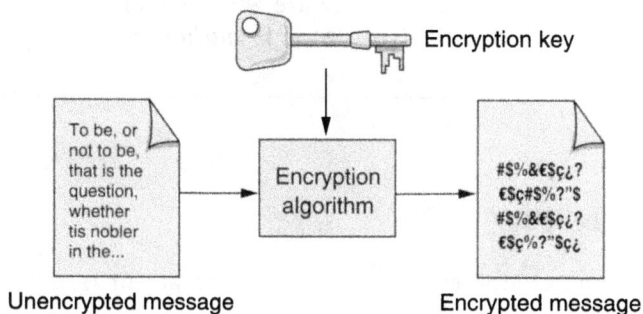

Unencrypted message   Encrypted message

Figure 15.1: Key-based encryption

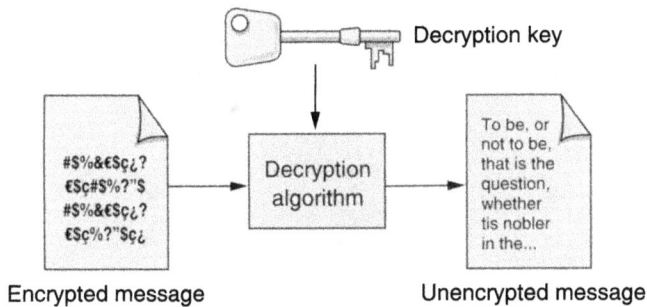

Figure 15.2: Key-based decryption

Now, we arrive at the encrypted message by adding both numbers:

```
  1 2 3 4 5 6 5 4 3 2 1
+ 4 2 3 2 4 2 3 2 4 2 3
-------------------------
  5 4 6 6 9 8 8 6 7 4 4
```

The resulting message (54669886744) is the encrypted message. We can decrypt following the inverse process: Repeating the key as many times as necessary to cover the message, and then *subtract* the key character by character:

```
  5 4 6 6 9 8 8 6 7 4 4
- 4 2 3 2 4 2 3 2 4 2 3
-------------------------
  1 2 3 4 5 6 5 4 3 2 1
```

Voilà! We're back at the unencrypted message! Notice how it is absolutely necessary to have the decryption key (in this case, the same as the encryption key) to be able to decrypt the message. This means that a malicious user would need both the message *and* the key to eavesdrop on our conversation.

Please note that this is a very trivial example. Current key-based algorithms are *much more* sophisticated (for starters, keys are much longer, and the encryption process is not as simple as "adding the message and the key"). However, these complex algorithms *are based* on the same basic principle shown in our example: a key is needed to encrypt/decrypt a message. Most modern algorithms, however, only depend on keeping the key a secret (while the algorithm is usually public and known by everyone).

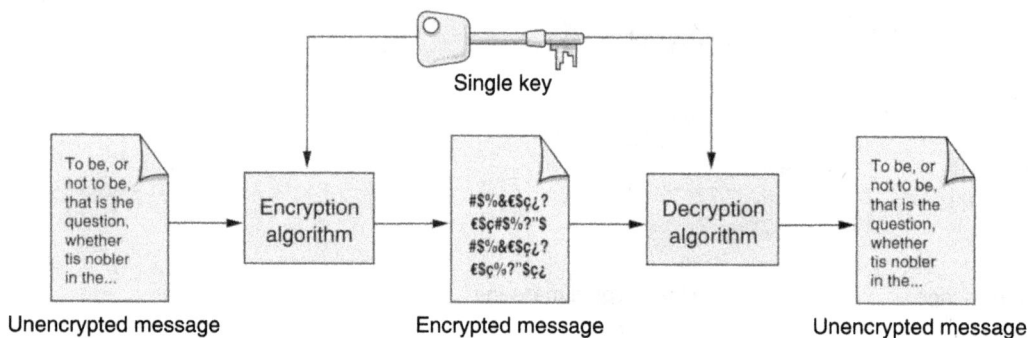

Figure 15.3: Key-based symmetric algorithm

15.2.2 Symmetric and Asymmetric Key-Based Algorithms

The example algorithm we've just seen falls into the category of *symmetric algorithms*. This type of algorithm uses *the same key* for encryption and decryption (Figure 15.3)

Although this type of algorithm is generally very fast and simple to implement, it also has several drawbacks. The main drawback is that they can only be used to guarantee privacy (integrity and authentication would have to be done some other way). Another drawback is that both the sender and the receiver need to agree on the key they will use throughout the secure conversation (this is not a trivial problem).

Secure systems nowadays tend to use *asymmetric algorithms*, where a different key is used to encrypt and decrypt the message. *Public-key algorithms*, which are introduced in the next section, are the most commonly used type of asymmetric algorithms. We will also see how, in practice, a combination of both symmetric and asymmetric algorithms is used to get "the best of both worlds".

15.3 Public-Key Cryptography

Public-key algorithms are *asymmetric* algorithms and, therefore, are based on the use of two different keys, instead of just one. In public-key cryptography, the two keys are called the *private key* and the *public key*

- **Private key**: This key must be known *only* by its owner.
- **Public key**: This key is known to everyone (it is *public*)
- **Relation between both keys**: What one key encrypts, the other one decrypts, and vice versa. That means that if you encrypt something with my public key (which you would know, because it's public :-), I would need my private key to decrypt the message.

15.3.1 A Secure Conversation Using Public-Key Cryptography

In a basic secure conversation using public-key cryptography, the sender encrypts the message using the receiver's *public* key. Remember that this key is known to everyone. The encrypted message is sent to the receiving end, who will decrypt the message with his *private* key. Only the receiver can decrypt the message because no one else has the private key. Also, notice how the encryption algorithm is the same at both ends: what is encrypted with one key is decrypted with the other key using the same algorithm (Figure 15.4)

15.3.2 Pros and Cons of Public-key Systems

Public-key systems have a clear advantage over symmetric algorithms: there is no need to agree on a common key for both the sender and the receiver. As seen in the previous example, if someone wants to receive an encrypted message, the sender only needs to know the receiver's public key (which the receiver will provide; publishing the *public* key in no way compromises the secure transmission). As long as the receiver keeps the private key secret, no one but the receiver will be able to decrypt the messages encrypted with the corresponding public key. This is due to the fact that, in public-key systems, it is relatively easy to compute the public key from the private key, but *very hard* to compute the private key from the public key (which is the one everyone knows). In fact, some algorithms need several *years* (or even decades) of constant computation to obtain the private key from the public key (the bigger the key, the longer it will take) (Figure 15.5)

Another important advantage is that, unlike symmetric algorithms, public-key systems can guarantee integrity and authentication, not only privacy. The basic communication seen above only guarantees privacy. We will shortly see how integrity and authentication fit into public-key systems.

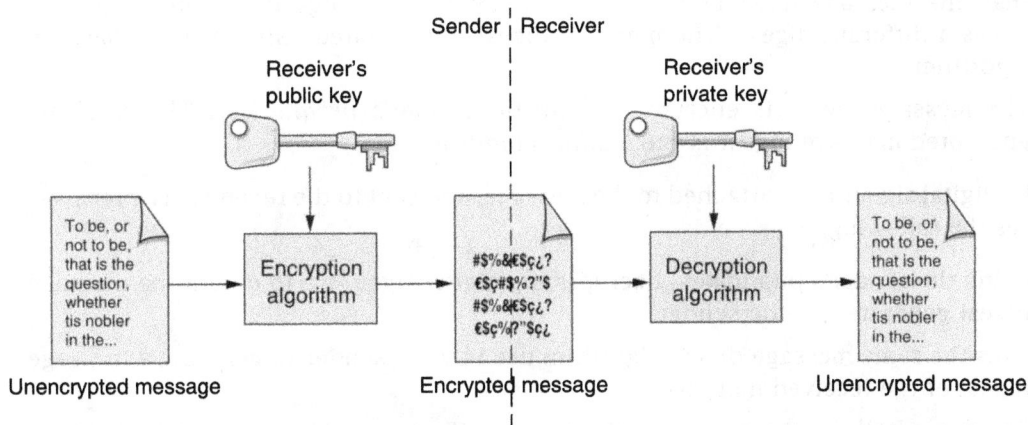

Figure 15.4: Key-based asymmetric algorithm

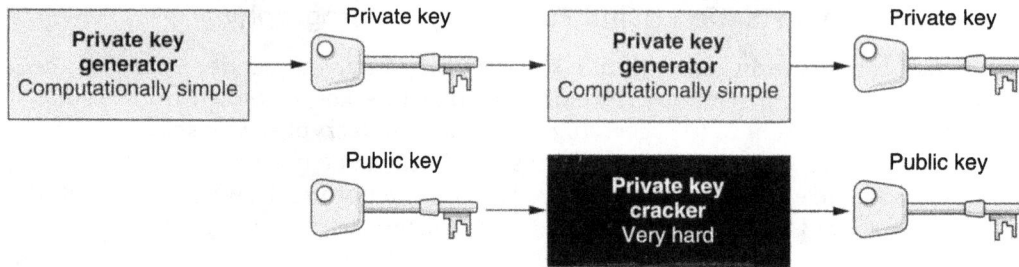

Figure 15.5: Public-key generation

The main disadvantage of using public-key systems is that they are not as fast as symmetric algorithms. This is why *hybrid algorithms* which combine symmetric and asymmetric algorithms are used in practice. These algorithms use an asymmetric algorithm to perform authentication and agree on a common key (usually called the *session key*). For the rest of the communication ("the session"), the common key is used with a symmetric algorithm (which is much faster).

15.3.3 Digital Signatures: Integrity in Public-key Systems

Integrity is guaranteed in public-key systems by using *digital signatures* (Figure 15.6). A digital signature is a piece of data which is attached to a message and which can be used to find out if the message was tampered with during the conversation (e.g. through the intervention of a malicious user).

The digital signature for a message is generated in two steps:

1. A *message digest* is generated. A message digest is a "summary" of the message we are going to transmit, and has two important properties: (1) It is always smaller than the message itself and (2) Even the slightest change in the message produces a different digest. The message digest is generated using a set of hashing algorithms.

2. The message digest is encrypted using the sender's *private* key. The resulting encrypted message digest is the *digital signature*.

The digital signature is attached to the message, and sent to the receiver. The receiver then does the following:

1. Using the sender's public key, decrypts the digital signature to obtain the message digest generated by the sender.

2. Uses the same message digest algorithm used by the sender to generate a message digest of the received message.

3. Compares both message digests (the one sent by the sender as a digital signature, and the one generated by the receiver). If they are not *exactly the same*, the message

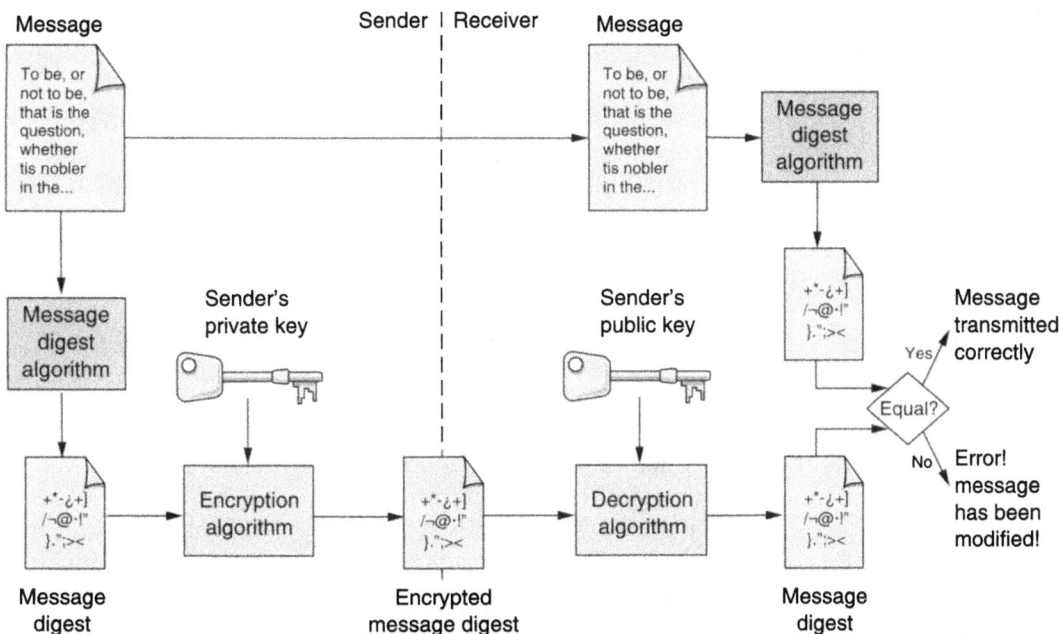

Figure 15.6: Digital signatures

has been tampered with by a third party. We can be sure that the digital signature was sent by the sender (and not by a malicious user) because *only* the sender's public key can decrypt the digital signature (which was encrypted by the sender's private key; remember that what one key encrypts, the other one decrypts, and vice versa). If decrypting using the public key renders a faulty message digest, this means that either the message or the message digest are not exactly what the sender sent.

Using public-key cryptography in this manner ensures integrity, because we have a way of knowing if the message we received is exactly what was sent by the sender. However, notice how the above example guarantees *only* integrity. The message itself is sent unencrypted. This is not necessarily a bad thing: in some cases we might not be interested in keeping the data private, we simply want to make sure it isn't tampered with. To add privacy to this conversation, we would simply need to encrypt the message as explained in the first diagram.

15.3.4 Authentication in Public-key Systems

The above example does guarantee, to a certain extent, the authenticity of the sender. Since *only* the sender's public key can decrypt the digital signature (encrypted with the sender's *private* key). However, the only thing this guarantees is that whoever sent the message has the private key corresponding to the public key we used to decrypt the digital signature.

Although this public key might have been advertised as belonging to the sender, how can we be absolutely certain? Maybe the sender isn't really who he claims to be, but just someone impersonating the sender.

Some security scenarios might consider that the 'weak authentication' shown in the previous example is sufficient. However, other scenarios might require that there is absolutely no doubt about a user's identity. This is achieved with *digital certificates*, which are explained below.

15.4 Certificates and Certificate Authorities

A *digital certificate* is a digital document that *certifies* that a certain public key is owned by a particular user. This document is signed by a third party called the *certificate authority* (or CA). Figure 15.7, might help you get an idea of what a digital certificate is.

Of course, the certificate is encoded in a digital format (no, you don't get a paper diploma so you can brag to your pals that "you really are who you claim to be" :-). The important thing to remember is that the certificate is *signed* by a third party (the certificate authority) which does not itself take place in the secure conversation. The signature is actually a digital signature generated with the CA's private key. Therefore, we can verify the integrity of the certificate using the CA's public key.

15.4.1 It's All About Trust

Having a certificate to prove to everyone else that your public key is really, truly, honestly yours allows us to conquer the third pillar of a secure conversation: authentication. If you digitally sign your message with your private key, and send the receiver a copy of your certificate, he can know for sure that the message was sent by *you* (because only your public key can decrypt the digital signature...and the certificate assures that the public key the receiver uses is yours and no one else's).

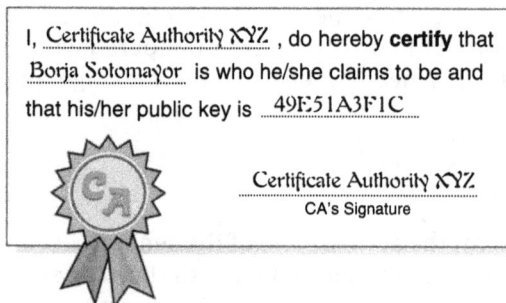

> I, Certificate Authority XYZ , do hereby **certify** that Borja Sotomayor is who he/she claims to be and that his/her public key is 49E51A3F1C
>
> Certificate Authority XYZ
> CA's Signature

Figure 15.7: A digital certificate

However, all this is true supposing you *trust* the certificate. To be more exact, you have to *trust the CA that signs the certificate*. Believe it or not, there are no fancy algorithms to decide when a CA is trustworthy...you must decide by yourself whether you trust or don't trust a CA. This means that the public-key system you use will generally have a list of 'trusted CAs', which includes the digital certificates of those CAs you will trust (each of these certificates, in turn, include the CA's public key, so you can verify digital signatures).

You have to decide which CAs make it into the list. This decision should be based on whether you trust the CA's processes and agree with its policies. Some CAs are so well known that they are included by default in many public-key systems (for example, web browsers usually include VeriSign (http://www.verisign.com) and GlobalSign (http://www.globalsign.com) certificates, because many websites use certificates issued by those companies to authenticate themselves to web browsers). Of course, you can add other CAs to the "trusted list". For example, if your department sets up a CA, and you *trust* that the department's CA will only issue certificates to trustworthy people, then you could add it to the list.

15.4.2   X.509 Certificate Format

Now that we've gone through the basics, let's take a look at the format in which digital certificates are encoded: the X.509 certificate format. An X.509 certificate is a file which includes a lot of information in a binary format. Of all the information we can find in a certificate, we will be mostly interested in the following:

- **Subject**: This is the "name" of the user. It is encoded as a *distinguished name* (the format for distinguished names will be explained next).

- **Subject's public key**: This includes not only the key itself, but information such as the algorithm used to generate the public key.

- **Issuer's Subject**: CA's distinguished name.

- **Digital signature**: The certificate includes a digital signature of all the information in the certificate. This digital signature is generated using the CA's private key. To verify the digital signature, we need the CA's public key (which can be found in the CA's certificate).

As you can see, the information we can find in an X.509 certificate is the same which was shown in Figure 15.7 (name, CA's name, public key, CA's signature). Notice how the certificate, however, does *not* include the private key, which must be kept separate from the public key. Remember that the certificate is a public document we want to be able to distribute to other users so they can verify our identity, so we don't want to include the private key (which must be known only by the owner of the certificate). When we are in possession of both a certificate and its associated private key, these two items are generally referred to as the user's credentials.

Distinguished Names

Names in X.509 certificates are not encoded simply as "common names", such as "Borja Sotomayor", "Lisa Childers", "Certificate Authority XYZ", or "Systems Administrator". They are encoded as *distinguished names*, which are usually represented as a comma-separated list of name-value pairs. For example, the following could be our distinguished names:

```
O=University of Chicago, OU=Department of Computer Science,
    CN = Borja Sotomayor


O=Argonne National Laboratory, OU=Mathematics and Computer Science Division,
    CN=Lisa Childers
```

So what do "O", "OU", and "CN" mean? A distinguished name can have several different attributes, and the most common are the following:

- **O**: Organization
- **OU**: Organizational Unit
- **CN**: Common Name (generally, the user's name)
- **C**: Country.

15.4.3   CA Hierarchies

We mentioned earlier that your 'trusted CA list' includes the certificates of all the CAs you decided to trust. At that point, you might have asked yourself: And who signs the CA's certificate? The answer is very simple: Another CA! (as we will see in a moment, the CA's certificate can also be signed by itself). This allows for hierarchies of CAs to be created, in such a way that although you might not explicitly trust a CA (because it's not in your list), you might trust the higher-level CA that signed its certificate (which makes the lower-level CA trustworthy). Figure 15.8, might make things a bit clearer.

In Figure 15.8 Borja's certificate is signed by Certificate Authority FOO. Certificate Authority FOO's certificate is, in turn, signed by Certificate Authority BAR. Finally, BAR's certificate is signed by itself (we'll get to this in a second).

If you receive Borja's certificate, and don't explicitly trust CA FOO (the issuer of my certificate), this doesn't automatically mean the certificate isn't trustworthy. You might check to see if CA FOO's certificate was issued by a CA you *do* trust. If it turns out that CA BAR is in your "trusted list", then that means that Borja's certificate is trustworthy.

However, notice that the higher-level CA (BAR) has signed its own certificate. This is not uncommon, and is called a *self-signed certificate*. A CA with a self-signed certificate is called a *root CA*, because there's "no one above it". To trust a certificate signed by this CA, it must necessarily be in your "trusted CA list".

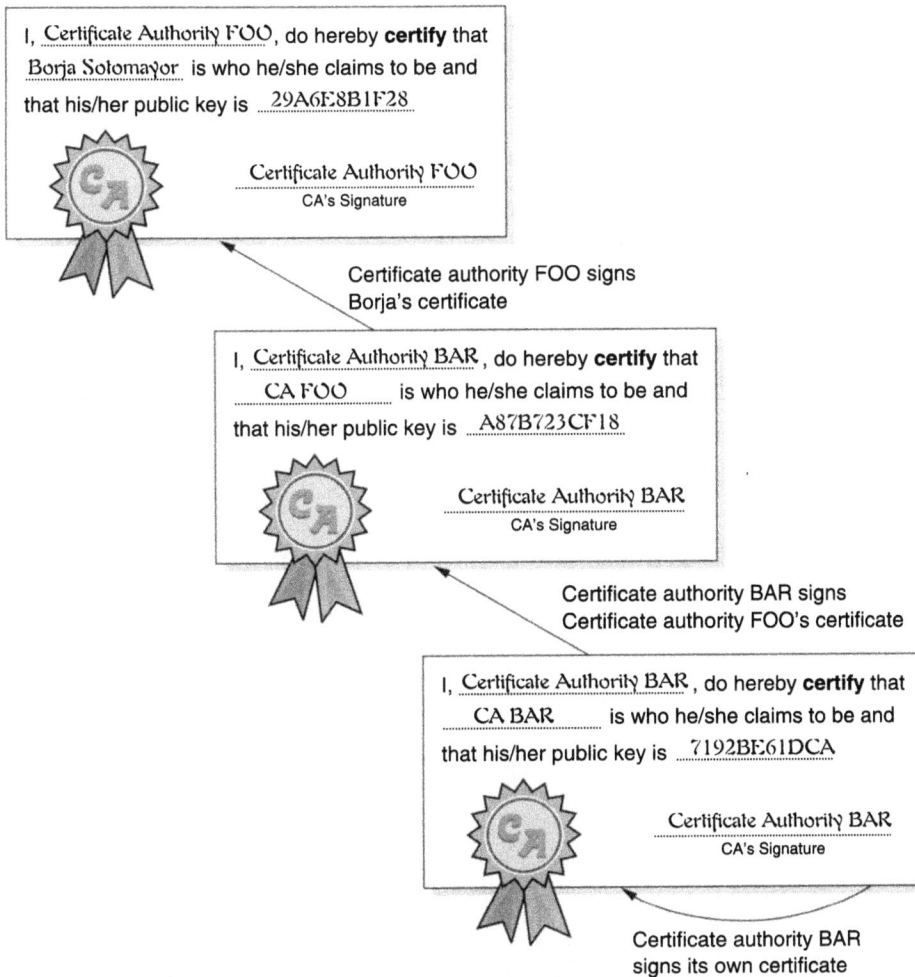

Figure 15.8: Digital certificate chain of verification

References

[1] Bruce Schneier. *Practical Cryptography*. John Wiley & Sons, 2003. http://www.schneier.com/book-practical.html.

[2] Bruce Schneier. *Applied Cryptography*. John Wiley & Sons, 1996. http://www.schneier.com/book-applied.html.

GSI: Grid Security Infrastructure

This chapter introduces the Grid Security Infrastructure, the basis for GT4's Security layer. A working knowledge of fundamental security concepts is assumed in this chapter. If you've read the previous chapter, you should be fine. If you haven't, but you know how public-key cryptography, certificates, and certificate authorities work, then you should also be fine.

16.1 Introduction to GSI

If you're familiar with Grid Computing, you probably know that security is one of the most important parts of a Grid application. Since a grid implies crossing organizational boundaries, resources are going to be accessed by a lot of different organizations. This poses a lot of challenges:

- We have to make sure that only certain organizations can access our resources, and that we're 100% sure that those organizations are really who they claim to be. In other words, we have to make sure that everyone in our grid application is properly *authenticated*.

- Depending on our application, we may also be interested in assuring data *integrity* and *privacy*.

- As we'll see later on, there will be cases when it will be necessary for a user to *delegate* his credentials to another user, so that other users will be able to perform certain actions on his behalf.

The Globus Toolkit 4 allows us to overcome the security challenges posed by grid applications through the *Grid Security Infrastructure* (or GSI). GSI is a family of components that include command-line tools to manage certificates, Java classes to easily integrate security into our web services, and higher-level services. GSI offers programmers the following features, which we will discuss in the next sections:

- Transport-level and message-level security
- Authentication through X.509 digital certificates
- Several authorization schemes
- Credential delegation and single sign-on
- Different levels of security: container, service, and resource.

16.2   Transport-Level and Message-Level Security

GSI allows us to enable security at two levels: the *transport* level or the *message* level. To explain the difference between these two levels, let's suppose we want our communication to be private. If we use transport-level security, as shown in Figure 16.1, then the complete communication (all the information exchanged between the client and the server) would be encrypted. If we use message-level security, as shown in Figure 16.2, then only the *content* of the SOAP message is encrypted, while the rest of the SOAP message is left unencrypted.

Both transport-level and message-level security in GSI are based on public-key cryptography and, therefore, can guarantee privacy, integrity, and authentication. However, not all communications need to have those three features all at once. As soon as we start programming secure services, we'll see how using these features is as easy as adding a few

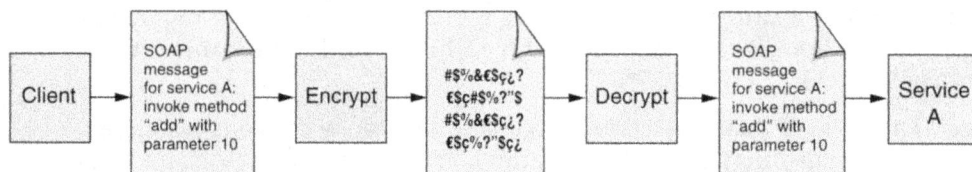

Figure 16.1: Transport-level security

Figure 16.2: Message-level security

lines in the client indicating that (for example) we want to use integrity, but not encryption during the communication.

ⓘ **Message-level vs. transport-level performance**

Transport-level security has been around for a long time and, in fact, chances are that you've already used it when browsing the Web, since secure websites rely on transport-level security. Message-level security in Web Services is relatively new and, although it offers more features than transport-level security, its performance still leaves a bit to be desired. So, even though we would ideally like to use message-level security for everything (because of its feature-rich goodness), we will sometimes have to consider using transport-level security if performance is an issue. In fact, transport-level security is used by default in the Globus Toolkit.

GSI offers two message-level protection schemes, and one transport-level scheme. The differences between these three schemes are highlighted in Table 16.1.

- **GSI Secure Message**: Provides message-level security and is based on the WS-Security standard.

- **GSI Secure Conversation**: Provides message-level security and is based on the WS-SecureConversation specification. When this method is chosen, a *security context* is first established between the client and the server. After an initial exchange of messages to establish the context, all the following messages can reuse that context, resulting in a better performance than GSI Secure Message (if the overhead of setting up the context is acceptable). Furthermore, GSI Secure Conversation is the only scheme that supports credential delegation (explained further on).

- **GSI Transport**: Provides transport-level security by using TLS (formerly known as SSL). It provides the best performance and is used by default in GT4.

These schemes are *not* mutually exclusive, although it is generally enough to use a single method for our communications.

	GSI Secure Conversation	GSI Secure Message	GSI Transport
Technology	WS-SecureConversation	WS-Security	TLS
Privacy (Encrypted)	YES	YES	YES
Integrity (Signed)	YES	YES	YES
Anonymous authentication	YES	NO	YES
Delegation	YES	NO	NO
Performance	Good if sending many messages	Good if sending few messages	Best

Table 16.1: Comparison of transport-level and message-level security

16.3 Authentication

GSI supports three authentication methods:

- **X.509 certificates**: All three protection schemes seen above can be used along with X.509 certificated to provide strong authentication (as seen in Section 15.4).

- **Username and password**: A more rudimentary form of authentication, using usernames and passwords, can also be used. However, when using usernames and passwords, we will not be able to use features like privacy, integrity, and delegation. This form of authentication is not covered in this book (you can refer to the official Globus documentation for more details on how to use it).

- **Anonymous authentication**: A client can request to be anonymous, or *unauthenticated*. Note that the server-side cannot use this type of authentication. Anonymous authentication generally makes sense when we are using more than one security scheme. For example, we can use GSI Secure Conversation (authenticated with X.509 certificates) and anonymous GSI Transport, so that we don't perform an additional (redundant) authentication.

In general, in terms of authentication, communications can fall into three categories:

- **Mutually authenticated**: Both parties (the server and the client) exchange authentication information.

- **Server-side only authentication**: The server provides authentication information, but the client is unauthenticated (uses anonymous authentication).

- **Completely unauthenticated**: Neither of the parties provides any authentication information. This can only be achieved by not using GSI at all (as we have been doing in the Java WS Core chapters).

> ☞ Since unauthenticated communications are not commonly used, the Globus literature generally uses the term *authentication methods* to refer directly to GSI Secure Conversation, GSI Secure Message, and GSI Transport. We will follow this same convention throughout the rest of the book.

16.4 Authorization

Although authorization is not one of the "fundamental pillars" of a secure conversation, it is nonetheless an important part of GSI. Authorization refers to who is *authorized* to perform a certain task. In a Web services context, we will generally need to know who is authorized to use a certain web service.

GSI supports authorization in both the server-side and the client-side. Several authorization mechanisms are already included with the toolkit, but we will also be able to implement our own authorization mechanisms. The default authorization mechanisms will be described in more detail in Chapter 20.

16.4.1 Server-Side Authorization

The server has six possible authorization modes. Depending on the authorization mode we choose, the server will decide if it accepts or declines an incoming request.

- **None**: This is the simplest type of authorization. No authorization will be performed.

- **Self**: A client will be allowed to use a service if the client's identity is the same as the service's identity.

- **Gridmap**: A gridmap is a list of 'authorized users' akin to an ACL (Access Control List). We will see them in detail in Chapter 20. When this type of authorization is used, only the users that are listed in the service's gridmap may invoke it.

- **Identity authorization**: A client will be allowed to access a service if the client's identity matches a specified identity. In a sense, this is like having a one-user gridmap (except that identity authorization is configured programmatically, whereas the gridmap is represented as a file in our system).

- **Host authorization**: A client will be allowed to access a service if it presents a host credential that matches a specified hostname. In other words, we will only allow requests coming from one particular host.

- **SAML Callout authorization**: We can delegate the authorization decision to an OGSA Authorization-compliant authorization service. OGSA-Authz (http://forge.gridforum.org/projects/ogsa-authz) is a GGF working group whose goal is to specify standard authorization components. One of the main technologies used in these components is SAML (Security Assertion Markup Language).

16.4.2 Client-Side Authorization

This allows the client to figure out when it will allow a service to be invoked. This might seem like an odd type of authorization, since authorization is generally seen from the server's perspective ("Do I allow client FOO to connect to grid service BAR?"). However, in GSI, clients have every right to be picky about the services they can access.

- **None**: No authorization will be performed.

- **Self**: The client will authorize an invocation if the service's identity is the same as the client.

- **Identity authorization**: As described above, the client will only allow requests to be sent to services with a specified identity.

▪ **Host**: The client will authorize an invocation if the service has a host credential. Furthermore, the client must be able to resolve the address of the host to the hostname specified in the host credential. Note that this is different from server-side host authorization, where we check if the hostname in the credential is equal to a host specified by us.

16.4.3   Custom Authorization

GSI provides an infrastructure to easily plug in our own authorization mechanisms. For example, our organization might be using a legacy authorization service that can't work out-of-the-box with the authorization methods provided by the toolkit. In this case, we can create a new authorization method that will allow GSI to make authorization decisions based on our organization's legacy service.

16.5   Delegation and Single Sign-on (Proxy Certificates)

Credential delegation and single sign-on are one of the most interesting features of GSI, and are possible thanks to something called *proxy certificates*. Before looking into these concepts in detail, let's first take a look at the problem they solve.

16.5.1   The Problem

Let's suppose that user Alice asks user Bob to perform a task (see Figure 16.3). Bob accepts to perform the task, but it turns out that task Z is very complex, and that one of its subtasks (Y) must be performed by a third user: Charlie. In this case, Bob will ask Charlie to perform subtask Y. However, we would ideally like Charlie to be aware that the original requestor is Alice. What should Charlie do? It has two options:

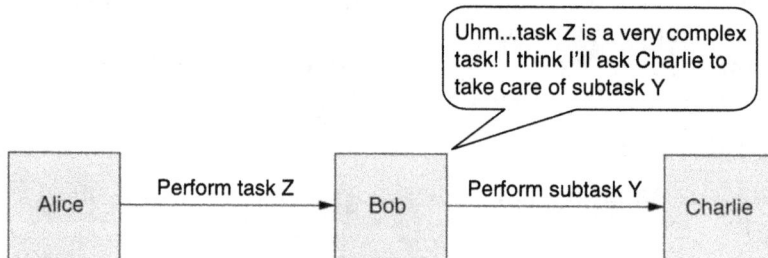

Figure 16.3: Alice, Bob, and Charlie

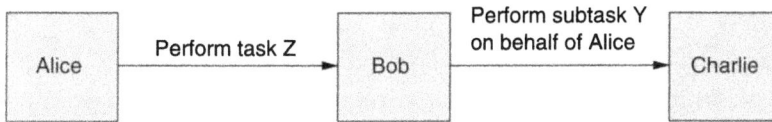

Figure 16.4: Alice, Bob, and Charlie (2)

- **Ignore who the original requestor is**. The user contacting Charlie is Bob, and that's that.

- **Contact Alice**. Bob could specify that the request is being performed on behalf of Alice (as shown in Figure 16.4), and Charlie could contact Alice to ask her, "Hey, did you really request this operation?"

It seems like, given that we want Charlie to be aware that the original requestor is Alice, the second choice seems like the logical one. However, having to contact the original requestor every time an operation is requested on behalf of someone is not an ideal solution. For example, what would happen if Alice has signed off by the time Charlie needs to ascertain if she made the original request? We need a solution that provides *autonomy*, in the sense that Alice can request that a task is performed, and is not expected to be available, or to provide any information (such as authentication information) at any point, except when she initially makes the request.

So, a more elegant solution would be to somehow make Charlie believe that Bob *is* Alice. In other words, it would be interesting to find a legitimate way for Bob to demonstrate that it is, in fact, acting on Alice's behalf. One way of doing this would be for Alice to "lend" its public and private key pair to Bob. However, this is absolutely out of the question. Remember, the private key has to remain *secret*, and sending it to other users (no matter how much you trust them) is a *big* breach in security. What we really need is a special type of certificate like the one shown in Figure 16.5.

Figure 16.5: A proxy certificate

16.5.2   The Solution: Proxy Certificates

The certificate shown in Figure 16.5 is a *proxy certificate*. Webster's Dictionary defines "proxy" as "The instrument by which a person is empowered to transact the affairs of another". As you can see in the picture, the proxy certificate allows the holder of the certificate to act on Alice's behalf. In fact, it's very similar to the X.509 digital certificates seen in Section 15.4, except that it's not signed by a Certificate Authority; it's signed by an end user. We can be sure that the certificate is authentic by checking its signature (Alice digitally signs the certificate, as described in Section 15.3).

But, what about the proxy certificate's public key? Whose public key is it? Alice's? Bob's? The answer is "neither". A proxy certificate has a private–public key pair generated specifically for the proxy certificate. This private–public key pair is mutually agreed upon by both parties (in this case, Alice and Bob), and Alice will only allow the holder of *that* private–public key pair to act on its behalf (in this case, Bob). The exact mechanism by which the proxy certificate is generated by Alice and Bob will be explained later on.

There is, however, something missing from the picture. Allowing someone to act *unconditionally* on your behalf is a risky affair. Sure, you might trust them now, for the particular task you want to do, but someone from Bob might use the proxy certificate in the future to carry out some mischievous deeds on your behalf. Therefore, the lifetime of the certificate is usually very limited (for example, to 12 hours). This means that, if the proxy certificate is compromised, the attacker won't be able to make much use of it. Furthermore, proxy certificates extend ordinary X.509 certificates with extra security features to limit their functionality even more (for example, by specifying that a proxy certificate can only be used for certain tasks). Summing up, a more correct representation of a proxy certificate would be the one shown in Figure 16.6.

16.5.3   What the Solution Achieves: Delegation and Single Sign-On (and more)

A proxy certificate allows a user to act on another user's behalf. This is more properly called *credential delegation*, since proxy certificates allow a user to effectively *delegate* a

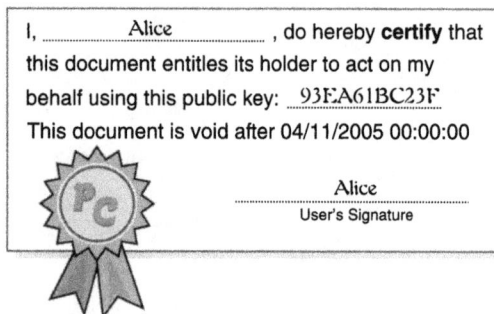

> I, _____Alice_____ , do hereby **certify** that this document entitles its holder to act on my behalf using this public key: __93EA61BC23F__
> This document is void after 04/11/2005 00:00:00
>
> _____Alice_____
> User's Signature

Figure 16.6: A proxy certificate with a limited lifetime

set of credentials (the user's identity) to another user. This solves the problem originally posed, since Bob could use a proxy certificate (signed by Alice, of course) to prove that it is acting on Alice's behalf. Charlie would then know that the original requestor is Alice, but without having to contact Alice herself to verify it.

By using proxy certificates we also get another desirable feature: *single sign-on*. Without proxy certificates, Alice would have to authenticate herself with all the organizations that receive requests "on behalf of Alice". In practice, this means that the user in Alice with permission to read the private key would have to access the key each time a mutual authentication is needed. Since private keys are usually protected by a password, this means that the user would have to *sign on* (provide the password) to access the key and perform authentication. Using proxy certificates, the user only has to sign in *once* to create the proxy certificate. The proxy certificate is then used for all subsequent authentications.

Finally, although we've centered on the advantages of proxy certificates for delegation, these certificates have other features that make them interesting for other purposes. For example, they can be used locally: generating a proxy certificate that authorizes myself to act on my behalf. This might sound silly, but is actually very useful since I can use the proxy certificate for all my secure conversations, instead of using my public–private key pair directly. This reduces the risk of having my conversations compromised because an attacker would only have a chance to crack the proxy's key pair, and not my personal one (which would only be used to generate the proxy certificate). We're not going to discuss all the added benefits of proxy certificates, since in this book we will be mainly concerned with delegation and single sign-on. However, you can check the references for this chapter if you are interested in reading more about proxy certificates.

16.5.4   The Specifics

At this point, you might be truly impressed at how masterfully proxy certificates allow us to delegate credentials in a completely secure manner. Then again, maybe not :-). If you are not willing to take a leap of faith when we say "Proxy certificates are really nifty!", and are not totally convinced that they are secure, this section gives a much more detailed look at the process of creation and validation of a proxy certificate. You can safely skip it unless you really, really, really need a more detailed explanation.

How a Proxy Certificate is Generated

We've said that a proxy certificate can be used to delegate a user's credentials to another, different user. How is this achieved in a secure manner? For example, let's suppose that (as shown in Figure 16.3) Bob needs Alice's credentials so it can make a request to Charlie. Bob, therefore, needs a proxy certificate signed by Alice. Let's take a close look at the process used to generate that certificate.

1. Bob generates a public–private key pair for the proxy certificate.
2. Bob uses the key pair to generate a certificate request, which will be sent to Alice using a secure channel. This certificate request includes the proxy's public key, but *not* the private key.

3. Supposing Alice agrees to delegate its credentials to Bob, Alice will use its private key to digitally sign the certificate request. This results in the creation of a new certificate (the proxy certificate).

4. Alice sends the signed certificate back to Bob using a secure channel.

5. Bob can now use the proxy certificate to act on Alice's behalf.

Notice how the proxy's private key is never transmitted between Alice and Bob. This is also true of Alice's private key.

Validation of a Proxy Certificate

Now let's take a look at Charlie. When Bob sends a request "on behalf of Alice", and sends Charlie the proxy certificate, how can Charlie validate the proxy certificate? In other words, how can Charlie be absolutely sure that Bob *is* acting on Alice's behalf?

The process of validating a proxy certificate is practically identical to the process of validating an ordinary certificate, as described in Section 15.4. The main difference is that the proxy certificate is not signed by a Certificate Authority, it's signed by a user. In our example, the proxy certificate is signed by Alice, which means that we need Alice's public key to test its authenticity. Since Charlie is unlikely to have Alice's certificate, a request that uses a proxy certificate generally also sends the delegator's certificate, so the proxy certificate can be validated. Since the delegator's certificate will be signed by a Certificate Authority, the only step left is to validate the Certificate Authority's signature. Figure 16.7 shows the chain of signatures that we could find in a proxy certificate.

More on Proxy Certificates

There's a lot more to proxy certificates than what has been explained in this chapter. For example, you can use proxy certificates to sign other proxy certificates. However, for the purposes of this book, the material covered here should be enough. If you want to take a closer look at proxy certificates, and everything that can be done with them, we highly recommend reading RFC 3820, Internet X.509 Public Key Infrastructure Proxy Certificate Profile, available at http://www.ietf.org/rfc/rfc3820.txt.

16.6 Container, Service, and Resource Security

Finally, it should be noted that many of the features described in this chapter can be specified at three levels: container, service, and resource level. Of special interest is the fact that we can configure security at the resource level. For example, we can set different authorization mechanisms for a service and its resources, so that stateless operations can be performed without authorization, but stateful operations do require an authorized user.

Throughout the following chapters, we will see exactly what can be configured at each of the three levels.

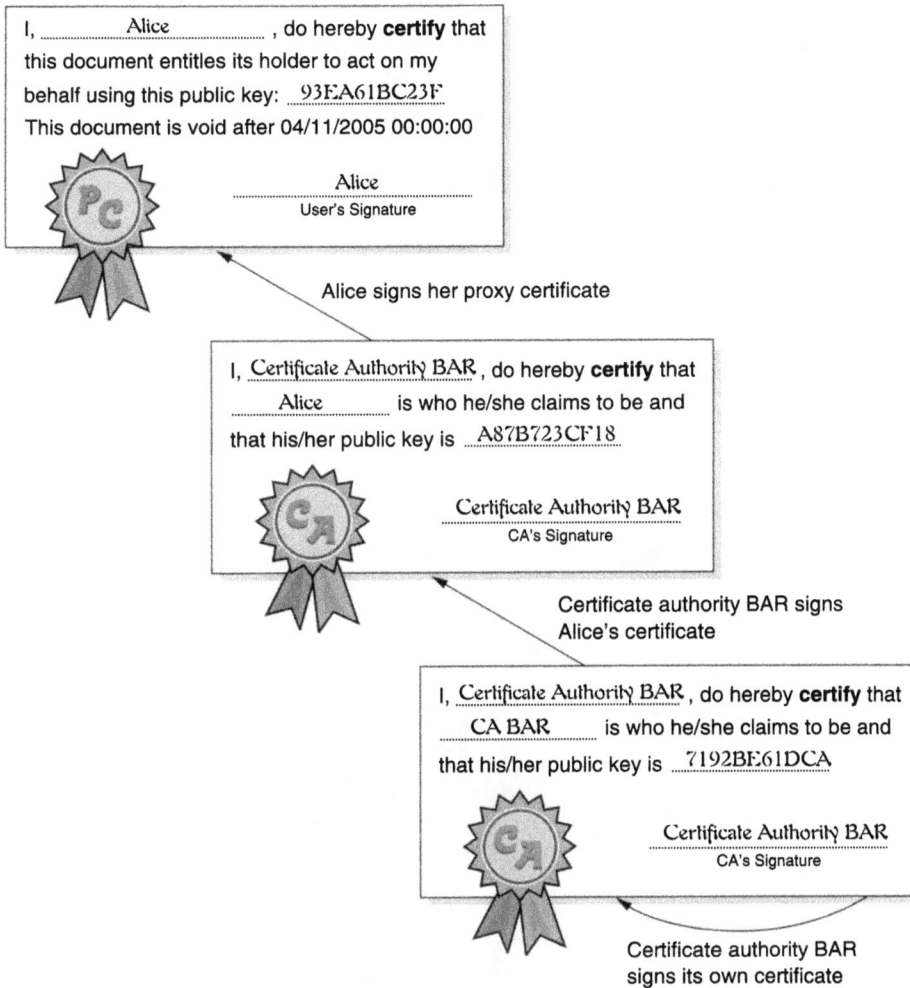

Figure 16.7: Validation of a proxy certificate

References

[1] *Official Globus Security Documentation.* http://www.globus.org/toolkit/docs/4.0/security/.

[2] *Globus Toolkit Version 4 Grid Security Infrastructure: A Standards Perspective.* Von Welch. December 8, 2004. http://www.globus.org/toolkit/docs/4.0/security/GT4–GSI–Overview.pdf.

[3] *RFC 3820 – Internet X.509 Public Key Infrastructure (PKI) Proxy Certificate Profile.* June, 2004. http://www.faqs.org/rfcs/rfc3820.html.

[4] "Web Services Secure Conversation Language (WS-SecureConversation)". IBM, et al., May, 2004. http://www-106.ibm.com/developerworks/library/specification/ ws-secon/.

[5] "WS-Security specification". 1.0. *Web Services Security (WSS) TC.* OASIS, January, 2004.

chapter **17**

Writing a Secure MathService

In this chapter we will add security to our MathService example. We will see that, once we have configured GSI, adding basic security to a service is very simple. The example in this chapter will highlight the changes necessary to make a service secure. In particular, the code will be similar to the singleton example seen in Chapter 7. In the following chapters, we will continue to build on this example as we take a closer look at more elaborate security scenarios.

> ☞ This chapter and all the following chapters assume that you have set up GT4 as explained in Appendix A, Installing the Globus Toolkit 4. In particular, to work through all the following examples, you will need to make sure you have two separate users: a special **globus** account and a normal user account which we will call **globus4user** (this can be your normal user account). The user account must have a valid digital certificate.

17.1 A Secure Service

17.1.1 The Service Interface

Adding security to a service does *not* affect the service interface. However, for the purposes of this example, and the following examples, we will be using a new MathService interface with 4 operations (**add**, **subtract**, **multiply**, and **divide**). We are simply doing this because, further on, it will allow us to configure each operation with a different security configuration (and four simply happens to be a convenient number of operations).

☞ The WSDL file for this example can be found here: **$EXAMPLES_DIR/schema/ examples/MathService_instance_4op/Math.wsdl**

17.1.2 The Service Implementation

At this point, we don't have to modify the service implementation either, since we will be able to add security simply by modifying the WSDD file. However, we *will* be adding a private method **logSecurityInfo** to the service class to print out certain security information.

☞ The code for the service can be found in **$EXAMPLES_DIR/org/globus/examples/services/security/first/impl/ MathService.java**

The code for the resource can be found in **$EXAMPLES_DIR/org/globus/examples/services/security/first/impl/ MathResource.java**

The code for the resource home can be found in **$EXAMPLES_DIR/org/globus/examples/services/security/first/impl/ MathResourceHome.java**

First, let's take a look at the **logSecurityInfo** method. This method will print out a lot of security information. At this point, we are only interested in a snippet of code that prints out the client's identity. This will allow us to verify that authentication is taking place and that the service correctly receives the client's credentials. In the following chapters, we will see what the rest of **logSecurityInfo** prints out, and what that information means.

```
private void logSecurityInfo(String methodName)
{
        Subject subject;
        logger.info("SECURITY INFO FOR METHOD '" + methodName + "'");


        // Print out the caller
        String identity = SecurityManager.getManager().getCaller();
        logger.info("The caller is:" + identity);


        // Print out more security information

}
```

Next, the implementation of the remote operations is exactly the same as in a non-secure service. The only difference is that we will be calling the **logSecurityInfo** method in each of them. For example, the **add** method looks like this:

```
public AddResponse add(int a) throws RemoteException {

    logSecurityInfo("add");


    MathResource mathResource = getResource();
    mathResource.setValue(mathResource.getValue() + a);
    mathResource.setLastOp("ADDITION");


    return new AddResponse();
}
```

Finally, remember that, strictly speaking, we are not modifying the Java files at all. We are simply adding some logging code to keep track of what's happening in the service. At this point, adding security will affect only the deployment files. Later on, more complicated security scenarios will require that we modify the service implementation.

17.2 The Security Descriptor

The heart of a secure service is its *security descriptor*. This file specifies the security configuration for a service. One of the really neat things about the security descriptor is that it centralizes practically all the security configuration for a service. So, if we decide to modify some security aspects of a service, we will only need to modify the security descriptor, *not* the Java files.

In the next chapter, we will take a much closer look at this special file and its syntax. For now, we will be using the following security descriptor:

```
<securityConfig xmlns="http://www.globus.org">


    <authz value="none"/>


</securityConfig>[-1pt]
```

> ☞ This is file **$EXAMPLES_DIR/org/globus/examples/services/security/first/etc/security-config-first.xml**

This security descriptor simply specifies that we will not be performing any authorization (**none**). As we will see in the next chapter, the fact that we have not specified anything else basically means that the client will be free to use any type of security it wants. For example, we will be configuring our client to use GSI Secure Conversation.

Of course, we'll need to tell our service that we want it to use that security descriptor. To do this, we have to add the following parameter to our service in the WSDD file. Notice that the path to the security descriptor is relative to **$GLOBUS_LOCATION**.

```
<service name="examples/security/first/MathService" provider="Handler"

    use="literal" style="document">


    <!-- Other parameters -->>


    <parameter name="securityDescriptor"

            value="etc/org_globus_examples_services_security_first/

                security-config-first.xml"/>


</service>
```

> ☞ The WSDD file for this service is **$EXAMPLES_DIR/org/globus/examples/services/ security/first/deploy-server.wsdd**
>
> Our service's name is **"examples/security/first/MathService"**. If you take a look at this file, you will see that it contains deployment information for more services. These are the services we will use in the following chapters. Notice how the only difference between each service (beside the service name) is the fact that they have different security descriptors. Again, since the security configuration is kept separate from the Java code, there is no need to modify the Java implementation if we decide to change the security configuration. We simply have to modify the security descriptor.

17.3 A Secure Client

The client used to invoke the secure service will be almost identical to all the clients seen so far. The only difference is that we will be instructing the client to use GSI Secure Conversation with encryption and no client-side authorization. Believe it or not, this requires two simple lines of code:

❶ `((Stub)math)._setProperty(Constants.GSI_SEC_CONV,Constants.ENCRYPTION);`

❷ `((Stub)math)._setProperty(Constants.AUTHORIZATION,`

`    NoAuthorization.getInstance());`

❶ We're telling the stub to use GSI Secure Conversation with encryption. In Chapter 19, we will see how to configure clients to use different authentication methods, such as GSI Secure Message and GSI Transport, and with different levels of protection (for example, using digital signatures to guarantee integrity, instead of using full-blown encryption).

❷ We're telling the stub to use no *client-side* authorization. Remember that there is a difference in GSI between client-side and server-side authorization (take a look at Section 16.4). It is important to understand that each side is configured separately: the server-side authorization is configured in the security descriptor, and client-side authorization is configured by setting the **Constants.AUTHORIZATION** property on the stub. In Chapter 20, we will take a closer look at authorization, including all the authorization methods available on the server and client side.

Besides those two lines, the rest of the client is practically identical to the ones we've already seen. The only difference is that we will be putting the calls to the remote operations inside **try...catch** blocks to observe how certain exceptions are raised in certain circumstances (we'll see this in the following chapters).

```
package org.globus.examples.clients.MathService_instance_4op;

import javax.xml.rpc.Stub;

import org.apache.axis.message.addressing.Address;
import org.apache.axis.message.addressing.EndpointReferenceType;
import org.globus.axis.util.Util;
import org.globus.examples.services.security.first.impl.MathConstants;
import org.globus.examples.stubs.MathService_instance_4op.MathPortType;
import org.globus.examples.stubs.MathService_instance_4op.service.
    MathServiceAddressingLocator;
import org.globus.wsrf.impl.security.authorization.NoAuthorization;
import org.globus.wsrf.security.Constants;
import org.oasis.wsrf.properties.GetResourcePropertyResponse;

public class Client_GSISecConv_Encrypt {

        public static void main(String[] args) {
                MathServiceAddressingLocator locator = new
                    MathServiceAddressingLocator();
```

```
GetResourcePropertyResponse valueRP;
String value;
try {

        String serviceURI = args[0];


        // Create endpoint reference to service
        EndpointReferenceType endpoint = new
            EndpointReferenceType();
        endpoint.setAddress(new Address(serviceURI));
        MathPortType math = locator.getMathPortTypePort
            (endoint);


        // Get PortType
        math = locator.getMathPortTypePort
            (endpoint);


        // Setup security options
        ((Stub)math)._setProperty(Constants.GSI_SEC_CONV,
            Constants.ENCRYPTION);
        ((Stub)math)._setProperty(Constants.AUTHORIZATION,
            NoAuthorization.getInstance());


        // Perform an addition
        try {
                math.add(60);
                System.out.println("Addition was successful");
        } catch (Exception e) {
                System.out.println("[add]        ERROR: "
                    + e.getMessage());
        }
```

```
                    /* Similar calls to subtract(), multiply(), divide(),
                            and getResourceProperty */


            } catch (Exception e) {
                e.printStackTrace();
            }
        }
    }
```

---

⑦ This file is **$EXAMPLES_DIR/org/globus/examples/clients/MathService_instance_**
  4op/Client_GSISecConv_Encrypt.java

17.4 Trying It Out

We are now ready to give this secure service a try.

Compile and Deploy

First of all, we'll need to build the service:

    ./globus-build-service.sh sec_first

Now, we have to deploy it. Remember that you have to do this from the **globus** account:

    globus-deploy-gar $EXAMPLES_DIR/org_globus_examples_services_security_
    first.gar

Starting the Container

At this point you might be thinking that we will now be running the container *without* the
-nosec flag we've been using so far to "deactivate security". Well, you thought wrong! :-).

    globus-start-container -nosec

At this point, we can clarify what the **-nosec** flag does. It only deactivates *transport-level*
security, but not message-level security. So, we can still use GSI Secure Conversation
and GSI Secure Message. The reason why we're not using transport-level security (yet)
is because, as part of our test of this service, we will be using a tool included with the
Globus Toolkit that can intercept the SOAP messages. However, this tool won't work if we
use transport-level security, so you should use the **-nosec** flag if you want to participate in
our little experiment. In the following chapters, on the other hand, you can use the **-nosec**
flag at your discretion (unless otherwise noted).

Compiling the Client

Let's compile the client:

```
javac \
-classpath ./build/stubs/classes/:$CLASSPATH \
org/globus/examples/clients/MathService_instance_4op/Client_GSISecConv_
    Encrypt.java
```

Running the Client

Before running the client, we will need to create a proxy certificate for our user account. We have to do this because the default behavior in the client-side is to use a proxy certificate for authentication. In the next chapter we will see how we can configure a client to use a specific set of credentials, instead of using a proxy certificate.

To create a proxy certificate, run the following from your user account:

```
grid-proxy-init
```

You will see the following:

```
Your identity: /O=Globus/OU=GT4 Examples/CN=Globus 4 User
Enter GRID pass phrase for this identity:
```

The password you must enter is the one you entered when creating your user certificate (as described in Section A.6, "Setting up user certificates"). Once you've entered the password, you will see the following:

```
Creating proxy ........................................ Done
Your proxy is valid until: Sun Apr 24 04:28:26 2005
```

> ⓘ Globus proxy certificates expire by default in 12 hours. If you get a "proxy expired" or "no valid credentials found" error message later on, this probably means that your proxy certificate has expired. Simply create a new one using **grid-proxy-init**.

Now, run the client:

```
java \
-classpath ./build/stubs/classes/:$CLASSPATH \
org.globus.examples.clients.MathService_instance_4op.Client_GSISecConv_
    Encrypt \
http://127.0.0.1:8080/wsrf/services/examples/security/first/MathService
```

If all goes well, you should see this in the client side:

```
Addition was successful

Subtraction was successful

Multiplication was successful

Division was successful

Current value: 20
```

And the following on the server side:

```
SECURITY INFO FOR METHOD 'add'

The caller is: /O=Globus/OU=GT4 Examples/CN=Globus 4 User


... other security information ...
```

> ✆ Remember that the **logSecurityInfo** will also print out a lot of other information. Don't worry about that information right now. It will be explained later on.

Notice how the service has correctly authenticated the client, and prints out its distinguished name:

```
/O=Globus/OU=GT4 Examples/CN=Globus 4 User.
```

17.5   Does This Really Work?

After all the work we've gone through to setup security, you might be a bit disappointed. After all, we've gone through all the trouble of setting up a CA and some certificates to end up writing a MathService client that behaves just like all the other MathService clients we've already seen in the book. Ho hum. You're probably asking yourself: "Yeah, but is this really doing all that encryption thingy?"

To empirically prove that it is doing the "encryption thingy", we are going to use an Apache Axis tool called TCPMonitor that is included with the toolkit. This tool allows us to intercept the data that are sent from the client to the server (and vice versa). We will see how the information is, in fact, encrypted.

To start TCPMonitor, run this:

```
java org.apache.axis.utils.tcpmon 8081 localhost 8080
```

This starts an instance of the TCPMonitor (Figure 17.1). What the monitor will do is listen on port 8081 and redirect all the traffic it receives on that port to port 8080 (which is where our container is listening). This means that TCPMonitor acts like a proxy, not like

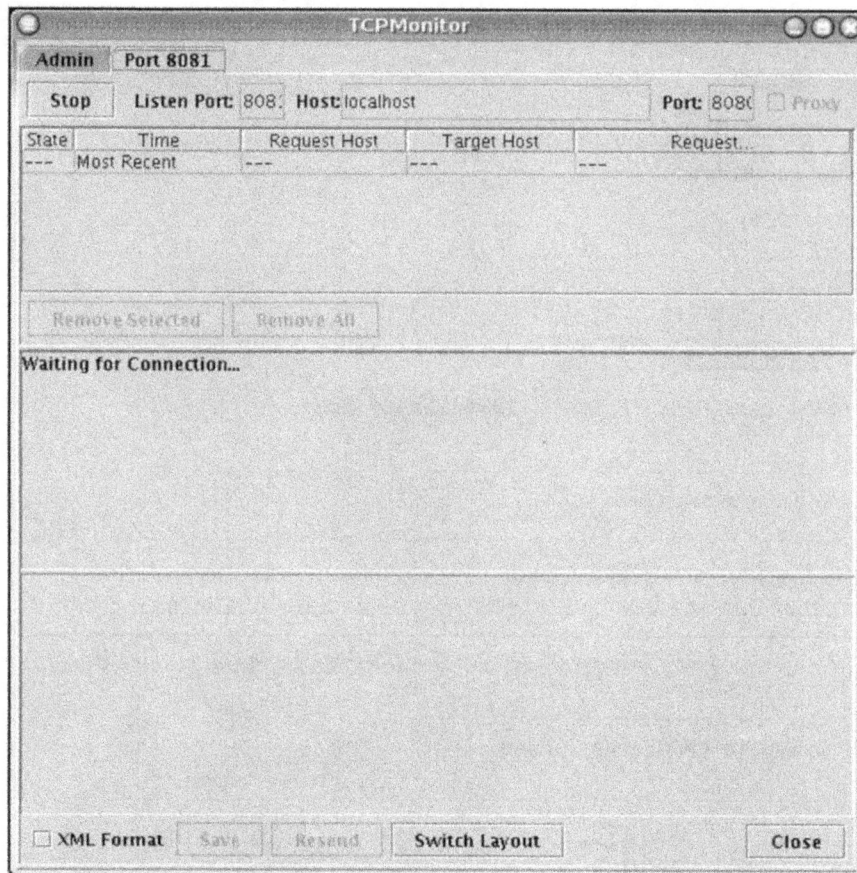

Figure 17.1: TCPMonitor interface (1)

a sniffer, so we'll have to tell our client to make the invocation on port 8081 to be able to see what kind of data are being sent.

> ☞ Make sure you check the "XML Format" box in TCPMonitor. This will make reading the messages much easier.

Let's run the client again. Make sure to change "8080" for "8081" so that the invocation will go through the TCPMonitor. Otherwise, we won't be able to see it.

```
java \
-classpath ./build/stubs/classes/:$CLASSPATH \
org.globus.examples.clients.MathService_instance_4op.Client_GSISecConv_
    Encrypt \
http://127.0.0.1: 8081 /wsrf/services/examples/security/first/MathService
```

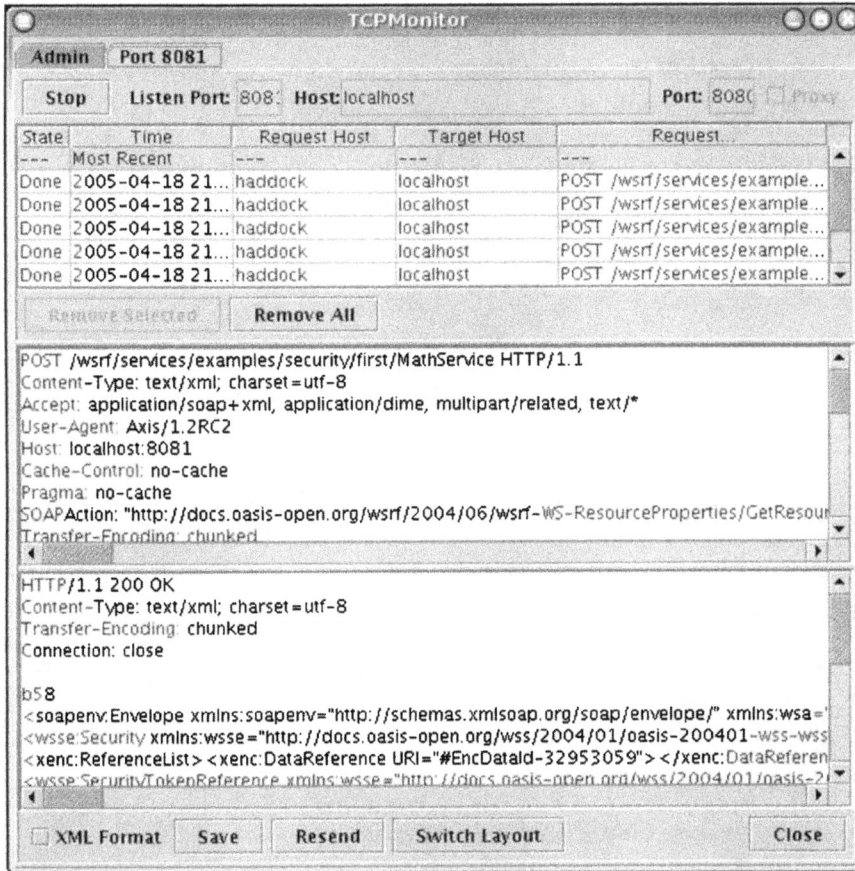

Figure 17.2: TCPMonitor interface (2)

Once you've invoked the service, the TCPMonitor will reflect that it has intercepted some connections on port 8081 (Figure 17.2). The top list shows a list of the connections. You can select any of them to see what was sent to the server (top text area) and what the server replied to the client (bottom text area).

ⓘ **Five calls and eight connections… huh?** TCPMonitor should show 8 connections. This might seem a bit odd considering that our client only makes *five* calls to MathService (**add**, **subtract**, **multiply**, **divide**, and **getResourceProperty**). However, remember that we're using GSI Secure Conversation.

As described in the previous chapter, GSI Secure Conversation involves the creation of a *security context* before the client and server can actually communicate. This accounts for the first three connections. The client and server are agreeing on the details of the secure context. Once the context is created, the calls can proceed as normal.

> In Chapter 19, we will see how to configure our client to use GSI Secure Message. At that point, you can use TCPMonitor again and see how there are no messages being sent to create a security context.

Let's take a look at the fourth connection, corresponding to the *add* invocation:

```
<soapenv:Envelope xmlns:soapenv="http://schemas.xmlsoap.org/soap/envelope/"
    xmlns:wsa="http://schemas.xmlsoap.org/ws/2004/03/addressing"
        xmlns:xenc="http://www.w3.org/2001/04/xmlenc# "
    xmlns:xsd="http://www.w3.org/2001/XMLSchema"
        xmlns:xsi="http://www.w3.org/2001/XMLSchema-instance">
<soapenv:Header>
    <wsse:Security
        xmlns:wsse="http://docs.oasis-open.org/wss/2004/01/oasis-200401-
            wss-wssecurity-secext-1.0.xsd"
        soapenv:mustUnderstand="1">
        <wsc:SecurityContextToken xmlns:wsc="http://schemas.xmlsoap.org/
            ws/2004/04/sc"
        xmlns:wsu="http://docs.oasis-open.org/wss/2004/01/
            oasis-200401-wss-wssecurity-utility-1.0.xsd"
        wsu:Id="SecurityContextToken-15021407">
        <wsc:Identifier>8439eb60-b079-11d9-bf45-98ad001497de</
            wsc:Identifier>
        </wsc:SecurityContextToken>
        <xenc:ReferenceList>
            <xenc:DataReference URI="#EncDataId-749304">
                </xenc:DataReference>
        </xenc:ReferenceList>
    </wsse:Security>
    <wsa:MessageID soapenv:mustUnderstand="0">uuid:837bf290-b079-11d9-
        a882-a1d8507fabe7</wsa:MessageID>
    <wsa:To soapenv:mustUnderstand="0">
      http://127.0.0.1:8081/wsrf/services/examples/security/first/
      MathService
```

```
        </wsa:To>
        <wsa:Action soapenv:mustUnderstand="0">
            http://www.globus.org/namespaces/examples/MathService_instance_4op/
                MathPortType/addRequest
        </wsa:Action>
        <wsa:From soapenv:mustUnderstand="0">
            <wsa:Address>http://schemas.xmlsoap.org/ws/2004/03/addressing/role/
                anonymous</wsa:Address>
        </wsa:From>
    </soapenv:Header>

<soapenv:Body>
    <xenc:EncryptedData Id="EncDataId-749304" Type="http://www.w3.org/2001/
        04/xmlenc#Content">
        <xenc:EncryptionMethod Algorithm="http://www.globus.org/2002/
            04/xmlenc#gssapi-enc"></xenc:EncryptionMethod>
        <ds:KeyInfo xmlns:ds="http://www.w3.org/2000/09/xmldsig#">
            <wsse:SecurityTokenReference
                xmlns:wsse="http://docs.oasis-open.org/wss/2004/01/
                    oasis-200401-wss-wssecurity-secext-1.0.xsd">
                    <wsse:Reference URI="#SecurityContextToken-15021407">
                    </wsse:Reference>
                </wsse:SecurityTokenReference>
        </ds:KeyInfo>
        <xenc:CipherData>
            <xenc:CipherValue>
                FwMAAYCNYHoPTT6WgG096yj0NPONpNXp3u8tVPbPBjZzqzFt
                x03Yh1tMEI6ebObR1Rvr8ihBk+EtBsCAUNuVXN7QAP/FrMIZJ
                zacALBaLpie0A1BfO8QjjDNGvv6KsDrydY2qywSuaZvqclUus
                2eAnPjW3ewanPqemntYfSHKW0X81wkIDI4oUx5WOOkYbKLl6
                Yg/R4osS2PR+/aqAwAb8vdZtzDdBkpyIDfCsMrQnZA
                1sarFbdZPT7buNIPRJ8vja3/icV5yB4WZg8sobm7K
```

7yrYkFT6g1nLHhgznsJj0pf67BcowXO+swpOuSAnjczNEyDRafk
6HaIPeeMpZWLGNL11BrfHM1pDGs0foDCvbFApfFJGz5v70DdAGQWz5
xsR6YQOBp8gcOh1B+hrsc6Wyf8RiQ/kxBfMYZ3hKY8fah4oRaq39/
sJvA8pXnfxvp1EKonQKhOh/yYYGkuzMI4whDOKsLAiEwjX3uOh
UdAF1zwwqyPK4zYBHsz1Qe0I81D2OmTjQw=
                         </xenc:CipherValue>
                       </xenc:CipherData>
                    </xenc:EncryptedData>
                 </soapenv:Body>

            </soapenv:Envelope>
Holy gibberish, Batman! :-).

Notice how only certain parts of the message are encrypted, not the *whole* message. Remember that this is because GSI Secure Conversation is a form of *message-level* security (explained in Section 16.2). This means that we only encrypt the contents of the message, but not the whole message. Notice how the message still reveals what the service URI is, along with the operation name, but the actual call itself is encrypted. If we wanted the whole message to be encrypted we would need to use *transport-level* security (GSI Transport). We will see how to do this in Chapter 19.

## chapter 18

The Security Descriptor

In the previous chapter we used a *security descriptor* to configure our service's security. This file can also be used to configure client-side security or to specify the security options of the standalone container. We can even specify security options at the resource level using a security descriptor. In this chapter we will take a first look at what can be done with the security descriptor.

18.1 Basic Structure

The security descriptor is an XML file with the following root element:

```
<securityConfig xmlns="http://www.globus.org">


        <-- options -->


</securityConfig>
```

Inside the **securityConfig** we will use tags to specify security options. Depending on whether we are writing a service, resource, client, or container security descriptor, we will be able to use different security options.

18.2 Common Options

The four types of descriptors have a set of common options. First of all, we can use the resource descriptor to specify what credentials must be used during a secure communication. We do this using the *credential* tag:

```
<securityConfig xmlns="http://www.globus.org">

    <credential>

        <key-file value="key_file"/>

        <cert-file value="certificate_file"/>

    </credential>

</securityConfig>
```

> ☞ Remember that *credentials* is a catch-all term referring to both a user's certificate and its associated private key.

On the server-side, the container will first check if a resource is configured to run with a specific set of credentials. If it isn't, then it checks the service's security descriptor. If no credentials are specified there, then the container's credentials are used. Finally, in case the container does not have its own certificate, it will rely on the proxy certificate of the user running the container.

On the client-side, the client will first check if the client security descriptor specifies what certificate must be used. If it doesn't, it will rely on the proxy certificate of the user running the client.

> ☞ In the previous example, remember how we had to create a proxy certificate before running the client. Now you know that we have to do this because we were not using a client security descriptor to specify a normal certificate for the client.

Another common option can be used to specify what proxy certificate (instead of a normal certificate) must be used, in case we don't want the container or client to look for a proxy certificate in the default location.

```
<securityConfig xmlns="http://www.globus.org">


    <proxy-file value="proxy_file"/>


</securityConfig>
```

Finally, both the container and service security descriptor can be configured to reject *limited proxies*. These will be discussed briefly in Chapter 22.

```
<securityConfig xmlns="http://www.globus.org">


    <reject-limited-proxy value="true"/>


</securityConfig>
```

18.3 The Service Security Descriptor

In the previous chapter we used the following security descriptor for our service:

```
<securityConfig xmlns="http://www.globus.org">


    <authz value="none"/>


</securityConfig>
```

> ☞ This is file **$EXAMPLES_DIR/org/globus/examples/services/security/first/etc/ security-config-first.xml**

Remember that, to tell the service that it has to use that file, we added a new parameter to the WSDD file:

```
<parameter name="securityDescriptor"
        value="etc/org_globus_examples_services_security_first/
        security-config-first.xml"/>
```

The simple security descriptor used in the previous chapter only specified that we didn't want any server-side authorization to take place. In the following chapters we will see that we can also use the service security descriptor to specify the following:

- Authentication method on a per-method basis. Remember that by "authentication method" we refer to GSI Secure Conversation, GSI Secure Message, or GSI Transport. We will also be able to specify a default authentication method. This is covered in Chapter 19.

- Server-side authorization. This is covered in Chapter 20.

- Run-as identity. We can specify whether the service should run using the resource, service, or container credentials. If the client has delegated its credentials, we can also choose to run using the caller's credentials. This is covered in Chapter 22.

18.4 The Resource Security Descriptor

We can specify what authentication method and what authorization method must be used at the resource level. This is covered in Chapter 21.

18.5 The Client Security Descriptor

In the previous chapter, we used the following two lines to specify what authentication and authorization methods had to be used by the client:

```
((Stub)math)._setProperty(Constants.GSI_SEC_CONV,Constants.ENCRYPTION);

((Stub)math)._setProperty(Constants.AUTHORIZATION,NoAuthorization.
    getInstance());
```

However, instead of configuring client-side security programmatically, we can also do so using a client security descriptor. The descriptor equivalent of these two lines would be the following:

```
<securityConfig xmlns="http://www.globus.org">


    <GSISecureConversation>
            <privacy/>
    </GSISecureConversation>


    <authz value="none"/>


</securityConfig>
```

> ☞ This is file **$EXAMPLES_DIR/org/globus/examples/clients/**
> **MathService_instance_4op/GSISecConv_Encrypt.xml**

To instruct the client to use a security descriptor, we simply have to use the following two lines:

```
String secDescFile = "path/to/security_descriptor.xml";

((Stub) stub_object)._setProperty(Constants.CLIENT_DESCRIPTOR_FILE, secDescFile);
```

> ☞ The path of the security descriptor can be absolute, or relative to the current directory from which we are running the client application.

This way, changing the security configuration for a client does not involve compiling it again. We only have to modify its security descriptor. As we will see in the next two chapters, the client security descriptor can be used to specify what authentication and authorization methods must be used in the client side.

☞ The examples bundle includes a client that reads its security configuration from a descriptor. It can be found at: **$EXAMPLES_DIR/org/globus/examples/clients/ MathService_instance_4op/Client_SecDesc.java**. This client expects the service's URI as its first parameter and the path to the security descriptor file as the second parameter. This path is relative to the current directory.
To compile this client:

```
javac \

-classpath ./build/stubs/classes/:$CLASSPATH \

org/globus/examples/clients/MathService_instance_4op/Client_SecDesc.java
```

A couple of example security descriptors are also included. For example, to run the previous chapter's client with a security descriptor, simply run the following:

```
java \

-classpath ./build/stubs/classes/:$CLASSPATH \

org.globus.examples.clients.MathService_instance_4op.Client_SecDesc \

http://127.0.0.1:8080/wsrf/services/examples/security/first/MathService \

org/globus/examples/clients/MathService_instance_4op/GSISecConv_Encrypt.xml
```

18.6 The Container Security Descriptor

This descriptor specifies the global security options that affect the whole container. The location of the descriptor is specified in the container's WSDD file:

```
<parameter

        name="containerSecDesc"

        value="etc/globus_wsrf_core/global_security_descriptor.xml"/>
```

☞ This is part of file **$GLOBUS_LOCATION/etc/globus_wsrf_core/server-config.wsdd**

18.6.1 Specifying the Container Credentials

If you take a look at the default container descriptor, you'll see that the only option specified is the credentials that the container must use. These credentials are created during the installation of the toolkit (as described in Appendix A, Installing the Globus Toolkit 4 or in the official installation guide).

```xml
<?xml version="1.0" encoding="UTF-8"?>

<securityConfig xmlns="http://www.globus.org">

    <credential>

        <key-file value="/etc/grid-security/containerkey.pem"/>

        <cert-file value="/etc/grid-security/containercert.pem"/>

    </credential>

</securityConfig>
```

> ☞ This is file **$GLOBUS_LOCATION/etc/globus_wsrf_core/global
> _security_descriptor.xml**

Of course, you can modify these values to use other credentials if you wish. You must make sure that both the private key file and the certificate file are readable by the user that will run the container.

18.6.2 Message-level Security Options

Two options allow us to control certain aspects of message-level security. The first option affects GSI Secure Conversation. Remember that, in this case, a security context is established before the communication takes place. The **context-lifetime** option allows us to control the maximum lifetime of the context. The default value is 10 minutes.

```xml
<?xml version="1.0" encoding="UTF-8"?>

<securityConfig xmlns="http://www.globus.org">


    <!-- ... -->


    <context-lifetime value="seconds"/>


    <!-- ... -->


</securityConfig>
```

The second option affects GSI Secure Message which is potentially vulnerable to a type of attack called *replay attack.* In this type of attack, a malicious user sends a copy of a message previously sent by one of the parties. To neutralize this attack, the container can keep track of received messages using a special message identifier. We can use the **replay-attack-interval** option to control how long each message must be tracked. If a message with the same identifier arrives more than once during that interval, it is discarded. The default interval is 5 minutes.

```
<?xml version="1.0" encoding="UTF-8"?>

<securityConfig xmlns="http://www.globus.org">


    <!-- ... -->


    <replay-attack-interval value="milliseconds"/>


    <!-- ... -->


</securityConfig>
```

18.6.3 Global Gridmap File

Gridmap authorization will be explained in more detail in Chapter 20. In that chapter we will see how to specify a gridmap file for a specific service. However, we can also specify a global gridmap file valid for all services. The container will first check if the resource security descriptor specifies a gridmap file. If it doesn't, it will check the service security descriptor. If a gridmap isn't specified there either, then the global gridmap file is used.

```
<?xml version="1.0" encoding="UTF-8"?>

<securityConfig xmlns="http://www.globus.org">


    <!-- ... -->


    <gridmap value="gridmap_file"/>


    <!-- ... -->


</securityConfig>
```

chapter **19**

Authentication

In Section 16.3 we saw how GSI supports three authentication methods: GSI Secure Conversation, GSI Secure Message, and GSI Transport. In this chapter we will see how we can use the service security descriptor to require that a certain authentication method is used. Next, we will see how we can set the client's authentication method programmatically or using a client security descriptor. Finally, we will see two simple examples that illustrate how server-side and client-side authentication works.

19.1 Service Authentication Options

Using the service security descriptor we can specify a default authentication method and also configure authentication on a per-method basis.

19.1.1 Setting the Default Authentication Methods

To specify a default authentication method we will use the **auth-method** tag. This tag can contain any of the following tags:

- **<GSISecureConversation/>**: Indicating that the client must use GSI Secure Conversation.
- **<GSISecureMessage/>**: Indicating that the client must use GSI Secure Message.
- **<GSITransport/>**: Indicating that the client must use GSI Transport.

For example, the following security descriptor specifies that the default authentication method is GSI Secure Conversation. This means that, if the client uses any other method, he will not be allowed to communicate with the service.

```
<securityConfig xmlns="http://www.globus.org">

    <!-- ... -->

    <auth-method>
            <GSISecureConversation/>
    </auth-method>

</securityConfig>
```

Note that we specify more than one authentication method. For example, in the following descriptor we are allowing GSI Secure Conversation *and* GSI Transport. If the client tried to use GSI Secure Message, it would receive an error message.

```
<securityConfig xmlns="http://www.globus.org">

    <!-- ... -->

    <auth-method>
            <GSISecureConversation/>
            <GSITransport/>
    </auth-method>

</securityConfig>
```

Finally, we can also use the <none/> tag to specify that no authentication is required. This tag cannot be combined with the other three tags seen above.

```
<securityConfig xmlns="http://www.globus.org">

    <!-- ... -->

    <auth-method>
            <none/>
    </auth-method>

</securityConfig>
```

19.1.2 Setting Per-Method Authentication

In a similar way, we can specify the authentication for each method. To do this, we use the **method** tag. This tag will contain an **auth-method** as above specifying the acceptable authentication methods. For example, the following security descriptor requires that **add** be invoked using GSI Secure Conversation, while **subtract** must be invoked using GSI Secure Message.

```
<securityConfig xmlns="http://www.globus.org">


        <method name="add">
                <auth-method>
                        <GSISecureConversation/>
                </auth-method>
        </method>


        <method name="subtract">
                <auth-method>
                        <GSISecureMessage/>
                </auth-method>
        </method>


</securityConfig>
```

Note that we can still specify a default authentication method for those methods for which we have not explicitly specified an authentication method.

19.1.3 Setting the Protection Level

Finally, we can use the **protection-level** tag to specify the protection level. This tag must be contained inside **<GSISecureConversation>**, **<GSISecureMessage/>**, and **<GSITransport/>** and can contain the following two tags:

- **<integrity/>**: Indicating that the client must use digital signatures, guaranteeing *only* integrity.

- **<privacy/>**: Indicating that the client must use encryption, guaranteeing privacy. Note that using encryption in GSI also guarantees integrity.

For example:

```
<securityConfig xmlns="http://www.globus.org">

    <method name="add">
      <auth-method>
        <GSISecureConversation>
              ❶
          <protection-level>
            <privacy/>
          </protection-level>
        </GSISecureConversation>
      </auth-method>
    </method>

    <method name="subtract">
      <auth-method>
        <GSISecureConversation>
              ❷
          <protection-level>
            <integrity/>
          </protection-level>
        </GSISecureConversation>
      </auth-method>
    </method>

    <method name="multiply">
      <auth-method>
        <GSISecureConversation>
              ❸
          <protection-level>
            <integrity/>
            <privacy/>
          </protection-level>
```

```
        </GSISecureConversation>

      </auth-method>

    </method>


  </securityConfig>
```

❶ The client must use encryption, but cannot use digital signatures alone.

❷ The client must use digital signatures, but not encryption.

❸ The client can use encryption *or* digital signatures (note that this option doesn't mean that the client must use both, it means that the client can choose between either).

19.2 Client Authentication Options

Authentication in the client can be set programmatically or by using a client security descriptor. In Chapter 17 we configured authentication programmatically by including the following line:

```
((Stub) math)._setProperty(Constants.GSI_SEC_CONV,Constants.ENCRYPTION);
```

In the previous chapter, we saw that an equivalent way of telling our client to use GSI Secure Conversation with encryption is to use the following security descriptor:

```
<securityConfig xmlns="http://www.globus.org">


    <GSISecureConversation>
              <privacy/>
    </GSISecureConversation>


    <authz value="none"/>


</securityConfig>
```

The only code we have to add to the client in this case is to tell it to use the security descriptor:

```
String secDescFile = "path/to/security_descriptor.xml";

((Stub) stub_object )._setProperty(Constants.CLIENT_DESCRIPTOR_FILE,
    secDescFile);
```

19.2.1   GSI Secure Conversation

To specify GSI Secure Conversation with encryption in the security descriptor, we must include the following:

```
<securityConfig xmlns="http://www.globus.org">


    <!-- ... -->


    <GSISecureConversation>
        <privacy/>
    </GSISecureConversation>


    <!-- ... -->


</securityConfig>
```

> ☞ Notice how, unlike the service security descriptor, there is no **protection-level** tag.

To enable GSI Secure Conversation with encryption programmatically, we must include the following in our client:

```
((Stub) stub_object )._setProperty(Constants.GSI_SEC_CONV,Constants.ENCRYPTION);
```

To enable GSI Secure Conversation with digital signatures, but not full-blown encryption, we must include the following in the security descriptor:

```
<securityConfig xmlns="http://www.globus.org">
    <!-- ... -->


    <GSISecureConversation>
            <integrity/>
    </GSISecureConversation>


    <!-- ... -->


</securityConfig>
```

To do it programmatically:

```
((Stub) stub_object)._setProperty(Constants.GSI_SEC_CONV,Constants.SIGNATURE);
```

19.2.2 GSI Secure Message

Using GSI Secure Message on the client is a bit more tricky than using GSI Secure Conversation. Remember how, unlike GSI Secure Conversation, this authentication method did not involve the creation of a security context first. To avoid this initial setup, GSI Secure Message depends on having the server's public key beforehand if we want to perform encryption. So, our client security descriptor must include the path to the container's certificate file (where its public key is stored). We do this using the **peer-credentials** tag.

```
<securityConfig xmlns="http://www.globus.org">


    <!-- ... -->


    <GSISecureMessage>

        <privacy/>

        <peer-credentials value="/etc/grid-security/containercert.pem"/>

    </GSISecureMessage>


    <!-- ... -->


</securityConfig>
```

> ☞ In the above example, we are assuming that the service will be using the container's credentials at **/etc/grid-security/containercert.pem**. However, if the service is running under a different set of credentials, you must make sure that the **peer-credentials** tag points to the appropriate certificate file.

Doing this programmatically is not as simple as before, since we have to load the certificate file into memory:

```
// Specify server's public key
String pkFile = "/etc/grid-security/containercert.pem";
Subject subject = new Subject();
X509Certificate serverCert = CertUtil.loadCertificate(pkFile);
EncryptionCredentials encryptionCreds = new EncryptionCredentials(
            new X509Certificate[] { serverCert });
subject.getPublicCredentials().add(encryptionCreds);
```

```
// Set stub options
```

```
((Stub) math)._setProperty(Constants.GSI_SEC_MSG, Constants.ENCRYPTION);
```

```
((Stub) math)._setProperty(Constants.PEER_SUBJECT, subject);
```

On the other hand, using GSI Secure Message with digital signatures is simpler because we do not have to use the server's public key.

> ☞ Remember that a digital signature is encrypted using our private key, not using the server's public key. This might be a good time to review Section 15.3.

If we want to use a security descriptor, we simply have to include the following:

```
<securityConfig xmlns="http://www.globus.org">


        <!-- ... -->


    <GSISecureMessage>
            <integrity/>
    </GSISecureMessage>


        <!-- ... -->


</securityConfig>
```

Programmatically we do the following:

```
((Stub) stub_object )._setProperty(Constants.GSI_SEC_MSG,Constants.SIGNATURE);
```

19.2.3   GSI Transport

When using GSI Transport, we must first make sure that the standalone container is running in secure mode. To do this, we just have to start it without the **-nosec** flag.

globus-start-container

Once the container has started, you will notice that the service URIs now use the HTTPS protocol and listen on the 8443 port (instead of port 8080). For example, the example seen in Chapter 17 would show up like this:

```
...

[26]: https://127.0.0.1:8443/wsrf/services/examples/security/first/MathService

...
```

On the client side, we must make sure that our client class includes the following bit of code so it will work correctly with transport-level security.

```
//...
import org.globus.axis.util.Util;
//...


public class Client {


        static {
                Util.registerTransport();
        }


        // ...


}
```

Finally, the only way to configure GSI Transport in the client is programmatically. If we want to use encryption, we will use the following:

```
((Stub) stub_object )._setProperty(Constants.GSI_TRANSPORT,Constants.ENCRYPTION);
```

If, on the other hand, we only want to use digital signatures to guarantee integrity, we must include the following:

```
((Stub) stub_object )._setProperty(Constants.GSI_TRANSPORT,Constants.SIGNATURE);
```

Note, however, that setting these options doesn't force the client to use GSI Transport. If the URI of the service uses the HTTP protocol, the client will not force HTTPS to be used instead. In other words, these options refer to whether digital signatures or encryption must be used *if* the URI uses the HTTPS protocol.

19.3 Examples

We will now see two examples that use the authentication methods explained above. These examples reuse all the code from the example seen in Chapter 17, except for the security descriptor. We will concentrate on looking at new, more complete, security descriptors and seeing how the service reacts when invoking the service with different security parameters.

> ☞ Remember that the WSDD file for the example seen in Chapter 17 included deployment information for several services. If you already deployed the example from that chapter, then you have already deployed the services we will explain right now (if not, refer to the instructions in Chapter 17).

19.3.1   Example #1

In this first example, we will configure each method with a different set of authentication methods. Then, we will invoke each method from two clients, one using GSI Secure Conversation and one using GSI Transport, observing whether the invocation fails and, if so, why.

The Security Descriptor

```
<securityConfig xmlns="http://www.globus.org">
```

❶

```
<authz value="none"/>
```

❷

```
<method name="add">
  <auth-method>
    <GSISecureConversation/>
  </auth-method>
</method>
```

❸

```
<method name="subtract">
  <auth-method>
    <GSISecureMessage/>
  </auth-method>
</method>
```

❹

```
<method name="multiply">
  <auth-method>
    <GSISecureConversation/>
    <GSISecureMessage/>
  </auth-method>
</method>
```

❺

```
<method name="divide">
  <auth-method>
    <GSITransport/>
  </auth-method>
</method>
```

❻

```
<auth-method>
  <GSISecureConversation/>
  <GSISecureMessage/>
  <GSITransport/>
</auth-method>


</securityConfig>
```

> ☞ This is file **$EXAMPLES_DIR/org/globus/examples/services/security/first/etc/ security-config-auth.xml**

❶ As in our first secure example, we specify that no server-side authorization must be performed. We will see how to perform authorization in the next chapter.

❷ The **add** method can only be invoked using GSI Secure Conversation.

❸ The **subtract** method can only be invoked using GSI Secure Message.

❹ The **multiply** method can be invoked using GSI Secure Conversation *or* GSI Secure Message.

❺ The **divide** method can only be invoked using GSI Transport (transport-level security).

❻ The rest of the methods can be invoked with any of the authentication methods. You might think that there are no "other methods", but we mustn't forget that our service will also include the **getResourceProperty** operation from the standard **GetResource-Property** portType. Remember that we do not implement this method ourselves and use operation providers instead. However, we still have to configure security for that method in our own security descriptor.

A new service, **examples/security/first/MathAuthService**, will have exactly the same deployment parameters as the example seen in Chapter 17, except we will use the security descriptor seen above:

```
<service name="examples/security/first/MathAuthService" provider="Handler"
    use="literal" style="document">


    <!-- ... -->


    <parameter name="securityDescriptor"
        value="etc/org_globus_examples_services_security_first/
            security-config-auth.xml"/>


    <!-- ... -->


</service>
```

> ⌖ Remember that this service was compiled and deployed along with our first
> secure MathService.

The GSI Secure Conversation Client

Now, we will invoke the service using the same client seen in Chapter 17. Remember that
this client was configured to use GSI Secure Conversation with encryption.

If you have not already compiled this client:

**javac **

**-classpath ./build/stubs/classes/:$CLASSPATH **

org/globus/examples/clients/MathService_instance_4op/

    Client_GSISecConv_Encrypt.java

Next, run the client:

**java **

**-classpath ./build/stubs/classes/:$CLASSPATH **

**org.globus.examples.clients.MathService_instance_4op.Client_GSISecConv_Encrypt **

http://127.0 .0.1:8080/wsrf/services/examples/security/first/MathAuthService

You can also run the client using the **Client_SecDesc** client, described in the previous
chapter, that uses a client security descriptor instead of programmatically setting the
client's security options.

```
java \
-classpath ./build/stubs/classes/:$CLASSPATH \
org.globus.examples.clients.MathService_instance_4op.Client_SecDesc \
http://127.0.0.1:8080/wsrf/services/examples/security/first/MathAuthService \
org/globus/examples/clients/MathService_instance_4op/GSISecConv_Encrypt.xml
```

You should see the following output:

❶

```
Addition was successful
```

❷

```
[subtract] ERROR: GSI Secure Message authentication required for
          "{http://www.globus.org/namespaces/examples/MathService_instance
               _4op}subtract" operation.
```

❸

```
Multiplication was successful
```

❹

```
[divide] ERROR: GSI Transport authentication required for
          "{http://www.globus.org/namespaces/examples/MathService_instance
               _4op}divide" operation.
```

❺

```
Current value: 20
```

❶ Addition is successful because the **add** method is configured to work with GSI Secure Conversation.

❷ Subtraction fails because the **subtract** method is configured to *only* accept calls that use GSI Secure Message.

❸ The **multiply** method is configured to accept either GSI Secure Conversation *or* GSI Secure Message. Since we use GSI Secure Conversation, the call is successful.

❹ Division fails because the **divide** method is configured to *only* accept calls using GSI Transport.

❺ Accessing the **Value** RP is successful because the default authentication method (which applies to **getResourceProperty**) is set to any of the three authentication methods.

The GSI Transport Client

We will now use a client configured to use GSI Transport.

> ✆ This client is **$EXAMPLES_DIR/org/globus/examples/clients/
> MathService_instance_4op/Client_GSITransport.java**

Compile the client:

```
javac \

-classpath ./build/stubs/classes/:$CLASSPATH \

org/globus/examples/clients/MathService_instance_4op/Client_GSITransport.java
```

Now, first of all, let's take a look at what happens if we try to run this client with a server with transport-level security deactivated. Make sure you start the container like this:

```
globus-start-container -nosec
```

Next, run the client:

```
java \

-classpath ./build/stubs/classes/:$CLASSPATH \

org.globus.examples.clients.MathService_instance_4op.Client_GSITransport \

http://127.0.0.1:8080/wsrf/services/examples/security/first/MathAuthService
```

You should get the following output:

❶

```
[add]      ERROR: GSI Secure Conversation authentication required for
           "{http://www.globus.org/namespaces/examples/MathService_
           instance_4op}add" operation.


[subtract] ERROR: GSI Secure Message authentication required for
           "{http://www.globus.org/namespaces/examples/MathService_
           instance_4op}subtract" operation.


[multiply] ERROR: GSI Secure Conversation or GSI Secure Message
           authentication required for "{http://www.globus.org/namespaces/
           examples/MathService_instance_4op}multiply" operation.
```

❷

```
[divide]     ERROR: GSI Transport authentication required for
             "{http://www.globus.org/namespaces/examples/MathService_instance_
             4op}divide" operation.


[getRP]      ERROR: GSI Secure Conversation or GSI Secure Message or GSI
             Transport authentication required for
             "{http://www.globus.org/namespaces/examples/MathService_instance_
             4op}getResourceProperty" operation.
```

❶ Addition, subtraction, and multiplication all fail because none of them are configured to accept GSI Transport.

❷ Division and accessing the **Value** RP *also* fail because, although they are configured to accept GSI Transport, we are accessing a server with transport-level security disabled. So, the client is unable to use GSI Transport.

Now, let's start the container with transport-level security activated (without the **-nosec** flag).

```
globus-start-container
```

Now, run the client again. Remember that, when the container runs in secure mode, the URIs use the HTTPS protocol and the port is 8443:

```
java \
-classpath ./build/stubs/classes/:$CLASSPATH \
org.globus.examples.clients.MathService_instance_4op.Client_GSITransport \
https://127.0.0.1:8443/wsrf/services/examples/security/first/MathAuthService
```

You should see·the following:

❶

```
[add]        ERROR: GSI Secure Conversation authentication required for
             "{http://www.globus.org/namespaces/examples/MathService_instance
             _4op}"add operation.


[subtract]   ERROR: GSI Secure Message authentication required for
             "{http://www.globus.org/namespaces/examples/MathService_instance
             _4op}subtract" operation.
```

```
[multiply] ERROR: GSI Secure Conversation or GSI Secure Message
             authentication required for
       "{http://www.globus.org/namespaces/examples/MathService_instance
       _4op}multiply" operation.
```

❷

```
Division was successful
```

```
Current value: 0
```

❶ Once again, addition, subtraction, and multiplication all fail because none of them are configured to accept GSI Transport.

❷ On the other hand, the calls to **divide** and **getResourceProperty** both work fine because the server is now running with transport-level security activated.

19.3.2   Example #2

In this example, all the methods (except one) will use GSI Secure Conversation with different levels of protection.

```
<securityConfig xmlns="http://www.globus.org">

<authz value="none"/>
```

❶
```
<method name="add">
  <auth-method>
    <GSISecureConversation>
      <protection-level>
        <integrity/>
        <privacy/>
      </protection-level>
    </GSISecureConversation>
  </auth-method>
</method>
```

❷
```
<method name="subtract">
  <auth-method>
    <GSISecureConversation>
      <protection-level>
        <integrity/>
      </protection-level>
    </GSISecureConversation>
  </auth-method>
</method>
```

❸
```
<method name="multiply">
  <auth-method>
    <GSISecureConversation>
      <protection-level>
        <privacy/>
          </protection-level>
    </GSISecureConversation>
  </auth-method>
</method>
```

❹
```
<method name="divide">
  <auth-method>
    <none/>
  </auth-method>
</method>
```

❺
```
<auth-method>
    <GSISecureConversation/>
</auth-method>

</securityConfig>
```

☞ This is file **$EXAMPLES_DIR/org/globus/examples/services/security/first/etc/**
security-config-auth_GSISecConv.xml

---

❶ The **add** method can be invoked with either encryption or digital signatures.

❷ The **subtract** method can *only* be invoked with digital signatures (not with encryption).

❸ The **multiply** method can *only* be invoked with encryption (using only digital signatures is not allowed).

❹ The **divide** method requires no security at all. Remember that we can still use security if we want to.

❺ The rest of the methods must use GSI Secure Conversation, but we don't specify if encryption or digital signatures are required. In practice, this is the same as allowing both (as we did in **add**).

We have a new service, **examples/security/first/MathAuthGSIService**, which will use this security descriptor:

```
<service name="examples/security/first/MathAuthGSIService" provider="Handler"
    use="literal" style="document">


    <!-- ... --->

    <parameter name="securityDescriptor"
        value="etc/org_globus_examples_services_security_first/
            security-config-auth_GSISecConv.xml"/>


    <!-- ... --->


</service>
```

Once again, we will use the client that uses GSI Secure Conversation with encryption.

```
java \
-classpath ./build/stubs/classes/:$CLASSPATH \
org.globus.examples.clients.MathService_instance_4op.Client_GSISecConv_Encrypt \
http://127.0.0.1:8080/wsrf/services/examples/security/first/MathAuthGSIService
```

> ☞ Note that the command above assumes that you are running the container with the **-nosec** option (port 8080). You can also run this example with a secure container(port 8443) and obtain the same results. Just make sure you use the correct URI (**https://127.0.0.1:8443/...**) when running the client.

You should see the following:

```
Addition was successful

[subtract] ERROR: GSI Secure Conversation (signature only)authentication
          required for
          "{http://www.globus.org/namespaces/examples/MathService_instance
          _4op}subtract" operation.

Multiplication was successful


Division was successful


Current value: 120
```

Notice how all the calls are successful, except subtraction, where we specified that *only* digital signatures could be used (not encryption).

chapter **20**

Authorization

The authorization mechanisms included in GSI were first introduced in Section 16.4. In this chapter we will review each mechanism and explain what changes must be made in our services to use them. We start by taking a brief look at what code must be added to a service's or resource's security descriptor to use server-side authorization, and what each type of authorization is commonly used for. Next, we will take a much closer look at one particular type of server-side authorization, gridmap authorization, by working through an example service that uses gridmaps. Then, we will take a look at the different types of client-side authorization. Finally, we will briefly discuss how GT4 allows us to implement our own custom authorization mechanisms.

20.1 Server-side Authorization

20.1.1 No Authorization

This is the simplest type of authorization, since *no* authorization decisions will be made.

```
<securityConfig xmlns="http://www.globus.org">

    <!-- ... -->

    <authz value="none"/>

    <!-- ... -->

</securityConfig>
```

20.1.2   Self Authorization

A client will be allowed to use a service if the client's identity is the same as the service's identity.

```
<securityConfig xmlns="http://www.globus.org">

    <!-- ... -->

    <authz value="self"/>

    <!-- ... -->

</securityConfig>
```

This type of authorization is generally useful when we create new resources and we want to make sure that only we have access to them. To create this kind of "ownership" relationship, we will need to delegate our credentials to the resource. This will be explained in Section 22.4.

20.1.3   Identity Authorization

A client will be allowed to access a service if the client's identity matches a specified identity. To use identity authorization, we must add the following tag to our security descriptor:

```
<securityConfig xmlns="http://www.globus.org">

    <!-- ... -->

    <authz value="identity"/>

    <!-- ... -->

</securityConfig>
```

The actual value of the identity that will be allowed to access that service will be placed in a **idenAuthz-identity** parameter in the service's WSDD file:

```
<service name="..." provider="Handler" use="literal" style="document">

    <!-- ... -->
```

```
<parameter name="idenAuthz-identity"

        value="/O=Globus/OU=GT4 Examples/CN=Globus 4 User"/>


    <!-- ... -->


</service>
```

20.1.4 Host Authorization

A client will be allowed to access a service if it presents a host credential that matches a specified hostname. In other words, we will only allow requests coming from one particular host. To use host authorization, we need to include the following in our security descriptor:

```
<securityConfig xmlns="http://www.globus.org">


    <!-- ... -->


    <authz value="host"/>


    <!-- ... -->


</securityConfig>
```

The actual hostname we are going to authorize must be specified through a **hostAuthz-url** parameter in the service's WSDD file:

```
<service name="..." provider="Handler" use="literal" style="document">


    <!-- ... -->


    <parameter name="hostAuthz-url"

        value="pc-johndoe.foobar.com"/>


    <!-- ... -->


</service>
```

20.1.5   SAML Callout Authorization

We can delegate the authorization decision on an OGSA Authorization-compliant authorization service. OGSA-Authz (http://forge.gridforum.org/projects/ogsa-authz) is a GGF working group whose goal is to specify standard authorization component. One of the main technologies used in these components is SAML (Security Assertion Markup Language). To use a separate authorization service, we need to add the following to our security descriptor:

```
<securityConfig xmlns="http://www.globus.org">

    <!-- ... -->

    <authz value="samlCallout"/>

    <!-- ... -->

</securityConfig>
```

The details regarding the authorization service to use are configured through parameters in the WSDD file. For example, to specify the URI of the authorization service, we would use the **samlAuthz-authzService** parameter:

```
<service name="..." provider="Handler" use="literal" style="document">

    <!-- ... -->

    <parameter name="samlAuthz-authzService"
            value="URI of authorization service"/>

    <!-- ... -->

</service>
```

A full discussion of how to work with OGSA Authz-compliant services is beyond the scope of this book. You can check out the official Globus security documentation for details on how to integrate your services with authorization services. Furthermore, the toolkit includes a sample authorization service. To take a look at the source code, you can either look at the source code included with the GT4 installer (**source-trees/wsrf/java/core/samples/authzService/**) or take a look at the Globus CVS server at http://viewcvs.globus.org/viewcvs.cgi/wsrf/java/core/samples/authzService/.

20.2 Gridmap Authorization

Gridmaps are one of the best-known forms of server-side authorization, playing an important role in higher-level services. A *gridmap* is basically an ACL (Access Control List) that allows us to specify what users have access to a service.

Adding gridmap authorization is easy. We just have to add two lines to the service's security descriptor (plus create the gridmap file). Although we could directly reuse most of the code of the previous chapters, we're going to start working in a new directory (**$EXAMPLES_DIR/org/globus/examples/services/security/gridmap/**) since this example will also be used as part of a larger example in Chapter 22.

20.2.1 The Gridmap File

First of all, we need to create the *gridmap file*. This file has a list of distinguished names that are allowed access to a service. The file also maps each distinguished name to a user account. However, this doesn't mean that our services will actually be running under that user account. This mapping feature is used by higher-level services, and doesn't play any role when we use GSI by itself.

The format of the file is very simple: one line for each user which is granted access. Each line has two fields separated by whitespace: the distinguished name and the user account. Since the distinguished name usually contains whitespace, it is placed between "quotation marks".

For example, a gridmap file which gave our user account (the **globus4user** account) access to a service could be the following:

```
"/O=Globus/OU=GT4 Examples/CN=Globus 4 User" globus4user
```

☞ Save this file as **$GLOBUS_LOCATION/etc/gridmapfile**.

20.2.2 Configuring Gridmap Authorization

To configure a service to use gridmap authorization, we first need to specify that the authorization mechanism is **gridmap**. We also need to specify what gridmap file must be used. This is done with the **gridmap** tag:

```
<securityConfig xmlns="http://www.globus.org">


        <auth-method>

                <GSISecureConversation/>

        </auth-method>
```

```
<authz value="gridmap"/>
<gridmap value="etc/gridmapfile"/>

</securityConfig>
```

> ☞ This is file **$EXAMPLES_DIR/org/globus/examples/services/security/gridmap/etc/**
> **security-config.xml**

Note that paths are interpreted to be relative to **$GLOBUS_LOCATION**. So, our gridmap is assumed to be in **$GLOBUS_LOCATION/etc/gridmapfile**. Should the gridmap file be outside the **$GLOBUS_LOCATION** directory tree, then you should include a complete (absolute) path.

20.2.3 The Service

Service Interface

The service interface is the same as the one used in the previous chapters (add, subtract, multiply, divide).

> ☞ The WSDL file is: **$EXAMPLES_DIR/schema/examples/MathService_instance_4op/**
> **Math.wsdl**

Service Implementation

The Java code is nearly identical to the one seen in the previous chapters. The only difference is that we will be producing less logging information. We are only interested in writing out the identity of the caller, along with the username that identity is mapped to in the gridmap.

```
private void logSecurityInfo(String methodName)
{
        String identity = SecurityManager.getManager().getCaller();
        logger.info("'" + methodName + "' invoked by: " + identity);
        logger.info("Mapped to " + SecurityManager.getManager().
            getLocalUsernames()[0]);
}
```

The shorter logging messages will come in handy when we reuse this service as part of the example in Chapter 22.

> ☞ The code for the service can be found in **$EXAMPLES_DIR/org/globus/examples/**
> **services/security/gridmap/impl/MathService.java**

> The code for the resource can be found in **$EXAMPLES_DIR/org/globus/examples/ services/security/gridmap/impl/MathResource.java**
>
> The code for the resource home can be found in **$EXAMPLES_DIR/org/globus/ examples/ services/security/gridmap/impl/MathResourceHome.java**

Compile and Deploy

Build the service:

```
./globus-build-service.sh sec_gridmap
```

And deploy it:

```
globus-deploy-gar $EXAMPLES_DIR/org_globus_examples_services_security_gridmap.gar
```

20.2.4 Testing the gridmap

We'll give the service a try with the same client used in the previous chapters (GSI Secure Conversation with encryption). If you haven't already done so, compile the client:

```
javac \
-classpath ./build/stubs/classes/:$CLASSPATH \
org/globus/examples/clients/MathService_instance_4op/
     Client_GSISecConv_Encrypt.java
```

> ☞ Before running the client, don't forget to create a proxy certificate using the **grid-proxy-init** command. Remember that the default behavior in the client-side is to use a proxy certificate for authentication, so we need to create one first.

Now, run the client:

```
java \
-classpath ./build/stubs/classes/:$CLASSPATH \
org.globus.examples.clients.MathService_instance_4op.Client_GSISecConv_Encrypt \
http://127.0.0.1:8080/wsrf/services/examples/security/gridmap/MathService
```

You should get a pretty normal output:

```
Addition was successful
Subtraction was successful
Multiplication was successful
Division was successful
Current value: 20
```

If you take a look at the server-side logs, you will see how our user is being correctly authenticated. Although we can tell that gridmap authorization is working because we have not been denied access to the service, you can find further proof by noting that the user's identity is being correctly mapped to the **globus4user** user:

'add' invoked by: /O=Globus/OU=GT4 Examples/CN=Globus 4 User

Mapped to globus4user

Now, open the **$GLOBUS_LOCATION/etc/gridmapfile** file and erase the single line from the file (or simply modify the identity so it won't map your user's identity). If you run the client again, you will get the following error:

[add]   ERROR: org.globus.wsrf.impl.security.authorization.exceptions.

AuthorizationException:

"/O=Globus/OU=GT4 Examples/CN=Globus 4 User" is not authorized

to use operation:

{http://www.globus.org/namespaces/examples/

MathService_instance_4op}add on this service

The error message speaks for itself: since the user running the client is not in the gridmap file, it has been denied access to the server.

> ☞ Note that we do not have to restart the container for the changes in the gridmap to take effect.

20.3 Client-side Authorization

20.3.1   No Authorization

This is the simplest type of client-side authorization, as no authorization decisions will be made based on the service's identity. To use this type of authorization we need to add the following to the client security descriptor:

```
<securityConfig xmlns="http://www.globus.org">

    <!-- ... -->

    <authz value="none"/>

    <!-- ... -->

</securityConfig>
```

We can also do this programmatically:

```
((Stub) stub_object )._setProperty(Constants.AUTHORIZATION,
    NoAuthorization.getInstance());
```

20.3.2 Self Authorization

The client will authorize an invocation if the service's identity is the same as the client. To use self authorization, we need to add the following to the security descriptor:

```
<securityConfig xmlns="http://www.globus.org">

    <!-- ... -->

    <authz value="self"/>

    <!-- ... -->

</securityConfig>
```

To do this programmatically:

```
((Stub) stub_object )._setProperty(Constants.AUTHORIZATION,
    SelfAuthorization.getInstance());
```

20.3.3 Identity Authorization

The client will only allow requests to be sent to services with a specified identity. To use identity authorization, we must set the **value** of the **authz** tag in the client security descriptor to the identity we will accept:

```
<securityConfig xmlns="http://www.globus.org">

    <!-- ... -->

    <authz value="/O=Globus/OU=GT4 Examples/CN=Globus 4 User"/>

    <!-- ... -->

</securityConfig>
```

If we want to do it programmatically, we need to set the stub property **AUTHORIZATION** to an **IdentityAuthorization** object. Notice that, unlike the other client-side authorization mechanisms, we do not use a static **getInstance** method but, rather, create the object ourselves. The parameter to the constructor will be the identity.

```
((Stub) stub_object )._setProperty(Constants.AUTHORIZATION,

    new IdentityAuthorization("/O=Globus/OU=GT4 Examples/CN=Globus 4 User"));
```

20.3.4 Host Authorization

The client will authorize an invocation if the service has a host credential. Furthermore, the client must be able to resolve the address of the host to the hostname specified in the host credential. Note that this is different from server-side host authorization, where we check if the hostname in the credential is equal to a host specified by us. To use host authorization, we must add the following to the client security descriptor:

```
<securityConfig xmlns="http://www.globus.org">


    <!-- ... -->


    <authz value="host"/>


    <!-- ... -->


</securityConfig>
```

To do it programmatically:

```
((Stub) stub_object )._setProperty(Constants.AUTHORIZATION,

    HostAuthorization.getInstance());
```

20.4 Custom Authorization Mechanisms

The authorization mechanisms included with the toolkit will allow you to deal with simple authorization scenarios. For more complex authorization scenarios, GT4 provides an infrastructure to easily implement your own authorization mechanisms to use in your services. The implementation of such a mechanism is beyond the scope of the book, but we provide here some pointers so you will get a general idea of what is involved in writing your own authorization mechanism. For more details, you can refer to the official Globus documentation.

The first thing we will have to do is to write a class that implements the **PDP** interface. PDP stands for "Policy Decision Point" which, in the Globus literature, is the more correct name for an authorization mechanism.

```
package org.globus.examples.services.security.custom_authz.impl;


org.globus.wsrf.security.PDP;
// Other imports


public class CustomPDP implements PDP
{
        /* Required by interface PDP */
        public boolean isPermitted(Subject peerSubject, MessageContext context,
            QName operation)
                throws AuthorizationException {
        {
                // ...
        }


        /* Required by interface PDP */
        public String[] getPolicyNames() {
                // ...
        }


        /* Required by interface PDP */
        public Node getPolicy(Node query)
                // ...
        }


        /* Required by interface PDP */
        public Node setPolicy(Node policy)
                // ...
        }
}
```

> ☞ The above class is not included with this book's examples bundle. It is only shown for illustrative purposes.

The most important method you'll need to implement is the **isPermitted**, which receives the subject of the user (the "peer") on which you have to make an authorization decision, along with the operation the user is trying to access, and a message context.

Once we have implemented that class, we can use it in our services by including the following in the security descriptor:

```
<securityConfig xmlns="http://www.globus.org">

    <!-- ... -->

    <authz value="example:org.globus.examples.services.security.
        custom_authz.impl.CustomPDP"/>

    <!-- ... -->

</securityConfig>
```

Notice how the name of our class includes a prefix (**example**). This is relevant for later on referring to our PDP, specially when specifying authorization options in the WSDD file. For example, we could include the following parameter in our WSDD file:

```
<service name="examples/security/custom_authz/MathService"
    provider="Handler" use="literal" style="document">

    <!-- Other parameters -->

    <parameter name="example-interestingParameter" value="FOOBAR"/>

</service>
```

Using the Globus API, our authorization class can retrieve the value of that parameter by requesting the **interestingParameter** parameter.

Again, for more details on how to implement the PDP interface and how to interact with your own custom authorization mechanism, please refer to the official Globus documentation.

chapter **21**

Resource-Level Security

Up to this point in the book, we have seen how we configure several security aspects at the service and client levels. In Chapter 18 we also touched briefly on the topic of container-level security. In this chapter we will see what security options are configurable at the resource level. We will start by seeing how we can configure resource security using a security descriptor, and how we can instruct a resource to use that descriptor. Next, we will briefly see how we can set security options programmatically, without the need for a security descriptor. Finally, we will see an example that showcases resource security. This example will be extended in Chapter 22, where we will see how to perform credential delegation to resources.

21.1 The Resource Security Descriptor

To configure security in an individual resource, we must first specify the security options for the resource in a security descriptor, similar to the ones seen in the previous chapters.

```
<securityConfig xmlns="http://www.globus.org">

        <!- ... ->

</securityConfig>
```

Through this security descriptor, we will be able to configure the following on a per-resource basis:

- Authentication: Using the **<auth-method>** element as described in Chapter 19.
- Authorization: Using the **<authz>** element as described in Chapter 20.

As with client security descriptors, we have to programmatically tell the resource to use a certain security descriptor. First of all, our resource must implement the **Secure-Resource** interface. This interface requires that we implement a **getSecurityDescriptor** method returning a **ResourceSecurityDescriptor** object representing the resource's descriptor:

```
public class MathResource implements SecureResource, ResourceIdentifier,

    ResourceProperties {


        /* Security descriptor */

        ResourceSecurityConfig config;


        // ...


        /* Required by SecureResource */

        public ResourceSecurityDescriptor getSecurityDescriptor() {

        return config.getSecurityDescriptor();

    }

}
```

For this method to work correctly, we will need to initialize the **config** attribute in the resource's constructor or **initialize** method:

```
public Object initialize() throws Exception {


        // ...


        config = new ResourceSecurityConfig("{resource descriptor file}");

        config.init();


        // ...


    }
```

21.2 Configuring Resource Security Programmatically

Resource security can also be configured programmatically using the **ResourceSecurity-Descriptor** class. In general, we will need to first create a new **ResourceSecurityDescriptor** object in the resource's constructor or **initialize** method, configure the security option, and then create a **ResourceSecurityConfig** object with the **ResourceSecurityDescriptor** instead of providing a security descriptor file:

```
ResourceSecurityDescriptor desc = new ResourceSecurityDescriptor();


// Use the Globus API to create a resource descriptor programatically


config = new ResourceSecurityConfig(desc);
config.init();
```

For a complete list of options that can be configured programmatically, refer to the official Globus documentation. For example, the following code creates a resource descriptor, and sets it up to use gridmap authorization, pointing the descriptor to a specific gridmap file:

```
ResourceSecurityDescriptor desc = new ResourceSecurityDescriptor();
desc.setGridMapFile("/etc/grid-security/gridmapfile");
desc.setAuthz("gridmap");
config = new ResourceSecurityConfig(desc);
config.init();
```

Another possibility is to programmatically create the gridmap, without the need for a gridmap file:

```
ResourceSecurityDescriptor desc = new ResourceSecurityDescriptor();
GridMap map = new GridMap();
map.map("/O=Globus/OU=GT4 Examples/CN=Globus 4 User", "globus4user");
desc.setGridMap(map);
desc.setAuthz("gridmap");
config = new ResourceSecurityConfig(desc);
config.init();
```

21.3 Example

We will now see an example where the service requires no security, but the resources do. In other words, stateful invocations will require security, while stateless invocations won't.

The code for this example will be based on the factory/instance service seen in Chapter 8. This example will be extended in Chapter 22 to show how we can delegate credentials to a resource.

21.3.1   The WSDL File

The service interface will be a simplified version of the WSDL file we've seen so far. First of all, the interface will include a single **Value** RP. Then, our interface will include an **add** operation and a stateless **helloWorld** operation. This will allow us to see how **add**, a stateful operation requiring a resource, requires a secure communication while **helloWorld** doesn't.

> ✐ The instance WSDL file is **$EXAMPLES_DIR/schema/examples/MathService_instance _helloworld/Math.wsdl**.
> The factory WSDL file is **$EXAMPLES_DIR/schema/examples/FactoryService/ Factory.wsdl**.
> Remember that we must add namespace mappings for these WSDL files. The supplied mappings file (**$EXAMPLES_DIR/namespace2package.mappings**) includes the necessary mappings.

21.3.2   Implementation Files

The Service Implementation

The service implementation is pretty straightforward, and simply includes small changes to accommodate the new interface. Also, the **logSecurityInfo** has been modified to print out information about the resource. However, this information will not be relevant until we extend the example in Chapter 22. The **add** method is the same as in previous examples:

```
public AddResponse add(int a) throws RemoteException {

        MathResource mathResource = getResource();


        logSecurityInfo("add", mathResource);


        mathResource.setValue(mathResource.getValue() + a);


        return new AddResponse();


}
```

The **helloWorld** method, on the other hand, is stateless, so we don't need to retrieve the current resource:

```
public String helloWorld(HelloWorld params) throws RemoteException {

        logSecurityInfo("helloWorld", null);


        return "Hello, world!";

}
```

☞ The instance service implementation is **$EXAMPLES_DIR/org/globus/examples/ services/security/resource/impl/MathService.java**

The Resource Implementation

Our resource security descriptor will require that the resource be accessed using GSI Secure Conversation;

```
<securityConfig xmlns="http://www.globus.org">


<auth-method>

    <GSISecureConversation/>

</auth-method>


<authz value="none"/>


</securityConfig>
```

☞ This file is **$EXAMPLES_DIR/org/globus/examples/services/security/resource/ etc/security-config-resource.xml**

As described earlier, we need to make sure our resource implements the **SecureResource** interface. Besides adding the **getSecurityDescriptor** method, we need to initialize the security descriptor in the resource's **initialize** method. Notice how we point the resource descriptor to the file described above.

```
config =
    new ResourceSecurityConfig("etc/org_globus_examples_services_security
        _resource/security-config-resource.xml");
config.init();
```

> ☞ The resource implementation is **$EXAMPLES_DIR/org/globus/examples/services/
> security/resource/impl/MathResource.java**

The Factory Service Implementation

The factory service implementation is the same as the one seen in Chapter 8. We only add a **logSecurityInformation** to print out some security information when the service is created.

> ☞ The factory service implementation is **$EXAMPLES_DIR/org/globus/examples/
> services/security/resource/impl/MathFactoryService.java**

The Resource Home Implementation

The resource home is exactly the same as the one seen in Chapter 8.

> ☞ The resource home implementation is **$EXAMPLES_DIR/org/globus/examples/
> services/security/resource/impl/MathResourceHome.java**

21.3.3   Deployment Descriptors

The deployment descriptor requires no additional parameters to accommodate resource-level security.

> ☞ The WSDD file is **$EXAMPLES_DIR/org/globus/examples/services/security/
> resource/deploy-server.wsdd**
> The JNDI deploy file is **$EXAMPLES_DIR/org/globus/examples/
> services/security/resource/deploy-jndi-config.xml**

21.3.4   Build and Deploy

Build the service:

    ./globus-build-service.sh sec_resource

And deploy it:

    globus-deploy-gar $EXAMPLES_DIR/org_globus_examples_services_wsrf_security_

    resource_self.gar

21.3.5 Trying it Out

To try this service out, we will use a resource creation client, an addition client, and a "Hello, world!" client. The addition and "Hello, world!" clients have a non-secure version and a secure version (using GSI Secure Conversation). The code for these clients is pretty straightforward, and will not be discussed here.

> ☞ If you need help understanding the source code of the clients, this might be a good time to review Chapter 8.

Let's start by using the creation client to create a new WS-Resource.

> ☞ The creation client is **$EXAMPLES_DIR/org/globus/examples/clients/ FactoryService_Math_helloworld/ClientCreate.java**.

Take into account that using resource-level security only mandates that we use security when *accessing* a resource. The resource security descriptor does not affect the *creation* of new resources. Using or not security to create the resource is up to you, although it is generally a good idea. If you take a peek at the source code of our creation client, you'll see that we choose to use security.

Let's compile the client:

```
javac \
-classpath ./build/stubs/classes/:$CLASSPATH \
org/globus/examples/clients/FactoryService_Math_helloworld/ClientCreate.java
```

And run it:

```
java \
-classpath ./build/stubs/classes/:$CLASSPATH \
org.globus.examples.clients.FactoryService_Math_helloworld.ClientCreate \
http://127.0.0.1:8080/wsrf/services/examples/security/resource/
    MathFactoryService
```

The EPR of the new WS-Resource will be written to an **epr.txt** file. Now, let's use that EPR to invoke the **add** operation.

> ☞ The addition client without security is
> **$EXAMPLES_DIR/org/globus/examples/clients/MathService_instance_helloworld/ ClientAdd_NoSec.java**.
> The addition client with security is
> **$EXAMPLES_DIR/org/globus/examples/clients/MathService_instance_helloworld/ ClientAdd_Secure.java**.

First of all, let's compile both clients:

```
javac \
-classpath ./build/stubs/classes/:$CLASSPATH \
org/globus/examples/clients/MathService_instance_helloworld/ClientAdd
    _NoSec.java


javac \
-classpath ./build/stubs/classes/:$CLASSPATH \
org/globus/examples/clients/MathService_instance_helloworld/ClientAdd
    _Secure.java
```

Now, let's use the secure client:

```
java \
-classpath ./build/stubs/classes/:$CLASSPATH \
org.globus.examples.clients.MathService_instance_helloworld.ClientAdd_Secure \
epr.txt \
10
```

The result should be pretty normal:

```
Addition was successful
Current value: 10
```

However, if we try to use the non-secure client:

```
java \
-classpath ./build/stubs/classes/:$CLASSPATH \
org.globus.examples.clients.MathService_instance_helloworld.ClientAdd_NoSec \
epr.txt \
10
```

We will see the following error messages:

```
[add]      ERROR: GSI Secure Conversation authentication required for
           "{http://www.globus.org/namespaces/examples/MathService_instance
               _helloworld}add"
           operation.
```

```
[getRP]    ERROR: GSI Secure Conversation authentication required for

           "{http://www.globus.org/namespaces/examples/MathService_instance

           _helloworld}getResourceProperty"

           operation.
```

This error message can be a bit deceitful, since it refers to the *operation* requiring GSI Secure Conversation. However, we did not specify any security options at the service level. The error is, in fact, being triggered by the resource, which requires GSI Secure Conversation.

To see how the resource is, in fact, the source of this error message, we will now invoke the service's stateless **helloWorld** operation.

☞ The "hello, world!" client without security is **$EXAMPLES_DIR/org/globus/examples/clients/MathService_instance_helloworld/ClientHelloWorld_NoSec.java**.
The "hello, world!" client with security is **$EXAMPLES_DIR/org/globus/examples/clients/MathService_instance_helloworld/ClientHelloWorld_Secure.java**.

We will be interested in seeing how the **helloWorld** operation reacts to being invoked without security, so let's compile the non-secure client:

```
javac \

-classpath ./build/stubs/classes/:$CLASSPATH \

org/globus/examples/clients/MathService_instance_helloworld/ClientHelloWorld

_NoSec.java
```

And now, run it:

```
java \

-classpath ./build/stubs/classes/:$CLASSPATH \

org.globus.examples.clients.MathService_instance_helloworld.ClientHelloWorld

  _NoSec \

http://127.0.0.1:8080/wsrf/services/examples/security/resource/MathService
```

Notice how we're not using the EPR file but, rather, supplying the service URI directly. Since this operation is stateless, there's no need to specify a resource (since none will be used). The client should output the following:

```
Hello, world!
```

However, notice what happens if we try to invoke **helloWorld** using the EPR file:

```
java \
-classpath ./build/stubs/classes/:$CLASSPATH \
org.globus.examples.clients.MathService_instance_helloworld.ClientHelloWorld
    _NoSec \
epr.txt
```

We will get the same error as before, telling us that GSI Secure Conversation is required:

```
[helloWorld] ERROR: GSI Secure Conversation authentication required for
            "{http://www.globus.org/namespaces/examples/MathService_instance
            _helloworld}helloWorld"
            operation.
```

The reason for this is that, despite the fact that **helloWorld** does not use a resource, we are using a *WS-resource-qualified endpoint reference*, so the container still checks if we're allowed to access the resource referred to in the EPR. When using only a URI (which results in a *WS-resource-non-qualified* EPR), the container makes no resource-level checks.

> ☞ If you're confused by the term *WS-resource-qualified endpoint reference*, this might be a good time to review Section 4.3.

## chapter 22

Run-as Modes and Delegation

We have finally arrived at the last security chapter. This chapter, longer than the previous ones, is where everything "clicks together". The two final examples of this chapter draw from everything we've seen previously to show how an adequate combination of authentication, authorization, and credential delegation can make our services pretty secure.

The chapter starts with a brief explanation of *run-as* modes, another parameter we can configure in the security descriptor and that makes the most sense in the context of credential delegation. Then, a trivial example of delegation is seen, followed by a more elaborate (and non-trivial) example of credential delegation. Next, we will see how we can delegate credentials to a specific resource. Finally, we will briefly talk about the GT4 Delegation Service.

22.1 Run-as Modes

Run-as modes allow us to control the credentials the service will use during the course of an invocation. Remember, from Chapter 18, that we can configure resources, services, and containers to use a specific set of credentials. In particular, during a call to a service, there are three distinct *subjects* in play:

- **System subject:** This is the identity the system (the container) is running under. We will generally specify this by setting a specific set of credentials in the container's security descriptor.

- **Service subject:** When a service is invoked, its identity depends on the credentials we've specified in the service security descriptor. If we haven't specified any, then the system's subject will be used. As we'll see further on, this subject can also be modified by using credential delegation.

■ **Resource subject:** Each resource can have its own credentials, either by using a resource security descriptor or by setting them programmatically. If the resource doesn't have its own credentials, then the service credentials will be used.

⌖ Remember that in our first secure example, seen in Chapter 17, we wrote a bunch of security-related information to the server's log. At that point, we were only interested in seeing the caller's identity, but still wrote other information that would be relevant "later on". Well, if you take a look at the `logSecurityInfo` method in the first example, you'll see that we're printing out some of the subjects described above.

We also have a special subject called the *invocation subject* which is specially relevant when we want to perform credential delegation, and depends on the run-as mode selected during a particular call. There are four different run-as modes:

■ **Run as caller:** This sets the invocation subject with the same value as the caller's subject (the client making the invocation).

■ **Run as system:** Sets the invocation subject to be the system subject.

■ **Run as service:** Sets the invocation subject to be the service subject.

■ **Run as resource**: Sets the invocation subject to be the resource subject.

The default is for methods to run using the resource's identity. Note that, if we don't specify credentials for the resource or the service, this means that the invocation subject will equal the system's subject.

To configure the run-as mode on a per-method basis, we simply have to include a **run-as** tag inside the **method** tag. This **run-as** tag will include either a **caller-identity**, **system-identity**, **service-identity**, or **resource-identity** tag. We can also specify a default run-as mode using a separate **run-as** tag (outside of any **method** tags).

The following security descriptor showcases all four run-as modes. As with the examples in Chapter 19, the service that uses this security descriptor is exactly the same as the one seen in Chapter 17, and was deployed along with that chapter's example. Please refer to that chapter if you have not yet deployed the service.

```
<securityConfig xmlns="http://www.globus.org">

<method name="add">

    <run-as>

        <caller-identity/>

    </run-as>
```

```
</method>

<method name="subtract">
    <run-as>
        <system-identity/>
    </run-as>
</method>

<method name="multiply">
    <run-as>
        <service-identity/>
    </run-as>
</method>

<method name="divide">
    <run-as>
        <resource-identity/>
    </run-as>
</method>

<run-as>
    <service-identity/>
</run-as>

<authz value="none"/>

</securityConfig>
```

☞ This is file **$EXAMPLES_DIR/org/globus/examples/services/security/first/etc/ security-config-runas.xml**

This security descriptor will be used by service **examples/security/first/ MathRunAsService**:

```
<service name="examples/security/first/MathRunAsService"
    provider="Handler" use="literal" style="document">


    <!-- ... --->

    <parameter name="securityDescriptor"
        value="etc/org_globus_examples_services_security_first/
            security-config-runas.xml"/>


    <!-- ... --->


</service>
```

Now, we will invoke each of the four methods in the service using the same client used in previous chapters (the one that uses GSI Secure Conversation with encryption). If you have not already compiled it:

```
javac \
-classpath ./build/stubs/classes/:$CLASSPATH \
org/globus/examples/clients/MathService_instance_4op/
    Client_GSISecConv_Encrypt.java
```

Now, run it:

```
java \
-classpath ./build/stubs/classes/:$CLASSPATH \
org.globus.examples.clients.MathService_instance_4op.Client
    _GSISecConv_Encrypt \
http://127.0.0.1:8080/wsrf/services/examples/security/
    first/MathRunAsService
```

If you look at the server log, you will first see how the **add** method is, in fact, running with its invocation subject set to the caller's identity.

```
SECURITY INFO FOR METHOD 'add'
The caller is:/O=Globus/OU=GT4 Examples/CN=Globus 4 User
```

INVOCATION SUBJECT

Subject:

       Principal: */O=Globus/OU=GT4 Examples/CN=Globus 4 User*

       Public Credential: [Ljava.security.cert.X509Certificate;@ec0962

SERVICE SUBJECT

Subject:

       Principal: /O=Globus/OU=GT4 Examples/CN=host/pc-johndoe.foobar.com

       Private Credential: org.globus.gsi.gssapi.GlobusGSSCredentialImpl@1ebf4ff

SYSTEM SUBJECT

Subject:

       Principal: /O=Globus/OU=GT4 Examples/CN=host/pc-johndoe.foobar.com

       Private Credential: org.globus.gsi.gssapi.GlobusGSSCredentialImpl@1ebf4ff

The rest of the methods, on the other hand, run under the system's identity. Although only **subtract** is explicitly set to run under the system's identity, the rest of the methods default to the system subject because we have not set any credentials for the service or the resource.

SECURITY INFO FOR METHOD 'subtract'

The caller is:/O=Globus/OU=GT4 Examples/CN=Globus 4 User

INVOCATION SUBJECT

Subject:

       Principal: */O=Globus/OU=GT4 Examples/CN=host/pc-johndoe.foobar.com*

       Private Credential: org.globus.gsi.gssapi.GlobusGSSCredentialImpl@1ebf4ff

SERVICE SUBJECT

Subject:

       Principal: /O=Globus/OU=GT4 Examples/CN=host/pc-johndoe.foobar.com

       Private Credential: org.globus.gsi.gssapi.GlobusGSSCredentialImpl@1ebf4ff

SYSTEM SUBJECT

Subject:

> Principal: /O=Globus/OU=GT4 Examples/CN=host/pc-johndoe.foobar.com
>
> Private Credential: org.globus.gsi.gssapi.GlobusGSSCredentialImpl@1ebf4ff

22.2   A First Approach at Delegation

We are now going to work through a simple example that shows what additional code is necessary to add credential delegation to a service. As such, the code will be based on our first secure service, seen in Chapter 17. All the modified files can be found in directory **$EXAMPLES_DIR/org/globus/examples/services/security/delegation_first/**. This example will allow us to see the basic mechanism that activates delegation and, using the server-side logs, we will verify that delegation is working properly.

> ☞ This might be a good time to review Section 16.5.

However, this first example doesn't allow us to see the full potential of delegation. This is why, after this example, we will write a more complex example based on Figure 16.4. The second example will include *two* services. The client will delegate its credentials on the first service, and that service will use those delegated credentials to invoke the second service. Furthermore, the second service will be configured to accept only the client's credentials so, when delegation is not activated, the example will not work (because the second service expects the client's credentials, not the first service's credentials). Then, once we activate delegation, we will see how everything works perfectly.

22.2.1   Activating Delegation on the Client Side

The first thing we have to do is modify the client to tell it to delegate its credentials to the service. First of all, we must make sure that the client performs some sort of client-side authorization. Otherwise, delegation will not work.

We can set the client to use two types of delegation: full or limited. Choosing limited delegation makes GSI use a *limited proxy* which can potentially be rejected by a service.

> ☞ Remember from Chapter 18 that we can configure a service, or the whole container, to reject limited proxies by using the **<reject-limited-proxy/>** tag.

To use full delegation, we must set the following stub property:

```
((Stub) stub_object)._setProperty(GSIConstants.GSI_MODE,GSIConstants.
    GSI_MODE_FULL_DELEG);
```

To use limited delegation:

```
((Stub) stub_object)._setProperty(GSIConstants.GSI_MODE,GSIConstants.
    GSI_MODE_LIMITED_DELEG);
```

Note that we can also explicitly say that we don't want any delegation, although this is the default value:

```
((Stub) stub_object)._setProperty(GSIConstants.GSI_MODE,GSIConstants.
    GSI_MODE_NO_DELEG);
```

We can also set the desired type of delegation using the client security descriptor.

```
<securityConfig xmlns="http://www.globus.org">

        <GSISecureConversation>
                <integrity/>
                <delegation value="full"/>
        </GSISecureConversation>


        <!-- ... -->

</securityConfig>
```

The delegation option can take on the values **full**, **limited**, or **none**.

> ☞ Our client will use full delegation and host authorization. The client can be found in **$EXAMPLES_DIR/org/globus/examples/clients/MathService_instance _4op/Client_DelegationFull.java**

22.2.2 Activating Delegation on the Server Side

Set the run-as Mode to caller-identity

The method to which we want to delegate credentials must be configured to run with the caller's identity. In other words, the *invocation subject* must be set to the caller's identity. As explained earlier, we will do this in the service's security descriptor by setting the run-as mode to **caller-identity**.

> ☞ For our example we will use the same security descriptor used in the run-as example. Only the **add** method will be configured to run with the caller's identity, while the rest of the methods will use other identities.
>
> This is file **$EXAMPLES_DIR/org/globus/examples/services/security/ delegation_first/etc/security-config.xml**

Setting the Service Owner

However, using the **caller-identity** run-as mode isn't enough to delegate the client's credentials to the service. We also have to tell the service to assume the identity of the caller. By doing this, we will make the service assume the invocation subject as its own subject. To do this, we have to add the following line in each method where we want to perform delegation:

```
SecurityManager.getManager().setServiceOwnerFromContext();
```

For example, in the **add** method:

```
public AddResponse add(int a) throws RemoteException {

    SecurityManager.getManager().setServiceOwnerFromContext();

    logSecurityInfo("add");


    MathResource mathResource = getResource();

    mathResource.setValue(mathResource.getValue() + a);

    mathResource.setLastOp("ADDITION");


    return new AddResponse();

}
```

☞ **setServiceOwnerFromContext** delegates the credentials to that service until the proxy certificate used for the delegation expires (i.e. you shouldn't think that the credentials are delegated only for that particular invocation, or delegated permanently). Unless used wisely, **setServiceOwnerFromContext** can result in some very kludgy delegations, and using the GT4 Delegation Service (described at the end of the chapter) is generally preferred when delegating credentials to a service.

22.2.3 Compile and Deploy

Now, let's build the service:

> **./globus-build-service.sh sec_delegation_first**

And deploy it:

> **globus-deploy-gar $EXAMPLES_DIR/org_globus_examples_services_security_**
>
> **delegation_first.gar**

22.2.4 Compiling and Running the Client

Let's compile the client:

```
javac \
-classpath ./build/stubs/classes/:$CLASSPATH \
org/globus/examples/clients/MathService_instance_4op/Client_DelegationFull.java
```

And run it:

```
java \
-classpath ./build/stubs/classes/:$CLASSPATH \
org.globus.examples.clients.MathService_instance_4op.Client_DelegationFull \
http://127.0.0.1:8080/wsrf/services/examples/security/delegation_first/MathService
```

> ! Since we are using *host authorization* for this example, the client might not work if your host certificate is not set up correctly (as described in Section A.4).
>
> Also, you will probably have to use your complete hostname (instead of 127.0.0.1) in the service URI. Otherwise, you will get an error similar to this:
>
> ```
> javax.xml.rpc.soap.SOAPFaultException: Operation unauthorized
>
> (Mechanism level: Authorization failed.
>
>     Expected "/CN=host/localhost.localdomain" target but received
>
>     "/O=Globus/OU=GT4 Examples/CN=host/ <your hostname>")
> ```
>
> If you get that error, then simply use **<your hostname>** instead of 127.0.0.1. Another way of finding out your hostname is to check the subject of your host certificate:
>
> ```
> grid-cert-info -s -file /etc/grid-security/hostcert.pem
> ```

The output on the client side should be pretty normal. We need to take a close look at the server side logs to verify that delegation is, in fact, working. Look at the **add** method (which runs under the caller's identity):

```
SECURITY INFO FOR METHOD 'add'
The caller is: /O=Globus/OU=GT4 Examples/CN=Globus 4 User


INVOCATION SUBJECT
Subject:
        Principal: /O=Globus/OU=GT4 Examples/CN=Globus 4 User
```

```
        Public Credential: [Ljava.security.cert.X509Certificate;@457235

        Private Credential: org.globus.gsi.gssapi.GlobusGSSCredentialImpl@14d3343
```

SERVICE SUBJECT

Subject:

```
        Principal: /O=Globus/OU=GT4 Examples/CN=Globus 4 User

        Public Credential: [Ljava.security.cert.X509Certificate;@457235

        Private Credential: org.globus.gsi.gssapi.GlobusGSSCredentialImpl@14d3343
```

SYSTEM SUBJECT

Subject:

```
        Principal: /O=Globus/OU=GT4 Examples/CN=host/pc-johndoe.foobar.com

        Private Credential: org.globus.gsi.gssapi.GlobusGSSCredentialImpl@13a3d36
```

Notice how the service subject is no longer equal to the system's (the container's) subject... it's the caller's identity! Holy identity theft, Batman! :-). This means that, during the method's invocation, the **add** method will be able to act as if it actually had the "Globus 4 User" credentials.

As for the rest of the methods, since they are not using the **caller-identity** run-as mode, the service subject continues to be the same as the system's subject. For example, this is the output for the **subtract** method:

SECURITY INFO FOR METHOD 'subtract'

The caller is:/O=Globus/OU=GT4 Examples/CN=Globus 4 User

INVOCATION SUBJECT

Subject:

```
        Principal: /O=Globus/OU=GT4 Examples/CN=host/pc-johndoe.foobar.com

        Private Credential: org.globus.gsi.gssapi.GlobusGSSCredentialImpl@13a3d36
```

SERVICE SUBJECT

Subject:

```
        Principal: /O=Globus/OU=GT4 Examples/CN=host/pc-johndoe.foobar.com

        Private Credential: org.globus.gsi.gssapi.GlobusGSSCredentialImpl@13a3d36
```

SYSTEM SUBJECT

Subject:

> Principal: */O=Globus/OU=GT4 Examples/CN=host/pc-johndoe.foobar.com*
>
> Private Credential: `org.globus.gsi.gssapi.GlobusGSSCredentialImpl@13a3d36`

So, we've seen that delegation actually *does* work. However, this example isn't exactly what you could call "exciting". However, we promise the next example is guaranteed to positively thrill you!

22.3 A More Elaborate Delegation Example

22.3.1 Overview

We are now going to start working on a more elaborate delegation example which uses *two* services:

- **PhysicsService:** This is a new service we will program from scratch.
- **MathService:** This is, in fact, the exact same service we saw in Section 20.2. We won't need to make a single modification to this service, but you must make sure that it is correctly deployed.

In our example, PhysicsService will be responsible for undertaking an extremely complex calculation. For this, it will need to invoke MathService several times. However, there's a catch:

- We will be invoking the PhysicsService from our user account. We will assume that this account has a certificate with subject `O=Globus,OU=GT4 Examples,CN=Globus 4 User`
- PhysicsService allows any user to access its methods. Therefore, the client application will have no trouble accessing PhysicsService.
- MathService, on the other hand, only allows one user to access its methods. Since we'll be using the same service and gridmap seen in Section 20.2, this service will only allow user **globus4user** to access the service.

This all means that, for the example to work, PhysicsService *must* invoke MathService using the `O=Globus,OU=GT4 Examples,CN=Globus 4 User` credential. Since PhysicsService is running in a container that has a different set of credentials (the container's credentials), PhysicsService will only be able to access MathService if the client application (run by the **globus4user** user account) delegates its credentials. In fact, to show that this is all true, we will test PhysicsService without delegation and then with delegation.

Figure 22.1, summarizes the whole example: PhysicsService has a single method **getAnswer** which will be invoked by the client application. This method, in turn, will invoke the **add** and **multiply** methods in MathService.

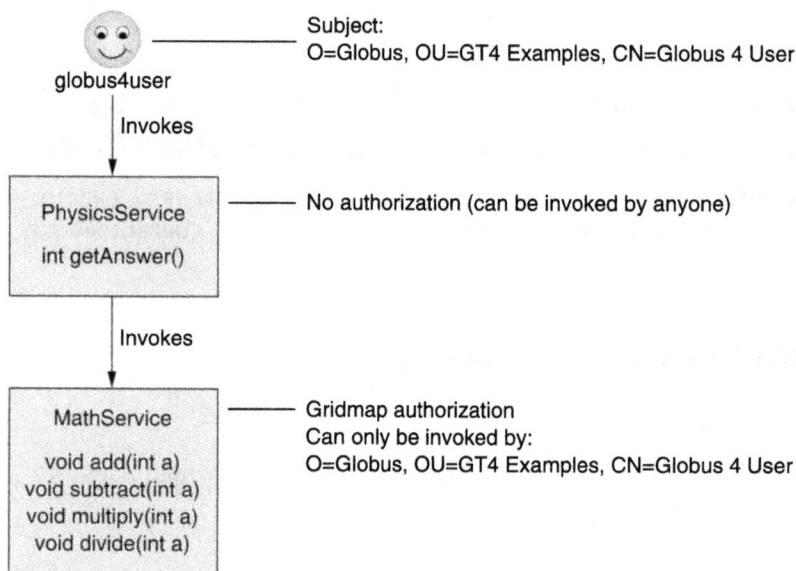

Figure 22.1: The PhysicsService example

22.3.2 PhysicsService

We will start by taking a look at the implementation of PhysicsService. All the code for this example can be found in **$EXAMPLES_DIR/org/globus/examples/services/security/delegation/**

Service Interface

The service interface of the PhysicsService is very simple, as it only has a single operation and no resource properties. It can be found here: **$EXAMPLES_DIR/schema/examples/PhysicsService/Physics.wsdl**

Service Implementation

The implementation of this services is going to be pretty long, since this is the first time we have a service that invokes another service. You can find the code here: **$EXAMPLES_DIR/org/globus/examples/services/security/delegation/impl/PhysicsService.java**

However, since this code is lengthy, we're going to take the time to take a look at it step-by-step. First of all, instead of fitting all the code into the **getAnswer** method, we're going to divide everything into several private methods. The "skeleton" of our implementation looks something like this:

```
package org.globus.examples.services.security.delegation.impl;


// Import statements


public class PhysicsService {

        static Log logger = LogFactory.getLog(PhysicsService.class);

        static final String mathURI =
                "http://127.0.0.1:8080/wsrf/services/examples/security/
                    first/MathService";

        public int getAnswer(GetAnswer request) throws RemoteException {
        }

        private void makeStubSecure(Object stub) {
        }

        private MathPortType getReferenceToMathService() throws Exception {
        }

        private void logSecurityInfo(String methodName) {
        }

    }
```

Let's take a look at what all these attributes and methods do.

mathURI **Attribute**

We keep the URI of the MathService we will invoke in a static final attribute:

```
static final String mathURI =
        "http://127.0.0.1:8080/wsrf/services/examples/
        security/first/MathService";
```

> ! We are hardcoding the URI of the MathService in our implementation for simplicity. You should never hardcode the address of a service in your Java code, and should instead rely on an index service to locate the MathService to use. Although index services are not covered in this book, we will briefly skim over them in Part IV and we will give you pointers to relevant documentation in the book's conclusion.

getAnswer **Method**

The **getAnswer** method will use MathService to find The Answer. The following is the complete code of this example. Refer to the callouts for a more detailed explanation of what each bit of code does.

```
public int getAnswer(GetAnswer request) throws RemoteException {


❶
try {
            SecurityManager.getManager().setServiceOwnerFromContext();
} catch (Exception e) {
        logger.warn("Unable to set service owner from context.");
        logger.warn("Did you forget to delegate credentials?");
}


❷
MathPortType math;
GetResourcePropertyResponse valueRP;
int answer = 0;
String answer_str;
```

❸

```
logSecurityInfo();

try {
        ❹
        math = getReferenceToMathService();
        makeStubSecure(math);

        ❺
        logger.info("Invoking add...");
        try {
                math.add(7);
                logger.info("add invoked successfully!");
        } catch (Exception e) {
                System.out.println("[add]          ERROR: " +
                    e.getMessage());
        }

        logger.info("Invoking multiply...");
        try {
                math.multiply(6);
                logger.info("multiply invoked successfully!");
        } catch (Exception e) {
                System.out.println("[multiply] ERROR: " +
                    e.getMessage());
        }

        ❻
        logger.info("Accessing Value RP...");
        try {
                valueRP = math.getResourceProperty(
                    MathConstants.RP_VALUE);
```

```
                                    answer_str = valueRP.get_any()[0].getValue();

                                    answer = Integer.parseInt(answer_str);

                                    logger.info("Value RP accessed correctly!");

                            } catch (Exception e) {

                                    System.out.println("[getRP]          ERROR: "

                                        + e.getMessage());

                            }



                    } catch (Exception e) {

                            e.printStackTrace();

                    }



                    ❼

                    return answer;

            }
```

❶ First off, we set the service subject to equal the invocation subject. Notice that this operation will fail if, while using the **caller-identity** run-as mode, the client does not delegate credentials. In fact, we will see how this part of **getAnswer** fails when we try to use a non-delegating client.

❷ Auxiliary variables.

❸ Before we invoke MathService, we print out some security information to check that delegation is taking place.

❹ We get a reference to the MathPortType and set the appropriate security stub options. This is done using two private methods which are discussed later on.

❺ We invoke the **add** and **multiply** operations in MathService, thus obtaining The Answer.

❻ We retrieve The Answer by accessing the **Value** RP in MathService.

❼ Finally, we return The Answer.

logSecurityInfo **Method**

The **logSecurityInfo** method is very similar to the one we used in previous examples, with a couple of minor modifications. We'll use it to write out the caller's identity, and the invocation, subject, and service subjects.

Other Private Methods

The rest of the private methods perform operations which we've seen in many of the client applications (getting a reference to a portType, making a stub secure, etc.).

The **getReferenceToMathService** obtains a **MathPortType** stub from the locator.

```
private MathPortType getReferenceToMathService() throws Exception {
        logger.info("Obtaining reference to MathService...");
        MathServiceAddressingLocator locator =
            new MathServiceAddressingLocator();
        EndpointReferenceType endpoint = new EndpointReferenceType();
        endpoint.setAddress(new Address(mathURI));
        MathPortType math = locator.getMathPortTypePort(endpoint);
        math = locator.getMathPortTypePort(endpoint);
        logger.info("Obtained reference to MathService!");


        return math;
    }
```

The **makeStubSecure** method sets the stub's security properties.

```
private void makeStubSecure(Object stub) {
        ((Stub) stub)._setProperty(Constants.GSI_SEC_CONV,
            Constants.ENCRYPTION);
        ((Stub) stub)._setProperty(Constants.AUTHORIZATION,
            NoAuthorization.getInstance());
    }
```

22.3.3 Compiling and Deploying

Deployment Descriptor

The WSDD file is pretty straightforward, and similar to the one used in previous examples. However, it will include two services: a PhysicsService that runs using the **caller-identity** run-as mode, and one that doesn't. This way, we will be able to see how MathService reacts when no delegation is taking place. The WSDD file can be found here: **$EXAMPLES_DIR/org/globus/examples/services/security/delegation/deploy-server. wsdd.**

The service that doesn't run as **caller-identity** will have the following security descriptor:

```
<securityConfig xmlns="http://www.globus.org">


<authz value="none"/>


<method name="getAnswer">
    <auth-method>
        <GSISecureConversation/>
    </auth-method>
</method>


<!-- Default for other methods -->
<auth-method>
    <GSISecureConversation/>
</auth-method>


</securityConfig>
```

☞ This file is **$EXAMPLES_DIR/org/globus/examples/services/security/ delegation/etc/security-config-nodeleg.xml**

The service that *does* run as **caller-identity** will have the following security descriptor:

```
<securityConfig xmlns="http://www.globus.org">


<authz value="none"/>


<method name="getAnswer">
    <auth-method>
        <GSISecureConversation/>
    </auth-method>
```

```
<run-as>

    <caller-identity/>

</run-as>


</method>


<!-- Default for other methods -->

<auth-method>

        <GSISecureConversation/>

</auth-method>


</securityConfig>
```

☞ This file is **$EXAMPLES_DIR/org/globus/examples/services/security/delegation/
etc/security-config.xml**

Compile and Deploy

Build the service:

./globus-build-service.sh sec_delegation

And deploy it:

globus-deploy-gar $EXAMPLES_DIR/org_globus_examples_services_security

   _delegation.gar

22.3.4 A non-delegating Client

First of all, we're going to use a client that doesn't perform delegation, along with the PhysicsService that doesn't run as **caller-identity**, to see how MathService denies access to PhysicsService because it isn't using the adequate credentials. The client itself is pretty simple. We'll just invoke the **getAnswer** in PhysicsService. The client's only parameter is the service's URI.

```
package org.globus.examples.clients.PhysicsService;


import javax.xml.rpc.Stub;
```

```java
import org.apache.axis.message.addressing.Address;
import org.apache.axis.message.addressing.EndpointReferenceType;
import org.globus.examples.stubs.PhysicsService.GetAnswer;
import org.globus.examples.stubs.PhysicsService.PhysicsPortType;
import org.globus.examples.stubs.PhysicsService.service.
    PhysicsServiceAddressingLocator;
import org.globus.wsrf.impl.security.authorization.HostAuthorization;
import org.globus.wsrf.security.Constants;

public class ClientNoDelegation {

    public static void main(String[] args) {
        PhysicsServiceAddressingLocator locator =
            new PhysicsServiceAddressingLocator();

        try {
            String serviceURI = args[0];

            // Create endpoint reference to service
            EndpointReferenceType endpoint =
                new EndpointReferenceType();
            endpoint.setAddress(new Address(serviceURI));
            PhysicsPortType physics =
                locator.getPhysicsPortTypePort(endpoint);

            // Get PortType
             physics = locator.getPhysicsPortTypePort(endpoint);

            // Set up security
            ((Stub) physics)._setProperty(Constants.GSI_SEC_CONV,
                        Constants.SIGNATURE);
```

```
((Stub) physics)._setProperty(Constants.AUTHORIZATION,
                    HostAuthorization.getInstance());


// Print out answer
System.out.println("Answer: " +
        physics.getAnswer(new GetAnswer()));


        } catch (Exception e) {
                e.printStackTrace();
        }
    }
}
```

☞ This file is **$EXAMPLES_DIR/org/globus/examples/clients/PhysicsService/**
ClientNoDelegation.java

Now, let's compile the client:

**javac **

**-classpath ./build/stubs/classes/:$CLASSPATH **

org/globus/examples/clients/PhysicsService/ClientNoDelegation.java

And run the client:

**java **

**-classpath ./build/stubs/classes/:$CLASSPATH **

**org/globus/examples/clients/PhysicsService/ClientNoDelegation **

http://127.0.0.1:8080/wsrf/services/examples/security/delegation/

PhysicsNoDelegService

☞ **examples/security/delegation/PhysicsNoDelegService** is the PhysicsService
that doesn't use the **caller-identity** run-as mode.

You should see the following:

Answer: 0

We are not seeing any error message because **getAnswer** is still configured to return successfully even if the call to MathService fails. If we take a look at the server log, we will see the following:

```
-------- BEGIN SECURITY INFO --------
Caller: /O=Globus/OU=GT4 Examples/CN=Globus 4 User
Invocation subject: /O=Globus/OU=GT4 Examples/CN=host/pc-johndoe.foobar.com
Service subject: /O=Globus/OU=GT4 Examples/CN=host/pc-johndoe.foobar.com
System subject: /O=Globus/OU=GT4 Examples/CN=host/pc-johndoe.foobar.com
-------- END SECURITY INFO --------


Obtaining reference to MathService...
Obtained reference to MathService!
Invoking add...
[add]      ERROR: org.globus.wsrf.impl.security.authorization.exceptions.
              AuthorizationException:
           "/O=Globus/OU=GT4 Examples/CN=host/pc-johndoe.foobar.com" is
              not authorized to use operation:
           {http://www.globus.org/namespaces/examples/
              MathService_instance_4op}add on this service


...
```

Since delegation is not taking place, the container will use the service subject (/O=Globus/OU=GT4 Examples/CN=host/pc-johndoe.foobar.com) to invoke MathService. However, that subject isn't in MathService's gridmap, and that's why we get an authorization error.

22.3.5   A Delegating Client

We will now use a client that will delegate its credentials to PhysicsService. The code for this client is exactly the same as the one for the non-delegating client, except that we will activate full delegation in the PhysicsPortType object.

> ☞ This code for the delegating client is **$EXAMPLES_DIR/org/globus/examples/clients/**
> **PhysicsService/Client.java**

Let's compile the client:

```
javac \
-classpath ./build/stubs/classes/:$CLASSPATH \
org/globus/examples/clients/PhysicsService/Client.java
```

And run it:

```
java \
-classpath ./build/stubs/classes/:$CLASSPATH \
org/globus/examples/clients/PhysicsService/Client \
http://127.0.0.1:8080/wsrf/services/examples/security/
    delegation/PhysicsService
```

> ☞ examples/security/delegation/PhysicsService is the PhysicsService that *does* use the **caller-identity** run-as mode.

Once you run the client, you should see the following output:

Answer: 42

> ☞ For the meaning of this number, please refer to [1].

If we take a look at the server logs, we'll see how delegation is really taking place. First, let's look at the initial security info written by the PhysicsService:

```
-------- BEGIN SECURITY INFO --------
Caller: /O=Globus/OU=GT4 Examples/CN=Globus 4 User
Invocation subject: /O=Globus/OU=GT4 Examples/CN=Globus 4 User
Service subject: /O=Globus/OU=GT4 Examples/CN=Globus 4 User
System subject: /O=Globus/OU=GT4 Examples/CN=host/pc-johndoe.foobar.com
-------- END SECURITY INFO --------
```

Notice how, this time, both the invocation subject *and* the service subject are the same as the caller's subject.

Next, let's see what happens during the invocation of the **add** method:

```
Invoking add...
Authorized "/O=Globus/OU=GT4 Examples/CN=Globus 4 User" to invoke
"{http://www.globus.org/namespaces/examples/MathService_instance_4op}add".
'add' invoked by: /O=Globus/OU=GT4 Examples/CN=Globus 4 User
```

Mapped to globus4user

add invoked successfully!

The emphasized lines are produced by MathService. Notice how MathService correctly reports that the call is being made using **globus4user**'s credentials, instead of the service or container credentials of PhysicsService.

22.4 Delegating Credentials to a Resource

We will now see an example of an interesting, and useful, security scenario that is solved with delegation. For an application, we might sometimes be interested in resources being accessed *only* by the users who create them. For example, imagine we have a service whose resources represent business transactions initiated by users. We want to make sure that only the user that starts the transaction is authorized to fiddle with the resource and potentially modify its resource properties.

To solve this problem, we can change the ownership of a resource so it will equal the identity of the user creating the resource. Similarly to changing the ownership of a service, this requires that the client delegate its credentials to the resource.

The code for this example is based on the example seen in Chapter 21. This example already included resource-level security by requiring that resources be accessed with GSI Secure Conversation. We will now see what changes are necessary to delegate credentials to a resource.

22.4.1 The Security Descriptors

We will start by seeing what changes are necessary in the resource descriptors. First of all, we need to change the authorization mechanism in the resource to **self**, so that only clients with its same identity will be able to access it.

```
<securityConfig xmlns="http://www.globus.org">


<auth-method>

        <GSISecureConversation/>

</auth-method>


<authz value="self"/>


</securityConfig>
```

> ☞ This file is **$EXAMPLES_DIR/org/globus/examples/services/security/ resource_self/etc/security-config-resource.xml**

The client's credentials will be delegated to the resource when the resource is created. Therefore, the run-as mode of the factory service will have to be **caller-identity** so that the delegated credentials can be passed over to the resource. Notice how we do not require any authorization in the factory.

```
<securityConfig xmlns="http://www.globus.org">


<method name="createResource">
    <auth-method>
        <GSISecureConversation/>
    </auth-method>
    <run-as>
        <caller-identity/>
    </run-as>
</method>


<authz value="none"/>


</securityConfig>
```

> ☞ This file is **$EXAMPLES_DIR/org/globus/examples/services/security/ resource_self/etc/security-config-factory.xml**

Finally, the **add** operation in the instance service will require GSI Secure Conversation. Notice that we can specify that no authorization will take place at this level, since the resource authorization mechanism will have precedence over the service one.

```
<securityConfig xmlns="http://www.globus.org">


<method name="add">
    <auth-method>
        <GSISecureConversation/>
    </auth-method>
</method>
```

```
<authz value="none"/>

</securityConfig>
```

> ☞ This file is **$EXAMPLES_DIR/org/globus/examples/services/security/
> resource_self/etc/security-config-instance.xml**

22.4.2 The WSDL File

The WSDL files for this example are exactly the same as the ones seen in Chapter 21.

> ☞ The instance WSDL file is **$EXAMPLES_DIR/schema/MathService_instance
> _helloworld/Math.wsdl.**
>
> The factory WSDL file is **$EXAMPLES_DIR/schema/FactoryService/Factory.wsdl.**

22.4.3 Implementation Files

The Service Implementation

The service implementation is exactly the same as the one seen in Chapter 21.

> ☞ The service implementation is **$EXAMPLES_DIR/org/globus/examples/services/
> security/resource_self/impl/MathFactoryService.java**

Even so, at this point we can take a closer look at the **logSecurityInfo** method, since it will allow us to verify that delegation is taking place. In particular, unlike previous examples, we will be printing out information on the resource's subject:

```
private void logSecurityInfo(String methodName, Resource resource) {


        // Print caller, invocation subject, service subject, system subject


        // Print out resource subject
        logger.info("RESOURCE SUBJECT");
        if (resource == null)
                logger.info("No resource");
        {
                try {
                        subject = SecurityManager.getManager().getSubject(resource);
```

```
            logger.info(subject == null ? "NULL" : subject.toString());
        } catch (Exception e) {
                logger.warn("Unable to obtain resource subject");
        }
    }
}
```

The Resource Implementation

The resource implementation is the same as the one seen in Chapter 21, except for the fact that we are now using a new resource security descriptor:

```
config =
    new ResourceSecurityConfig("etc/org_globus_examples_services_security
        _resource_self/security-config-resource.xml");

config.init();
```

> ☞ The resource implementation is **$EXAMPLES_DIR/org/globus/examples/services/security/resource_self/impl/MathResource.java**

The Factory Service Implementation

The service implementation is exactly the same as the one seen in Chapter 21. Although we've said that credential delegation takes place during the resource creation (through the factory service), this doesn't affect the implementation of the factory service. We will only need to modify the resource home, which is directly responsible for resource creation.

> ☞ The factory service implementation is **$EXAMPLES_DIR/org/globus/examples/services/security/resource_self/impl/MathFactoryService.java**

The Resource Home Implementation

We need to modify the resource home so that, after the resource is created, we make the client the owner of the new resource.

```
public ResourceKey create() throws Exception {
        // Create a resource and initialize it
        MathResource mathResource = (MathResource) createNewInstance();
        mathResource.initialize();
```

```
// Get key
ResourceKey key = new SimpleResourceKey(keyTypeName, mathResource.getID());

// Security
ResourceSecurityDescriptor desc = mathResource.getSecurityDescriptor();
SecurityManager.getManager().setResourceOwnerFromContext(desc);

// Add the resource to the list of resources in this home
add(key, mathResource);
return key;
}
```

> ☞ The resource home implementation is **$EXAMPLES_DIR/org/globus/examples/
> services/security/resource_self/impl/MathResourceHome.java**

Deployment Descriptors

Since the factory and instance services now have their own security descriptors, we must make sure to include them in the WSDD file. No changes are necessary in the JNDI file.

```xml
<?xml version="1.0" encoding="UTF-8"?>
<deployment name="defaultServerConfig"
    xmlns="http://xml.apache.org/axis/wsdd/"
    xmlns:java="http://xml.apache.org/axis/wsdd/providers/java"
    xmlns:xsd="http://www.w3.org/2001/XMLSchema">

    <!-- Instance service -->
    <service name="examples/security/resource_self/MathService"
        provider="Handler" use="literal" style="document">

    <!-- ... -->

    <parameter name="securityDescriptor"
        value="etc/org_globus_examples_services_security_resource
            _self/security-config-instance.xml"/>
```

```
<!-- ... -->


</service>


<!-- Factory service -->
<service name="examples/security/resource_self/MathFactoryService"
    provider="Handler" use="literal" style="document">


    <!-- ... -->


    <parameter name="securityDescriptor"
        value="etc/org_globus_examples_services_security_resource_self/
            security-config-factory.xml"/>


    <!-- ... -->


</service>


</deployment>
```

☞ The WSDD file is **$EXAMPLES_DIR/org/globus/examples/services/security/
resource/deploy-server.wsdd**

The JNDI deploy file is **$EXAMPLES_DIR/org/globus/examples/services/
security/resource/deploy-jndi-config.xml**

22.4.4 Build and Deploy

Build the service:

> **./globus-build-service.sh sec_resource_self**

And deploy it:

> **globus-deploy-gar $EXAMPLES_DIR/org_globus_examples_services_wsrf
> _security_sec_resource_self.gar**

22.4.5   Trying it Out

Remember from the example in Chapter 21 that we had several clients for this service. To try our new service, we will first create a new service using a creation client that delegates its credentials. Then we will try to invoke the new WS-Resource using a secure addition client using the user account that created the resource, and then with a different user, to observe how it is denied access to the resource.

> ☞ The instance creation client, with delegation activated, is **$EXAMPLES_DIR/org/ globus/examples/clients/FactoryService_Math_helloworld/ClientCreate_ Deleg.java.**

Compile the creation client:

```
javac \
-classpath ./build/stubs/classes/:$CLASSPATH \
org/globus/examples/clients/FactoryService_Math_helloworld/
    ClientCreate_Deleg.java
```

And run it:

```
java \
-classpath ./build/stubs/classes/:$CLASSPATH \
org.globus.examples.clients.FactoryService_Math_helloworld.ClientCreate_Deleg \
http://127.0.0.1:8080/wsrf/services/examples/security/resource_self/
    MathFactoryService
```

The recently created WS-Resource's EPR will be written to file **epr.txt**. Now, we will use the addition client.

> ☞ The addition client with security is **$EXAMPLES_DIR/org/globus/examples/clients/ MathService_instance_helloworld/ClientAdd_Secure.java.**

Compile the client:

```
javac \
-classpath ./build/stubs/classes/:$CLASSPATH \
org/globus/examples/clients/MathService_instance_helloworld/
    ClientAdd_Secure.java
```

And run it:

```
java \
-classpath ./build/stubs/classes/:$CLASSPATH \
```

```
org.globus.examples.clients.MathService_instance_helloworld.ClientAdd_Secure \
epr.txt \
10
```

You should see the following:

```
Addition was successful
```

```
Current value: 10
```

Ok, no surprises there. However, if you take a look at the server-side logs, you'll see how the resource's subject is, in fact, set to the same subject that created the resource (and that is now running the addition client).

```
SECURITY INFO FOR METHOD 'add'
```

The caller is:*/O=Globus/OU=GT4 Examples/CN=Globus 4 User*

```
INVOCATION SUBJECT
```

```
Subject:
```

```
        Principal: /O=Globus/OU=GT4 Examples/CN=Globus 4 User
```

```
        Public Credential: [Ljava.security.cert.X509Certificate;@170b6d
```

```
        Private Credential: org.globus.gsi.gssapi.GlobusGSSCredentialImpl@ef2e7c
```

```
SERVICE SUBJECT
```

```
Subject:
```

```
        Principal: /O=Globus/OU=GT4 Examples/CN=host/pc-johndoe.foobar.com
```

```
        Private Credential: org.globus.gsi.gssapi.GlobusGSSCredentialImpl@1d4f355
```

```
SYSTEM SUBJECT
```

```
Subject:
```

```
        Principal: /O=Globus/OU=GT4 Examples/CN=host/pc-johndoe.foobar.com
```

```
        Private Credential: org.globus.gsi.gssapi.GlobusGSSCredentialImpl@1d4f355
```

```
RESOURCE SUBJECT
```

```
Subject:
```

```
        Principal: /O=Globus/OU=GT4 Examples/CN=Globus 4 User
```

```
        Public Credential: [Ljava.security.cert.X509Certificate;@170b6d
```

```
        Private Credential: org.globus.gsi.gssapi.GlobusGSSCredentialImpl@ef2e7c
```

If, on the other hand, you try to run the addition client with a different identity, you will get an error message indicating that you cannot access the resource. For example, let's suppose the **globus** user is set up with a certificate with identity **/O=Globus/OU=GT4 Examples/CN=Globus 4 Administrator**. If we use that user to run the addition client, we would see the following:

```
[add]        ERROR: org.globus.wsrf.impl.security.authorization.exceptions
                 .AuthorizationException:
             "/O=Globus/OU=GT4 Examples/CN=Globus 4 Administrator" is not
                 authorized to use operation:
             {http://www.globus.org/namespaces/examples/
                 MathService_instance_helloworld}add
             on this service


[getRP]      ERROR: org.globus.wsrf.impl.security.authorization.exceptions
                 .AuthorizationException:
             "/O=Globus/OU=GT4 Examples/CN=Globus 4 Administrator" is not
                 authorized to use operation:
             {http://www.globus.org/namespaces/examples/
                 MathService_instance_helloworld}getResourceProperty
             on this service
```

So, as you can see, only the user that created the resource will have access to it. Pretty nifty, huh?

22.5   The Delegation Service

All through this chapter we have seen how to delegate credentials programmatically. However, it is also possible to do this at a higher level, by using a Web services interface. GT4 supplies a *delegation service* that will allow us to delegate credentials to any service that is deployed in the same container as the delegation service. To do this, the client must tell the delegation service that it wants to delegate its credentials to a certain service. Then, the service that wants to use those credentials must contact the delegation service to retrieve them.

This service also provides an interface to easily refresh the delegated credentials. Remember that delegation is possible thanks to proxy certificates, which have a limited lifetime. So, the delegation service could be a good option whenever we want to delegate credentials for an unspecified amount of time (and want to periodically refresh the delegation, instead of issuing a proxy with a longer time limit).

More details on the delegation service can be found on the official Globus documentation [2].

References

[1] Douglas Adams. *The Hitchhiker's Guide to the Galaxy*. Del Rey. September 27, 1995.

[2] *GT4.0. Security: Delegation Service (Official documentation)*. http://www.globus.org/toolkit/docs/4.0/security/delegation.

part **IV**

The FileBuy Application

Previous chapters of this book have focused on features included in the Java WS Core and Authentication & Authorization components of GT4. The chapters used a simple example, MathService, to illustrate fundamentals of service development in GT4. Although MathService is a good way of making first contact with GT4, its simplicity does not allow for interesting higher-level discussions.

And so the final chapters of this book are built around a new example application called *FileBuy*. The FileBuy system is composed of multiple services deployed across several machines. The additional complexity in FileBuy enables us to highlight a few design patterns commonly found in GT4-based systems. It should be noted that in order to maintain focus on GT4, many details of a real-world system have been intentionally simplified in our example.

The FileBuy section is composed of two chapters, the first of which focuses on design considerations. The second chapter includes a discussion of implementation details and instructions on how to deploy the application. The source code for FileBuy can be downloaded from the book's website (http://www.gt4book.com/).

chapter **23**

Design

In this chapter we present an overview of the design of FileBuy. FileBuy is a *resource brokering* system, and so we begin with a conceptual overview of resource brokering. Then, using a simplified form of UML, we walk through three usage scenarios of the system. The chapter concludes with a brief discussion on security considerations and a review of the important design concepts seen in this chapter.

> ☞ This might be a good time to review Chapter 1, (unless you are already familiar with Grid computing). In particular, you should be familiar with what a *virtual organization* is.

23.1 Resource Brokering Overview

A resource brokering system is a construct common to many Grid deployments. Such systems track available resources in a virtual organization and mediate their use. When a service on the Grid (a *resource consumer*) requires a resource, it will contact a *resource broker*, specifying the type of resource it needs. The resource broker then matches the request against available resources.

For example, a service might need to locate a machine with at least 10 GB of available disk space to store the result of a computation. Given this request, the resource broker checks the list of resources in the virtual organization, and matches the request to the best possible resource.

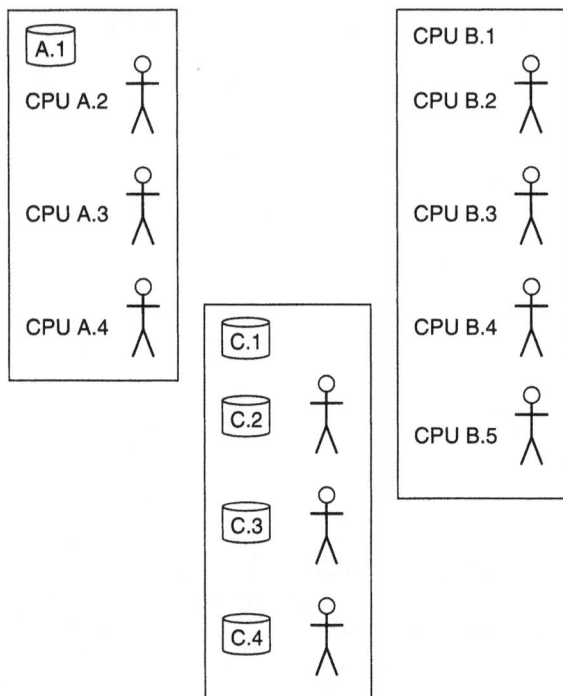

Figure 23.1: Three organizations with resources

> ☞ Note that in this chapter, we use the term *resource* loosely, referring to "resources on the Grid" (such as CPUs, clusters, network storage, etc.). We are not referring to the more formal *WS-Resource*, as defined in the WS-Resource Framework specification, though in practice "resources" are often *represented* as WS-Resources in a deployed grid.

To illustrate more fully the way resource brokers work, consider a VO that includes participants from three organizations (see Figure 23.1). These organizations share two types of resources: CPUs and storage capacity. As is common in Grid computing, not all resources owned by a participating organization are shared in the VO. Hence, our example VO includes a subset of all possible resources (see Figure 23.2). In this chapter we refer to the pool of resources designated for sharing as the set of *available resources*. Remember that the membership of this set is dynamic: resources in a VO often come and go.

Information on available resources in a VO can be maintained through the use of a central *index service*, as shown in Figure 23.3.

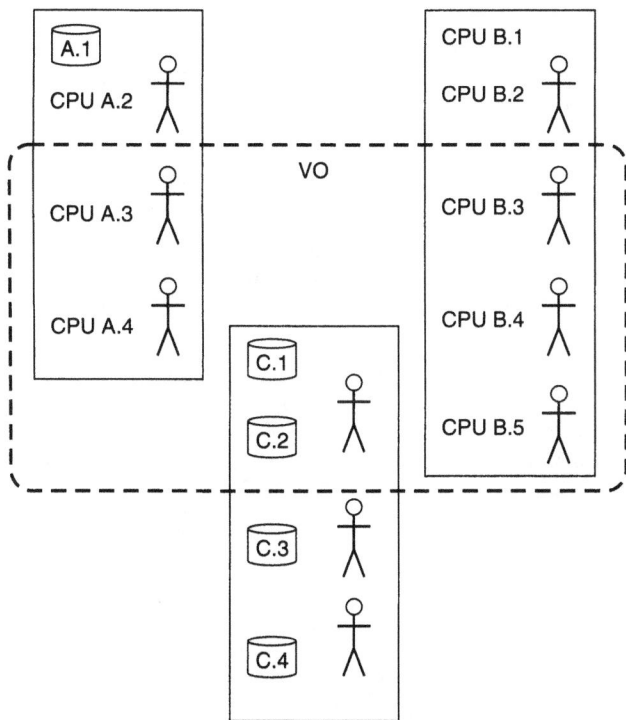

Figure 23.2: A virtual organization based on our three organizations

> ☞ While a general discussion on information service infrastructure is out-of-scope for this book, it is important to understand that VO information systems can be quite complex. Sophisticated systems might include multiple index services linked in a structured way, replicas and elaborate mechanisms to ensure the integrity of entries.

An index service alone usually isn't enough to perform efficient resource brokering. Often there is a gateway service in front of the index, called the *broker*, which is responsible for interpreting requests and enforcing VO policies on resource access. Brokers can hide the many details involved in locating suitable resources.

Interactions in a typical resource brokerage can include (also, see Figure 23.4.

1. Available resources *register* with a broker. This can be viewed as a way of *advertising* a resource to the VO. (Note that the term '*resource producers*' is sometimes applied to these entities.)

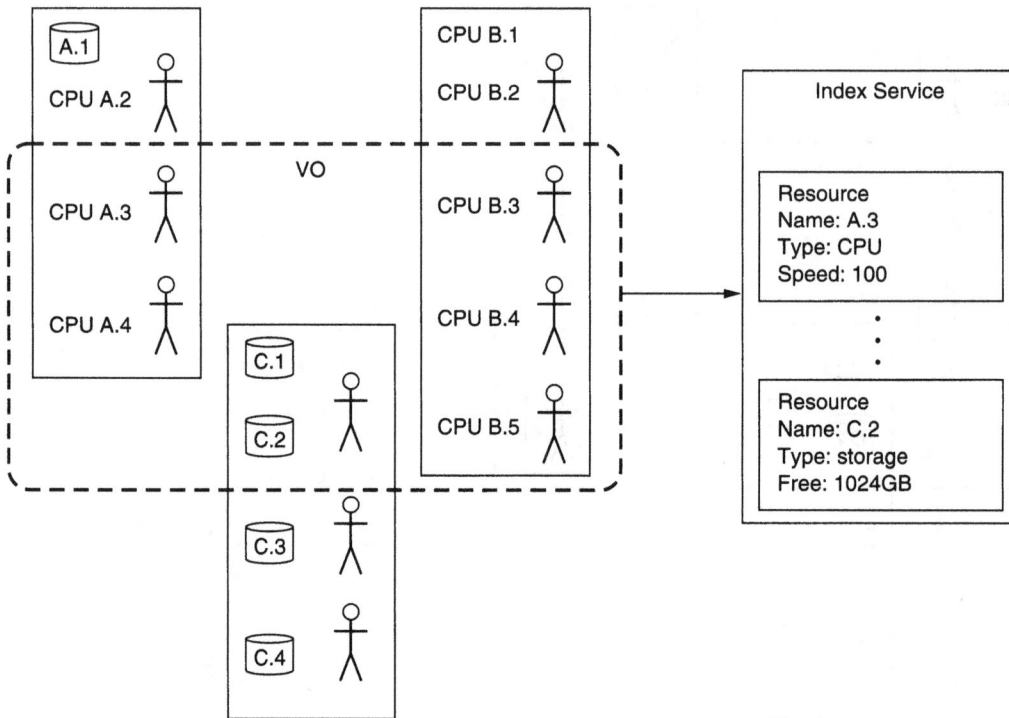

Figure 23.3: Index service

2. The resource broker's index service collects, or *aggregates*, information about avail-able resources. Brokers often include mechanisms to track resources in order to ensure accurate information is available.

3. A *resource consumer* contacts the broker service, requesting a resource that meets some parameters. For example, a service might seek storage capacity of at least 10 GB of available disk space. Finding a resource based on its attributes is often referred to as the process of *discovery*.

4. The broker might query an index service to find a resource matching the requested criteria. Our FileBuy example follows very simple rules for resource discovery, based on filename and price. However, matching a request to a resource in a real-world system can be quite complex, as other factors sometime must be taken into account (authorization policies, reservation availability, accounting, etc.).

5. The broker might return a match by pointing the consumer directly to a resource. In this case the resource consumer might then contact the resource producer directly, although in some Grid architectures the resource broker still acts as an intermediary.

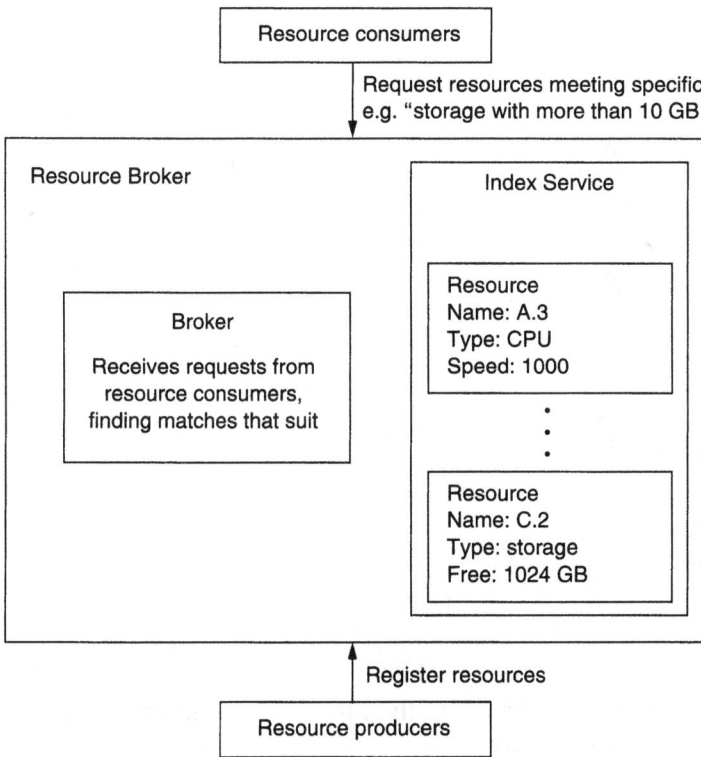

Figure 23.4: Resource brokering

> ☞ Figure 23.4 shows the index service as being the "Broker's Index Service". Although the index service can be tightly coupled to the resource broker, this is not always the case. In fact, the index service in a VO is usually not used exclusively by the resource broker.

Now that you have an understanding of brokering fundamentals, we shift the discussion to the specifics of our example application.

23.2 FileBuy System Overview

FileBuy is a resource brokering system that enables buyers to purchase files from sellers linked by a wide-area network. In our system the sellers represent resource producers and the buyers represent resource consumers. Interactions between the two are mediated by the *FileBuy Broker*. The "resources" in a FileBuy VO are not CPUs nor storage capacity, but data files. For the purpose of our example , the content of these files is irrelevant.

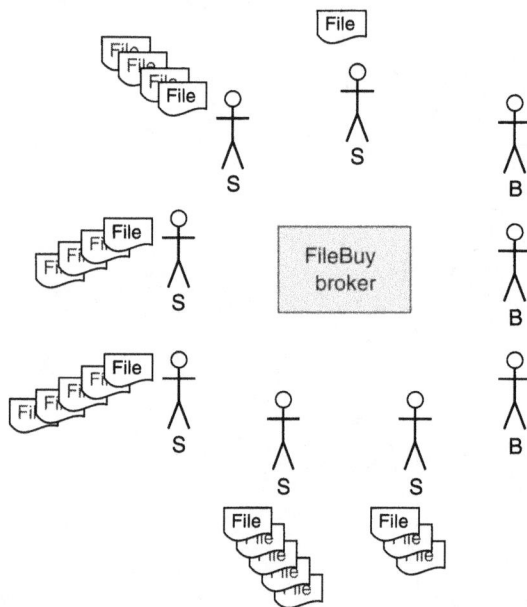

Figure 23.5: Example FileBuy VO

A FileBuy VO is made up of one broker and (potentially) hundreds of buyers, sellers, and files. An example FileBuy VO is shown in Figure 23.5.

23.3   Use Cases

In this section we further explore the design details and behavior of FileBuy. To this end we consider three key use cases of the system: (1) advertising a file, (2) finding a file and (3) purchasing a file (Figure 23.6).

We begin by walking through the sequence of component interactions for each use case. A brief explanation of key design decisions follows. Then each uses case study concludes with highlights of important general concepts.

23.3.1   Usage Scenario 1: Advertising a File

Overview

We now describe the first use case: advertising a file. Figure 23.7 shows the sequence diagram for this use case:

1. The sequence begins with a seller's desire to advertise the existence of a file for sale. The seller runs an **AddFile** client application on his local machine, providing

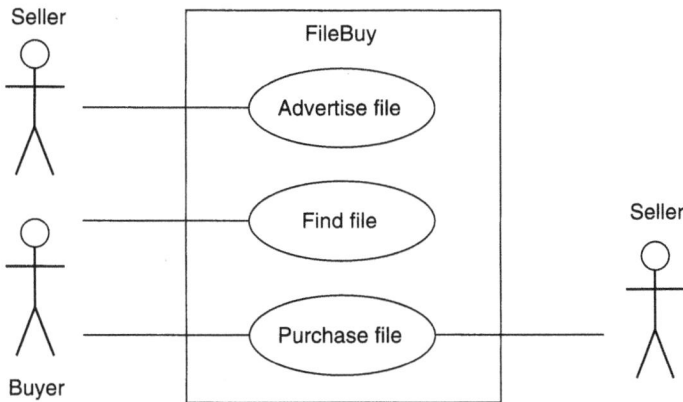

Figure 23.6: FileBuy use cases

(1) a universally recognized name for the file, (2) the location of the file on the seller's machine and (3) its selling price.

2. The **AddFile** client invokes the **FilesForSale** service, which runs in the seller's container. This service provides the interface for sellers to manage the files they advertise. In particular, at this point the seller invokes the **Add** operation, requesting that the file be included in the list of files advertised by this seller.

3. The **Add** operation of **FilesForSale** triggers the creation of a WS-Resource called **File**. Each file for sale on disk is represented by a **File** resource in the seller's container.

4. Upon creation, **File** registers with a **FilesForSale Index** running locally on the seller's container. Note that this is *not* the broker's index service but, rather, a local index with information on the files in the seller's machine.

5. After some time, the local registrations will propagate to the broker's **FileBuy Index**, which will also cache the data stored in the seller's local index. As explained in Section 23.1, this is known as *aggregating* the information in our virtual organization.

Design Details

Figure 23.7, provides a high-level view of the interactions between the components involved in advertising a file. Key design decisions include:

- **Creation pattern for the File resource:** In our application, a buyer can advertise multiple files, which means the system must support multiple **File** resources. Following the factory model covered in Chapter 8, the **FilesForSale** component is implemented as two services (the factory service and the instance service).

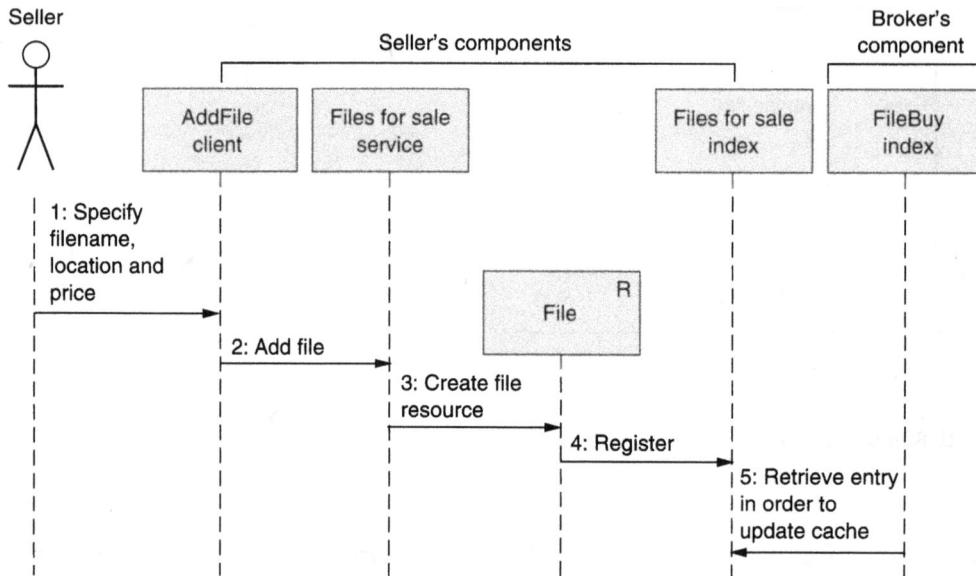

Figure 23.7: Sequence diagram for advertising a file

■ **Resource persistence:** Our `File` resources are *persisted* so they will survive container restarts. In this case we decided that persisting was worth the cost in performance because of the central importance of `File` resources to the system. If these resources were lost, it would be very difficult to reconstruct them. See Chapter 12 for additional information on persisting resources.

■ **The seller's index and the broker's index:** Fortunately, we will not need to implement an index service ourselves, as GT4 already includes an Index Service implementation. When the WS MDS component is installed (either by specifying the "all" or "wsmds" targets on the GT4 installer) a local index is deployed by default into the Java WS container. In Grid deployments a local index service is often used to maintain a registry of interesting services and/or resources running in that container. In our scenario, a seller's local resources of interest include the files for sale.

Furthermore, GT4 Index services can be configured to register with an *upstream index* which automatically aggregates the data of all *downstream indexes*. In our system the broker's index serves as the top-level upstream index for the VO. Because all the seller's indexes will register with it, the broker maintains a registry of interesting resources for the entire VO.

Note that GT4's Index service is versatile enough that it can serve both as a local index or a VO index. Although the GT4 Index service is not covered in this book, we will see in the next chapter that the code required to support these usage scenarios is relatively simple.

- **Handling sellers that become unavailable:** We want to minimize situations in which the broker lists files that are no longer available. Such situations can occur when sellers experience network problems or their containers shut down. To this end, the lifetimes of sellers' registrations in the broker's index are *lease-based*. Lease-based lifetime management is described in Chapter 11.

General Concepts

- FileBuy is not a static system. Rather, it is a dynamic system where sellers can add new files at any time, and sellers can enter and leave the VO as they please. Therefore, many of our design decisions are centered on creating a robust information structure.

- As described in Section 23.1 the brokering system provides a 'single point of entry' for the seller. Instead of implementing a complex seller component that must discover all the potential buyers on its own, this task is delegated (with minimal overhead for the seller) to a broker service.

23.3.2   Usage Scenario 2: Finding a File

Overview

We now switch to the buyer's perspective, and explore what happens when a buyer needs to find a file. Figure 23.8, shows the sequence diagram for this use case:

1. The sequence begins with a buyer's desire to find a file for purchase. The buyer runs a **FindFile** client on his local machine, providing (1) a universally recognized name for the file, and (2) the maximum price he is willing to spend on the file.

2. The **FindFile** client invokes the **Find** operation on the **FileBuy Broker**, which is deployed on the broker's container.

3. The **FileBuy Broker** performs a query against the broker's **FileBuy Index**, searching for entries matching the name and price requirements of the buyer.

4. If there is at least one entry returned from the search, **FileBuy Broker** creates a **File Order** resource.

5. **FileBuy Broker** adds the least expensive seller's file to the **File Order** resource. Internally, the **File Order** stores the EPR of the **File** resource returned from the search.

6. **FileBuy Broker** then returns the **File Order** EPR along with the cost of the file to the **FindFile** client.

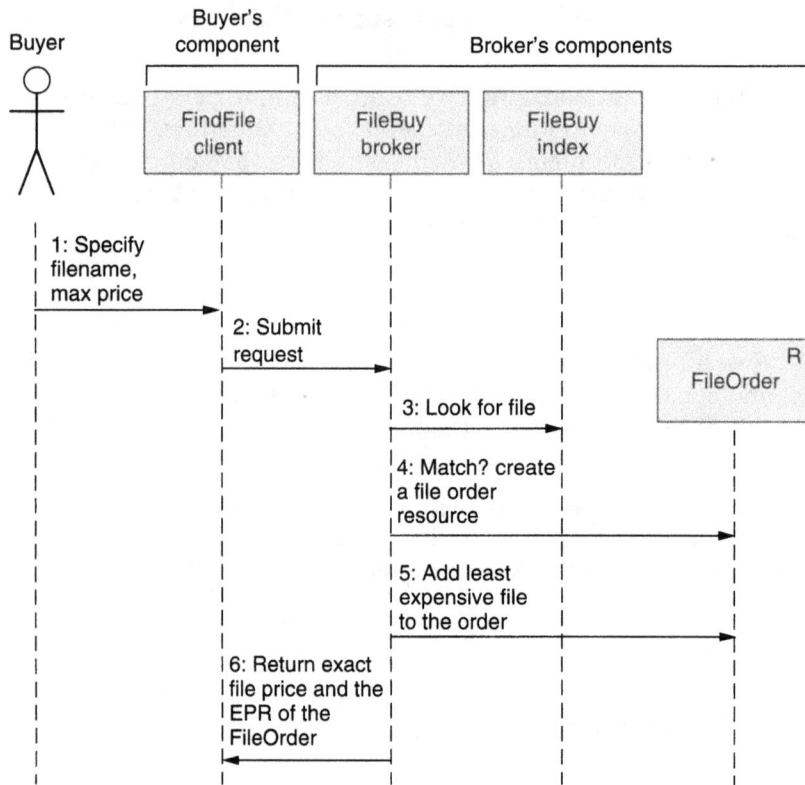

Figure 23.8: Sequence diagram for finding a file

Design Details

Design highlights include:

- **Creation pattern for the File Order resource:** The broker contains a resource factory that creates **File Orders** upon finding a match for a buyer's request. Given the implicit nature of the factory we chose not to use a separate factory instance service in the implementation.

- **Resource persistence:** For the purpose of discussion we have chosen not to persist the File Order resource. For each type of resource in a system, designers must decide if the overhead of persistence is worth the benefits.

  In our simple system recovery from the loss of a File Order is relatively painless, as the buyers need only execute a single search to recreate it. The effort to recover File resources, however, can be non-trivial as the seller must re-register a potentially large number of files.

■ **Service composition:** From the client's perspective the FileBuy Broker is a single service, though in actuality the broker is a suite of services. The approach of building higher-level functionality through the composition of multiple lower-level services is a hallmark of service-oriented architectures.

Advantages of this approach include encouraging service reuse and easing the task of integrating new implementations of existing functionality. Costs of this approach include an increased overhead on communications within the higher-level service.

General Concepts

■ This scenario illustrates the process of *discovery*, in which resources are identified based on their attributes (as opposed to using EPRs directly). The ability to discover resources is a fundamental requirement of Grid computing, as it enables the formation of dynamic systems that do not depend on the existence of specific resources.

■ As described in Section 23.1, the buyer (or resource consumer) uses the brokering system to access resources offered by many sellers. The brokering system saves the buyer the work of interacting with the sellers individually.

23.3.3   Usage Scenario 3: Purchasing a File

Overview

The final scenario puts everything together, showing a client's purchase of a seller's file. Figure 23.9 shows the sequence diagram for this use case:

1. The sequence begins with a buyer initiating a purchase using a **FileBuy** client running on the buyer's machine.

2. The client invokes the **Purchase** operation on the **FileBuy Broker**, providing the EPR of the **File Order** returned from the **Find** operation in scenario 2.

3. The **Purchase** operation triggers the retrieval of the file entry from the File Order.

4. Using the EPR of the **File** resource, the **FileBuy Broker** invokes the **FillOrder** operation on the seller's resource, passing the EPR of the buyer's **FileBuy** client as an parameter.

5. When called to fill an order, **FilesForSale** invokes the **Transfer** operation on a locally running **FileTransfer** service, providing details of the file and the buyer's **FileBuy** client EPR as parameters.

6. The buyer's **FileBuy** client receives the transfer from the seller's **FileTransfer** service.

7. The **FileBuy** client reports the results of the transfer to the **FileBuy Broker**.

8. If the transfer succeeded, the broker destroys the resource.

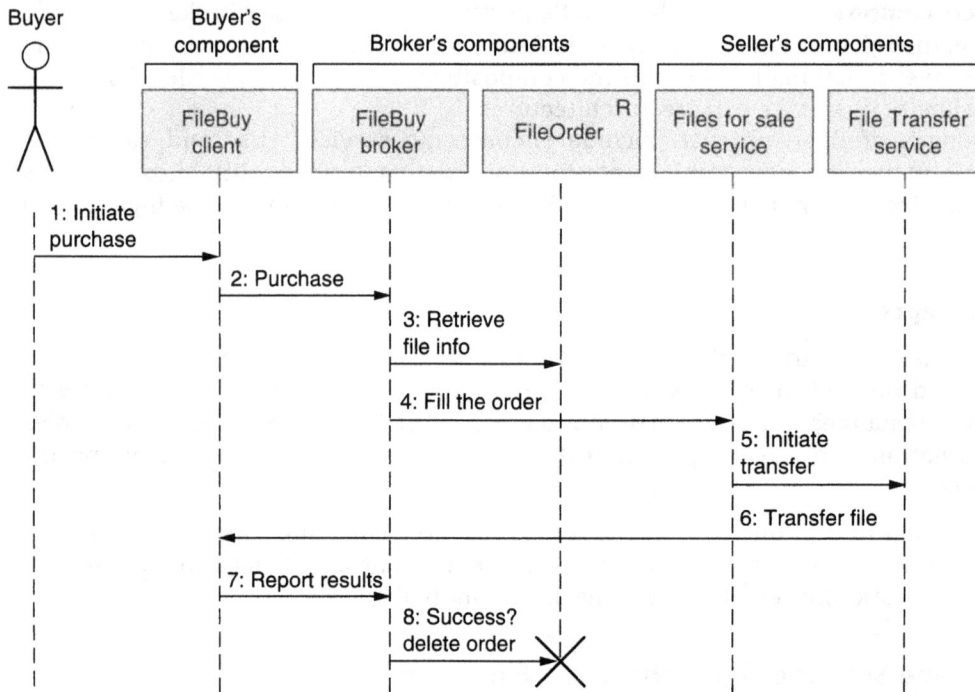

Figure 23.9: Sequence diagram for purchasing a file

Design Details

- **FileBuy client:** There is more to the FileBuy client than might first meet the eye. Because it must handle "transfer file" messages, the FileBuy client is implemented as a service. It might seem strange for a service to also act as a client, but this is in fact quite common in distributed computing. For instance the File-Buy broker acts as a client of the FileBuy Index when it queries the index for files.

- **File transfer service:** In our demo application the file transfer functionality is tightly coupled with the FileBuy client. In other words, FileBuy contains a FileTransfer implementation that only knows how to transfer files to FileBuy clients. In a real Grid deployment this would not be a particularly wise design decision.

  For non-trivial Grid deployments it is recommended that you reuse existing general-purpose services where possible. Services like the *Reliable File Transfer (RFT) service* included in GT4 are generic enough to be applied across many different problem domains and are generally more robust than ad hoc solutions.

- **Immediate destruction of the File Order:** FileBuy assumes that a `File Order` resource is limited to a single file and that, once the file is purchased, the need for the File Order goes away. Given these semantics it makes sense to use immediate destruction to destroy the resource after the purchase. Refer to Chapter 11 for a discussion on immediate destruction.

- **Monetary debits and credits:** Our Files have a cost associated with them in order to demonstrate that resource consumers can impose constraints on brokering system requests. Though outside the scope of this book, a real-world application would contain robust financial services infrastructure to deal with monetary exchanges.

General Concepts

- This usage scenario, more than others, illustrates the importance of writing loosely coupled services, as this makes it easier to reuse our services in other applications. As mentioned, our file transfer service is tightly coupled to the FileBuy implementation, which means our file transfer service will *only* work with File-Buy. Instead, we could develop a more loosely coupled service, or better yet use an existing one such as RFT. An added advantage is that this makes it easier to change file transfer services down the road, as the impact on other services would be minimal.

- A client doesn't necessarily have to be implemented as a Java client application. Sometimes it makes sense to implement a client as a service, especially when the client will itself be invoked by other services. In general, the line between clients and services is a very thin one. Just consider that many of the services in this application invoke other services, which technically also makes them clients.

23.4 Deployment Architecture

Unlike the MathService example seen throughout the book, the deployment of FileBuy is more complex as it involves multiple hosts. With MathService, we were quite content to deploy the service on our local container, and invoke it from our own machine. FileBuy, on the other hand, is intended to be deployed across three types of platforms: the buyer, the broker, and the seller.

> ☞ Of course, in practice, you will be able to deploy our implementation on a single machine. However, we encourage you to try it out (if possible) on several machines.

Figure 23.10, contains an overview of the components deployed on each platform, and the relationship between each component. The straight arrows represent communication dependencies, while the dotted dependencies represent creation of WS-Resources.

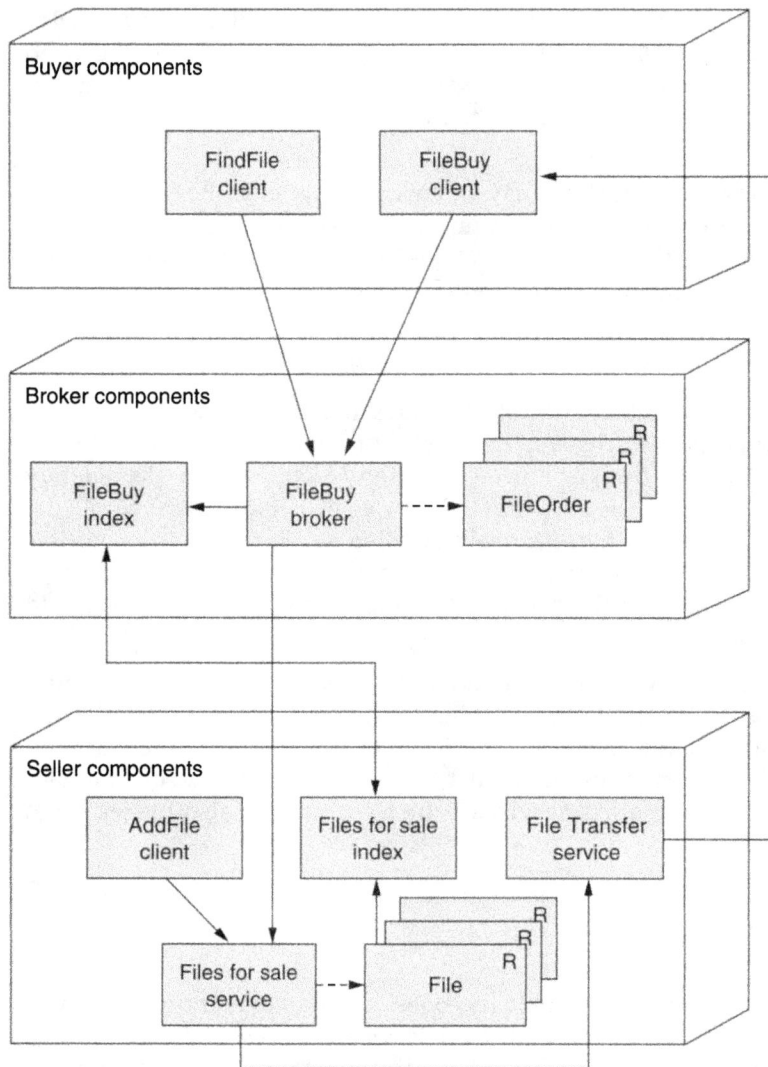

Figure 23.10: FileBuy deployment diagram, with communication dependencies

23.5 Security Considerations

Security is a primary concern in the context of Grid computing, as Grid-based collabora-
tions involve people from multiple administrative domains sharing important resources.
While participants in a VO agree in principle to work together, that openness increases the
importance of protecting the system from naive or intentional misuse.

So why not lock everything down with a full complement of security mechanisms? The answer is simple: runtime security adversely affects performance. The challenge for the system designer is to minimize the potential for exploits while at the same time optimizing for performance. In practice the correct design decisions are highly dependent on the requirements imposed by the problem domain and the policies of the participants.

We use this section to explain key decisions made in securing FileBuy. Our goal is to highlight a few of the issues the designer must consider when developing a security model. It should be noted that GT4 includes a full suite of state-of-the-art security features, many of which are not addressed here.

23.5.1 Authentication

As we saw in Chapter 16 and then in Chapter 19 secure communications are always mutually authenticated, except when the client decides to use anonymous authentication. We need to consider if we want everyone to be properly authenticated, or if we will allow certain users to access the application anonymously.

In our case, we have decided to avoid anonymous authentication. As we will discuss below, we are interested in *auditing* who uses FileBuy, which requires that clients always authenticate themselves.

As for the authentication method to use, performance will be a big issue in our application as we will be moving a potentially large number of files around. The best performing authentication method is GSI Transport (see Section 16.2 and Table 16.1) so we choose that method.

23.5.2 Privacy and Integrity

Regardless of the authentication method we choose, we will have to decide whether we want communications to use digital signatures (guaranteeing integrity but not privacy) or encryption (guaranteeing integrity and privacy). In our case, we assume that the content of the files is not critical, and that having someone eavesdrop on a communication does not pose a security risk. On the other hand, we are interested in making sure that no one tampers with a communication. In other words, we are not concerned about privacy, only about integrity. So, we decide to use GSI Transport with digital signatures and no encryption (see Chapter 19).

23.5.3 Authorization

We will also need to decide if users will need to be authorized to access certain services or WS-Resources. In our case, we will want to make sure that, once a File Order resource has been created during a "find file" operation, only the creator is authorized to use that resource (to avoid malicious users from tampering with another user's order). We can do this as described in Section 22.4. However, the technique described in that section uses delegation, and GSI Transport does not support delegation. We can circumvent this in any of the following ways:

- We can use GSI Secure Conversation (which *does* support delegation) along with GSI Transport. However, this would adversely affect the performance of our application.

- We can use the delegation service (see Section 22.4) to delegate our credentials.

- We can limit access to the resource creator without having to use delegation. One possibility is to use the Globus API (as described briefly in Section 21.2) to dynamically create a gridmap (with a single entry corresponding to the resource creator) when the resource is created, and specify that the gridmap must be used to perform authorization.

Since we have not demonstrated how to work with the delegation service, and performance is an issue in our application, we choose the third option.

Note that we have singled out this particular decision as it showcases an authorization technique seen previously in the book. In a real system, we would probably have to deal with a lot of other authorization decisions. For example, we would probably want to make sure that only a set of known buyers, previously registered in our VO, have access to the File Broker service. We could do this using an external authorization service (e.g. using SAML Callout authorization, as described in Section 20.1.5), or using the Globus-supplied Community Authorization Service (CAS) [1].

Auditing

Finally, we need to decide if we want to keep logs of key component interactions for auditing purposes. These logs can help identify and track problems, as well as resolve disputes should they occur. Keeping such a history is useful, as problems often go unnoticed until well after the offending event occurred. Thus FileBuy logs the following events:

- Registrations of sellers' index services to the broker's index.
- Purchase requests from the FileBuy client to the broker.
- Reports of file transfer results from the FileBuy client to the broker.

23.6 Summing Up

23.6.1 Design is Good!

Notice how, at this point, we have not written a single line of code and, nonetheless, we have pondered some very important issues regarding how our application will be implemented. As you can see, it is important to write up the design of our application before we start writing code (of course, this is true of most computer applications, not just Grid-based ones). This way, all the important decisions regarding our application will be made before we start implementing it. "Should I use lease-based lifetime management, or immediate destruction?," "What services should I deploy in each container?", "Should I use resource-level security, or will service-level security be enough?", Changing your mind on these and other issues is easy when your application is still on paper. Changing your mind once the application is implemented, on the other hand, can be painful and time-consuming.

Of course, we didn't come up with all this "design is good" mumbo-jumbo. If you're familiar with application design, you'll recognize that we've simply repeated some very well-known design principles. If you're not familiar with application design, we encourage you to get well acquainted with it. Believe us, it'll be worth it in the long run. For a quick introduction to software design, check out [2]. For more comprehensive texts, two frequently recommended books are [3] and [4]. For object-oriented applications, you should consider getting up to speed with UML [5] and taking a look at a classic favorite [6], where you will find a lot of useful design patterns.

Cost vs. Benefit

In particular, many of the design decisions you'll have to face are those which require you to analyze the cost of using a certain feature in relation to its potential benefits. More specifically, some design decisions necessarily have to take performance into account, and should not be based solely on the functionality provided by a feature. For example, if we didn't care about performance, we could argue that we should *always* use persistent resources. After all, who doesn't want resources to survive container restarts? But we *do* care about performance, and this feature comes at a price: resources are stored on disk, and the container will have to eventually read from and write to disk (which is not as fast as memory). The other alternative, using in-memory resources, also has its drawbacks, as we could exhaust a machine's memory if we have a lot of resources. As you can see, these are things worth pondering.

Leverage Existing Services

Finally, it is important to leverage existing services (both Globus and non-Globus) in your application. Several times throughout this book, we have reminded you that you *cannot* program Grid applications using *only* the Java WS Core and security components of the toolkit. Thanks to the FileBuy application, we hope you get a much clearer picture of the importance of using higher-level services in your applications. For example, we *could* have implemented an index service all by ourselves, but it turns out GT4 already includes one. We also include our own file transfer service, but saw that our application would benefit greatly from using an existing service such as Reliable File Transfer (which, being out of the scope of this book, we cannot use in our implementation).

In general, during the design of your application you should determine what services you should program yourself and which ones can be "filled in" by an existing service. The Globus Toolkit includes many such services (as seen in Chapter 5), and there is a myriad of general-purpose services out there developed by other projects. Once you know what existing components you're going to use, you can *integrate* them with your own services using Java WS Core.

The conclusion of the book will provide you with a couple of pointers to documentation resources you can use to get better acquainted with all the higher-level services available for use in your applications.

References

[1] *Community Authorization Service documentation.* http://www.globus.org/toolkit/docs/4.0/security/cas/.

[2] David Gustafson. *Schaum's Outline of Software Engineering.* McGraw-Hill, June 24, 2002.

[3] Ian Sommerville. *Software Engineering.* Addison-Wesley Professional, 7th edition, 2004.

[4] Roger Pressman. *Software Engineering: A Practitioner's Approach.* McGraw-Hill Science/Engineering/Math, 6th edition, 2004.

[5] Martin Fowler. *UML Distilled: A Brief Guide to the Standard Object Modeling Language.* Addison-Wesley Professional, 3rd edition, 2003.

[6] Erich Gamma, Richard Helm, Ralph Johnson, and John Vlissides. *Design Patterns: Elements of Reusable Object-Oriented Software.* Addison-Wesley Professional, 1995.

chapter **24**

Implementation

After seeing the design of the FileBuy application, we are now ready to see its implementation. This chapter is meant as a *roadmap* to the FileBuy code, and not a comprehensive explanation of every single action that takes place in the implementation. As such, this chapter is meant to be read with the FileBuy code in front of you (otherwise, this chapter will seem unusually terse at times). The reason for this is that most of the code should be easy to read if you have read all the previous chapters (or, at the very least, the Java WS Core chapters). The main appeal of this code is that it involves several services interacting with each other, so it'll be interesting to see how the sequence diagrams in the previous chapter translate to code, with control flowing from one service to another (while, in all the MathService examples control never flowed from one service to another, except in the PhysicsService example). Even so, there are a few bits and pieces of code that are completely new, specially those that deal with the GT4 Index Service, and we will provide an explanation for those.

Remember that a complete implementation is available for download at the book's website (http://www.gt4book.com/). Each of the four services explained in the previous chapter can be found in the following directories:

- File Broker service: **$EXAMPLES_DIR/org/globus/examples/services/filebuy/ broker/**

- File Seller service: **$EXAMPLES_DIR/org/globus/examples/services/filebuy/seller/**

- File Buyer service: **$EXAMPLES_DIR/org/globus/examples/services/filebuy/buyer/**

- File Transfer service: **$EXAMPLES_DIR/org/globus/examples/services/ filebuy/transfer/**

Furthermore, the WSDL files for these services can be found in **$EXAMPLES_DIR/schema/ examples/filebuy/**.

> ⓘ **Check for updated versions!**
>
> The version of FileBuy described in this chapter is version **1.0**. However, we will continue to improve and expand FileBuy to showcase more design patterns, more GT4 features, etc. These new versions can be downloaded from the book's website. You should still be able to use this chapter to walk through future versions, as any new features included in FileBuy will be fully documented in the book's website.
>
> ## GT4.0.1, or Higher, Required
>
> The FileBuy application requires at least version 4.0.1 of the toolkit. A small bug in GT4.0.0 prevents some of the code from compiling and running correctly.

24.1 Setting Up

Before we start walking through each of the three scenarios, we have to perform some basic setup, mostly related to the GT4 Index Service. First of all, FileBuy should ideally be deployed in at least three machines (one broker, at least one seller, and at least one buyer). Although we will also see how to deploy the application on a single machine (see below), the deployment instructions are given assuming three machines, each with a full GT4 install:

- **pc-broker.gt4book.com**
- **pc-seller.gt4book.com**
- **pc-buyer.gt4book.com**

> ☞ A full GT4 install is not strictly required. However, a core-only install will not be enough as it does not include the GT4 Index Service necessary to run FileBuy. When running the GT4 installer, you must specify the target **wsmds**:
>
>   globus$ make wsmds install

On the seller's machine, you will need to register the local index with the broker's VO index. To do this, you must add the following to the file **$GLOBUS_LOCATION/etc/globus_wsrf_mds_index/hierarchy.xml**:

```
<config>

    <upstream>https://pc-broker.gt4book.com:8443/wsrf/services/
        DefaultIndexService</upstream>

</config>
```

By default, the broker's index (the *upstream* index) will collect new data from the seller's index (the *downstream* index) every 10 minutes. Although this is generally a good refresh interval, in our case we will need to shorten it (unless you want to wait 10 minutes to check if an example is running correctly!). We will set the interval to 20 seconds. To do this, make the following modification to file **$GLOBUS_LOCATION/etc/ globus_wsrf_mds_index/upstream.xml** on the seller machine:

```
<ServiceGroupRegistrationParameters

    xmlns="http://mds.globus.org/servicegroup/client" >


    <!-- Specifies that the registration will be renewed every 600

        seconds (= 10 minutes) -->

    <RefreshIntervalSecs> 600 </RefreshIntervalSecs>


    <Content xsi:type="agg:AggregatorContent"

        xmlns:xsi="http://www.w3.org/2001/XMLSchema-instance"

        xmlns:agg="http://mds.globus.org/aggregator/types">


        <agg:AggregatorConfig xsi:type="agg:AggregatorConfig">
            <agg:GetResourcePropertyPollType

                xmlns:wssg= "http://docs.oasis-open.org/wsrf/2004/06/wsrf-WS-
                    ServiceGroup-1.2-draft-01.xsd">
                <!-- Specifies that the upstream index should refresh information
                    every 10 minutes -->
                <!-- Change this to 20000 (20 seconds) >-->
                <agg:PollIntervalMillis> 20000 </agg:PollIntervalMillis>


                <!-- specified that the upstream index should collect the
                    Entry resource properties from this index -->
                <agg:ResourcePropertyName>wssg:Entry</agg:ResourcePropertyName>


            </agg:GetResourcePropertyPollType>
        </agg:AggregatorConfig>
        <agg:AggregatorData/>
```

```
        </Content>

</ServiceGroupRegistrationParameters>
```

24.1.1 Running FileBuy on a Single Machine

Of course, since it is possible you won't have access to three machines with GT4 installed on them, you can also run the application on a single machine. However, you will still need to be running two containers simultaneously. The reason for this is that we will need two distinct Index Services, one for the broker and one for the seller (remember that the broker's index acts as a VO index which the seller's local index registers with). This means that you will need to have two installations of the Globus Toolkit 4 present in your system. Although you can perform a second installation in a different directory, one quick way of getting a second GT4 installation is to simply make a complete copy of your current $GLOBUS_LOCATION to a new directory.

> ⓘ Making a complete copy of **$GLOBUS_LOCATION** is a very crude way of getting a second installation. You should only do this for the purposes of getting FileBuy running on your machine. If you ever do need to perform additional installations of the toolkit, follow the normal installation procedures to do so.

For example, let's suppose that GT4 is installed in **/usr/local/gt4**, and that you make a copy in **/usr/local/gt4-clone**. You can use the "cloned" installation to host the broker's index, and your original installation to deploy all the services. You must run each container on a different port. We suggest that you have the broker's index listen on the default port (8443) and the original container listen on port 8444. You can do this by running **globus-start-container** with the **-p** option, like so:

```
globus-start-container -p 8444
```

> ☞ You must have a separate shell for each of the two containers. In each shell, make sure that the environment variable **GLOBUS_LOCATION** is set to the appropiate location. Also, take into account that we recommend you use the cloned installation to run *only* the broker's index, but not the broker itself. Although you can certainly deploy the broker to that container, and the other components to the other container, you will have to make sure that **GLOBUS_LOCATION** is pointing to the cloned installation directory whenever you run **globus-deploy-gar**.

24.2 Usage Scenario 1: Advertising a File

We begin by taking a look at the implementation of the first usage scenario. You should review Figure 23.7 to see how the sequence of events described here matches the one shown in the sequence diagram. However, take into account that, as in all the previous examples in the book, we will defer the explanation of the client applications to the very end, as they only perform very simple invocations. The interesting code will mainly be in the services, not the client applications.

This scenario only involves the seller components. Although step 5 (as shown in Figure 23.7) involves the broker's index, this step is not performed by us. The broker's index automatically retrieves the data in the seller's local index because we configured the broker's index as the upstream index (see above). We will take a look at the **Files-ForSale** service, and then see how we can deploy the seller components and run this scenario.

24.2.1 The FilesForSale Service

As described in the previous chapter, this service is actually composed of a factory service and an instance service. In this scenario we are only interested in the **addFile** operation in the factory service, which will be the one responsible for creating **File** resources. This operation expects three parameters: the name of the file to add, the location of the file, and the price at which it will be offered.

> ☞ The implementation of the factory service can be found in **$EXAMPLES_DIR/org/ globus/examples/services/filebuy/seller/impl/ FilesForSaleFactoryService.java**
>
> Since the resource creation actually takes place in the resource home, we will also be interested in looking at what happens there: **$EXAMPLES_DIR/org/ globus/examples/services/filebuy/seller/impl/FileResourceHome.java**

Once the **addFile** operation is invoked, three interesting things happen:

1. We first create a new **File** resource. This resource will be used to store the file's information, so it will have three resource properties: **Name**, **Location**, **Price**.

2. In the resource home, we will need to make sure that we register the resource in the seller's local index. This is explained below.

3. Finally, we return the EPR of the new WS-Resource. If you take a look at the code, you'll see that this is not done exactly the same way as in previous examples. This is also explained below.

Interesting Code Snippets

The Instance Service Path When the WS-Resource's EPR is created, we obtain the instance service's path through a *configuration object* instead of using the resource home.

Remember that, in previous examples, we had something similar to this in our JNDI file:

```
<?xml version="1.0" encoding="UTF-8"?>
<jndiConfig xmlns="http://wsrf.globus.org/jndi/config">


<!-- Instance service -->
<service name="examples/core/factory/MathService">
        <resource name="home" type="org.globus.examples.services.core.factory.
            impl.MathResourceHome">
        <resourceParams>


                <!-- Other parameters -->
        <parameter>
                <name>instanceServicePath</name>
                <value>examples/core/factory/MathService</value>
        <parameter>


        </resourceParams>
        </resource>
</service>


<service name="examples/core/factory/MathFactoryService">
        <resourceLink name="instanceHome" target="java:comp/env/services/
            examples/core/factory/MathService/home"/>
</service>


</jndiConfig>
```

> ☞ You might want to review Section 8.7.2 if this doesn't ring a bell.

In brief, the instance service's path was included as a parameter in the resource home, which the factory service was able to access by using the **instanceHome** link. Although this is a valid way of "gluing" the factory and instance service together, in the FileBuy application we are using a much cleaner and more elegant approach. Instead of storing the instance service's path in the resource home, we are putting all configuration information in a separate object which can be retrieved using JNDI. So, our JNDI deployment file will look like this:

```
<service name="examples/filebuy/seller/FilesForSaleFactory">

    <resource name="configuration" type="org.globus.examples.services
        .filebuy.seller.impl.FilesForSaleConfiguration">
    <resourceParams>

            <parameter>
                    <name>factory</name>
                    <value>org.globus.wsrf.jndi.BeanFactory</value>
            </parameter>

            <parameter>
                    <name>instanceServicePath</name>
                    <value>examples/filebuy/seller/FilesForSale</value>
            </parameter>

            <parameter>
                    <!-- Insert the URI of the file transfer service
                        here -->
                    <name>transferURI</name>
                    <value>https://127.0.0.1:8444/wsrf/services/examples/
                        filebuy/seller/FileTransfer</value>
            </parameter>

    </resourceParams>
    </resource>
</service>
```

☞ This is part of file **$EXAMPLES_DIR/org/globus/examples/services/filebuy/seller/ deploy-jndi-config.xml**

This requires that we implement a simple **FilesForSaleConfiguration** class with **instanceServicePath** and **transferURI** attributes and corresponding get/set methods (the

transferURI attribute will be relevant in scenario (3). The configuration class looks like this:

```
package org.globus.examples.services.filebuy.seller.impl;
// imports


public class FilesForSaleConfiguration {
        private String instanceServicePath;
        private String transferURI;

        public String getInstanceServicePath() {
                return instanceServicePath;
        }

        public void setInstanceServicePath(String instanceServicePath) {
                this.instanceServicePath = instanceServicePath;
        }

        public String getTransferURI() {
                return transferURI;
        }

        public void setTransferURI(String transferURI) {
                this.transferURI = transferURI;
        }

        static final FilesForSaleConfiguration getConfObject()
            throws Exception {

                // Code to lookup the configuration object using JNDI

        }
}
```

> ☞ This is file **$EXAMPLES_DIR/org/globus/examples/services/filebuy/seller/impl/**
> **FilesForSaleConfiguration.java**

So, when constructing the WS-Resource's EPR, we retrieve the instance service's path from the configuration object:

```
FilesForSaleConfiguration config = FilesForSaleConfiguration.getConfObject();

String instanceService = config.getInstanceServicePath();
```

Take a look at the **getConfObject** in the **FilesForSaleConfiguration** class to see the actual JNDI code used to lookup the configuration object. Also, notice how the instance service's path is also used to lookup the resource home (take a look at the **getInstanceResourceHome** method in the factory service implementation).

Registration in the Index Service To register the resource in the local index, we will use the Globus-supplied **ServiceGroupRegistrationClient** class. This class is used to register WS-Resources in a *service group*. Remember that one of the WSRF specifications, WS-ServiceGroup, deals with how to aggregate several WS-Resources together. The GT4 Index Service, in fact, relies on this specification.

> ☞ The resource implementation is **$EXAMPLES_DIR/org/globus/examples/services/**
> **filebuy/seller/impl/FileResource.java**

To register our resource in the local index, we will need to include a private **Timer** attribute, including get/set methods for that attribute.

```
Timer regTimer;
```

This Timer attibute will be used by the Globus-supplied **ServiceGroupRegistrationClient** (which we will use in the resource home) to register the resource with an index service.

Next, we need to write a registration configuration file specifying what information must be aggregated by the local index. In our case, since the buyer will only perform searches based on the file's name and price, it only makes sense to aggregate the **Name** and **Price** resource properties (but not **Location**).

```
<ServiceGroupRegistrationParameters

    xmlns:sgc="http://mds.globus.org/servicegroup/client"

    xmlns:xsd="http://www.w3.org/2001/XMLSchema"

    xmlns:xsi="http://www.w3.org/2001/XMLSchema-instance"

    xmlns:wsa="http://schemas.xmlsoap.org/ws/2004/03/addressing"

    xmlns:agg="http://mds.globus.org/aggregator/types"

    xmlns="http://mds.globus.org/servicegroup/client" >
```

```
<!-- Specifies that the registration will be renewed every 30
        seconds -->
<RefreshIntervalSecs> 30 </RefreshIntervalSecs>


<!-- <Content> specifies registration specific information -->
<Content xsi:type="agg:AggregatorContent"
    xmlns:agg="http://mds.globus.org/aggregator/types">


    <agg:AggregatorConfig xsi:type="agg:AggregatorConfig">
        <agg:GetMultipleResourcePropertiesPollType
            xmlns:ffs="http://www.globus.org/namespaces/examples/filebuy/
                FilesForSale">
            <!-- ffs: FilesForSale -->


            <!-- Specifies that the index should refresh information
                    every 20000 milliseconds (once every 20 seconds) -->
            <agg:PollIntervalMillis> 20000 </agg:PollIntervalMillis>


            <!-- Specifies the resource property that should be aggregated -->
            <agg:ResourcePropertyNames>ffs:Name</agg:ResourcePropertyNames>
            <agg:ResourcePropertyNames>ffs:Price</agg:ResourcePropertyNames>


        </agg:GetMultipleResourcePropertiesPollType>
    </agg:AggregatorConfig>
    <agg:AggregatorData/>
</Content>
</ServiceGroupRegistrationParameters>
```

☞ This file is **$EXAMPLES_DIR/org/globus/examples/services/filebuy/seller/etc/
registration.xml**

Now, we need to make sure that when a new resource is created, it is registered in the local index. To do this, we need to override the **add** method in the resource home so we can include our registration code:

```
protected void add(ResourceKey key, Resource resource) {
❶
    super.add(key, resource);

❷
    ServiceGroupRegistrationClient regClient=ServiceGroupRegistrationClient.
        getContainerClient();

❸
    // Construct EPR of this resource, and store it in a variable called "epr"
    // [Code omitted]

❹
    String regPath = ContainerConfig.getGlobusLocation()
                    + "/etc/org_globus_examples_services_filebuy_seller/
                        registration.xml";
❺
    try {
            FileResource fileResource = (FileResource) resource;
            ServiceGroupRegistrationParameters params =
                ServiceGroupRegistrationClient.readParms(regPath);
            params.setRegistrantEPR(epr);
            Timer regTimer=regClient.register(params);
            fileResource.setRegTimer(regTimer);
    } catch (Exception e) {
            logger.error("ERROR: Couldn't register File resource in local
                index.");
            throw new RuntimeException("ERROR: Couldn't register File
                resource in local index.", e);
    }
}
```

> ☞ This is part of **$EXAMPLES_DIR/org/globus/examples/services/filebuy/seller/impl/FileResourceHome.java**

❶ We are overriding the **add** method provided by the parent class (**ResourceHomeImpl**). However, we have to invoke **ResourceHomeImpl**'s **add** method to make sure that the resource is correctly added.

❷ We get the resource's **ServiceGroupRegistrationClient** object.

❸ To register the resource in the container's local index, we will need to supply the WS-Resource's EPR. We construct the EPR, and store it in a variable called **epr**. We omit the code here as it is nearly identical to the code used in previous examples when constructing an EPR (e.g. when a factory service returns the EPR of a new WS-Resource).

❹ We construct the path to the service's registration configuration file.

❺ Finally, we register the resource. Notice how we first read the parameters from the configuration file, and then specify the EPR to be registered. Also, notice how the registration returns a **Timer** object which is then assigned to the resource's **regTimer** attribute. Later on, we will able to use this timer to cancel the registration.

Finally, we also have to make sure that a resource's registration is cancelled if it is destroyed. We do this using the **RemoveCallback** interface's **remove** method in the resource:

```
public void remove() throws ResourceException {
        logger.info("Resource " + this.getID() + " is going to be removed.");
        regTimer.cancel();
        getPersistenceHelper().remove(this.key);
}
```

Persistence

Remember that one of our design decisions regarding the **File** resource was that we wanted it to be persistent. If you look at the resource's implementation, you'll notice that we've included all the necessary code to make it persistent (as seen in Chapter 12).

24.2.2 The AddFile Client

The **AddFile** client is the one responsible for invoking the **addFile** operation in the **Files-ForSale** service. The client has no noteworthy code, and is similar to clients seen in previous chapters.

> ☞ The **AddFile** client can be found in **$EXAMPLES_DIR/org/globus/examples/clients/filebuy/FilesForSale/AddFileClient.java**

24.2.3 Trying it Out

To test this scenario, we are going to advertise a file. Create a file named **example.txt** in the seller machine's **/tmp** directory, and write any random text in that file. Now, build the FilesForSale service:

```
./globus-build-service.sh filebuy_seller
```

And deploy it:

```
globus-deploy-gar $EXAMPLES_DIR/org_globus_examples_services_filebuy

    _seller.gar
```

Compile the **AddFile** client:

```
javac \

-classpath ./build/stubs/classes/:$CLASSPATH \

org/globus/examples/clients/filebuy/FilesForSale/AddFileClient.java
```

Now, before you run the client, you have to make sure that the broker's container is running. Even though we have not deployed any broker components, we still need the broker's index service up and running. Of course, the seller's container must also be running.

The client expects three parameters: the file's name, the location of the file, and the price at which you will be offering it. For example:

```
java \

-classpath ./build/stubs/classes/:$CLASSPATH \

org.globus.examples.clients.filebuy.FilesForSale.AddFileClient \

https://pc-seller.gt4book.com:8443/wsrf/services/examples/filebuy/seller/

    FilesForSaleFactory \

example.txt \

/tmp/example.txt \

25
```

If all goes well, you should see the following:

```
Endpoint reference written to file File-example.txt.epr
```

Although we will not use this EPR in the following scenarios, you can use it to experiment with the **File** resource (getting its resource properties, destroying it, etc.).

If you check the container's log, you should see the following:

```
Added new file. NAME=example.txt, LOCATION=/tmp/example.txt, PRICE=25.0

File has been added by user '/O=Globus/OU=GT4 Examples/CN=Globus 4 User'
```

24.3   Usage scenario 2: Finding a File

This scenario, described in Figure 23.8 involves a client application in the buyer's machine and two services deployed in the broker's machine. One service, the File Broker service, is implemented by us, while we use GT4's Index Service to act as the broker's index.

24.3.1   The File Broker Service

This service provides several operations. Right now, we are only interested in the **Find** operation, which is responsible for finding a file of a certain name meeting a price restriction. As such, the operation expects two parameters: the file's name and maximum price of the file. If we are successful in finding a file meeting the specified criteria, a new File Order WS-Resource is created and its EPR is returned, along with the price of the file. Otherwise, a null EPR is returned.

However, as mentioned in the design, this particular service is not divided into a factory service and instance service. Back in Section 8.2, one of the points we made is that there are many ways of implementing the WS-Resource factory pattern. The one used in previous chapters (and in the previous scenario) is a particularly good way, as it cleanly separates the code responsible for creating the new resource ("the factory service") and the code that actually manipulates the resource ("the instance service"). However, a simpler way of implementing the WS-Resource factory pattern is to have all the code in a single service. This results in simpler code, but one that forces us to have the "factory code" and the "instance code" in the same container.

The File Broker service implementation is: **$EXAMPLES_DIR/org/globus/examples/ services/filebuy/broker/impl/FileBrokerService.java**

If you look at the implementation of the **find** method, you will see that it is a pretty long method. It is divided into the following main blocks:

1. First of all, we query the Index Service to see if there are any files with the specified name. This is done using the **QueryResourceProperties** portType.

2. If the query doesn't return anything, the method ends there and we return a **null** EPR.

3. If the Index Service returns more than one file, the we find the cheapest file.

4. If the cheapest file meets the price restriction, we create a **FileOrder** resource and return its EPR.

5. If the cheapest file doesn't meet the price restriction, we return a **null** EPR.

The **FileOrder** is used in the next scenario to complete the purchase of the file found in this scenario. Therefore, we will be interested in storing the **File** WS-Resource's EPR in the **FileOrder** resource (as a resource property), so we can later refer to it and request that it be transferred to the buyer. We will also store the file's name in the **FileOrder** resource.

This might seem redundant (we could use the **File**'s EPR to access the name), but it will save us an extra trip to the **File** WS-Resource in the next scenario. Storing a redundant piece of information is sometimes acceptable, if the performance gain outweights the cost of storing that information (in our case, a string).

We will also include an **OrderStatus** resource property indicating the status of our order. This property has four possible values: **NEW**, **TRANSFERING**, **FAILED**, and **COMPLETED** (note that this last value will only occur for a short while right before the **File**). Although we will not use this value for anything, it could be used, for example, to obtain a list of all the current orders that have a certain status.

Interesting Code Snippets

The Index Service URI The File Broker service needs to know the URI of the VO index service. In general, our VO might have a central index service separate from any of the brokering services, so we should not assume that the broker components and the broker's index are deployed on the same host (although, in FileBuy they *are* deployed in the same host). As in the previous scenario, we will use a *configuration object*, accessible through JNDI, to store the index service's URI:

```
<service name="examples/filebuy/broker/FileBroker">


    <!-- "home" resource -->
    <resource name="configuration" type="org.globus.examples.services.
        filebuy.broker.impl.FileBrokerConfiguration">
    <resourceParams>


        <parameter>
                <name>factory</name>
                <value>org.globus.wsrf.jndi.BeanFactory</value>
        </parameter>


        <parameter>
                <!-- Insert the URI of the VO index service here -->
                <name>indexURI</name>
                <value>https://pc-broker.gt4book.com:8443/wsrf/
                    services/DefaultIndexService</value>
```

```
        </parameter>


    </resourceParams>
    </resource>
</service>
```

☞ This is part of file **$EXAMPLES_DIR/org/globus/examples/services/filebuy/
broker/deploy-jndi-config.xml**

Similarly to the previous scenario, we will have to implement a **FileBrokerConfiguration**
class with an **indexURI** attribute and corresponding get/set methods. Right at the beginning of the **find** method, we retrieve the configuration object and retrieve the index URI
contained in it.

Querying the Index Service   To query the Index Service we will use the QueryResourceProperties portType. We briefly touched upon this portType in Chapter 10. Although
we did not see this portType in detail, the code used to invoke it is very similar to the
one used in other WS-ResourceProperties portTypes. It simply involves a **query** operation
that is used to send an XPath query to the Index Service. However, as mentioned back in
Chapter 10, a full explanation of XPath, and how we can use it to query the Index Service, is
beyond the scope of this book. So you will have to take a leap of faith and believe that the
following XPath query returns all the entries in the Index Service that refer to files named
example.txt:

```
"//*[local-name()='Entry'][./*/*/*[local-name()='Name']/text()=example.txt]"
```

The **find** method will construct a similar query based on the name specified by the buyer.

Processing the Query Results   The query returns 0..N *entries* from the Index Service. In
general, we will process them like this:

```
MessageElement[] entries = queryResponse.get_any();


for (int i = 0; i < entries.length; i++) {
        // Access information contained in the entry. First of all,
        // we need to deserialize the entry...
        EntryType entry = (EntryType) ObjectDeserializer.toObject(entries[i],
            EntryType.class);

        // ... access its content ...
        AggregatorContent content = (AggregatorContent) entry.getContent();
```

```
      // ... then the data ...

      AggregatorData data = content.getAggregatorData();


      // Process the data

  }
```

The data, in general, contains 0..N elements. These elements are the actual resource properties which have been aggregated by the Index Service. In our case, we configured the registration (in the **registration.xml** shown in the previous scenario) so the following data would be aggregated:

```
<agg:ResourcePropertyNames>ffs:Name</agg:ResourcePropertyNames>

<agg:ResourcePropertyNames>ffs:Price</agg:ResourcePropertyNames>
```

So, to retrieve the price of the file, we need to access the second element in the data:

```
String price_str = data.get_any()[1].getValue();

float price = Float.parseFloat(price_str);
```

Of course, this code could be written more elegantly. Instead of hardcoding that we want to access the second element contained in the data, we could search through the aggregated resource properties and find the element called **Price**. This, however, would require additional code.

Creating the WS-Resource As mentioned previously, this service is not separated into two services (a factory service and an instance service). If you look at the code that creates the **FileOrder** resource, and returns the EPR of the new WS-Resource you will notice that it is simpler than the one seen in previous chapters. The main reason is that we don't need to find out what the path of the instance service is, as the EPR of the new WS-Resource will include the URI of the FileBuy Broker service, and the key of the new resource.

24.3.2 The FindFile Client

FindFile is a simple client application that invokes the **find** operation in the **FileBroker** service. As in the previous scenario, this client contains no noteworthy code, and you should be able to read its source code without problems.

> ☞ The **FindFile** client is **$EXAMPLES_DIR/org/globus/examples/clients/filebuy/ FileBroker/FindFileClient.java**

Trying it Out

We will now run through this scenario to try and find the file advertised in the previous scenario. We will also see what happens when we ask for the file but specify that we are not willing to pay the 25 monetary units at which the file is offered.

Before building the FileBuy Broker service, make sure you modify its JNDI file to include the URI of the index service, as explained above.

```
<resource name="configuration" type="org.globus.examples.services.filebuy.
    broker.impl.FileBrokerConfiguration">
        <resourceParams>
        <!-- Other parameters -->
        <parameter>
                <!-- Insert the URI of the file transfer service here -->
                <name>indexURI</name>
                <value>https://pc-broker.gt4book.com:8443/wsrf/services/
                    DefaultIndexService</value>
        </parameter>
        </resourceParams>
</resource>
```

> ☞ This file is **$EXAMPLES_DIR/org/globus/examples/services/filebuy/broker/
> deploy-jndi-config.xml**
> If you are using a one-machine setup, the hostname and port should be
> **127.0.0.1:8443**

Once we have done this, we start by building the FileBuy Broker:

```
./globus-build-service.sh filebuy_broker
```

Next, deploy it:

```
globus-deploy-gar $EXAMPLES_DIR/org_globus_examples_services_filebuy
    _broker.gar
```

Now, compile the **FindFile** client:

```
javac \
-classpath ./build/stubs/classes/:$CLASSPATH \
org/globus/examples/clients/filebuy/FileBroker/FindFileClient.java
```

Before running the client, make sure that the broker's container is running. The client expects three parameters: The URI of the FileBuy Broker, the name of the file we want so search for, and the maximum price we're willing to pay. Let's ask for the **example.txt** file advertised in the previous scenario, and let's say that we're willing to pay 100 monetary units (more than the 25 units at which it is offered)

```
java \
-classpath ./build/stubs/classes/:$CLASSPATH \
org.globus.examples.clients.filebuy.FileBroker.FindFileClient \
    https://pc-broker.gt4book.com:8443/wsrf/services/examples/filebuy/broker/
        FileBroker
example.txt \
100
```

You should see the following:

```
A file has been found! (price=25.0)
EPR of your order has been written to FileOrder-example.txt.epr
Remember to use this EPR to complete the purchase.
```

In the next scenario (purchasing a file), we will use the EPR written to disk to refer to the **FileOrder** WS-Resource for which we want to initiate a purchase. Remember that the **FileOrder** resource, in turn, contains the EPR of the **File** we will be purchasing.

Also, if you look at the broker's container's logs, you will see the following:

```
Created new file order for file NAME=example.txt, PRICE=25.0
FileOrder has been created for user '/O=Globus/OU=GT4 Examples/CN=Globus
    4 User'
```

Finally, you can try to run the client again, but specifying a price less than 25 (so the broker will return no files):

```
java \
-classpath ./build/stubs/classes/:$CLASSPATH \
org.globus.examples.clients.filebuy.FileBroker.FindFileClient \
    https://pc-broker.gt4book.com:8443/wsrf/services/examples/filebuy/broker/
        FileBroker \
example.txt \
10
```

Now, you should see the following:

```
No file meeting the given price constraint has been found.
```

24.4   Usage Scenario 3: Purchasing a File

In this final scenario, described in Figure 23.9, we will purchase the file found in the previous scenario. Although there are few interesting code snippets, this scenario involves the three set of components in our application: the buyer, the broker, and the seller. As we "jump" around from one service to another, you should read the code for each operation involved in this scenario, to see how the flow of events described in the sequence diagram is coded.

24.4.1   The FileBuyer Service: The Purchase Operation

The purchase of a file begins in the "FileBuy client" which, as explained in the design, will be responsible for initiating the purchase in the File Broker, but will also be responsible for receiving the file from the File Transfer service. As explained in the detail, this means that we will implement the FileBuy client as a service, not a client application. This service will have a simple **purchase** operation that invokes the **purchase** operation on the FileBroker using the EPR obtained in the previous scenario. When invoking the FileBroker service, the buyer will send along its own EPR, which will eventually make its way to the File Transfer service.

As a simple precaution against receiving unexpected transfers, we will make this service stateful and we will store the name of the file which we expect to receive from the File Transfer service. However, there is really no need to publish this information as a resource property, as it will only be used internally by the FileBuy service (and no other service). So, this service showcases how we can have a stateful service that uses a resource to store its state but has no resource properties.

Finally, take into account that despite implementing the FileBuy client as a service, there will still be a simple client application that will invoke the **purchase** operation on the FileBuy client. As mentioned earlier, this operation will access the FileBroker service and, since we want the broker to log what user is performing the purchase, our client application will need to delegate its credentials to the FileBuy service. Otherwise the broker will log that the initiator of the purchase is the user running the FileBuy service, which will usually be a generic **globus** account, not a user account.

The **FileBuy** service is: **$EXAMPLES_DIR/org/globus/examples/services/filebuy/buyer/impl/FileBuyerService.java**

24.4.2   The FileBroker Service: The **purchase** Operation

This operation does little more than relay information to the seller. In particular, the File EPR is retrieved from the FileOrder resource. This EPR is used to invoke the **fillOrder** operation on the seller's **FilesForSale** service. In this call we relay the buyer's EPR, which the seller will then pass on to the File Transfer service.

The File Broker service implementation is: **$EXAMPLES_DIR/org/globus/examples/ services/filebuy/broker/impl/FileBrokerService.java**

24.4.3 The FilesForSale Service: The **fillOrder** Operation

The **fillOrder** operation retrieves the name and location of the file to transfer from the **File** resource, which are sent to the File Transfer service, along with the buyer's EPR. The transfer service's URI is obtained from the FilesForSale configuration object, which was described in the first scenario.

> ☞ The implementation of the FilesForSale service can be found in **$EXAMPLES_DIR/ org/globus/examples/services/filebuy/seller/impl/ FilesForSaleFactoryService.java**

24.4.4 The FileTransfer Service: The **transfer** Operation

The File Transfer service is a stateless service with a single operation (**transfer**) responsible for sending a file to the specified buyer EPR by invoking the **transfer** operation on the FileBuy service.

The implementation of the **FileTransfer** service is: **$EXAMPLES_DIR/org/globus/ examples/services/filebuy/transfer/impl/FileTransferService.java**

This service does have an interesting snippet of code in which we read the file from disk. Whenever we want to transfer binary data, we will need to read the file into an array of **byte**'s. As we will see next, this array is sent when invoking the **transfer** operation on the FileBuy service (which expects "binary data").

```
byte[] fileBytes = null;

try {

        File file = new File(location);

        FileInputStream fis = new FileInputStream(file);

        fileBytes = new byte[fis.available()];

        fis.read(fileBytes);

} catch (IOException e) {

        logger.error("ERROR: Unable to open file to transfer.");

        throw new RemoteException("ERROR: Unable to open file to transfer.", e);

}
```

24.4.5 The FileBuyer Service: The **transfer** Operation

The **transfer** operation in the FileBuyer service expects the file's name and the file's data. The steps performed in this operation are the following:

1. Check if the expected name matches the received name. Remember that we stored the expected file's name in the FileBuyer's resource to be able to make this check.

2. We write the file to disk.

3. We invoke the **report** operation on the FileBroker service to report if the transfer was successful.

The only interesting snippet of code in this operation is how we actually declare a Web service operation to receive binary data. We do so using the XML Schema type **base64Binary**:

```
<xsd:element name="transfer">
        <xsd:complexType>
        <xsd:sequence>
                <xsd:element name="name" type="xsd:string"/>
                <xsd:element name="data" type="xsd:base64Binary"/>
        </xsd:sequence>
        </xsd:complexType>
</xsd:element>
<xsd:element name="transferResponse">
        <xsd:complexType/>
</xsd:element>
```

> ☞ This is part of file **$EXAMPLES_DIR/schema/examples/filebuy/FileBuyer.wsdl**

In Java this translates to an array of **byte**'s:

```
public TransferResponse transfer(Transfer params) throws RemoteException {
        String name = params.getName();
        byte data[] = params.getData();


        // ...


        String filePath = System.getProperty("java.io.tmpdir")
                        + File.separatorChar + "File-" + name;
```

```
try {

        FileOutputStream fos = new FileOutputStream(filePath);

        fos.write(data);

        fos.flush();

        reportCode=0; // Success

} catch (IOException e) {

        logger.error("ERROR: Unable to write file to disk.");

        reportCode=-1; // Error

}


        // ...

}
```

24.4.6 The FileBroker Service: The **report** Operation

Finally, we arrive at the end of the road. In this operation, the **FileOrder** resource is destroyed if the transfer was completed successfully. Otherwise, the order's status (the **OrderStatus** resource property) is set to **FAILED**.

24.4.7 Trying it Out

Before we try out this final scenario, make sure that the FilesForSale's JNDI deployment file includes the URI of the transfer service:

```
<resource name="configuration" type="org.globus.examples.services.filebuy.
    seller.impl.FilesForSaleConfiguration">

        <resourceParams>


        <!-- Other parameters -->


        <parameter>

                <!-- Insert the URI of the file transfer service here -->

                <name>transferURI</name>

                <value>https://pc-seller.gt4book.com:8443/wsrf/services/

                        examples/filebuy/seller/FileTransfer</value>
```

```
        </parameter>

      </resourceParams>

  </resource>
```

☞ This file is **$EXAMPLES_DIR/org/globus/examples/services/filebuy/seller/
deploy-jndi-config.xml**
If you are using a single-machine setup, the address and port should be
127.0.0.1:8444.

Now, we will need to build and deploy the seller components (if you have modified the JNDI file as described above), the buyer components, and the file transfer service:

./globus-build-service.sh filebuy_seller

./globus-build-service.sh filebuy_buyer

./globus-build-service.sh filebuy_transfer

**globus-deploy-gar $EXAMPLES_DIR/org_globus_examples_services_filebuy_
    seller.gar**

globus-deploy-gar $EXAMPLES_DIR/org_globus_examples_services_filebuy_buyer.gar

**globus-deploy-gar $EXAMPLES_DIR/org_globus_examples_services_filebuy_
    transfer.gar**

To initiate the purchase through the FileBuyer service, we will use a simple client application that invokes the **purchase** operation. We compile the client:

**javac **

**-classpath ./build/stubs/classes/:$CLASSPATH **

org/globus/examples/clients/filebuy/FileBuyer/FileBuyClient.java

This client expects two parameters, the FileBuyer's URI, and the name of the file containing the FileOrder's EPR (created in the previous scenario). Run the client:

**java **

**-classpath ./build/stubs/classes/:$CLASSPATH **

org.globus.examples.clients.filebuy.FileBuyer.FileBuyClient

**https://pc-buyer.gt4book.com:8443/wsrf/services/examples/filebuy/buyer/
    FileBuyer **

FileOrder-example.txt.epr

If all goes well, you should see the following:

A request to purchase the file has been sent.

You should receive the file shortly.

The file should be saved in your system's temporary directory, with the prefix **File-**. In our case, the file should show up in **/tmp/File-example.txt**. It should contain the same data as the file you advertised in the first scenario.

Finally, if you check the logs on the broker's container, you will see the following:

Going to purchase file example.txt

Purchase requested by user '/O=Globus/OU=GT4 Examples/CN=Globus 4 User'

And, after that, the following:

Received report of transfer of file example.txt

Report code: 0

Order completed successfully.

Conclusion

So, here we are: the end of the book. We've covered a great deal of material! time to sit back, relax, and give yourself a pat on the back. Unless you have skipped straight from the Preface to this Conclusion, you should now have a working knowledge of how to program Java services using the Globus Toolkit 4. However, as we've pointed out several times throughout the book, you cannot develop Grid applications using only that knowledge you've gained from this book. While you've taken a good first step, what should you do next?

One approach is to deepen your understanding of how components can be combined to create interesting Grid applications. Although the FileBuy application does this to a certain extent, Grid applications are usually much more complex. To see some examples of this, we highly recommend Lee Liming's "Globus Primer", available for download at `http://www-unix.mcs.anl.gov/~liming/primer/`. This primer, not to be confused with Ian Foster's "GT4 Primer", puts the Globus Toolkit in context and shows how it can be used in a variety of applications.

You might also broaden your understanding of the toolkit and related technologies by studying the information contained on the Globus Alliance website, located at `http://www.globus.org/`. Detailed technical information on each of the GT components, including sample programs, can be found in the official release manuals, located at `http://www.globus.org/toolkit/docs/4.0/`. Finally, don't forget the community-driven website, the Globus Documentation Project (GDP), where members of the Globus community are encouraged to contribute GT-related documentation. The GDP can be found at `http://gdp.globus.org/`

Certainly you should go forth and gain more hands-on experience with this exciting technology. Create some interesting services and combine them in cool ways. Build systems using some of the higher-level services included in the Globus Toolkit. Join the Globus community forums to share your ideas and findings, helping to advance the state of the art. By collaborating as we build the Grid, the extraordinary is within our reach!

part V

Appendices

Installing the Globus Toolkit 4

This appendix will guide you through the installation of the Globus Toolkit 4. Since this book only covers the Java WS Core and GSI components of the toolkit, we will only see how to set up those particular components. The official installation guide, available on the Globus website, includes instructions on how to set up other components.

Take into account that this guide is written with version **4.0** in mind. Newer versions of the toolkit (released after the book is published) *might* work by following these same instructions. However, to be on the safe side, please follow the official installation guide if you want to install a version newer than 4.0.

The installation guide is divided into seven sections. To be able to run the examples described in Part II you must perform all the steps described in the first five sections (up to and including Section A.5). This will involve configuring some security aspects of the toolkit (despite the fact that we don't touch on security in Part II). You should be able to complete the security configuration even if you don't know about security concepts like "certificate authorities", "certificates", etc. However, if you do want to have more information about what we are actually doing, you might want to first read Chapter 15. That chapter is written to be completely self-contained, so you can read it to learn about fundamental security concepts even if you haven't read the previous chapters yet.

To run the examples described in Part III you will need to perform the steps described in Section A.6. You can skip that section if you do not intend to work through the security examples.

Finally, the last section briefly describes how to test your installation by running the Globus standalone container.

A.1 Software Prerequisites

A.1.1 Required Software

First of all, you will need to download the Globus Toolkit 4.0 Installer from the Globus website (http://www-unix.globus.org/toolkit/downloads/). Before we actually run the installer, you must make sure you have installed the following software packages on your system:

- JDK 1.4.2+. You can use JDK's from:

    Sun (http://java.sun.com/j2se)

    IBM (http://www.ibm.com/developerworks/java/jdk)

    BEA (http://www.bea.com/)

    However, you cannot use GCJ (http://gcc.gnu.org/java/).

- Ant 1.5.1+ (http://jakarta.apache.org/ant). Do not use the version of Ant distributed with Fedora Core 2. Also, if you are going to use Java 1.5, make sure you install Ant 1.6.1+.

The following software packages are also required, although they are generally included in most UNIX distributions. However, you should check that they are installed and, in some cases, that you have the right version:

- C compiler. If using gcc (http://gcc.gnu.org/), avoid version **3.2**. Versions 3.2.1 and 2.95.x are ok.
- GNU tar (http://www.gnu.org/software/tar/tar.html)
- GNU sed (http://www.gnu.org/software/sed/sed.html)
- zlib (http://www.gzip.org/zlib/)
- GNU Make (http://www.gnu.org/software/make/).

A.1.2 Optional Software

- Apache Tomcat (http://jakarta.apache.org/tomcat/).

A.1.3 Platform Notes

You will be able to follow this installation guide if you are using GNU/Linux, Windows, or MacOS. If you are using another UNIX OS (such as HP/UX, Solaris, etc.) make sure you check the platform notes included in the official installation guide. These platform notes are also available in the **INSTALL** file included in the GT4 installation tar or zip file.

A.2 Installing the Toolkit

You can choose between making a full install of the toolkit, or installing just the Java WS Core component. If you are using Windows, then you will only be able to install Java WS Core. In both cases, there are a set of common steps you must follow.

1. [UNIX only] Create a user named **globus**. This non-privileged user will be used to perform administrative tasks such as starting and stopping the container, deploying services, etc. Pick an installation directory (e.g. **/usr/local/gt4/**, and make sure this account has read and write permissions in the installation directory.

   > ☞ You might need to create the target directory as **root**, then chown it to the **globus** user:
   >
   > # `mkdir /usr/local/gt4`
   >
   > # `chown globus.globus /usr/local/gt4`

   This user doesn't necessarily have to be called **globus**, but it *must* be a *non-root* user.

2. [UNIX only] Throughout the book, we will also be relying on a *user* account that will be used to compile the examples, and to run the example clients (as opposed to the **globus** user which should *only* be used for Globus-related administrative tasks). This account could be your own user account, or you could choose to create a new account specifically for the purposes of this book. We will refer to this account as **globus4user**.

   > ⓘ At this point, you might be thinking: "Sure, having two separate users seems like the right thing to do, but this is just an introductory text... I guess I can work with just one user". If this is so, vanquish that thought from your head immediately. It is certainly possible to work through all the examples using just one user (for both the container and the client programs), but doing so might 'mask' errors and pitfalls that will reveal themselves when you run the examples in a more real situation: having the container on one machine, run by a certain user, and having the client programs running in a different machine with a completely different user.

3. Download and install the required software listed above.

   > ☞ Be aware that Apache Ant will use the Java referred to by **JAVA_HOME**, not necessarily the first Java executable on your **PATH**. Be sure to set **JAVA_HOME** to the top-level directory of your Java installation before installing.

   Also, if your OS already includes Ant, your **/etc/ant.conf** is probably configured to use GCJ, which will fail to compile the Toolkit.

A.2.1 Installing the Full Toolkit [UNIX Only]

1. From the GT4 download page (http://www.globus.org/toolkit/downloads/4.0.0/), download a binary or source installer. The steps you must follow for both types of installers are the same. However, take into account that if you choose the source installer, the toolkit can take several hours to build, while a binary install takes about 10–15 minutes to install.

2. In a temporary directory, untar the GT4 installer file. This will create a directory with all the installation files. We will call this directory **$INSTALL_DIR**.

3. In this guide we will assume that you are installing to **/usr/local/gt4**, but you may replace **/usr/local/gt4** with whatever directory you wish to install to.

   As the **globus** user, in **$INSTALL_DIR**, run:

   ```
   globus$ export GLOBUS_LOCATION=/usr/local/gt4
   ```

   ```
   globus$ ./configure --prefix=$GLOBUS_LOCATION
   ```

   You can use command line arguments to **./configure** for a more custom install. However, none of these options is relevant to the components covered in this book. To see what the different options are, simply run **./configure --help** or refer to the official Globus installation guide.

4. Now, to build and install the toolkit, run the following as the **globus** user:

   ```
   globus$ make
   ```

   Note, however, that this builds the *complete* toolkit, including a lot of components which are not used in this book. If you are using the source installer, the full install can take *several hours*, so if you simply want to do a quick install, with the components covered in the book, run the following:

   ```
   globus$ make wsjava globus-gsi postinstall
   ```

   If you wish to have a log file of the build, use **tee**:

   ```
   globus$ make 2>&1 | tee build.log
   ```

   or:

   ```
   globus$ make wsjava globus-gsi postinstall 2>&1 | tee build.log
   ```

   > ☞ The syntax above assumes a Bourne shell. If you are using another shell, redirect stderr to stdout and then pipe it to **tee**.

A.2.2 Installing Java WS Core [UNIX and Windows]

> ☞ If you are using a UNIX OS, and have already installed the full toolkit as described above, you don't have to install Java WS Core on top of that, as it is already included in the full install. You can skip to the next step.

1. From the GT4 download page (http://www.globus.org/toolkit/downloads/4.0.0/), download a Java WS Core binary or source installer.

2. If you are using a source installer:

   a. Untar or unzip the installer in a temporary directory. This will create a directory called **ws-core-4.0.0**. The following instructions are relative to that new directory.

   b. Set the **GLOBUS_LOCATION** environment variable to the absolute path of the target directory of your installation. On Windows:

      set GLOBUS_LOCATION=c:\gt4

      On a UNIX system with a BASH shell:

      export GLOBUS_LOCATION=/usr/local/gt4

      On a UNIX system with a CSH shell:

      setenv GLOBUS_LOCATION /usr/local/gt4

      Note that, if **GLOBUS_LOCATION** is not set, an **install** directory will be created under the current directory.

   c. Run the following:

      ant all

3. If you are using a binary installer:

   a. Untar or unzip the installer straight to the directory where you want to install Java WS Core. The installation archive will create a directory called **ws-core-4.0.0**. So, if you untar/unzip the installer in directory **/usr/local**, the directory where Java WS Core will be installed is **/usr/local/ws-core-4.0.0**. Of course, you can change the name of this directory. We will assume that you want to install the toolkit in directory **/usr/local/gt4**. For Windows users, we will assume you want to install the toolkit in directory **c:\gt4**.

   b. Set the **GLOBUS_LOCATION** environment variable to the absolute path of the directory where Java WS Core is installed. On Windows:

      set GLOBUS_LOCATION=c:\gt4

      On a UNIX system with a BASH shell:

      export GLOBUS_LOCATION=/usr/local/gt4

      On a UNIX system with a CSH shell:

      setenv GLOBUS_LOCATION /usr/local/gt4

A.2.3   Setting Environment Variables

Finally, In order for the system to know the location of the Globus Toolkit commands you just installed, you must set an environment variable and source the **globus-user-env** script in every console that will use the Globus commands and libraries (this includes both the **globus** user and your user account). Although you can do this every time you open a new console, we recommend you modify your shell's startup script to automatically set these environment variables up when you open a new console.

1. As the **globus** user, set **GLOBUS_LOCATION** to the directory where you installed the Globus Toolkit. Assuming you installed in **/usr/local/gt4**:

   - Using Bourne shells:

     ```
     globus$ export GLOBUS_LOCATION=/usr/local/gt4
     ```

   - Using CSH:

     ```
     globus$ setenv GLOBUS_LOCATION /usr/local/gt4
     ```

   - Using Windows:

     ```
     set GLOBUS_LOCATION=c:\gt4
     ```

2. Source the **globus-user-env** script:

   - Use .sh for Bourne shell:

     ```
     globus$ source $GLOBUS_LOCATION/etc/globus-user-env.sh
     ```

   - Using csh:

     ```
     globus$ source $GLOBUS_LOCATION/etc/globus-user-env.csh
     ```

> ☞ The Java WS Core installation does not include the **globus-user-env** script. However, if you are only going to use this component, you will only need to make sure you include **$GLOBUS_LOCATION/bin** in your **PATH**. This is not strictly required, but will allow you to run Globus commands without having to type their full path.

A.3   Setting Up GT4 to Work with a CA

The Globus Toolkit requires a set of *digital certificates* to work properly. To obtain these certificates, we need to configure GT4 to work with a *certificate authority* (which we can use to obtain the certificates)

> ☞ Remember that, even if we are not going to use security in our examples, we still need to configure some security aspects of the toolkit. If you have no idea of

what we just said in the previous paragraph (i.e. if you don't know what a "digital certificate" is and what a "certificate authority" is), you have two options:

1. Read Chapter 15, Fundamental Security Concepts. This chapter provides a self-contained introduction to fundamental security concepts.

2. If you're pressed for time, you should be able to follow the instructions described in the rest of the installation guide, even if you have no idea of what we're talking about. However, we recommend that you choose option (1).

We can set up GT4 to work with a CA in three different ways:

- Setting up our own CA (SimpleCA).
- Using an existing CA.
- Using the Globus Certificate Server.

All three options are described. Throughout the book, we have used the SimpleCA certificate authority included with GT4. If you choose to use an existing CA (e.g. your organization's CA) or the Globus Certificate Server, this will only affect certain parts of the installation guide (which we will point out). The book examples are independent of the CA you choose, except that the subject names of your certificates will obviously differ from the ones we create using SimpleCA.

> ☞ SimpleCA is not a part of the Java WS Core install, so Windows users will have to use an existing CA or use the Globus Certificate Server.

A.3.1 Setting Up SimpleCA

SimpleCA is a basic certificate authority package included with GT4. It can be used to manage certificates when a full-blown CA is not needed (e.g. when developing an application). Production-quality applications, however, will probably have to end up using a more complete CA.

To setup SimpleCA we need to run an installation script. Once GT4 is installed, simply run the following as the **globus** user:

```
$GLOBUS_LOCATION/setup/globus/setup-simple-ca
```

You should see the following output:

```
         C e r t i f i c a t e    A u t h o r i t y    S e t u p


This script will setup a Certificate Authority for signing Globus
users certificates. It will also generate a simple CA package
that can be distributed to the users of the CA.
```

The CA information about the certificates it distributes will
be kept in:

/home/globus4/.globus/simpleCA/

The unique subject name for this CA is:

cn=Globus Simple CA, ou=simpleCA-<*your hostname*>, ou=GlobusTest, o=Grid

Do you want to keep this as the CA subject (y/n) [y]:

The script is asking us to define the subject that will appear in the CA's digital certificate. Although you can certainly keep the default subject name, we're going to change it. Answer 'n' to the question. You should now see this:

Enter a unique subject name for this CA:

We will use the following subject name:

cn=Globus Simple CA, ou=GT4 Examples, o=Globus

Now you should see the following:

Enter the email of the CA (this is the email where certificate

requests will be sent to be signed by the CA):

If you are going to use SimpleCA only for the purpose of running the book examples, then you can enter any e-mail you want, since we're not actually going to use it. However, if you intend to allow other users to request certificates from your SimpleCA, you should enter an e-mail address, since this is the e-mail they'll be instructed to send certificate requests to.

Once you've entered the e-mail address, you should see the following:

The CA certificate has an expiration date. Keep in mind that

once the CA certificate has expired, all the certificates

signed by that CA become invalid. A CA should regenerate

the CA certificate and start re-issuing ca-setup packages

before the actual CA certificate expires. This can be done

by re-running this setup script. Enter the number of DAYS

the CA certificate should last before it expires.

[default: 5 years (1825 days)]:

We won't be too concerned about the expiration date of the CA certificate, so we can safely press enter here to select the default value (5 years).

Now, the install script will ask you to enter the password for the CA certificate's private key. You will also need to confirm it.

```
Enter PEM pass phrase:

Verifying - Enter PEM pass phrase:
```

Any time we need to access the CA's private key, we will need to provide this password. For example, since the private key is needed to digitally sign certificates, we'll need to provide the password each time the CA issues a certificate.

After you enter the password and confirm it, you will be asked no more questions. You will see a rather lengthy output which you can safely ignore. However, let's take a close look at some particular messages which basically confirm that we've successfully set up a CA:

```
A self-signed certificate has been generated

for the Certificate Authority with the subject:


/O=Globus/OU=GT4 Examples/CN=Globus Simple CA


If this is invalid, rerun this script


/usr/local/gt4/setup/globus/setup-simple-ca


and enter the appropriate fields.


-------------------------------------------------------------------


The private key of the CA is stored in /home/globus4/.globus/simpleCA

//private/cakey.pem

The public CA certificate is stored in /home/globus4/.globus/simpleCA

//cacert.pem
```

This message confirms that the CA's certificate has, in fact, been created. We are also told where the certificate can be found, along with the private key. If you try to open the certificate, you'll see that its contents look like gibberish. If you want to take a peek at all the values it contains, you can use a very handy tool included with the toolkit called grid-cert-info:

```
grid-cert-info -file ~/.globus/simpleCA/cacert.pem
```

```
The distribution package built for this CA is stored in
```

```
/home/globus4/.globus/simpleCA//globus_simple_ca_e4da69c0_setup-0.17.tar.gz
```

```
This file must be distributed to any host wishing to request
certificates from this CA.
```

```
CA setup complete.
```

You will also see the following message in the final output, which tells us that the setup isn't quite complete yet:

```
********************************************************************************
```

```
Note: To complete setup of the GSI software you need to run the
following script as root to configure your security configuration
directory:
```

```
/usr/local/gt4/setup/globus_simple_ca_e4da69c0_setup/setup-gsi
```

```
For further information on using the setup-gsi script, use the -help
option. The -default option sets this security configuration to be
the default, and -nonroot can be used on systems where root access is
not available.
```

```
********************************************************************************
```

The **setup-gsi** finishes the setup of GSI on our system. To do this, it creates a set of configuration files in the /etc directory, so this command should be run as **root**. However, in systems without root access, you can use a **-noroot** argument to specify an alternate location which is non-root writable. Let's suppose you do have root access, and run the command. You should see the following:

```
setup-gsi: Configuring GSI security

Making /etc/grid-security...

mkdir /etc/grid-security

Making trusted certs directory: /etc/grid-security/certificates/

mkdir /etc/grid-security/certificates/

Installing /etc/grid-security/certificates//grid-security.conf.e4da69c0...

Running grid-security-config...

Installing Globus CA certificate into trusted CA certificate directory...

Installing Globus CA signing policy into trusted CA certificate directory...

setup-gsi: Complete
```

A.3.2 Using an Existing CA

If you are going to use an existing CA in your organization, then your system administrator should provide all the files and instructions to set up your GT4 installation so it will recognize the CA.

A.3.3 Using GCS

The Globus Alliance provides a CA service to provide low-quality certificates to users. This CA, known as the Globus Certificate Service (GCS), should only be used for testing purposes and when no other option is available. (given a choice, it is generally better to install SimpleCA). Instructions on how to obtain a GCS certificate can be found in the GCS website: http://gcs.globus.org:8080/gcs.

A.4 Obtaining a Host Certificate

We must now obtain a digital certificate for the host that will be running the Globus standalone container. Many Globus services depend on the existence of this certificate to verify that a host is who it truly claims to be.

We will request the certificate from SimpleCA. If you are using your organization's CA, you will have to follow your organization's procedures for requesting a host certificate (check with your system administrator to find out what steps to follow). If you are using GCS, the GCS website includes instructions on how to request host certificates.

As **root**, run:

```
# grid-cert-request -host 'hostname'
```

⏚ You must specify your computer's hostname. If your computer is a standalone machine, you should be able to use your computer's local name. If your computer is part of a network, you should find out what its *fully qualified domain name* (FQDN) is (e.g. **pc-johndoe.foobar.com**). In both cases, you should be fine using the standard **hostname** command.

Also, take into account that **grid-cert-request** will generally not be in **root**'s PATH, so you might have to run the following instead:

```
$GLOBUS_LOCATION/bin/grid-cert-request -host 'hostname'
```

If you use your computer's local name, you will get the following message:

```
The hostname pc-johndoe does not appear to be fully qualified.

Do you wish to continue? [n]
```

You can safely answer "yes", but take into account that your host certificate will only be valid for *local* use. In other words, if other machines try to access your services and check your host certificate, they will complain about it because it isn't a FQDN. So, don't use your local hostname unless you simply want to try out your services locally.

Next, the certificate request will be generated.

```
Generating a 1024 bit RSA private key

....++++++

..............++++++

writing new private key to '/etc/grid-security/hostkey.pem'
```

You will see some intermediate messages, and then the following:

```
A private host key and a certificate request has been generated
with the subject:


/O=Globus/OU=GT4 Examples/CN=host/<your hostname>


-----------------------------------------------------------


The private key is stored in /etc/grid-security/hostkey.pem
The request is stored in /etc/grid-security/hostcert_request.pem


Please e-mail the request to the Globus Simple CA <CA e-mail>
```

You may use a command similar to the following:

```
cat /etc/grid-security/hostcert_request.pem | mail <CA e-mail>
```

Only use the above if this machine can send AND receive e-mail. if not, please mail using some other method.

Your certificate will be mailed to you within two working days.

If you receive no response, contact Globus Simple CA at*<CA e-mail>*

Remember that we won't actually be mailing our request to anyone, since we are in control of the CA. We simply care that the following files have been created:

- **/etc/grid-security/hostkey.pem**: The host certificate private key.
- **/etc/grid-security/hostcert_request.pem**: The host certificate request.
- **/etc/grid-security/hostcert.pem** The host certificate (initially empty)

We now have to sign the host certificate request. Using the **globus** user, run:

grid-ca-sign -in /etc/grid-security/hostcert_request.pem -out

hostcert_signed.pem

You will be asked to enter a "password for the CA key". This is the password you entered when setting up SimpleCA.

To sign the request

please enter the password for the CA key:

Next, you will see the following:

The new signed certificate is at: /home/globus/.globus/simpleCA

//newcerts/01.pem

The new certificate will also be placed in the file **hostcert_signed.pem** in the current directory. As **root**, move the signed host certificate to **/etc/grid-security/hostcert.pem**. The certificate should be owned by root, and read-only for other users. The key should be read-only by root.

A.5 Setting Up the Container Certificate

The private key of the host certificate (**/etc/grid-security/hostkey.pem**) is only readable by root. However, the container will be running as a non-root user (the **globus** user) and in order to have a set of host credentials which are readable by the container, we need to copy the host certificate and key and change the ownership to the **globus** user.

As root, run:

```
# cd /etc/grid-security
```

```
# cp hostkey.pem containerkey.pem
```

```
# cp hostcert.pem containercert.pem
```

```
# chown globus.globus containerkey.pem containercert.pem
```

At this point the certificates in /etc/grid-security should look something like this:

```
# ls -l *.pem
-rw-r--r-- 1 globus globus 1785 Oct 14 14:47 containercert.pem
-r-------- 1 globus globus  887 Oct 14 14:47 containerkey.pem
-rw-r--r-- 1 root   root   1785 Oct 14 14:42 hostcert.pem
-r-------- 1 root   root    887 Sep 29 09:59 hostkey.pem
```

A.6   Setting Up User Certificates

We will now request a *user certificate* for user **globus4user**. Remember, this is the user we will use to compile the examples, and to run the example clients. This user needs its own certificate so the clients will be able to identify themselves when contacting the server. Otherwise, we will not be able to use authorization in our examples.

> ☞ Remember that **globus4user** is the arbitrary name we've chosen for our "user account". You can use your own user account instead of **globus4user**.

As user **globus4user**, run:

```
grid-cert-request
```

You will see the following output:

```
A certificate request and private key is being created.
You will be asked to enter a PEM pass phrase.
This pass phrase is akin to your account password,
and is used to protect your key file.
If you forget your pass phrase, you will need to
obtain a new certificate.
```

```
Generating a 1024 bit RSA private key

.........................++++++

..++++++

writing new private key to '/home/globus4user/.globus/userkey.pem'
```

You will be asked for a password to protect your private key. Don't confuse this password with the one we provided when configuring SimpleCA. That password protects the CA's private key. The one we're being asked for now will protect the private key of **globus4user**'s certificate. We will need this password each time we want to access our certificate's private key.

```
Enter PEM pass phrase:

Verifying - Enter PEM pass phrase:
```

After you enter and confirm the password, you should see some intermediate output, and finally the following:

```
A private key and a certificate request has been generated with the subject:

/O=Globus/OU=GT4 Examples/CN=Globus 4 User


If the CN=Globus 4 User is not appropriate, rerun this

script with the -force -cn "Common Name" options.


Your private key is stored in /home/globus4user/.globus/userkey.pem

Your request is stored in /home/globus4user/.globus/usercert_request.pem


Please e-mail the request to the Globus Simple CA <CA e-mail>

You may use a command similar to the following:


  cat /home/globus4user/.globus/usercert_request.pem | mail <CA e-mail>


Only use the above if this machine can send AND receive e-mail. if not, please

mail using some other method.


Your certificate will be mailed to you within two working days.

If you receive no response, contact Globus Simple CA at <CA e-mail>
```

As with the host certificate, we won't need to mail the request to anyone since the **globus** user (in the same machine) controls the CA. Also, note that our certificate's common name is **Globus 4 User**. This is the UNIX description of user **globus4user**, so you should expect a different common name in your certificate.

At this point, we will have the following files:

- **~/.globus/usercert.pem**: The user certificate (initially empty).
- **~/.globus/userkey.pem**: The user certificate's private key.
- **~/.globus/usercert_request.pem**: The user certificate request.

No, as user **globus**, run:

```
grid-ca-sign
        -in /home/globus4user/.globus/usercert_request.pem
        -out usercert_signed.pem
```

You will be asked for the CA key's password. Remember this is the password you entered when setting up SimpleCA, *not* the password we just entered when requesting the user certificate.

```
To sign the request
please enter the password for the CA key:
```

After entering the password, you will see the following:

```
The new signed certificate is at: /home/globus/.globus/simpleCA
//newcerts/02.pem
```

Additionally, a **usercert_signed.pem** file will be created in the current directory. Now, using the **globus4user** user, copy the signed certificate to **~/.globus/** and rename it as **usercert.pem**. The certificate should be owned by the **globus4user**, and read-only for other users. The key should be read-only by **globus4user**.

Finally, to make sure that the certificate is correctly installed, you can try to create a proxy certificate (proxy certificates are introduced in Section 16.5) by running the following as **globus4user**:

```
grid-proxy-init -verify
```

You will see the following:

```
Your identity: /O=Globus/OU=GT4 Examples/CN=Globus 4 User
Enter GRID pass phrase for this identity:
```

At this point, you need to enter the password you entered when creating the **globus4user** user certificate. If the certificate is correctly installed, you will see the following:

```
Creating proxy ................................... Done
Your proxy is valid until: Tue Apr 19 07:51:38 2005
```

A.7 The Globus Standalone Container

To test that the Globus Toolkit is correctly installed, you can try to start the Globus standalone web services container. We will use this container in all the examples in the book, so we need to be sure that it works properly.

To start the container, run the following using the **globus** user:

```
globus-start-container
```

If the toolkit is correctly installed, you should see the following:

```
Starting SOAP server at: https://111.222.333.444:8443/wsrf/services/
With the following services:
[1]: https://140.221.57.104:8443/wsrf/services/IndexFactoryService
[2]: https://140.221.57.104:8443/wsrf/services/TriggerFactoryService
[... more services listed ...]
[47]: https://140.221.57.104:8443/wsrf/services/ManagedJobFactoryService
[48]: https://140.221.57.104:8443/wsrf/services/TestServiceRequest
```

> ☞ Do not worry if you see the following error message:
>
> ```
> 2005-05-10 16:49:06,485 ERROR service.ReliableFileTransferImpl
> [main,<init>:73]
> Unable to setup database driver with pooling.
> Connection refused.
> Check that the hostname and port are correct and that the
> postmaster is accepting TCP/IP connections.
> ```
>
> It simply means that the RFT component is not fully configured. Since we won't be using that component, we can safely ignore this. Please refer to the official Globus documentation if you need to configure any component not covered in this book (such as RFT).

You can find more details on the **globus-start-container** command in Appendix C. That appendix also includes information on **globus-stop-container**, which will allow you to stop the container.

A WSDL Primer

This appendix shows you how to write a simple WSDL description of a portType in a step-by-step fashion. Although it should be easy to follow those same steps to create other simple WSDL files, this is not meant as an exhaustive WSDL guide. Anyone seeking to write more complex portTypes (for example, passing complex classes instead of primitive types -int. string, etc.- as parameters or return values) should definitely consider learning WSDL and XML Schema. A couple of references are provided at the end of the appendix in case you want to learn more.

That said, let's start writing WSDL! We are going to write the WSDL description corresponding to the following Java interface:

```java
public interface Math
{
    public void add(int a);

    public void subtract(int a);

    public int getValueRP();
}
```

Furthermore, our portType will have two resource properties: "value" of type integer and "lastOp" of type string. This is the interface used in many of the book's examples.

B.1   The Bare Bones of Our WSDL File

First of all, we have to write the root element of the WSDL file, which is <definitions>.

```
<?xml version="1.0" encoding="UTF-8"?>

<definitions name="MathService"
    targetNamespace="http://www.globus.org/namespaces/examples/
    MathService_instance"
    xmlns="http://schemas.xmlsoap.org/wsdl/"
    xmlns:tns="http://www.globus.org/namespaces/examples/MathService_instance"
    xmlns:wsdl="http://schemas.xmlsoap.org/wsdl/"
    xmlns:wsrp="http://docs.oasis-open.org/wsrf/2004/06/
        wsrf-WS-ResourceProperties-1.2-draft-01.xsd"
    xmlns:xsd="http://www.w3.org/2001/XMLSchema">


</definitions>
```

This tag has two important attributes:

- **name**: The "name" of the WSDL file. Not related with the name of the portType.
- **targetNamespace**: The target namespace of the WSDL file. This means that all the PortTypes and operations defined in this WSDL file will belong to this namespace.

ⓘ **XML Namespaces**

XML namespaces are basically a way of grouping similar "things" together. We're using the somewhat vague term "things" because XML Namespaces are used not only in WSDL, but in many XML languages, so just about anything can be grouped into an XML Namespace (not only portTypes and operations, which are specific to WSDL). The XML Namespace has to be a valid URI, but it doesn't necessarily have to be real (in fact, if you try to point your web browser to the URI we're using, you'll get a Page Not Found error).

The root element is also used to declare all the namespaces we are going to use. Notice how the **tns** namespace is the Target NameSpace. The rest of the namespace declarations should be copied verbatim.

☞ Notice above how the Globus namespaces and the official Oasis WSRF namespaces include versioning information. For example, the **wsrp** namespace includes the date when that particular draft of the specification was published

(2004/06) along with the version of the draft (**1.2-draft-01**). It is usually a good idea to include versioning information in your own namespaces if you need a way of tracking the version of your WSDL files.

B.2 The Port Type

Now we're going to define our portType, using the **<portType>** tag:

```xml
<?xml version="1.0" encoding="UTF-8"?>
<definitions ... >


<portType name="MathPortType"
wsrp:ResourceProperties="tns:MathResourceProperties">

    <operation name="add">
        <input message="tns:AddInputMessage"/>
        <outputmessage="tns:AddOutputMessage"/>
    </operation>


    <operation name="subtract">
        <input message="tns:SubtractInputMessage"/>
        <output message="tns:SubtractOutputMessage"/>
    </operation>


    <operation name="getValueRP">
        <input message="tns:GetValueRPInputMessage"/>
        <output message="tns:GetValueRPOutputMessage"/>
    </operation>


</portType>


</definitions>
```

The <portType> tag has two important attributes:

- **name**: Name of the PortType.

- **wsrp:ResourceProperties**: This attribute specifies what the service's resource properties are. The meaning of this attribute is explained further on.

ⓘ Make sure you read the warning regarding the WSDL Preprocessor in Section 6.1.2.

Inside the **<portType>** we have an **<operation>** tag for the three operations exposed in our web service: **add**, **subtract**, and **getValueRP**. They are all very similar, so let's just take a closer look at **add**'s **<operation>** tag:

```
<operation name="add">

    <input message="tns:AddInputMessage"/>

    <output message="tns:AddOutputMessage"/>

</operation>
```

The **<operation>** tag has an **<input>** tag and an **<output>**. These two tags have a **message** attribute, which specifies what message should be passed along when the operation is invoked (input message) and when it returns successfully (output message). So, we'll need to define the messages of our operations.

B.3 The Messages

The following are the messages for the **add** operation. The messages for the **subtract** and **getValueRP** operations are identical.

```
<?xml version="1.0" encoding="UTF-8"?>
<definitions ... >


<message name="AddInputMessage">
        <part name="parameters" element="tns:add"/>
</message>
<message name="AddOutputMessage">
        <part name="parameters" element="tns:addResponse"/>
</message>


<!-- PortType -->


</definitions>
```

Notice how the name of each message has to be the same as the one written in the message attribute of the **<input>** and **<output>** tags. However, it turns out messages are composed of **<part>**s! Messages have a single part, in which a single XML element is passed along. For example, the **AddOutputMessage** will contain the addResponse element (notice how it is part of the **tns** namespace, the target namespace).

B.4 The Response and Request Types

The definition of these elements is done using XML Schema inside a new tag: the **<types>** tag. The following would be the definition of the **add** and **addResponse** elements:

```
<?xml version="1.0" encoding="UTF-8"?>
<definitions ... >


<types>
<xsd:schema targetNamespace="http://www.globus.org/namespaces/examples/
    MathService_instance"
    xmlns:tns="http://www.globus.org/namespaces/examples/MathService_instance"
    xmlns:xsd="http://www.w3.org/2001/XMLSchema">


        <!-- REQUESTS AND RESPONSES -->


        <xsd:element name="add" type="xsd:int"/>
        <xsd:element name="addResponse">
                <xsd:complexType/>
        </xsd:element>


        <!-- more type definitions -->


</xsd:schema>
</types>


<!-- Messages -->


<!-- PortType -->


</definitions>
```

The **\<types\>** tag contains an **\<xsd:schema\>** tag. The attributes of the **\<xsd:schema\>** should be copied verbatim, except the **targetNamespace**, which should be the same as the target namespace of the WSDL document.

The **add** element (which, remember, is part of the *input* message of the **add** operation) represents the single input parameter of our add operation, and thus has an attribute specifying its type (notice how the type attribute is equal to **xsd:int**, the integer type in XML Schema).

If we had wanted our add operation to receive two parameters, we would have to declare the **add** element like this:

```
<xsd:element name="add">

    <xsd:complexType>

    <xsd:sequence>

        <xsd:element name="a1" type="xsd:int"/>

        <xsd:element name="a2" type="xsd:int"/>

    </xsd:sequence>

    </xsd:complexType>

</xsd:element>
```

In this case we're saying that the add operation has two parameters (a1 and a2) of type integer. Notice that to specify multiple parameters we need to use the XML Schema **complexType** tag.

As for the **addResponse** element (part of the output message of the add operation, i.e. the return value), it contains an empty **complexType**, since the add operation doesn't return anything.

The type definitions for the **subtract** is defined similarly. The types for **getValueRP** operation are slightly different, as this operation doesn't expect any parameters, but returns an integer value:

```
<xsd:element name="getValueRP">

        <xsd:complexType/>

</xsd:element>

<xsd:element name="getValueRPResponse" type="xsd:int"/>
```

B.5 Declaring the Resource Properties

We are very nearly done. There is only one thing left to do: declare our service's resource properties. This is also done in the **\<types\>** part of the WSDL document, inside the **\<schema\>** tag along with all the declarations we have just seen.

First of all, let's take another quick look at our portType:

```
<portType name="MathPortType"
    wsdlpp:extends="wsrpw:GetResourceProperty"
    wsrp:ResourceProperties="tns:MathResourceProperties">


        <!-- operations -->


</portType>
```

The **wsrp:ResourceProperties** attribute specifies what the service's resource properties are. This attribute must refer to a single element and, in our case, that element will be called **MathResourceProperties** which we must declare in the **<types>** part of the WSDL document.

```
<types>
<xsd:schema targetNamespace="http://www.globus.org/namespaces/examples/
    MathService_instance"
    xmlns:tns="http://www.globus.org/namespaces/examples/MathService_instance"
    xmlns:xsd="http://www.w3.org/2001/XMLSchema">


        <!-- Requests and responses declarations-->


            <xsd:element name="Value" type="xsd:int"/>
        <xsd:element name="LastOp" type="xsd:string"/>


        <xsd:element name="MathResourceProperties">
        <xsd:complexType>
            <xsd:sequence>
                    <xsd:element ref="tns:Value" minOccurs="1"
                        maxOccurs="1"/>
                    <xsd:element ref="tns:LastOp" minOccurs="1"
                        maxOccurs="1"/>
            </xsd:sequence>
        </xsd:complexType>
        </xsd:element>
```

```
</xsd:schema>

</types>
```

This declaration specifies that **MathResourceProperties** contains two resource properties, **Value** and **LastOp**, each of which appear only once (we could specify array resource properties by changing the values of **maxOccurs**). You must make sure that the resource properties are declared as *global elements* (this is explained further in Section 6.1.2).

B.6   Summing Up...

The whole WSDL file would be:

```
<?xml version="1.0" encoding="UTF-8"?>
<definitions name="MathService"
    targetNamespace="http://www.globus.org/namespaces/examples/
        MathService_instance"
    xmlns="http://schemas.xmlsoap.org/wsdl/"
    xmlns:tns="http://www.globus.org/namespaces/examples/MathService_instance"
    xmlns:wsdl="http://schemas.xmlsoap.org/wsdl/"
    xmlns:wsrp="http://docs.oasis-open.org/wsrf/2004/06/
        wsrf-WS-ResourceProperties-1.2-draft-01.xsd"
    xmlns:xsd="http://www.w3.org/2001/XMLSchema">


<!================================================================


                        T Y P E S


    ================================================================>
<types>
<xsd:schema targetNamespace="http://www.globus.org/namespaces/examples/
    MathService_instance"
    xmlns:tns="http://www.globus.org/namespaces/examples/MathService_instance"
    xmlns:xsd="http://www.w3.org/2001/XMLSchema">

        <!-- REQUESTS AND RESPONSES -->

        <xsd:element name="add" type="xsd:int"/>
```

```
<xsd:element name="addResponse">
        <xsd:complexType/>
</xsd:element>

<xsd:element name="subtract" type="xsd:int"/>
<xsd:element name="subtractResponse">
        <xsd:complexType/>
</xsd:element>

<xsd:element name="getValueRP">
        <xsd:complexType/>
</xsd:element>
<xsd:element name="getValueRPResponse" type="xsd:int"/>


<!-- RESOURCE PROPERTIES -->


<xsd:element name="Value" type="xsd:int"/>
<xsd:element name="LastOp" type="xsd:string"/>


<xsd:element name="MathResourceProperties">
<xsd:complexType>
        <xsd:sequence>
                <xsd:element ref="tns:Value" minOccurs="1"
                    maxOccurs="1"/>
                <xsd:element ref="tns:LastOp" minOccurs="1"
                    maxOccurs="1"/>
        </xsd:sequence>
</xsd:complexType>
</xsd:element>


</xsd:schema>
</types>
```

```
<!===============================================================


                        M E S S A G E S


   ==============================================================>
<message name="AddInputMessage">
        <part name="parameters" element="tns:add"/>
</message>
<message name="AddOutputMessage">
        <part name="parameters" element="tns:addResponse"/>
</message>


<message name="SubtractInputMessage">
        <part name="parameters" element="tns:subtract"/>
</message>
<message name="SubtractOutputMessage">
        <part name="parameters" element="tns:subtractResponse"/>
</message>


<message name="GetValueRPInputMessage">
        <part name="parameters" element="tns:getValueRP"/>
</message>
<message name="GetValueRPOutputMessage">
        <part name="parameters" element="tns:getValueRPResponse"/>
</message>


<!===============================================================


                        P O R T T Y P E


   ==============================================================>
<portType name="MathPortType"
        wsrp:ResourceProperties="tns:MathResourceProperties">
```

```
        <operation name="add">

            <input message="tns:AddInputMessage"/>

            <output message="tns:AddOutputMessage"/>

    </operation>


        <operation name="subtract">

            <input message="tns:SubtractInputMessage"/>

            <output message="tns:SubtractOutputMessage"/>

    </operation>


        <operation name="getValueRP">

            <input message="tns:GetValueRPInputMessage"/>

            <output message="tns:GetValueRPOutputMessage"/>

    </operation>



    </portType>


    </definitions>
```

Summing up, the basic steps involved in writing a WSDL file for a WSRF web service would be the following:

1. Write the root element **<definitions>**
2. Write the **<portType>**
3. Write an input and output **<message>** for each operation in the PortType.
4. Write the **<types>**. This includes declaring the request and response elements, along with the resource properties.

As any experienced WSDL writer should be able to tell you, there are many ways of writing WSDL (ways that allow you to write more compact WSDL). However, this is the most step-by-step method, which is probably best for beginners. Furthermore, remember this is just a very brief guide on how to write very basic WSDL. You should have no trouble adding basic operations such as void multiply(int a). To deal with more complex scenarios, we are including a list of books and websites where you can learn more about WSDL and XML Schema.

References

[1] Ethan Cerami. *Web Services Essentials.* O'Reilly, 2002.

[2] Eric van der Vlist. *XML Schema.* O'Reilly, June, 2002.

[3] *W3 Schools – WSDL Tutorial.* http://www.w3schools.com/wsdl/.

[4] *W3 Schools – XML Schema Tutorial.* http://www.w3schools.com/schema/.

Command-Line Clients

This appendix provides a reference guide of all the Globus command-line clients seen in the book. First, we include a table summarizing the common parameters to most of the clients, and a table with parameters that can allow us to configure security in the clients. Next, we provide an overview of clients related to resource properties (as seen in Chapter 10, resource lifetime (as seen in Chapter 11, notifications (as seen in Chapter 13), and general GT4 management commands. Finally, usage examples for some of the common parameters are provided.

C.1 The Common Parameters

Parameter	Description
-h, --help	Displays a help message.
-d, --debug	Activates debugging messages. If this option is not specified, the client will not print out a full stack trace if an error is produced.
-e, --eprFile <file>	Specifies the endpoint reference of a resource. **file** must be an XML representation of the endpoint reference.
-s, --service <uri>	Specifies a service's URI. This option can be used alone if we are addressing a singleton resource. Otherwise, it must be used with **-k** to specify the key of the resource.
-k, --key <key_name> <key_value>	Specifies a resource key. **key_name** is the QName of the key. **key_value** is the value of the key.

Table C.1: Common command-line parameters

C.2 Resource Property Clients

C.2.1 wsrf-get-properties

This command uses the **GetResourceProperties** portType to access the value of several resource properties at once. The resource properties must be specified using their QNames.

Usage

```
wsrf-get-properties [common options] <resource property 1> [<rp 2> ... <rp N>]
```

Example

```
wsrf-get-properties \
    -s http://127.0.0.1:8080/wsrf/services/examples/core/rp/MathService \
    {http://www.globus.org/namespaces/examples/MathService_instance_rpValue} \
    {http://www.globus.org/namespaces/examples/MathService_instance_rpLastOp} \
Expected output:
    <ns1:Value xmlns:ns1="http://www.globus.org/namespaces/examples/
        MathService_instance_rp">0</ns1:Value>
    <ns2:LastOp xmlns:ns2="http://www.globus.org/namespaces/examples/
        MathService_instance_rp">NONE</ns2:LastOp>
```

C.2.2 wsrf-update-property

This command uses the **SetResourceProperties** portType to update the value of one or several resource properties.

Usage

```
wsrf-update-property [common options] <updateFile>
```

Where **updateFile** must be a file with the following format:

```
<updateFile>
    <tns:ResourcePropertyName xmlns:tns="namespace">
    new_value
    </tns:ResourcePropertyName>
</updateFile>
```

Parameter	Description
-f, --descriptor <file>	Specifies a client security descriptor. Overrides all other security settings.
-a, --anonymous	Enables anonymous authentication. Only supported with transport security or GSI Secure Conversation authentication mechanism.
-g, --delegation <mode>	Enables delegation. <mode> can be either limited or full. Only supported with GSI Secure Conversation authentication mechanism.
-l, --contextLifetime <time>	Sets the lifetime of the client security context. Value is in milliseconds. Only supported with GSI Secure Conversation authentication mechanism.
-m, --securityMech <type>	Specifies the authentication mechanism. type can be 'msg' for GSI Secure Message, or 'conv' for GSI Secure Conversation.
-c, --serverCertificate <file>	Specifies the server's certificate file used for encryption. Only needed for GSI Secure Message authentication mechanism.
-p, --protection <type>	Specifies the protection level. type can be 'sig' for signature or 'enc' for encryption.
-z, --authorization <type>	Specifies authorization type. type can be 'self', 'host', or 'none'.

Table C.2: Security parameters

Note that several resource property updates can be included inside the **updateFile** element.

Example

We will update the **Value** RP and change its value to 100. Our **updateFile** would look like this.

```
<updateFile>
    <tns:Value xmlns:tns="http://www.globus.org/namespaces/examples/
        MathService_instance_rp">
    100
    </tns:Value>
</updateFile>
```

Assuming we've saved the file with the name **update.xml**:

```
wsrf-update-property \
    -s http://127.0.0.1:8080/wsrf/services/examples/core/rp/MathService \
    update.xml
```

You should not expect any output if the command is successful. To see that the update has been performed, you can use **wsrf-get-property** to access the **Value** RP. You should get the following:

```
<ns1:Value xmlns:ns1="http://www.globus.org/namespaces/examples/
    MathService_instance_rp">100</ns1:Value>
```

C.2.3   wsrf-insert-property

This command uses the **SetResourceProperties** portType to insert one or several new resource properties.

Usage

```
wsrf-insert-property [common options] <insertFile>
```

Where **insertFile** must be a file with the following format:

```
<insertFile>
    <tns:ResourcePropertyName xmlns:tns="namespace">
    new_value
    </tns:ResourcePropertyName>
</insertFile>
```

Note that several resource property updates can be included inside the **insertFile** element.

Example

We will insert two new **RecentOps** RPs. Our **insertFile** would look like this:

```
<insertFile>
    <tns:RecentOps xmlns:tns="http://www.globus.org/namespaces/examples/
        MathService_instance_rp_complex">
    ADDITION
    </tns:RecentOps>
```

```
<tns:RecentOps xmlns:tns="http://www.globus.org/namespaces/examples/
    MathService_instance_rp_complex">
SUBTRACTION
</tns:RecentOps>
</insertFile>
```

Assuming we've saved the file with the name **insert.xml**:

wsrf-insert-property \

    -s http://127.0.0.1:8080/wsrf/services/examples/core/rp_complex/MathService \

    insert.xml

You should not expect any output if the command is successful. To see that the update has been performed, you can use **wsrf-get-property** to access the **RecentOps** RP. You should get the following:

```
<tns:RecentOps xmlns:tns="http://www.globus.org/namespaces/examples/
    MathService_instance_rp_complex">
ADDITION
</tns:RecentOps>
<tns:RecentOps xmlns:tns="http://www.globus.org/namespaces/examples/
    MathService_instance_rp_complex">
SUBTRACTION
</tns:RecentOps>
```

C.2.4 wsrf-delete-property

This command uses the **SetResourceProperties** portType to delete all occurrences of a resource property. The resource property must be specified using its QName.

Usage

    wsrf-delete-property [common options] <resource property>

Example

    wsrf-delete-property \

        -s http://127.0.0.1:8080/wsrf/services/examples/core/rp_complex/MathService

    \

```
{http://www.globus.org/namespaces/examples/MathService_instance_rp_complex}
    RecentOps
```

You should not expect any output if the command is successful. To test that the deletion has been performed, you can use the **wsrf-get-property** to access the **RecentOps** RP. The command should simply output the following, indicating that there are no **RecentOps** RPs:

```
null
```

C.2.5 wsrf-query

This command uses the **QueryResourceProperties** portType to query the resource properties document. Currently, the only query dialect supported (and, therefore, the default) is XPath.

Usage

```
wsrf-query [common options] [query] [query dialect]
```

Example

The following query retrieves all the **RecentOps** RPs with a value greater than or equal to 20:

```
wsrf-query \
    -s http://127.0.0.1:8080/wsrf/services/examples/core/rp_complex/MathService \
    "/*/*[local-name()='RecentValues'][text()>=20]"
```

Expected output:

```
<ns1:RecentValues xmlns:ns1="http://www.globus.org/namespaces/examples/
    MathService_instance_rp_complex">
        20
</ns1:RecentValues>
<ns1:RecentValues xmlns:ns1="http://www.globus.org/namespaces/examples/
    MathService_instance_rp_complex">
        30
</ns1:RecentValues>
<ns1:RecentValues xmlns:ns1="http://www.globus.org/namespaces/examples/
    MathService_instance_rp_complex">
```

```
        4242
</ns1:RecentValues>
```

C.3 Resource Lifetime Clients

C.3.1 wsrf-destroy

This command uses the **ImmediateResourceTermination** portType to destroy a resource.

Usage

```
wsrf-destroy [common options]
```

Note: This command has no specific parameters. The common options must be used to specify what resource has to be destroyed.

Example

Assuming we have an EPR written to a file called **epr.txt**:

```
wsrf-destroy -e epr.txt
```

C.3.2 wsrf-set-termination-time

This command uses the **ScheduledResourceTermination** portType to schedule the destruction of a resource.

Usage

```
wsrf-set-termination-time [common options] ( <seconds> | "infinity" )
```

If **seconds** are specified, then the resource is scheduled to be destroyed that many seconds in the future. If **infinity** is specified, any scheduled destruction is canceled (the resource must now be explicitly destroyed, or another termination time must be scheduled).

Example

Once again, assuming we have an EPR written to a file called **epr.txt**, the following command sets its termination time 100 seconds in the future:

```
wsrf-set-termination-time -e epr.txt 100
```

The expected output is:

Parameter	Description
-b, --subEpr <file>	Saves the EPR of the **Subscription** resource to **file**

Table C.3: Parameters specific to **wsn-subscribe**

> requested: DATE TIME
>
> scheduled: DATE TIME

☞ In this case, the scheduled time should be 100 seconds in the future, relative to the current system time. Note that the requested and scheduled termination times will usually be the same.

To cancel the scheduled destruction:

> wsrf-set-termination-time -e epr.txt infinity

Expected output:

> requested: infinity
>
> scheduled: infinity

C.4   Notification Clients

C.4.1   wsn-subscribe

This client allows us to subscribe to a topic and see the raw XML sent in the notification, without having to write a client for a specific service. The topic must be specified using its QName.

Usage

> wsn-subscribe [common options] <topic>

Example

> wsn-subscribe \
>
> -s http://127.0.0.1:8080/wsrf/services/examples/core/notifications/MathService \
>
> "{http://www.globus.org/namespaces/examples/MathService_instance_notif}Value"

Expected output:

```
Subscription successful
Address: http://127.0.0.1:8080/wsrf/services/SubscriptionManagerService
Reference property[0]:
<ns1:SubscriptionKey xmlns:ns1="http://www.globus.org/namespaces/2004/06/core">
3135e260-a4ae-11d9-ad9d-a9c044fad770
</ns1:SubscriptionKey>
```

When the **Value** RP is modified, the following will be output by **wsn-subscribe**:

```
Received:
<ns5:Value xmlns:ns5="http://www.globus.org/namespaces/examples/
    MathService_instance_notif">10</ns5:Value>
```

C.4.2 wsn-get-current-message

This client allows us to inspect the latest message sent out to the subscribers of a topic. The topic must be specified using its QName.

Usage

```
wsn-get-current-message [common options] <topic>
```

Example

```
wsn-get-current-message \
-s http://127.0.0.1:8080/wsrf/services/examples/core/notifications/MathService \
"{http://www.globus.org/namespaces/examples/MathService_instance_notif}Value"
```

Expected output:

```
<ns1:ResourcePropertyValueChangeNotificationType xmlns:ns1="http://docs.oasis-
    open.org/wsrf/2004/06/wsrf-WS-ResourceProperties-1.2-draft-01.xsd">
 <ns1:OldValue>
  <ns2:Value xmlns:ns2="http://www.globus.org/namespaces/examples/
  MathService_instance_notif">0</ns2:Value>
 </ns1:OldValue>
 <ns1:NewValue>
```

Parameter	Description
-h, --help	Displays a help message.
-d, -debug	Activates debugging messages. If this option is specified, the container will print out a full stack trace if an error is produced.
-p <port>	Specifies an alternate port for the container to listen on. The default is 8443.
-quiet	Does not display a list of services on startup.
-nosec	Starts a non-secure container. This means that the server will listen on port 8080 and will not use GSI Transport. However, GSI Secure Conversation and GSI Secure Message can still be used.
-containerDesc <file>	Specifies an alternate security descriptor file for the container.

Table C.4: Parameters specific to `globus-start-container`

```
<ns3:Value xmlns:ns3="http://www.globus.org/namespaces/examples/
    MathService_instance_notif">10</ns3:Value>
  </ns1:NewValue>
</ns1:ResourcePropertyValueChangeNotificationType>
```

C.5 Globus Management

C.5.1 Globus-start-container

Starts the Globus standalone web services container.

Usage

```
globus-start-container [options]
```

This command supports the options described in Table C.4.

C.5.2 globus-stop-container

Stop the Globus standalone web services container.

Usage

```
globus-stop-container [options]
```

This command supports the options described in Table C.4.

Note that, to stop the container, **globus-stop-container** must be run with the same set of credentials as the container itself (typically the container credentials, as described in Section A.5). If you followed the installation appendix included in the book, then the **globus** user has its own credentials, but also has access to the container's credentials. So, we can stop the container by using a proxy certificate obtained from the container credentials. For example, using BASH, we would run the following:

```
globus$ grid-proxy-init -cert /etc/grid-security/containercert.pem \
                    -key /etc/grid-security/containerkey.pem \
                    -out containerproxy.pem

globus$ export X509_USER_PROXY=containerproxy.pem


globus$ globus-stop-container


globus$ unset X509_USER_PROXY


globus$ rm containerproxy.pem
```

Using CSH:

```
globus$ grid-proxy-init -cert /etc/grid-security/containercert.pem \
                    -key /etc/grid-security/containerkey.pem \
                    -out containerproxy.pem

globus$ setenv X509_USER_PROXY containerproxy.pem


globus$ globus-stop-container


globus$ unsetenv X509_USER_PROXY


globus$ rm containerproxy.pem
```

Finally, note that the **globus-stop-container** uses transport-level security by default. If you started the container with the **-nosec** option, you will need to stop the container using GSI Secure Message or GSI Secure Conversation:

```
globus-stop-container -s http://127.0.0.1:8080/wsrf/services/ShutdownService
    -m msg
```

Or:

```
globus-stop-container -s http://127.0.0.1:8080/wsrf/services/ShutdownService
    -m conv
```

C.6 Usage Examples

C.6.1 The **-s** (**--service**) Parameter

As mentioned above, this parameter is used to specify the URI of the service we want to access. It can be used alone if we are addressing a singleton resource. Otherwise, it must be used with **-k** to specify the key of the resource (see below for an example).

For example, let's assume we want to access the **Value** resource property of the service seen in Chapter 10. Since this service has a singleton resource, we only need to specify the service's URI:

```
wsrf-get-property \
    -s http://127.0.0.1:8080/wsrf/services/examples/core/rp/MathService  blslash
    {http://www.globus.org/namespaces/examples/MathService_instance_rp}Value
```

C.6.2 The **-e** (**--eprFile**) Parameter

This parameter is used to specify the EPR of the WS-Resource we want to address. This EPR must be in the form of a file containing an XML representation of an EPR. In Section 8.9 we saw how we can write an EPR to a file.

```
wsrf-get-property \
    -e epr.txt \
    {http://www.globus.org/namespaces/examples/MathService_instance}Value
```

C.6.3 The **-k** (**--key**) Parameter

Through this parameter we can specify the identifier of the resource we want to access. This parameter must be used with the **-s** (**--service**) parameter so we can address a WS-Resource. As mentioned throughout the book, it is not common to manipulate the resource identifier directly on the client side, so this option is provided mainly for debugging purposes.

For example, let's assume we have the following EPR:

```
<ns1:MathResourceReference xsi:type="ns2:EndpointReferenceType"
    xmlns:ns1="http://www.globus.org/namespaces/examples/MathService_instance"
```

```
xmlns:xsi="http://www.w3.org/2001/XMLSchema-instance"
xmlns:ns2="http://schemas.xmlsoap.org/ws/2004/03/addressing">


<ns2:Address xsi:type="ns2:AttributedURI">
    http://127.0.0.1:8080/wsrf/services/examples/core/factory/MathService
</ns2:Address>


<ns2:ReferenceProperties xsi:type="ns2:ReferencePropertiesType">
  <ns1:MathResourceKey>1137a200</ns1:MathResourceKey>
</ns2:ReferenceProperties>


<ns2:ReferenceParameters xsi:type="ns2:ReferenceParametersType"/>


</ns1:MathResourceReference>
```

We would use the **-k** option like this:

wsrf-get-property \

    -s http://127.0.0.1:8080/wsrf/services/examples/core/factory/MathService \

    -k *http://www.globus.org/namespaces/examples/*

      MathService_instanceMathResourceKey 1137a200 \

{http://www.globus.org/namespaces/examples/MathService_instance}Value

Notice how we have to include the QName of the resource identifier. This QName is specified in the service's JNDI deployment file (see Section 8.7.2).

Examples

D.1 Service Interfaces

D.1.1 FactoryService

WSDL file

$EXAMPLES_DIR/schema/examples/FactoryService/Factory.wsdl

Namespace

http://www.globus.org/namespaces/examples/FactoryService

Operations

- createResource

  Parameters: None

  Returns: wsa:**EndpointReference** (an endpoint reference)

Resource properties

None.

Extends

This interface doesn't extend from any other portTypes.

Chapters in which this interface is used

- Chapter 8, Multiple resources
- Chapter 11, Lifecycle management
- Chapter 21, Resource-level security
- Chapter 22, Run-as modes and delegation (in Section 22.4).

D.1.2 MathService_instance

WSDL file

$EXAMPLES_DIR/schema/examples/MathService_instance/Math.wsdl

Namespace

http://www.globus.org/namespaces/examples/MathService_instance

Operations

- **add**

  Parameters: 1 parameter of type **xsd:int** (integer)

  Returns: nothing

- **subtract**

  Parameters: 1 parameter of type **xsd:int** (integer)

  Returns: nothing

- **getValueRP**

  Parameters: None

  Returns: **xsd:int** (integer)

Resource properties

- **Value**

  Type: **xsd:int** (integer)

  Cardinality: [1..1]

- **LastOp**

  Type: **xsd:string** (string)

  Cardinality: [1..1]

Extends

This interface doesn't extend from any other portTypes.

Chapters in which this interface is used

- Chapter 6, Writing your first stateful web service in 5 simple steps
- Chapter 7, Singleton resources
- Chapter 8, Multiple resources.

D.1.3 MathService_instance_4op

WSDL file

$EXAMPLES_DIR/schema/examples/MathService_instance_4op/Math.wsdl

Namespace

http://www.globus.org/namespaces/examples/MathService_instance_4op

Operations

- **add**

  Parameters: 1 parameter of type **xsd:int** (integer)

  Returns: nothing

- **subtract**

  Parameters: 1 parameter of type **xsd:int** (integer)

  Returns: nothing

- **multiply**

  Parameters: 1 parameter of type **xsd:int** (integer)

  Returns: nothing

- **divide**

  Parameters: 1 parameter of type **xsd:int** (integer)

  Returns: nothing

Resource properties

- **Value**

  Type: **xsd:int** (integer)

  Cardinality: [1..1]

- **LastOp**

  Type: **xsd:string** (string)

  Cardinality: [1..1]

Extends

- **GetResourceProperty** (WS-ResourceProperties)

Chapters in which this interface is used

- Chapter 17, Writing a Secure Math Service
- Chapter 18, The Security Descriptor
- Chapter 19, Authentication
- Chapter 20, Authorization
- Chapter 22, Run-as modes and delegation.

D.1.4 **MathService_instance_helloworld**

WSDL file

$EXAMPLES_DIR/schema/examples/MathService_instance_helloworld/Math.wsdl

Namespace

http://www.globus.org/namespaces/examples/MathService_instance_helloworld

Operations

- **add**

  Parameters: 1 parameter of type **xsd:int** (integer)

  Returns: nothing

- **helloWorld**

  Parameters: None

  Returns: **xsd:string** (string)

Resource properties

- Value

    Type: **xsd:int** (integer)

    Cardinality: [1..1]

Extends

- **GetResourceProperty** (WS-ResourceProperties)

Chapters in which this interface is used

- Chapter 21, Resource-level security
- Chapter 22, Run-as modes and delegation.

D.1.5 MathService_instance_notif

WSDL file

$EXAMPLES_DIR/schema/examples/MathService_instance_notif/Math.wsdl

Namespace

http://www.globus.org/namespaces/examples/MathService_instance_notif

Operations

- add

    Parameters: 1 parameter of type **xsd:int** (integer)

    Returns: nothing

- subtract

    Parameters: 1 parameter of type **xsd:int** (integer)

    Returns: nothing

Resource properties

- Value

    Type: **xsd:int** (integer)

    Cardinality: [1..1]

- **LastOp**

  Type: **xsd:string** (string)

  Cardinality: [1..1]

Extends

- **NotificationProducer** (WS-BaseNotification)

  SubscriptionManager (WS-BaseNotification)

Chapter in which this interface is used

- Chapter 13, Notifications

Notes

This interface also defines an element **BigValueChangeNotificationMessage** which is used to send a custom notification message containing:

- **BigValue**

  Type: **xsd:int** (integer)

  Cardinality: [1..1]

- **NewValue**

  Type: **xsd:int** (integer)

  Cardinality: [1..1]

- **Op**

  Type: **xsd:string** (string)

  Cardinality: [1..1]

D.1.6 MathService_instance_remotelog

WSDL file

$EXAMPLES_DIR/schema/examples/MathService_instance_remotelog/Math.wsdl

Namespace

http://www.globus.org/namespaces/examples/MathService_instance_remotelog

Operations

- **add**

  Parameters: 1 parameter of type **xsd:int** (integer)

  Returns: nothing

- **subtract**

  Parameters: 1 parameter of type **xsd:int** (integer)

  Returns: nothing

Resource properties

- **Value**

  Type: **xsd:int** (integer)

  Cardinality: [1..1]

- **LastOp**

  Type: **xsd:string** (string)

  Cardinality: [1..1]

Extends

- **GetResourceProperty** (WS-ResourceProperties)

  RemoteLogging (see Section D.1.11, "**RemoteLogging**")

Chapter in which this interface is used

- Chapter 14, Implementing your own operation providers.

D.1.7 MathService_instance_rl

WSDL file

$EXAMPLES_DIR/schema/examples/MathService_instance_rl/Math.wsdl

Namespace

http://www.globus.org/namespaces/examples/MathService_instance_rl

Operations

- **add**

  Parameters: 1 parameter of type **xsd:int** (integer)

  Returns: nothing

- **subtract**

  Parameters: 1 parameter of type **xsd:int** (integer)

  Returns: nothing

- **multiply**

  Parameters: 1 parameter of type **xsd:int** (integer)

  Returns: nothing

- **divide**

  Parameters: 1 parameter of type **xsd:int** (integer)

  Returns: nothing

Resource properties

- **Value**

  Type: **xsd:int** (integer)

  Cardinality: [1..1]

- **LastOp**

  Type: **xsd:string** (string)

  Cardinality: [1..1]

Extends

- **GetResourceProperty** (WS-ResourceProperties)

  ImmediateResourceTermination (WS-ResourceLifetime)

  ScheduledResourceTermination (WS-ResourceLifetime)

Chapters in which this interface is used

- Chapter 11, Lifecycle management
- Chapter 12, Persistent resources.

D.1.8 MathService_instance_rp

WSDL file

$EXAMPLES_DIR/schema/examples/MathService_instance_rp/Math.wsdl

Namespace

http://www.globus.org/namespaces/examples/MathService_instance_rp

Operations

■ add

Parameters: 1 parameter of type **xsd:int** (integer)

Returns: nothing

■ subtract

Parameters: 1 parameter of type **xsd:int** (integer)

Returns: nothing

Resource properties

■ Value

Type: **xsd:int** (integer)

Cardinality: [1..1]

■ LastOp

Type: **xsd:string** (string)

Cardinality: [1..1]

Extends

■ **GetResourceProperty** (WS-ResourceProperties)

GetMultipleResourceProperties (WS-ResourceProperties)

SetResourceProperties (WS-ResourceProperties)

QueryResourceProperties (WS-ResourceProperties)

Chapter in which this interface is used

■ Chapter 10, Resource Properties.

D.1.9 MathService_instance_rp_complex

WSDL file

$EXAMPLES_DIR/schema/examples/MathService_instance_rp_complex/Math.wsdl

Namespace

http://www.globus.org/namespaces/examples/MathService_instance_4op

Operations

- **add**

  Parameters: 1 parameter of type **xsd:int** (integer)

  Returns: nothing

- **subtract**

  Parameters: 1 parameter of type **xsd:int** (integer)

  Returns: nothing

- **multiply**

  Parameters: 1 parameter of type **xsd:int** (integer)

  Returns: nothing

- **divide**

  Parameters: 1 parameter of type **xsd:int** (integer)

  Returns: nothing

Resource properties

- **Value**

  Type: **xsd:int** (integer)

  Cardinality: [1..1]

- **LastOp**

  Type: **xsd:string** (string)

  Cardinality: [1..1]

- **RecentValues**

    Type: **xsd:int** (integer)

    Cardinality: [0..unbounded]

- **RecentOps**

    Type: **xsd:string** (string)

    Cardinality: [0..unbounded]

- **SystemStats**

    Type: Complex type containing **CpuSpeed** (type **xsd:float**), **Mem** (type **xsd:int**), **Status** (type **xsd:string**)

    Cardinality: [1..1]

Extends

- **GetResourceProperty** (WS-ResourceProperties)

    GetMultipleResourceProperties (WS-ResourceProperties)

    SetResourceProperties (WS-ResourceProperties)

    QueryResourceProperties (WS-ResourceProperties)

Chapters in which this interface is used

- Chapter 17, Writing a Secure Math Service
- Chapter 18, The Security Descriptor
- Chapter 19, Authentication
- Chapter 20, Authorization
- Chapter 22, Run-as modes and delegation.

D.1.10 **PhysicsService**

WSDL file

$EXAMPLES_DIR/schema/examples/PhysicsService/Physics.wsdl

Namespace

http://www.globus.org/namespaces/examples/PhysicsService

Operations

- getAnswer

    Parameters: None.

    Returns: **xsd:int** (integer)

Resource properties

None.

Extends

This interface doesn't extend from any other portTypes.

Chapter in which this interface is used

- Chapter 22, Run-as modes and delegation.

D.1.11 RemoteLogging

WSDL file

$EXAMPLES_DIR/schema/examples/MathService_instance_remotelog/

RemoteLogging.wsdl

Namespace

http://www.globus.org/namespaces/examples/utils/RemoteLogging

Operations

- log

    Parameters: 1 parameter of type **xsd:string** (string)

    Returns: nothing

Resource properties

- LastLog

    Type: **xsd:string** (string)

    Cardinality: [1..1]

Extends

This interface doesn't extend from any other portTypes.

Chapter in which this interface is used

- Chapter 14, Implementing your own operation providers.

D.2 Services

Table D.1 summarizes all the services seen in the book. The meaning of each column is as follows:

- **Name**: This is the name of the service as it appears in the WSDD file and the JNDI deployment file. For example:

```
<?xml version="1.0" encoding="UTF-8"?>

<deployment name="defaultServerConfig" xmlns="http://xml.apache.org/

    axis/wsdd/">


    <service name="examples/core/first/MathService" provider="Handler"

        use="literal" style="document">


        <! Parameters -->


    </service>


</deployment>
```

- **Directory**: The directory where the implementation for this service can be found. To keep these paths short, we define **$SERVICES_DIR** as **$EXAMPLES_ DIR/org/globus/examples/services/**
- **Interface**: Interface implemented by this service (see Section D.1, for more details on each interface).

- **Impl.Type** ("Implementation type"):

  Serv: The service and the resource are implemented in the same class, as described in Chapter 6.

  Singl: The service and the resource are implemented in separate classes. The service is limited to work with a singleton service, as described in Chapter 7.

  Multi: The service is configured to work with multiple resources, which results in having a separate factory service and instance service, as described in Chapter 8.

  SLess: The service is stateless (doesn't interact with any resources).

- **Chapter**: Chapter in which this service is described.

- **Factory service**: If the implementation type is **Multi** (multiple resources), this column refers to the name of the factory service.

globus-build-service Script Reference

This appendix provides a reference guide for the **globus-build-service** used throughout the book to build services. The latest version of this guide can be found in the official GSBT (Globus Service Build Tools) website at http://gsbt.sourceforge.net/.

E.1 Parameters

The parameters accepted by the script are listed in Table E.1. Also, you can see the list of parameters from the command line by running **globus-build-service** with the **-h** parameter

```
./globus-build-service.sh -h
```

E.2 Shorthand Notation

The script offers a convenient shorthand way of building services without having to type the service directory and schema file every time. You must have a **build.mappings** file in the same directory as the build script, with one line for each service using the following format:

```
<service_id>,<service_dir>,<schema_file>
```

<service_id> must be a unique identifier (without whitespace). To use the shorthand notation, you simply have to run the script like this:

```
./globus-build-service <service_id>
```

Although there is usually no need to take a look at the contents of the **build** directory, you might occasionally want to check if the stub files are being generated correctly. The stub source files are generated in:

$BUILD_DIR/build/stubs-*<gar_id>*/src

The compiled stub files are placed in:

$BUILD_DIR/build/stubs-*<gar_id>*/classes

Index

A

Access Grid, 10
add (method)
  in FilesForSale service, 389
  overriding in resource home, 410, 412
  secure service, 285, 340
Adder/addition client
  compiling, 128, 206, 228
  custom notification messages, 235, 237
  multiple resources, 126–128
  persistent resources, 205–207
  resource property change notification, 227–229
  running, 128, 206–207, 229, 237
  without security, 343–345
  with security, 376–378
AddFile client, 388, 389, 412, 413
  compiling, 413
  running, 413
addFile operation, 405, 412
Advertising, resource, 385
Aggregation, of resource information, 386, 390
Allocation services, 9

AllowedMethods parameter, 68, 69
Anonymous authentication, 274
Ant, 71–72, 432, 433
Apache Ant, 71–72, 432, 433
Apache Axis, 27
Apache HTTP server, 27
Apache Jakarta Commons Logging see Jakarta Commons Logging
Apache Jakarta Commons Project, 129
Apache Jakarta Tomcat, 27, 42, 432
Apache Software Foundation, 71
Application server, 27
Applications layer, 10
Asymmetric algorithms, 262, 264
Attributes, names, 60–61
Auditing
  in FileBuy, 398
  see also logging
Authentication, 259, 305–323
  anonymous, 274
  client authentication options, 309–313

setting programmatically, 309
setting with security descriptor, 309
see also GSI Secure Conversation; GSI Secure Message; GSI Transport
examples, 313–323
  with different authentication methods, 314–320
  with different protection levels, 320–323
  in FileBuy, 397
  in GSI, 275
  in GT4, 43
  in public-key systems, 265
  service authentication options, 305–309
  setting default authentication methods, 305–306
  setting per-method authentication, 307
  setting protection level, 307–309
  vs. authorization, 259
Authentication methods, 274
auth-method tag, 305–306

495

Authorization, 259, 325–336
  client-side, 275–276, 286,
    287, 332–334
    no authorization, 332–333
  custom, 276, 334–336
  in FileBuy, 398–399
  in GSI, 274–276
  in GT4, 43
    see also Community
      Authorization
  server-side, 275, 287, 325,
    329, 334
    no authorization, 325
  vs. authentication, 259
  see also gridmap
    authorization; host
    authorization; identity
    authorization; SAML
    Callout authorization;
    self authorization
AUTHORIZATION stub property,
    334
Available resources, 383–386

B
base64Binary XML Schema
    type, 422
Binary data, receiving, 422
Bindings, 55
Bootstrap, of interaction with
    web services, 74
Broker's index, 386, 387, 389,
    390, 391, 398
build directory, 493–494
Buildfiles, 71
build.mappings file, 491, 493
byte arrays, 421, 422

C
Cache interface, 210
Caching, 208–210
caller-identity tag, 348, 353
CAS, 40, 398
C compiler, 432
Certificate authorities (CAs),
    266–269
  hierarchies of, 268–269
  root, 268
  setting up GT4 to work with,
    436–441

SimpleCA, 40, 437–441
  trusted, 267
Child topics, 214
ClassName, 69
Clients, 19
  calling WSRF portTypes,
    149–154
    with additional resource
      properties, 159–166
    compiling, 149
    running, 149
  with security descriptor,
    300–301
  for service with remote
    logging, 252–253
  see also adder/addition
    client; command-line
    clients; creation client;
    credential delegation
    clients; GSI Secure
    Conversation client; GSI
    Transport client; listener
    client; non-delegating
    client
Client stubs, 24–25
Collective layer, 9
Command-line clients, 461–473
  common parameters, 462,
    472–473
  -e (–eprFile) parameter, 462,
    472
  Globus management,
    470–472
  in GT4
    notification testing,
      238–239
    resource destruction, 190
    resource property
      access/modification,
      171–176
    resource termination time
      modification, 190–192
  -k (–key) parameter, 462,
    472–473
  multiple resources, 119–122
    compiling, 121–122
    with immediate
      destruction, 180–183
    running, 122
    with scheduled
      destruction, 187–190

notification clients, 468–470
  resource lifetime clients,
    467–468
  resource property clients,
    462–467
  security parameters, 463
  singleton resource, 74–79
    compiling, 77
    running, 78–79
  -s (–service) parameter, 462,
    472
  usage examples, 471–473
Common Runtime, 42
Community Authorization
    Service (CAS), 40, 399
Community authorization, 40
Community Scheduler
    Framework, 41
complexType tag, 454
Configuration objects, 405, 415
Connectivity layer, 8–9
Constants (class), 118
Constants.AUTHORIZATION
    property, 287
Constructor implementation,
    61–62
Consumer, of events, 211
Container, Java Web services
    see standalone container
Container certificate, setting
    up, 443–444
context-lifetime option, 302
Control domains, 6
createResource operation, 97,
    98, 102–103, 106
Creation client
  compiling, 125, 191, 205
  with delegation activated,
    376
  multiple resources, 122–125,
    191, 192
  persistent resources,
    205–206
  for resource-level security
    example, 343
  running, 205–206
Credential delegation,
    278–279, 347, 348,
    353, 372
  delegating credentials to
    resource, 370–378

building and deploying, 375
implementation files, 372–375
security descriptors, 370–372
trying it out, 376–378
WSDL file, 372
delegation service, 378–379
full, 352
limited, 353
single service example, 352–357
   activating delegation on client side, 352–353
   activating delegation on server side, 353–354
   compiling and deploying service, 354
   compiling and running client, 355–357
two service example, 357–370
   compiling and deploying, 363–365
   delegating client, 368–370
   non-delegating client, 365–368
   overview, 357–358
   PhysicsService implementation, 358–363
see also proxy certificates
Credential delegation clients, 355–357, 368–370
compiling, 355, 369
running, 355–357, 369–370
Credential management, 40
Credentials, 267, 298
C Runtime, 42
Cryptography, 259–266
key-based algorithms, 260–262
   asymmetric, 262
   hybrid, 264
   symmetric, 262
public-key, 262–266
   authentication in, 266
   integrity in, 264–266
   pros and cons, 263–264
   secure conversation using, 263

CSF, 41
CurrentTime resource property, 184, 185, 186
C WS Core, 43

D

Data Management, 40–41
Data management services, 9
Data Replication Service see DRS
Decryption key, 260
Delegation
in GT4, 40
see also credential delegation
Delegation service, in GT4, 378–379
deliver method, 223, 226, 227, 235
parameters, 227
deploy-jndi-config, 70, 93, 116, 187, 209
Deployment
custom notification messages, 235
FileBuy services, 413, 418, 424
first web service, 74
gridmap, 331
multiple resources, 118
   with lifecycle modifications, 180, 187
persistent resources, 205
PhysicsService, 365
resource property change notification, 223
secure service, 289
   with credential delegation to resource, 375
   with resource-level security, 342
   with simple delegation, 354
service implementing four WSRF portTypes, 149
   with additional resource properties, 159
service with own operation provider, 252
singleton resource, 94

Deployment configuration
first web service, 67–70
singleton resource, 92–94
Deployment descriptor see WSDD file
Deserializing, 26
Design
cost vs. benefit, 399
importance, 395, 396, 399
leveraging existing services, 399–400
destroy operation, 177, 179, 180
DestroyProvider operation, 179, 222
Digital certificates, 266–267, 269
self-signed, 268
setting up, 436–437, 439, 443–446
X.509 certificate format, 267–268
Digital signatures, 264–267
specifying requirement, 307
Discovery service, 21, 386, 393
Distinguished names, 267, 268
attributes, 268
Document/literal bindings, 63
effect on parameters, 63–64
Downstream indexes, 390, 403
DRS, 41

E

eDiaMoND, 10
EGEE Project, 5, 10
Encryption, specifying requirement, 307
Encryption key, 260
Endpoint references (EPRs), 33–34, 95
as opaque pointers, 34
WS-Resource-non-qualified, 34, 346
WS-Resource qualified, 33, 34, 346
EndpointReferenceType, 75
Environment variables, setting, 436
Examples directory ($EXAMPLES_DIR), 48

Exception handling, 77
Execution Management, 41

F

Fabric layer, 8
Factory/instance pattern, 95
    see also WS-Resource factory
        pattern
FactoryPortType, 105
Factory service, 95–97,
    475–476
    see also FilesForSale service
Factory service
        implementation, 102–107
    with resource-level security,
        343, 370
Faults, representation, 36
FileBrokerConfiguration
        class, 416
File Broker service *see* FileBuy
        Broker service
FileBuy
    deployment architecture,
        395, 396
    design, 383–399
    file advertising scenario,
        388–390, 404–413
        design details, 389–390
        general concepts, 391
        overview, 388
        trying it out, 413
        see also AddFile client;
            FilesForSale service
    file finding scenario,
        392–394, 414–420
        design details, 391
        general concepts, 393
        overview, 391–393
        trying it out, 418–420
        see also FileBuy Broker
            service; FindFile client
    file purchasing scenario,
        394–396, 420–425
        design details, 393
        general concepts, 395
        overview, 393
        trying it out, 423–425
        see also FileBuy Broker
            service; FileBuy client;
            FilesForSale service;
            FileTransfer service

GT4 versions required, 402
    implementation, 401–425
    running on single machine,
        404
    security considerations,
        395–398
        auditing, 398
        authentication, 397
        authorization, 399–398
        privacy and integrity, 397
    setting up, 402–403
    system overview, 387
    versions, 402
FileBuy Broker service,
        391–393, 393, 414–417
    composition, 392
    creating WS-Resource, 417
    Find operation, 391, 414
    index service URI, 415–416
    processing query results,
        416–417
    Purchase operation, 393,
        420–421
    querying index service, 416
    report operation, 422, 423
FileBuy client, 393, 420, 424
    compiling, 424
    implementation as service,
        394, 420
    purchase operation, 420, 424
    running, 424–425
    transfer operation, 422
FileBuy Index, 389, 391
FileInputStream class, 204
FileOrder resource, 391, 414,
        417, 419, 423
    creation pattern, 391
    immediate destruction, 394
FileOutputStream class,
        201–202
FilePersistenceHelper class,
        198–200
File resources, 389, 392
    creation pattern, 389–391
FilesForSaleConfiguration
        class, 407–409
FilesForSale Index, 389
FilesForSale service, 389,
        393, 405–412, 421
    addFile operation, 405, 412
    Add operation, 389

factory service,
        implementation,
        405
    fillOrder operation, 393,
        421
    implementation as two
        services, 389
    instance service, path,
        405–409
    persistence, 412
    registration in index service,
        409–412
FileTransfer service, 394,
        421
    transfer operation, 421
fillOrder operation, 393,
        421
Find (operation), 392, 414
FindFile client, 391, 417
    compiling, 418
    running, 419–420
findSingleton method, 91
Flattening, 144
Fully qualified domain name
        (FQDN), 442

G

GAR file, 71, 493
    creation, 70–73
GCJ, 432, 433
GCS, 441
getAnswer method, 357, 359,
        360–362, 368
getConfObject, 409
GetCurrentMessageProvider
        operation, 222
getID method, 109
getInstanceResourceHome
        method, 106, 117–118,
        409
getKeyASFile method,
        199–200, 204
getLog method, 132
GetMultipleResourceProperties
        operation, 153–154
GetMultipleResourceProperties
        portType, 144
getReferenceToMathService
        method, 363
getResource method, 88, 108

getResourceProperty
operation, 150–151, 315
with complex RP, 164–166
with unbounded RPs,
160–161
GetResourceProperty
portType, 144
exposing, 140–144
GetResourcePropertyResponse
object, 151, 161
GetRPProvider operation, 222
getSecurityDescription
method, 338
Get/set methods, 59
modification for persistent
resources, 202
names, 61
getTopicList method, 219
Global Grid Forum (GGF), 14
Global gridmap file, 303
Global Service Build Tools
(GSBT), 72
GlobalSign certificates, 267
globus4user user, creation,
433
Globus Alliance, 15
website, 427
Globus API, 339, 398
globus-build-service script
and buildfile, 72,
491–494
build directory, 493–494
first web service, 73
GAR file, 493
multiple resources, 118
parameters, 491, 492
shorthand notation, 491–493
singleton resource, 94
Globus Certificate Service
(GCS), 441
Globus Documentation Project
(GDP), 427
"Globus Primer", 427
globus-start-container
command, 77, 470
globus-stop-container
command, 78, 470–472
Globus Toolkit 4 see GT4
globus user, creation, 433
GNU Make, 432
GNU sed, 432

GNU tar, 432
GRAM, 41
Grid, The, 7
Grid architecture, 7–10
Applications layer, 9
Collective layer, 9
Connectivity layer, 8
Fabric layer, 8
Resource layer, 9
Grid Archive file see GAR file
Grid Café, 3
Grid computing, definition, 7
GridFTP, 40
Gridmap authorization,
329–332
configuring, 329–330
programmatically creating
gridmap, 339
service, 330–331
testing, 331–332
Gridmap file, 329
gridmap tag, 329
Grid Resource Allocation &
Management (GRAM), 41
Grid Security Infrastructure
see GSI
Grid systems
definition, 6–7
examples, 10
Grid Telecontrol Protocol, 41
GSBT, 72
GSI, 271–280
authentication see
authentication
authorization see
authorization
delegation and single
sign-on, 276–280
message-level security,
272–273, 296
security levels, 280
transport-level security,
272–273
deactivation, 289
see also resource-level
security
GSI Secure Conversation, 273,
286–287, 293
context lifetime control, 302
security context, 273, 293

specifying with digital
signatures, 310
specifying with encryption,
310
GSI Secure Conversation client,
286–289, 316–317,
322–323, 350–352
compiling, 290, 316, 350
gridmap testing, 331–332
running, 290–291, 316–317,
323, 350–352
GSI Secure Message, 273
replay attack neutralization,
303
specifying with digital
signatures, 312
specifying with encryption,
311–312
GSI Transport, 273
client configuration, 313
in FileBuy, 397
specifying with digital
signatures, 313
specifying with encryption,
313
standalone container
configuration, 312
GSI Transport client, 318–320
compiling, 318
running, 318–320
GT4, 16–17
component overview, 39–43
high-level services, 16
installation, 433–436
full toolkit, 434
Java WS Core, 434–435
setting environment
variables, 436
testing, 447
non-WS components, 16
obtaining host certificate,
441–443
official release manuals,
427
platform notes, 432
second installation on single
machine, 404
service overview, 43
setting up container
certificate, 443–444

GT4 (*continued*)
  setting up to work with CA, 436–441
    setting up SimpleCA, 437–441
    using existing CA, 441
    using GCS, 441
    setting up user certificates, 444–446
  software prerequisites, 432
GT4 Index Service, 403, 404, 411

H

HandlerClass parameter, 68, 69
hashCode method, 110
"hello, world!" client, 345–346
helloWorld method, 341
Host authorization
  client-side, 334, 355
  server-side, 327
hostAuthz-url parameter, 327
Host certificate, obtaining, 441–443
Hostname, finding, 355
Hostname/resource_class directory, 199
HTTP, 23
HTTP server, 27
Hybrid algorithms, 264
HyperText Transfer Protocol
  see HTTP

I

IBM Websphere, 27
idenAuthz-identity parameter, 326–327
Identity authorization
  client-side, 333–334
  server-side, 326–327
Immediate destruction, 177–183
ImmediateResourceTermination portType, 177
Index service, 384–387
  in GT4, 41, 391
indexURI attribute, 416
Information protocols, 9
Information Services, 41
  see also MDS

InitialContext class, 100, 118
initialize method, 84, 110, 338, 339, 341
  tweaking for persistent resources, 196–198
In-memory resources, 112, 193–194
  vs. persistent resources, 193–194
instanceHome link, 408
Instance service, 95–97
  see also FilesForSale service
Instance service implementation, 107–109
  with resource-level security, 341
instanceServicePath attribute, 112, 407–408
Integration of services, 400
Integrity, 258, 264
  in FileBuy, 381
  in public-key systems, 264–266
integrity tag, 307
Invocation subject, 348, 350, 353, 354, 362
isPermitted method, 336

J

Jakarta Commons Logging
  architecture, 129–130
  guide, 130
Jakarta Tomcat, 27, 42, 432
Java Runtime, 42, 43
Java Web services container
  see standalone container
Java WS Core, 43
  installation, 431–437
Jave Naming and Directory Interface *see* JNDI
JDK, 432
JNDI, 117
JNDI deployment file with credential delegation to resource, 374, 375
  FileBuy seller service, 409, 425–426
  first web service, 47
  multiple resources, 114

with lifecycle modifications, 177
persistent resources, 208, 193–195
service implementing four WSRF portTypes, 149, 159
singleton resource, 82, 88, 91, 94
Jobs, 9, 41

K

Key-based algorithms, 260–262
  asymmetric, 262
  hybrid, 264
  symmetric, 262

L

Large Hadron Collider, 3–4
Layered diagram of OGSA, GT4, WSRF, and Web Services, 17
Lease, 183, 391, 399
  renewal, 183
Lease-based lifecycle management, 183
Lifecycle management, 177–192
  immediate destruction, 177, 184, 187
  lease-based, 183
  performing action when resource destroyed, 190
  scheduled destruction, 183–184, 192
Limited proxies, 352
  rejection, 299, 352
Listener client, 223–227
  changes for custom notification messages, 235–236
  compiling, 228, 237
  delivery part, 223, 226–227
  with ReflectionResource-Property, 231
  running, 228–229, 237
  subscription part, 223–226
load method, 195, 197, 202
Load on startup, 69
Local names, 56

log (operation), 252
Log4j Logging Engine, 129, 130
LogFactory, 132
Logging, 129–135
  adding to MathService,
    130–132
  in FileBuy, 381
  filtering options, 133
  levels, 129–133
  viewing output, 133–135
  see also Jakarta Commons
    Logging
Logging engines, 130
logSecurityInfo method, 284,
    340, 362, 372
Loosely coupled systems, 20,
    395
LRUcache class, 210

M
makeStubSecure method, 363
Management protocols, 9
Mappings files, 55
Marshaling, 25
MathAuthGSIService, 322
MathAuthService, 315–319, 322
MathConstants interface, 62,
    84, 250
MathFactoryService class, 106
MathResource class, 86, 110
MathResourceHome class, 81,
    91, 93, 98, 106, 107, 111,
    112, 114, 116
MathService, 47–48
  examples, 478–489
    MathService_instance,
      478–479
    MathService_instance_
      4op, 477
    MathService_instance_
      helloworld, 478
    MathService_instance_
      notif, 479
    MathService_instance_
      remotelog, 480, 486
    MathService_instance_rl,
      481
    MathService_instance_rp,
      483, 484
    MathService_instance_
      rp_complex, 484

with four operations, 283
  internal logic, 47
  summary table, 490–491
MathService class, 59, 67, 90,
    108
mathURI attribute, 360
MDS, 41, 390
MDS2, 41
Message digests, 264
Message-level security,
    272–273, 289, 296
Message-orientation, 20
Message wrapper, 233, 235
method tag, 307, 348
Monetary debits and credits,
    395
Monitoring and Discovery
  System see MDS
Monitoring services, 9
MyProxy, 40

N
Namespace mappings, 55
  factory service, 105–106
  first web service, 47
Namespaces, 450, 451, 453,
    455, 456
NEESit, 10
Non-delegating client, 365, 368
  compiling, 355, 363
  running, 355
-nosec option, 77, 78, 289
NoSuchResourceException, 183
Notification brokers, 215
NotificationConsumer
  portType, 225
NotificationConsumerManager
  class, 225
Notification consumers, 36,
    214
NotificationProducer
  portType, 222, 225
Notification producers, 214
Notifications, 211–239
  command-line clients for,
    238
  custom notification
    messages, 231–232
  description, 211–213
  in GT4, 215

notifying changes in resource
  property, 216–227
  subscription/registration
    step, 212
  using ReflectionResource-
    Property instead of
    SimpleResource-
    Property, 229–231
  see also WS-Notifications
Notify (operation), 214, 215,
    225
NotifyCallback interface, 223,
    226
OASIS, 15
ObjectDeserializer class,
    128, 166, 236
ObjectInputStream object, 204
ObjectOutputStream object,
    201
ObjectSerializer class, 124
OGSA, 13–17
  relation with WSRF, 15
OGSA-DAI, 41
OGSI instance services, 96–97
Open Grid Services
  Architecture see OGSA
Operation providers, 147
  implementing your own,
    241–253
  Java implementation,
    244–247
  plugging operation
    provider into service,
    247–251
  RemoteLogging provider
    description, 241
  trying it out, 252–253
  WSDL file, 242
  shorthand notation, 251
  using, 147–148
OrderStatus resource
  property, 415, 423

P
PauseSubscriptionProvider
  operation, 222
PDP interface, 335–336
peer-credentials tag, 311
Performance considerations,
    194, 208, 400

PersistenceCallback
  interface, 195
PersistentResource interface,
  194–196
Persistent resources, 112,
  193–210
  adding persistence to
    MathService, 196–207
  cleaning up, 204
  load method, 195, 197, 202
  store method, 195, 197,
    200, 206
  trying it out, 205
  tweaking initialize
    method, 196
  using
    FilePersistenceHelper,
    198
  in FileBuy, 391, 393
  performance disadvantage,
    194, 208
  resource cache, 208–210
  vs. in-memory resources,
    193–194, 207
PhysicsService, 357, 485
  implementation, 358–360,
    372
  summary table, 490–491
Pointers, 33
  opaque, 34
Policy Decision Point (PDP), 335
Polling, 211–212
PortType(s), 49, 76
  exposing, 140
  in WS-ResourceProperties,
    143–144
portType element, 54, 453–454
  wsrp:ResourceProperties
    attribute, 54, 451, 452,
    455, 458
Privacy, 258
privacy tag, 307
Private key, 262
Producer, of events, 211
protection-level tag, 307–309
Proxy certificates, 276–280
  creation, 293
  expiration, 290
  generation, 279–280
  validation, 280–281
Public key, 262

Public-key algorithms, 262
  authentication in, 265
  integrity in, 264
  pros and cons, 263
  secure conversation using,
    263
purchase operation, 393, 420,
  424
Python Runtime, 42
Python scripts, 73
Python WS Core, 43

Q
QNames, 56
QNames interface, 56–57
Qualified names (QNames), 56
query operation, 416
QueryResourceProperties
  portType, 140, 145, 414,
  416

R
ReflectionResourceProperty,
  62, 138, 158
  benefits, 166
  resource property change
    notification, 216–217
Registration, resource, 385
  lease-based lifetimes, 391
reject-limited-proxy tag, 352
Reliable File Transfer (RFT), 41,
  394, 399
RemoteExceptions, 76, 77
RemoteLogging interface,
  246–247, 488–489
RemoteLogging provider
  description, 241
  Java implementation, 241
  WSDL file, 242–243
Remotely accessible methods
  implementation, 62
RemoveCallback interface, 190,
  194–196, 412
remove method, 190, 195–196,
  204–205, 412
Replacement algorithms, 208
  LRU (Least Recently Used),
  208
Replay attack, 303
replay-attack-interval
  option, 303

Replica Location Service
  see RLS
report operation, 422–423
Resource(s), 30–31, 82
  available see available
    resources
  in-memory, 112, 193
  in-memory vs. persistent,
    193
  keys, 30
  persistent see persistent
    resources
  see also WS-Resources
Resource brokering
  overview, 383–393
  see also FileBuy
Resource brokers, 384
Resource cache, 208–210
Resource consumers, 387, 395
ResourceContext class, 91,
  117, 118
ResourceException, 195,
  200–205
Resource home(s)
  multiple resources, 95–128
  singleton resource, 81
  usefulness, 91
ResourceHomeImpl class,
  110–112, 194–195, 412
Resource home
  implementation
  with credential delegation to
    resource, 373–374
  multiple resources, 95–128
  with resource-level security,
    342
  singleton resource, 90–92
ResourceIdentifier interface,
  109
resource-identity tag, 348
Resource implementation
  with credential delegation to
    resource, 373
  custom notification
    messages, 231–237
  multiple resources, 95–128
  with lifecycle
    modifications, 177
  with resource-level security,
    341–342

resource property change
notification, 216–217
service implementing four
WSRF portTypes, with
additional resource
properties, 156–158
service with own operation
provider, 247–250
singleton resource, 82, 88,
91, 94
Resource interface, 58
Resource layer, 9
Resource-level security,
337–346
configuring
programmatically, 339
example, 339–346
resource security descriptor,
300, 337–338, 341
for credential delegation to
resource, 370–372
ResourceLifetime interface,
185
Resource producers, 385
Resource properties (RPs), 35,
54, 137–176
accessing right way, 145–154
more elaborate example,
154–166
command-line clients in GT4,
171–176
global declaration, 54–55
information types stored, 35
notifying changes in,
216–229
using standard WSRF
portTypes, 140–144
WS-ResourceProperties
portTypes, 144–145
see also
SimpleResourceProperty
class
ResourceProperties interface,
58
Resource property documents,
138–140
accessing, 140
ResourcePropertySet, 138
ResourcePropertyTopic class,
219, 221, 227

ResourceProperty
ValueChange
NotificationType type,
227
Resource registries, 9
ResourceSecurityConfig
object, 338, 339
Resource security descriptor,
300, 337–338, 341
for credential delegation to
resource, 370–372
ResourceSecurityDescriptor
object, 338, 339
Resource subject, 348
ResumeSubscriptionProvider
operation, 222
RFT, 41, 394, 395
RLS, 41
Root CA, 268
Run-as modes, 347–352
run as caller, 348
run as resource, 348
run as service, 348
run as system, 348
run-as tag, 348

S
SAML Callout authorization,
328, 398
Scheduled destruction,
183–190
ScheduledResourceTermination
portType, 184
Scope parameter, 68, 69
Secure communication,
257–259
pillars of, 257–259
see also authorization
Security
in GT4, 39–40
authentication and
authorization, 39
community authorization,
40
credential management, 40
delegation, 40
see also GSI
Security context, 273, 293, 294
Security descriptor, 285–286,
297–303
basic structure, 297

client, 300–301
delegation options, 353
common options, 298–299
container, 301–303
credentials, 302
global gridmap file, 303
message-level security
options, 302–303
with different authentication
methods, 314–316
with different protection
levels, 320–323
with different run-as modes,
348–350
resource, 300, 337–338, 341
for credential delegation to
resource, 370–372
secure service, 285–286
service, 299
SecurityResource interface,
338
Self authorization
client-side, 333
server-side, 326
Self-signed certificates,
268–269
Seller's index, 390
Serializing, 25
Server, 19
Server stubs, 24–25, 27
Service base directory, 72–73
Service building
custom notification
messages, 235
FileBuy services, 415, 420,
421
first web service, 70–73
gridmap, 331–332
multiple resources, 108
with lifecycle
modifications, 177
persistent resources, 205
PhysicsService, 365
resource property change
notification, 216
secure service, 289
with credential delegation
to resource, 373
with resource-level
security, 343

Service building (*continued*)
secure service (*continued*)
with simple delegation,
354
service implementing four
WSRF portTypes, 147
with additional resource
properties, 158
service with own operation
provider, 247–252
singleton resource, 94
Service data values, 35
metadata about, 35
Service deployment *see*
deployment
Service description, 22
ServiceGroupRegistration-
Client class, 409
Service groups, 409
service-identity tag, 348
Service implementation
custom notification
messages, 234–235
first web service, 56–67
constructor, 61–62
effect of document/literal
bindings, 63–64
QNames interface, 56–57
remotely accessible
methods, 62
thread safety issues, 62–63
gridmap, 330–331
multiple resources *see*
factory service
implementation; instance
service implementation
PhysicsService, 358–363
resource property change
notification, 221
secure service, 284–285
with credential delegation
to resource, 372–373
with resource-level
security, 340
singleton resource, 87–90
thread safety issues, 87
Service implementation file, 87
Service interface definition
examples, 475–487
first web service, 49–56
bindings, 55

in Java, 49–50
namespace mappings,
55–56
resource properties, 54–55
WSDL code, 50–54
PhysicsService, 358
secure service, 283–285
Service invocation, 23
Service name, 68
Service processes, 22
Service request, 19, 20
ServiceResourceHome, 82–83
Service response, 19
Services, summary table,
491–492
Service subject, 347–348
Session key, 264
SetResourceProperties
operation
to delete, 163–164
to insert, 162–163
to update, 151–153
SetResourceProperties
portType, 145
setServiceOwnerFromContext,
354
SetTerminationTime operation,
187, 189
SetTerminationTimeProvider
operation, 187, 222
SimpleCA, 40, 437–441
Simple Object Access Protocol
see SOAP
SimpleResourceProperty class,
166–169, 219–221
accessing RPs if
implementation split up,
169–170
SimpleResourceProperty-
MetaData class, 186
SimpleTopicList class, 220,
221, 233
single sign-on, 276, 278–279
SingletonResourceHome class,
90–91
SOAP, 21–27
request, 22
response, 22
SOAP engine, 27
Standalone container, 42
secure mode, 312

starting, 78, 289, 449
stopping, 78–79
without security, 77–78
Standardization, reeason for,
14
startListening method, 225
Stateful interactions, 30
Statefulness, 30
Statelessness, 29–30
State management information,
35
store method, 195, 197,
200–202, 206
Strongly coupled systems, 20
Stub classes, 55–56, 63–64, 71,
77
"boxing" in, 63–64
placement of examples, 56
Stubs, 24–25
client, 24–25
server, 24–25
Subjects, 347–348
Subscribe operation, 214, 216
SubscribeProvider operation,
222
SubscribeResponse type, 224,
225
SubscriptionManager
portType, 216, 218, 226
Subscription resource, 214,
216, 226
Symmetric algorithms, 262
Synchronization, 62–63
synchronized, 62, 63, 87
SystemFault topic, 214
system-identity tag, 348
SystemLoadHigh topic, 214–215
System subject, 347

T
TCPMonitor, 291–296
connections list, 293–294
data from add invocation,
294–296
XML Format box, 292
TeraGrid, 10
TerminationTime resource
property, 184, 185, 186
Thread safety, 62–63, 87
timeout parameter, 210
Timer attribute, 409, 412

TLS, 273
TopicExpressionType object, 225
TopicListAccessor interface, 219
TopicList attribute, 219
Topics, 213–214
    child, 213
Topic trees, 213
transfer operation, 421, 422
transferURI attribute, 407–408
Transport, 23
Transport-level security, 272–273
    deactivation, 289
Trigger service, 41
Try/catch blocks, 76, 287

U
Undeploy command, 74
Uniform Resource Identifiers see URIs
Uniform Resource Locators see URLs
Unmarshaling, 26
Upstream indexes, 391, 403, 405
URIs, 23, 24
URLs, 23
User certificates, setting up, 444–446
UUIDGen class, 110
UUIDGenFactory class, 110

V
Vector objects, 157
VeriSign certificates, 267
Virtual organizations (VOs), 5, 383
    see also resource brokering

W
Weather Web Service, 23–24
WebMDS, 41
Web Service Deployment Descriptor see WSDD
Web services, 19–28
    addressing, 23–24
    advantages, 20
    disadvantages, 20–21

in practice, 24–26
self-describing, 22
server software, 26–27
typical invocation, 21–22, 25–26
    see also WSRF Web Services
Web Services Architecture, 15, 22–23
Web services container, 27, 67
    see also standalone container
Web Services Description Language see WSDL
Web Services Resource Framework see WSRF
Website authentication, 267
Workspace Management, 41
World Wide Web Consortium, 23
WS-Addressing, 33, 36
    namespace, 105
    Schema file, 105
WS-BaseFaults, 36
WS-BaseNotification, 214–215
WS-BrokeredNotification, 215
WSDD, 67
WSDD file
    authorization options, 336
    with credential delegation to resource, 373
    first web service, 67–69
    multiple resources, 114–116
    PhysicsService, 365–367
    with resource-level security, 343
    resource property change notification, 216–218
    secure service, 286
    service implementing four WSRF portTypes, 147, 148–149
    with additional resource properties, 158
    service with own operation provider, 250–251
    singleton resource, 91–92
WSDL, 22, 24, 449–460
    declaring resource properties, 454–456
    language-neutrality, 55
    messages, 452–453
    portType, 451–452

response and request types, 453–454
root element, 450
whole file, 456–459
WSRF and Globus-specific features, 54–55
WSDL file
    custom notification messages, 231–233
    example, 456–459
    first web service, 69
    multiple resources
        with lifecycle modifications, 183–184
        with resource-level security, 341, 373
    own operation provider (RemoteLogging), 242–244
    resource property change notification, 216–219
    service implementing four WSRF portTypes, 147–148
        with additional resource properties, 155–156
    service with own operation provider, 247–249
    singleton resource, 82
WSDL Preprocessor, 142–144
wsn-get-current-message client, 239, 469–470
WS-Notifications, 36, 213–215
wsn-subscribe client, 238–239, 468–469
WS-Resource factory pattern, 95–97
    implementation in GT4, 97–102
        alternative scenarios, 102
        resource creation, 98–100
        resource invocation, 100–102
WS-ResourceLifetime, 35, 178
WS-ResourceProperties, 35
    portTypes, 144–145
    WSDL file, 145
WSResourcePropertiesService AddressingLocator class, 153

WS-Resources, 33–34, 383–384
  addressing, 31–34
WSRF, 15, 29–37
  related specifications, 36
  relation with OGSA, 15
  resource approach to
    statefulness, 30–31
  specifications, 35–36
  statefulness vs.
    statelessness, 29–30
  see also resource properties;
    WS-Resources
wsrf-delete-property
  command, 174–175,
  465–466
wsrf-destroy command, 191,
  469
wsrf-get-properties
  command, 171–172, 462

wsrf-get-property command,
  171
wsrf-insert-property
  command, 173–174,
  464–465
WSRF.NET, 17
wsrf-query command, 140,
  175–176, 466–467
wsrf-set-termination-time
  command, 191–192,
  469–470
wsrf-update-property
  command, 172–173,
  462–464
WSRF Web Services
  writing and deployment
    steps, 48
  see also deployment;
    deployment

configuration; service
  building; service
  implementation; service
  interface definition
wsrp:ResourceProperties
  attribute, 54, 455
WS-SecureConversation, 273
WS-Security, 273
WS-ServiceGroup, 35–36, 409
WS-Topics, 213–214

X
X.509 certificate format,
  267–268
XML namespaces, 450

Z
Zlib, 432